Recreating sexual politics
Men, feminism and politics

Victor J. Seidler

London and New York

First published 1991
by Routledge
11 New Fetter Lane, London EC4P 4EE

Simultaneously published in the USA and Canada
by Routledge
a division of Routledge, Chapman and Hall, Inc.
29 West 35th Street, New York, NY 10001

© 1991 Victor J. Seidler

Typeset by
NWL Editorial Services, Langport, Somerset, England

Printed and bound in Great Britain by Mackays of Chatham PLC, Kent

British Library Cataloguing in Publication Data

Seidler, Victor, J. (Victor Jeleniewski) *1945–*
    Recreating sexual politics: men, feminism and politics.
    1. Feminism. Role of men
    I. Title
    305.42

Library of Congress Cataloging in Publication Data

Seidler, Victor J., 1945–
    Recreating sexual politics: men, feminism and politics/
    Victor Jeleniewski Seidler
    p. cm.
    Includes index.
    1. Men – Psychology. 2. Feminism. 3. Masculinity (Psychology)
    I. Title
    HQ1090.S435   1991
    305.3 – dc20
                   90–45014
                      CIP

ISBN 0–415–05853–8
ISBN 0–415–05854–6 (pbk)

Contents

Preface and acknowledgements

This book stretches over more than one political generation. Some of its original hopes and fears were set in 1968 at the horrendous moment when the young philosophy student Jan Palach burnt himself alive as a protest against the Russian tanks smashing the dreams for democracy that were set by the Prague Spring. It was a terrible moment. It was also an act of courage that nourished a resistance to stand firm against the lies that were to come to power in its wake. It is a moment that I shall never forget, for as a young graduate student in philosophy myself, it left its mark on both my personal and political life. In a harsh way it showed that the personal and the political are inseparable and that politics is not simply about power and interests, but also about our deepest beliefs and convictions. It is about who we are as human beings and how we can choose to live our lives with each other.

If some of this writing has its source in some of the events of 1968 it was brought to conclusion in the hopes that have been fired again by the revolutions in Eastern Europe in the closing moments of the 1980s. The people of Prague were to meet on the same spot where Palach gave his life, to remember and to celebrate. They could only live in truth if they honoured the past. The regime had lived a lie for over twenty years as it had failed to acknowledge the events of the Prague Spring for what they were. This had left a mark on each individual's soul as each person had grown accustomed to accept what they had known to be false. As Václav Havel (1987) recognises, people can live within a lie without really accepting it for 'it is enough for them to have accepted their life with it and in it'.

This is the way that each individual confirms an authoritarian system, for everyone 'in his or her own way is both a victim and a supporter of the system'. The difficulties of living in truth have a different resonance within capitalist democracies where we too become accustomed to the lie as almost second nature. As long as we can get away with it, it can seem preferable to lie, especially if we are not in fact breaking any law and if we can convince ourselves that to tell the truth could hurt someone. Within an Enlightenment heritage we are so used to separating the private from the public, the personal from the political, that lying easily becomes institutionalised. It is as if we do not expect the truth to be told to us for we know that politicians seem to have their interests well served by secrecy.

It has been a strength of feminist theory and practice to assert that 'the personal is political'. This is not simply a comment about the workings of power and subordination within our personal relations that have traditionally been taken as an arena of love and individual choice, but a radical challenge to the terms of a rationalist modernity that has insisted on separating private from public relations. In this sense, feminism provides an enduring challenge to our moral and political traditions that continue to be largely moulded within the terms set by the Enlightenment. This is not to reduce the importance of personal life and relationships, though a misplaced challenge to privacy was one of the false paths of a 1960s libertarian politics.

Rather it connects the personal to the rest of our lives so that a double standard should not apply that defends freedom and independence of men at the expense of women. As men we were being challenged to take greater responsibility for our relationships and emotional lives. It was hard to learn to be more honest and truthful because we were not used to identifying our emotional needs and desires. We were so used to having our wishes met or telling others what they wanted to hear, that we had never really learnt to be truthful with ourselves. Within a rationalist culture of self-denial, masculinity had been identified with independence and self-sufficiency. As men we had learnt to live a lie, for we had learnt to deny our own needs. At best we could be shoulders to support others. In truth it was hard to support and nourish others if we had never learnt how to nourish or give to ourselves. The emergence of sexual politics opened up a way to begin to understand processes of diconnections in our relationships, and the ways that we need to develop more fruitful relationships with ourselves in order to relate more honestly to others.

Feminism had helped many women to become more honest with themselves. Consciousness-raising provided a context in which women could share their feelings of suffering, joy and oppression. It was a context in which you could learn the importance of being true to yourself, knowing that your experience would be validated. This challenged the pervasive Enlightenment distinction between reason and emotions as women learnt to trust their feelings rather than discounting them automatically because they did not fit the precepts of reason. In learning to recognise that their personal feelings were shared, women did not have to turn their feelings against themselves in guilt and shame but could learn how they are connected to structured relations of power and subordination.

As women learnt that they needed the strength and support of other women to transform these structures of domesticity, work and childcare, so feminism recovered a dialectical grasp of historical materialism, reworked within the visions of sexual politics, for personal change was inseparably connected to political change. They could not be ripped apart or placed in separate spheres as our inherited moral and political traditions would have us do. In this sense, feminism promised a renewal of socialism, for it connected it to the validity of people's everyday experience. It potentially helped both women and men to a trust in their own voices as they learnt to identify their own needs and fulfilment.

It went beyond a Marxist tradition that identified fulfilment with creative labour, for it acknowledged love and relationships as discrete areas of human needs and fulfilment. It set to heal the split between the public and the private, recognising them both as potential sources of value, meaning and fulfilment for men and women. Ecological politics has taken this further by questioning the Enlightenment vision of history and progress as identified with the control and domination of nature. It helps us rework our relationship with our natural selves and inner lives as well as to spiritual insights and needs that have been too easily discounted within narrow materialistic traditions.

If we take seriously the challenges which feminism and ecological politics make to our inherited moral and political traditions, we recognise the limitations of a political framework that would blindly set Soviet-styled communism against capitalism so that the revolutions in Eastern Europe can be interpreted exclusively as a victory for capitalism. It is important to recognise the integrity of different libertarian traditions of socialism, so that we refuse to think that freedom and liberty are possessions of conservative politics. It might seem to some that the language of socialism has been so degraded by the state bureaucracies in Eastern Europe that it might be preferable to forsake this language altogether. It might take considerable time and effort to recover its meaningfulness for us again.

To the extent that political language has become empty and rhetorical, we should be wary of it. It is a strength of consciousness-raising continually to question gaps that arise between language, feelings and actions and so to ground our language in our experience. If this is a crucial insight in Wittgenstein's later philosophy, it was also given practical effect in a sexual politics that insisted on truth and honesty in the way that politics was to be lived in both our personal and political lives. In the struggle against rhetoric and moralism, it held important truths. It refused to deny a creative individuality in its challenge to possessive individualism that flourished within a capitalist ethic. It insisted that socialism should not set the society as a higher moral ideal against the needs and fulfilment of individuals.

If politics were to become a form of self-sacrifice and self-denial within the Left, it would soon lose its meaning, as it so often did in the radical politics of the 1960s and 1970s, when people lived for a future while losing a sense of what relationships and institutions they were struggling to create. As people lose a sense of their own individual needs and desires, it is hard to keep contact with what matters to others. But it is also crucial that needs and desires are not simply treated as given, as they are within a Fabian rationalist tradition which is largely set within utilitarian terms. Within an emerging sexual politics, people have to explore their own needs as they learn to recognise and validate what is important to them. This is not to discount consumer goods as able to meet real needs, but to recognise the ways they can also operate as substitutes within a capitalist consumer culture.

It has become common within post-structuralist theory to assume that identities are largely created out of available discourses and consumer goods. In the 1980s, style has assumed a new significance as the purveyor of identities. It has seemed that people can create their own identities out of what is culturally available. People do not have to accept the meanings that are already encoded, but can somehow subvert them to their own individual ends. In part this is a glorification of appearances and a validation of individuality and freedom as they can be expressed within a consumer culture. It insists that identities are no longer given and fixed and that we live in a culture of 'post-modernity' that has broken once and for all with the essences of a Cartesian ego.

So it is that nothing is fixed but everything is in flux, as we are constantly remaking and reconstituting our identities out of what has been made culturally available. This captures something of the broad social changes that have been wrought with technological change, but it can also blind us in its relativism and its incapacity to consider truth and morality. I want to address and insist on the importance of a social theory which can focus on the importance of relationship rather than merely the construction of identities. In a culture in which anything goes, it is hard to recognise the poverty of one's experience and relationships. As relationships crack, we fail to take responsibility for ourselves emotionally as we move on to the next event. We learn to conceal the hurt. We never learn from our experience, for it is a category that has been discounted within post-structuralist forms of social theory, taken as it is to be exclusively a construction of language or discourse.

In Eastern Europe, this deification of appearances and denial of essences has taken on a different, if no less brittle, form. In the denial of any distinctions between 'appearances' and 'essences' there is the denial of truth. It becomes an effect of power, as it unfortunately remains in so much of Foucault's writings. If it is important to learn to be more truthful with ourselves, then these traditions need to be questioned as we recognise that relativism is not the only alternative to absolutist notions of truth. Václav Havel talks about how the post-totalitarian system 'defended the integrity of the world of appearances in order to defend itself', knowing that as long as it seals off the entire society, it appears to be made of stone.

> But the moment someone breaks through in one place, when one person cries out 'the Emperor is naked!' – when a single person breaks the rules of the game, thus exposing it as a game – everything suddenly appears in another light.
>
> (Havel 1987)

With the dominance of Thatcher and Reagan in the West, we have lived under the spell of the market as the source of all value. The poverty and suffering this is continually causing has fallen out of view as people have learnt to accept that people only have themselves to blame. The glitter of consumerism has produced powerful images that have served to silence and to banish those who are forced to live a different reality in such a class-divided society.

Without an alternative vision, the Left can only think of running capitalism more effectively. Socialism continues to be trapped by a Fabian rationalism that can only talk a language of priorities. We are left bereft of a moral vision as we are told that, without power, the Left cannot do anything. The public and the private remain resolutely separate. It is through reason alone that our goals and ends are to be discerned and it is then through reason that the most effective means are to be chosen. This turns politics into an instrumental affair that does not have to touch our lives. It becomes a job that is best left to the politicians. As the possessors of reason, they supposedly know best and can legislate for others.

At best this gives us a limited vision of democracy for it serves to discount the experience and expression of most people, especially women and ethnic minorities who have an ambiguous and qualified relationship to the public sphere. Traditionally, this is the sphere of men, and politics has been a conversation between men about a public world that is largely formed within the image of men. Feminism, ecology and sexual politics have challenged the terms of this tradition and recognised that needs and desires are not given as part of a utilitarian calculation but have to be carefully explored and discerned. It is essentially a democratic process for it is something that individuals have to do for themselves, both individually and collectively. It is not simply an issue of administration. In this crucial sense, politics remains inseparable from morality within a sexual politics that can extend and learn from the insights of ecology.

This can help account for a widespread distrust of politics and politicians. People have learnt not to trust what they hear. Too often, words have no weight. The restoration and validation of the personal within a recreated sexual politics gives a different hope to politics. For if people are talking for themselves out of their own experience, it can be easier to detect cant and hypocrisy. As people learn to share the contradictions of their own experience, say the difficulties of both working and developing close relationships as fathers to our children, we recognise that these contradictions cannot be resolved in our minds alone. They might mean working less, or working less responsibly for a while, for these are contradictions in the ways we live, not simply in the ways that we think.

If we lose a sense of the dialectical tension between language and experience, on the widespread rationalist assumption that experience is not 'real' in itself but is provided for by either reason or language, so we will also lose a grip on the contradictions of our experience. We will be tempted by a determinism that would discount individual experience as a function of social structure or language, rather than be able to validate the individuality of experience.

It is a strength of sexual politics to be able to *confirm* and *validate* experience while recognising that its meanings are to be investigated, as well as to recognise that as its social and historical sources are explored, it does not cease to be any the less individual. It is not a matter of shifting responsibility from individuals to society, thereby abandoning notions of individual responsibility. If anything, we have to learn to take greater responsibility for our emotional, sexual and work lives as the relationship between personal and political is reformulated.

Language is crucial in this process. As we learn to explore the contradictions of our everyday experience within a capitalist society, we learn to acknowledge our emotions and feelings, rather than discounting them because they do not fit the way we have learnt to think things should be. This is to recognise a relationship between masculinity and the spirit of capitalism. It is to connect self-denial to a Protestant ethic that has informed political traditions of both Left and Right. As Weber understood it, as money becomes an end in itself, our working lives become a means to ends that exist independently of us. Protestantism helps us to take for granted a vision of rationality that reverses the relationship between means and ends. This is an irrational form of rationality, as the meaning of our lives is situated in something external.

So it is that salvation as something external is replaced within a secular capitalist culture by individual achievement and success. Life becomes an endless struggle and we are denied any sense of intrinsic fulfilment and satisfaction. We are locked into competitive relationships with others and plagued by feelings that whatever we do is not good enough. So it is that the Protestant ethic legislates a particular relationship to emotionality, which in turn constrains political vision.

Politics becomes appropriated into a form of instrumentalism because it operates within the context of a structure of negation of emotionality which inevitably constitutes a blindness to reality itself. Politics is defined as a feature of the public realm alone – supposedly it is a matter of reason, power and interests. So it is that politics becomes a matter of achieving power to legislate for goals that have been set by reason alone. As power becomes an end in itself, we lose a sense of what we are struggling for, for politics has been separated from morality and emotional life, which have been relegated to the private and the individual. As socialism is recast in these terms, it loses its vision of a more equal and humane society.

Feminism and sexual politics potentially break through these Protestant assumptions which underpin Enlightenment modernity and social theory. What I present is not an instance of sexual politics but rather an argument that sexual politics is a mode of development of a dialectical politics which allows for a reformulation of historical materialism. Marx's vision was partly trapped by Enlightenment notions of reason and progress so that oppression and exploitation could only be recognised within the public sphere. It was only here that freedom and justice could flourish, for the private realm was not a concern of politics.

In challenging the relationship between the personal and the political, sexual politics awakens us to the contradictory nature of our experience and the crucial importance of truth and honesty in facing ourselves. In recognising the importance of our taking responsibility for our emotional lives and personal relationships, it recognises the importance of both reason and emotions as the source of human values.

It is easy for us to betray the knowledge of what is important to us, thinking that we are thereby pleasing others. It is possible for people to lose touch with the sources of their own creativity and work. An orthodox Marxism too often abandoned the insights of the early Marx as it sought to explain the sources of change as essentially external. It lost a sense of the need for people to empower themselves as they learn to take control of their own lives. Learning to think for ourselves, as Simone Weil recognised, is a crucial aspect of this process.

In recognising that Enlightenment modernity has been largely formed as a secular form of Protestantism, I have sought to rethink the relationship of Marx to Weber, rather than seeing them as autonomous traditions. This fosters a reformulation of social and political theory in the sense that both liberalism and orthodox Marxism have been cast within a rationalistic vision that tended to reinforce the relation to self which Weber identifies as something that needs to be thought about critically. One theme is the particular relationship that men have with this structure of culture and the way that it constructs dominant masculinities in its own image.

But this is not all it does, for these processes of capitalist modernity presuppose and reinforce the subordination of the individual through its self-policing within this structure of relationship to emotions, feelings and desires. It leaves both men and women having constantly to struggle against feelings of being worthless and undeserving. This is why therapy, to the extent that it brings these assumptions and ways of relating into question, can be essentially radical, rather than simply another instance of the operation of the Protestant ethic itself. Similarly, ecological insight can be crucial in bringing into question the notion that progress lies in the domination of both inner and outer nature. So it is that the process of healing ourselves becomes inseparable from healing and repairing the damage that we have done to the planet. So it is that red and green have become inseparable, if politics is to be recreated.

If the recreation of sexual politics is to be part of such a larger process, then we need to recognise this does not just concern the oppression and subordination of women, gays and lesbians. It is because of the broader implications of sexual politics that it cannot be 'left to women', although the nature of men's contribution is clearly open to discussion. But sexual politics is also about men and the powers of masculinities. It is not enough for men to give support to women in their struggles for change. If men are to take the insights of feminism to heart, then sexual politics has to push beyond a realm exclusive to women, whilst taking care not to trivialise or marginalise the work of women, as happens all too often.

It is also crucial, as I argue, for men to reconsider their inherited forms of masculinity and how to *change* themselves, both individually and collectively. If this is to happen, then men have to learn to trust and support each other in new ways. As the personal and the political are brought into new relationships with each other, so will our sense of the place and limits of politics in our lives be transformed. As we learn to trust more aspects of our experience, so we will become clearer about how we need others. As we learn to take greater responsibility for our lives, so the relationship between state and civil society will be set in different terms.

This writing has stretched over many years and many people have helped in the formulation of these ideas. Some of the early chapters had their origin in discussions in the editorial collective of *Achilles' Heel*, which at different times included amongst others Paul Atkinson, Mel Cairns, Tony Eardley, Steve Gould, Martin Humphries, Andy Metcalf, Paul Morrison, Andy Moye, Chris Nickolay, John Rowen, James Swinson, Steve Turner, Tom Weld, Ian Wolstenholme and Nick Zenau. Some of us had been involved in a period of intensive political activity in the early 1970s in the context of East London Big Flame, which slowly disintegrated with the economic crisis in 1976. Different people went their individual ways, but we all confronted the difficulties of recovering a sense of individual needs and direction after such a period of collective activity.

Some of these issues were articulated in the context of Red Therapy, as an attempt to develop self-help therapy in a way that was sensitive to issues of class, race and gender. These were exciting days, even if we still carry some of the scars. I learnt enormously from these experiences, though I also lost touch with different aspects of myself. It seemed crucial to grasp the ways that activist socialist politics seemed to produce its own culture of self-denial. Even though we continually talked of needs and desires, it proved difficult to sustain much connection with the reality of this vision. I wrote some of the early drafts for the chapters on morality and self-denial as a way of coming to terms with this experience. It was a way of grasping the ways that a Protestant ethic remained powerful within a secular culture, even one which took itself to be challenging its bourgeois foundations. It was all the more significant for being invisible and unnamed. It was taken for granted in a way that compromised the insight and vision of our challenge to capitalist social relations.

These chapters have been through different incarnations and I have tried to rework them in a way that resonates with the predicaments we face in the 1990s. Hopefully they help us grasp how issues relating to masculinity, Protestantism and modernity prepare important ground for a recreation of feminist, socialist and ecological politics that can also speak to the transformations of masculinity. If we turn aside from our histories and experience, rather than share them, we will surely repeat the same mistakes. This is a period for asking questions, for many of the old certainties have gone. It is also a time for raising new questions and concerns so that we can learn as much as we can from the experience of others in different traditions. We need to be wary of a moralism that has all too often blocked honesty and clear thinking.

As Václav Havel warns us in his essay 'An Anatomy of Reticence', we need to be wary of

> the moment when the artefact, the project for a better world, ceases to be an expression of man's responsible identity and begins, on the contrary, to expropriate his responsibility and identity . . . when the abstraction ceases to belong to him and he instead begins to belong to it.
>
> (1987: 175)

If sexual politics teaches us to question the gender in which these sentiments are expressed, it can also help us to a broader analysis of a modernity that has made such blinding abstractions and a corresponding self-denial a pervasive temptation for us. If we are to live in truth, this has to start in relationship with ourselves and our partners, for unless we heal the wounds that have separated the personal from the political, it will be hard to trust what we have to say.

I would also like to thank others who shared this particular path, as well as those who have encouraged me to keep writing in dark times. Memory creates its own imagined communities, so I would like amongst others to remember Larry Blum, David Boadella, Terry Cooper, Sheila Ernst, Jane Foot, Lucy Goodison, Ian Hextall, Sally Inman, Marina Lewyzka, Tom Monk, Caroline Ramazanoglu, Sheila Rowbotham and Joanna Ryan. We are certainly all a little older, if not a little wiser. I would also like to thank Uxa Pierie for her sense that the issues of self-denial could also speak to the experience of women, and Ed Mason who made useful suggestions on an earlier draft. More recently, Janet Ransom has helped with insight and understanding in the completion of this manuscript. The 'Men for Men' group at Spectrum, London, has continually reminded me of the strength, love and support men can both give and receive from each other. Anna Ickowitz and our children Daniel and Lily have brought light and joy into the difficult moments of completion. Like many writers, I thought I was destined to carry some of these chapters in my desk drawer until the end of time, so it is wonderful for these ideas to see the light of day. Hopefully they will shed some insight as they find their own homes in the world.

1   Introduction
Identity, politics and experience

POLITICS AND VISION

In the last twenty years there has been a growing sense of the importance of sexual and personal politics. These questions have become central within contemporary politics and culture. People have learnt to take up quite different and challenging positions but within a shared sense of the crucial importance of these issues themselves. This is equally true on the political Right where issues of family, sexuality and morality have become critical. It could be said that Thatcherism in England and Reaganism in the United States took the initiative in moral and political issues that the traditional Left had too long marginalised as unimportant. These concerns were to be articulated within a Right libertarian language of rights and choice that was to provide a challenge to the statist conceptions on the Left. There is a growing feeling that socialism has to be redefined if it is to be able to make its own a concern with freedom, equality and community. It is important to learn from how the language of freedom was appropriated.

For many, the ascendancy of the libertarian Right in British and American politics in the 1980s was in large part an understandable reaction to the excesses and permissiveness represented by the 1960s. People look back with cynicism or with nostalgia but there has been little attempt to share some of the insight, enthusiasm and understandings of that time. And yet we still live in a very different world, partly because of the impact of those times. The attempts to bring the personal and political together in contemporary feminist struggles, in local government politics and in the peace and ecology movements, all have their source in the 1960s. This is equally true of the growth of vegetarianism, animal rights movements and the growing interest in alternative medicines and health care. These concerns are no longer the exclusive concern of the libertarian Left but have become central issues for mainstream thought and politics.

I want to set up some of the guiding ideas of the 1960s so as to begin a fuller dialogue between the generations and a clearer evaluation of those times. Too often we take these times for granted as the shared experience of a political generation. It is long overdue for this discussion to be opened up so that people can engage with these ideas and concerns for themselves in the very different political climate we live in now. This is not simply of historical interest, for it helps reveal the source of tensions and concerns within contemporary culture and politics. This should be part of redefining the nature of freedom, democracy and justice in critical relationship to the challenges of feminism and sexual politics, rather than seeking for a renewal of socialist theory and politics in a return to a pre-1968 consensus.

In the 1990s, we need to think about politics again. We need to rediscover its meaning if socialism is to become a meaningful tradition. This means asking basic questions. It means learning from the movements that have developed since the 1960s. This needs to be a collective project. It involves learning to share an experience so that different generations on the Left can begin to learn from each other. I want to show how this involves grasping the ambivalence of the politics of this period, seeing that whilst at one level it laid the foundations for the emergence of contemporary radical movements, at the same time it sustained a vision of politics grounded in will and determination. This vision was fed by a bourgeois inheritance and a particular form of masculine identity.

The year 1968 was a watershed. It released enormous energies and insight. I remember the excitement of the times. You could feel that the world was going to change. It became difficult to capture this feeling in the economic and social crisis of the 1970s and 1980s. Thatcherism gained an astounding victory. It was able to take an important moral and political initiative. It seemed to promise individual freedom and control. It grasped the deep disillusionment with socialism which had come to be identified with bureaucracy and red tape. The pragmatic politics of the Labour Party had simply served to dig its own grave. It had demanded the sacrifices of working-class people but could no longer promise to provide the economic and social benefits that had become an integral aspect of social democratic politics.[1]

In the 1980s we are confronting new social and political realities. The different movements such as feminism, the gay and lesbian movement, ecology and Green politics which have emerged since the 1960s have each, in their own way, reflected this new reality. They offer us new insights about the making of socialism. These have still to be integrated into our political understanding. In the mid-1970s there was a decisive turn against the hopes and aspirations of 1960s politics. This was understandable given all the dashed hopes and disappointments. We needed a broader historical and theoretical vision and understanding. Unfortunately, this turn to theory in terms of an interest in Althusser and structuralist Marxism, often meant that people had denied their own experience and understanding, even with the intensive community and industrial politics that had taken place in this time. Whatever understanding this rediscovery of theory brought, it did not make it easier to learn from the different movements which had emerged. In many ways it seemed to make this kind of learning more difficult.[2]

POLITICS AND UNREALITY

In 1968 I was a graduate student. I was frustrated with the abstractness of my thinking and feeling. The student movement offered me a different sense of involvement and participation. It gave me a sense of the meaningfulness of collective practice. We could get together and we could change things. We could *affect* the quality of our education through challenging the social relations of power we had taken for granted within education. I could change my relationship to the social world. I got a different sense of the relationship between theory and practice. I remember watching the events in Paris on the TV. They showed that modern capitalism was not the kind of stable castle that we were brought up to accept. A different reality could be brought into existence.

We were asking basic questions. Whose values? What was a relevant education? What was worth learning about? Knowledge could no longer simply be accepted as a commodity that we were accumulating. There was a different understanding in the air. Knowledge was to be related to understanding. It was to help us grasp our experience within the social world we had been brought up to take very much for granted. This was not simply a question of what we learnt. It was also a matter of the relationships of teaching and learning. These could no longer be incidental.

There was a recognition of the difference between different kinds of learning. We wanted to learn for ourselves. We knew that this would make a difference to the kinds of lives we would live. In this way, learning became threatening. It challenged our sense of ourselves and our assumptions about the social world we lived in. It was because we could not believe what politicians and teachers were saying about the war in Vietnam that we had to learn for ourselves. We learnt that the forms of learning implicitly embodied and reproduced particular values. If we wanted to challenge these values, then we had to challenge these forms of learning. We had to discover different ways of learning, which meant challenging traditional styles of academic argument. It was not simply a matter of the confrontation of disembodied ideas.

Another aspect of this was the feeling that we only exist through others. We live in the image of others. There is the common experience of feeling that you are a different person with different people. Our individuality seems to lack a centre. We can easily experience ourselves as fragmented, as existing in separate pieces that seem to have very little relationship with each other. This was a reality that we seemed to be living with in bureaucratic capitalism. There was little that could help us understand this experience. Often these feelings had to be kept to ourselves since they did not fit with what was presented to us as the prevailing social reality. It was within the new movements that these experiences could be identified and named. In part this fragmentation accounted for Laing and Cooper's popularity, in that they seemed to be saying something important about the everyday reality of life in the society we lived in. They seemed to recognise a reality that conventional knowledge and understanding dismissed.[3]

We began to question competitiveness and individual ambition. It was felt that people could only prove themselves through putting other people down. The education system was organised in a way to foster these kinds of invidious comparisons and to make people feel worthless if they did not succeed. Against this there was a recognition of the importance of people's relationships with each other, as an area of life in which meaning was to be sought. We began to value our relationships with each other and to question a society which readily subordinated human relationships to the search for profit and individual ambition.

We began to recognise the ways in which competitiveness worked to undermine our relationships with others. We felt that more equal relationships would be meaningful because each of us would feel validated and confirmed in our own individual experience. Laing's work helped us to feel the *validity* of our individual experience. This helped us discern the ways in which we felt systematically undermined and invalidated through the social relations of capitalist society and led us to challenge competitive institutions because of the quality of human relationships they fostered. If there was a risk of becoming moralistic and even rhetorical, the emerging politics nevertheless held insights into the changing quality of relationships in the larger society.

There was a prevailing feeling, growing up in the 1950s and 1960s, of the 'unreality' of life. You would often hear people say 'I feel unreal', 'Nothing seems to be real to me.' This was related to the quality of individual lives within monopoly capitalism. Hard work and effort had lost their meaning. They had been overtaken by the everyday reality of working in a bureaucratic organisation. Work had become simply a question of obeying the rules of the organisation. A tension emerged between the replaceability of people in the work process and people's sense of their own individuality. The social relations of bureaucratic life seemed to drain our lives of whatever meaning and significance they might otherwise have had.

POLITICS AND EXPERIENCE

Politics and experience were brought into relationship with each other as we learnt the value of individual experience. It was an axiom of the 1960s that we mattered equally. This was to go beyond the liberal idea of the equal respect that was owed to all. If it was sometimes confused with an unrealistic notion that we all have the same capacities and abilities and should all be able to learn different skills equally, the belief in the equal significance of people nevertheless helped to strengthen our confidence in ourselves. This was part of a challenge to the hierarchical division between mental and manual labour, and part of developing a fuller conception of human equality.

We realised that it was important to be able to develop both mental and manual skills. This was part of a developing sense of what it means to grow and develop as an individual, and is an example of how personal experience can be grasped as political. It was also a rejection of the workings of competitive institutions which made us feel that we should not attempt to learn to do something unless we were going to be good at it – better than others. This simply worked to undermine people's sense of themselves and made them feel incapable and worthless. We became aware of the workings of the Protestant ethic, not only within capitalism but within a socialist theory and practice that was often blind to its own cultural inheritance. This was not understood abstractly but in its bearings upon our everyday experience and relationships.

But this was also a challenge to liberal democratic political theory. It questioned the notion that competitiveness would bring out the best in individuals and help us develop our full capacities and abilities. There was a recognition of the ways hierarchical and competitive institutions threatened to undermine democracy and democratic institutions, as well as the hopes and aspirations of liberal political theory. Crucially, it did not help people believe in themselves; rather, it fostered, if unwittingly, the idea that some people are better, or more important, than others. It worked to make us feel inadequate and incompetent and so was at odds with, and even undermined, the democratic ideal of everyone having equal, if different, contributions to make. So we learnt that our conception of democracy had to go beyond formal conceptions of representative democracy and a language of individual rights, to be related to a sense of individual experience fostering a sense of individual validity and value.

The challenge to liberal theory also involved challenging the distinction between the public and the private. It could no longer be thought that the private realm could be loving and supportive while the public realm was competitive. We had to learn to think about the quality of people's experience, which involved thinking about *both* the public and the private and finding ways of relating them. It was recognised that the family could work as an oppressive institution, especially for women and children. Private and personal relationships were also relationships of power and subordination. They were not simply relationships of love. Rather the quality and meaningfulness of these emotional relationships could only be fully grasped if we understood them also as relationships of power and dependency. This involved a recognition of the personal as political. It threatened our conception that politics was what happened in the public world. There was also a politics of everyday life and of personal relationships.[4]

Liberal theory had prevented us from thinking about this seriously. It encouraged us to think that our personal lives were 'free' because they were simply areas of individual decision and resolve, and that institutions of representative democracy gave people freedom and control over their public lives through the legal and political rights they are guaranteed as citizens. This vision was to be challenged.[5] We were forced to recognise a tension between formal and substantial conceptions of freedom and that, whatever the rhetoric, we did not have effective *control* over our lives. Just as workers did not have power over the organisation of their work, students had little control over the character and organisation of their education. The notion of 'control' became important as the desire to connect freedom to the control of different areas of our lives was conceived. This involved an implicit challenge to the moral and political theory of liberalism.

There was a developing understanding that personal change involved developing different kinds of relationships with others and so a challenge to prevailing liberal conceptions of individualism and individuality. There was a recognition of the importance of developing more egalitarian relations with others as part of the critique of personal relationships as 'possessive'. Different kinds of relationship between people were imagined in which people would be able to learn to relate to each other more equally. Distributive conceptions of justice were brought into question as we realised it was not simply a matter of making sure that people were earning the same. Rather, we needed more concern for the quality of human relationships. This was not something easily achieved, but had to be learnt through people being more open and honest in their feelings and responses to each other. In this way, it was grasped that personal change involved the support and criticism of others. We need others to change, and it is through developing different kinds of relations with others that change is made possible. So conceptions of personal change had to be firmly grounded in social relations.

As it turned out, we had a very optimistic – many would now say naïve – conception of personal change. We tended to think that it would follow more or less automatically, as long as we were open and honest. We tended to think that the mere fact of living collectively and so reorganising the social relations we lived in, would bring about important changes in the kind of persons we were, through giving us an experience of relating differently to others. But the experience of this period can still help us think more creatively about different conceptions of personal and social change that have often remained implicit within the socialist movement. At one level it can help us question the liberal idea that we can change through acts of will and determination alone. It also challenges an orthodox Marxism which would assume that once the economic organisation was transformed, other social and personal changes would follow more or less automatically.

THE PERSONAL AND THE POLITICAL

Within the Black movement and the student movement there was a language of power and liberation that went beyond liberal notions of guaranteeing certain legal and political rights, however important these are. A different and challenging conception of the forms of politics was taking place in the 1960s, which still resonates in contemporary culture. This involved connecting the personal with the political, the everyday reality of our individual experience with the larger structures of power and subordination. It was a struggle to redefine our inherited liberal conceptions of freedom and equality as people sought to live a more human life within a society that was more clearly identified as oppressive and unjust. So, initially within the Black Power movement in the US, there was an awareness of the connection between one's identity and consciousness as a black person and one's oppression and powerlessness within the larger society.

Black people had to learn to *value* their experience, culture and history as black people. This was recognised as an aspect of the struggle against oppression and integral to defining the possibilities of freedom.

This involved people both individually and collectively learning to redefine an experience and history that had so often been degraded and diminished within the larger society. It meant developing a different sense of self and involved a process of personal and individual change. Others could not go through these changes for you, however important they could be for you, which meant that individuality could never be subordinated to an abstract collectivity. In a very real sense, you had to make these connections for yourself; so a process of consciousness-raising became extremely important within the women's movement and gay liberation movement as well as within the movements for sexual politics more generally.

This redefinition of politics involved a new grasp of the relationship of individuals to the larger society, as it was built around an understanding of the conceptions of freedom and oppression. Capitalist society brings us up to think of ourselves as individuals with a unique set of qualities and abilities. It teaches us that we are responsible for the quality and meaningfulness of our individual lives and that, if we are unhappy or miserable, then we have only ourselves to blame.[6] If we do not like the kind of life we have, then we should have worked harder at school, or else we just do not have the abilities and capacities to achieve more in our lives. This is the way in which we come to validate our experience within a liberal moral culture.

We inherit a conception of freedom as non-interference by others and a vision of equality as the equal respect for others and the right to be treated as equal human beings. This is supposedly granted to us regardless of the relations of power and subordination which exist in the larger society. Rather we show our respect for others by being prepared to abstract from the everyday realities of social life. This makes it very difficult to understand how much of our lives and experiences are influenced through the social relations of power and subordination.[7] If anything, it can easily leave us feeling inadequate and worthless because of the workings of competitive and hierarchical institutions which remain largely unchallenged.

The Black movement, women's movement and gay movement which developed in the late 1960s and the early 1970s were important in the ways they challenged the moral psychology of liberalism. They also recognised the difficulties presented by the different levels of our experience of ourselves so often ignored within a liberal theory which assumes that our ends or goals are provided by reason alone. This renders invisible issues about *whose* standards we are to judge ourselves by. So it was important for the Black movement to ask 'What does it mean to be black in this society?' 'How are blacks oppressed?' 'How is their experience to be validated?'[8] It is so easy for people to feel that they are not good enough, that they are lacking, and cannot live up to prevailing standards. Often these are standards that prevail in white male society. They are so often taken for granted as 'normal' that others find themselves 'lacking' or 'defective' when judging themselves according to these standards not of their own making.

This makes it very difficult in different ways for black people, Jews, women, gay men and lesbians to validate their experience. There is little toleration or understanding of difference, which within liberal theory is often only recognised as individual difference of purpose or preference. There is little grasp of the different experiences people live in society. In part this shows the depths of the Protestant tradition, and the ways its universalism has been given a secular form in liberal democratic societies. Often we do not need others to judge us because we are so hard and self-critical ourselves. Often we grow up feeling that we deserve very little for ourselves. It is not for the powerless and the oppressed to talk, simply to listen. It is as if, somewhat paradoxically within a liberal culture that prides itself in offering representation to all, people are left feeling that they do not deserve to have a voice of their own.

The Black movement and the women's and gay movements challenged accepted definitions of social reality. Both liberal individualism and prevailing conceptions of socialist morality had to be reassessed. A different sense of morality was emerging as it was recognised that different oppressed groups had to find their own voices which would grow out of their own history and culture. This challenged the assumed universalism and the singularity of the moral voice of reason.

Rather than learning to define experience against the prevailing standards of moral behaviour, these standards had themselves to be related to the power of white masculinity within the larger society. Just as black people had had to recover a sense of their own identity which meant rejecting the expectations of white society, so women and lesbians learnt to challenge the prevailing conceptions of femininity which dominant forms of masculinity had prepared for them. Women did not any longer simply want to live solely in relation to men and children. They were searching for their own voice, and seeking to define a different conception of identity and meaning in their lives. This involved a challenge to established relations of sexual power and subordination.

For men, the feminist challenge meant questioning assumed notions of masculinity. We had to recognise that as men we could no longer call on the automatic support of women, but had to find a way of relating more openly and emotionally to each other. We had to explore our own desires to control and dominate in relationships. Through coming to a deeper understanding of growing up as men, we could recognise the strength of sexual politics to render visible the structures that underlie the universal voice of reason which we easily appropriate as men before learning to speak for ourselves as gendered subjects. We could begin to explore different notions of masculinity. This was not an easy process.

As men, especially middle-class men, we found it easier to intellectualise our emotions and feelings rather than share them more openly. It was easy to respond with guilt to the challenges of the women's movement, thinking that all we could do as men would be to reject our masculinity, for this was directly expressive of a relationship of power. This rejection appeared as a way of supporting the demands of the movement.[9] It could endorse feelings of self-hatred and self-rejection that are never far from the surface within a Protestant culture. Only later in the mid-1970s, in the context of the *Achilles' Heel* collective, were there also glimpses of a more creative kind of politics which would begin to develop a deeper grasp of men's experience, working for more positive ways men could relate. This involved coming to terms with traditional notions of heterosexuality and the fear many of us had about developing closeness with other men. It also involved accepting the validity of our own sexual expression as heterosexual, rather than feeling that it had to be essentially oppressive to women and gay men. This did not have to involve ignoring or denying the power of heterosexual norms within the larger society.

THEORY AND EXPERIENCE

In the darker times of the 1980s, it became difficult to communicate the enormous excitement at the new forms of politics that were developing in the late 1960s and early 1970s. There was a desire for people to live differently and to see these changes as an integral aspect of their politics. It was through the different experiments in communal living and collective community projects that we thought we would deepen our political grasp, insights and understanding. We were suspicious of abstract theory, possibly too suspicious. There was a wisdom of the day that there was more to be learnt from a 'politics of experience'. This did not mean accepting things as they were or adopting a passive relationship to our experience of the social world. In its own way it challenged traditional empiricist conceptions of experience. It was searching for a different conception of experience, and promised a way of grounding our politics.

This period carried with it a positive distrust of notions that we had not experienced for ourselves, which related to a deeper awareness about the quality of experience within corporate capitalism. Often our experience is mediated. We become the passive consumers and observers of a spectacle we assimilate through the different forms of media.[10] Ours was the first generation that had been brought up on TV, which had been popularised in the mid-1950s. We had seen everything. The world lay before us waiting to be consumed. This produced its own form of controlled excitement. The world was not to be touched but to be looked at. Often it felt as if we were not supposed to live our lives – we were to experience our lives as if we were observers of them. This is also especially related to the experience of masculinity. We can discover ourselves watching, even commenting on the ways we are with people, even making love to them. It is as if we are moved to a point outside our own experience, trapped into a position of 'observer'. It is little wonder that this becomes the dominant image of impartiality and truth within the social sciences.

The notion of trusting our experience was developing as a critical idea. It did not mean accepting what we had been brought up to be, but it involved a critical relationship to traditional notions of femininity and masculinity, grasping these as embedded in relations of power and subordination. It meant we could come to a different sense of ourselves as 'individuals' if we could share what it had been for us to grow up into the society as 'women' or 'men'. We came to realise that the individual experience that liberal moral and political theory represents as 'private' and 'unique' is also a shared social and historical experience. The particular ways we related to cultural expectations and relations of power might depend upon our early experience within the family, and this also needed to be understood. There was a developing interest in different forms of therapy and psychoanalytic theory and a renewed theoretical interest in the historical attempts to bring Marx and Freud into fruitful relationship with each other.[11]

This did not mean submerging notions of 'individuality'. Rather these were given a new meaning and setting. This is extremely important for socialist theory. It was a way of recognising whatever emancipatory truths are expressed within liberal notions of 'individuality'. It gave the liberal idea that as individuals we have to choose what we want to do with our lives, a new meaning. At the same time, women were recognising that this was never a choice open to them. So the demand to be treated as a person in your own right, able to make individual decisions for yourself and be recognised as having an individual life of your own, was powerfully challenging to the social relations of power and subordination. It also meant that socialist theory would have to come to terms with individual differences, and had to acknowledge that people

had a different experience and would want different things out of life.
This was in no way a regression to bourgeois theory. Rather, it was a
critique of the naïve assumptions about the 'sameness' of people that
had for so long crippled the advance of socialist theory.[12]

But this also brought forward a deeply democratic strand. It meant
recognising that people had to learn to trust their own experience.
Others cannot learn for us. We have to learn for ourselves. A socialist
movement has to encourage the equal participation and development of
all of us. This involves a recognition of the differences that exist between
us. People need to be acknowledged for the differences in their
sexualities, ethnic and racial backgrounds. We have to take seriously
what it means being black in a predominantly white society, a woman in
male society, a gay man or lesbian within a society that normalises
heterosexuality, a Buddhist, Jew, Hindu or Muslim within a predominantly Christian society. People do not want to feel that these parts of
themselves have to be denied or acknowledged in a patronising way as if
they are not a real and important aspect of people's identity, culture and
history.

Liberalism too often marginalises these sources of identity in casting
these aspects of people's experience into the 'private realm', or seeing
them as forms of determination or unfreedom that people will want to
leave behind as they become free and autonomous individuals able to
make their own individual choices, regardless of class, race, ethnicity or
gender. Supposedly, they have little consequence for the respect people
are owed as individuals in the arena of social and political life.
Liberalism all too often thinks it is treating people equally in its very
readiness to ignore these aspects of people's experience, wanting to treat
people as 'equals' despite these differences. Not only does this deny us
an understanding of the structures of oppression and subordination, but
it leaves us with a limited vision of freedom, equality and justice. If
politics is to be renewed, these issues have to be taken seriously.

2   Consciousness-raising

MEN AND CONSCIOUSNESS-RAISING

Consciousness-raising has a different significance and meaning for men than for women, but it is no less important. It provides men with a way of exploring the interrelationship of the personal and the political, the emotional and the structural. It is not unproblematic for men because we have often been brought up to be wary of engaging emotionally with other men so that often it is easier for us to intellectualise our experience rather than share it. It is exactly here that we have traditionally been dependent on women, though we often fail to identify the dependency for what it is, so used are we to identifying our masculinity with being independent and self-sufficient. It becomes almost second nature to us.[1] We learn to pride ourselves in not needing others, which is partly what makes it so difficult to acknowledge, let alone identify and name, our needs within relationships.

It has become important to reassert the significance of the felt knowledge we draw from consciousness-raising because it stands in contrast to the dominant rationalistic culture. Too often we assume that we can guide our lives and control ourselves through reason alone. Often this leaves us with a limited conception of our possibilities as men. At the same time, there is an enduring tendency to treat consciousness-raising as if it were inherently subjective and personal, unconcerned with the larger structures of sexual power and domination, or as a practice that has outlived itself. But consciousness-raising has been crucial (although its power has not been fully appreciated) in that it represents a personal and political practice which focuses on the relationship between identity and historical experience. People have come together to understand what is shared in their individual experience.

Nevertheless, for many of us, the very idea of men's consciousness-raising groups and of a men's politics can seem awkward and strange. It seems to go against the important realisation that the culture, politics and forms of association we inherit have been created *for* men and *by* men. Both reformist and revolutionary political movements have acknowledged that the power and privileges that accrue to men are a problematic aspect of our society. Feminism reminds us that this is a power which has been systematically withheld from women, whose oppression is institutionalised in the family, law, politics, sexuality and culture. Feminists have emphasised the pervasive nature of this power, insisting that it is important to see that it formulates a reality which women experience walking in the streets in the middle of the day, let alone coming home at night. The whistle can signal the power any man has to objectify any woman, regardless of her class position. And if she is not flattered or does not like it, this only shows there is something wrong with her.

Yet the questions this raises for men have not been adequately approached, let alone dealt with, in mainstream socialist politics.[2] How are we, as men, to respond to the oppression of women? How can we relate to feminism? Are we to see ourselves solely as oppressors? How are we to relate to the social power we have, as men, within the larger society? I want to think here about the contribution consciousness-raising can make to our engagement with these questions.

MEN AND FEMINISM

Since the late 1960s, we have been challenged by feminism, for the ways we have been brought up to be, as men. Women were no longer prepared to subordinate their individual needs to servicing us. They wanted to live their own independent lives. They were no longer prepared to do more housework or childcare. Women rejected the notion that they were somehow born for domesticity and motherhood. For many women it was no longer acceptable for a man to bring back the wages and act the boss at home, waiting for his wishes to be met. Women were no longer prepared to discount their relationships with their women friends, nor did they always want to be ready to support us emotionally once we had come home.

Women had identities of their own, jobs of their own, minds of their own, sexualities of their own. Through consciousness-raising, women were gaining a sense of their individuality and their power. This was scary and threatening for us, as men. So much of our sense of male identity is tied up with our sense of control that we did not know *how* to be. It is in this connection that men's consciousness-raising can be an important developmental facet of a contribution to sexual politics. It can be part of a process of struggling with the sources of masculinity, and not simply another practice for consolidating male power.

Those of us who experienced this challenge directly were brought face to face with the years of accumulated anger and frustration which had been created through the years of subordination. Many relationships cracked up. But these were also years of intense political and personal exploration and discovery as men and women were trying to learn to have more equal relationships. These are experiences we should be learning from, however painfully they ended, not discounting as 'naïve'. For example, we can learn something about our own relationship to our experience through thinking about the ways we tried to develop an alternative radical morality. Even if our expectations for change were falsely grounded, we have to learn the ease with which we became 'moralistic' about the 'correct equal non-monogamous, non-possessive relationship'. We were more deeply gripped by notions of an inherited moral culture than we would want to admit. In the 1980s, we learnt a new humility as we looked back to the confidence and hopes of an earlier, more prosperous, time. We have to learn to trust the lessons of our experience, rather than forsake our experience for some abstract theory. Consciousness-raising can help us to build on, rather than disregard, these lessons.

In the early days of consciousness-raising, men would often admit that they did not really like men and that their closest relationships were with women. We had been brought up so relentlessly to compete with each other that it just did not feel safe to open up with men. We could not *trust* each other as men, nor did we have much idea of how to create such a trust. So men would say, 'I don't really know what I am doing here because I don't really get on with men as a group.' It is always scary to change, especially if we do not know what is going to happen. We desperately need to maintain control even though we declare otherwise.

Within consciousness-raising groups, control was often maintained by taking 'sexism' to be a 'struggle' that was completely external. It became a cause that could be organised around. It did not have to challenge the very terms of our politics. Sexism did not have to do with us, with the relationships that were going on between us as men in the room. The depths of our rationalism made it hard to talk personally and directly, and often we did not know how to identify the difficulties we felt. We did not want people coming too close.

The other option was for men to maintain a distance from consciousness-raising completely. It was easy to echo the feminist argument that men getting together was simply another way of men reorganising their power. A 'holier-than-thou' deference to feminism could be used to put down other men who were becoming involved in consciousness-raising; yet to maintain a distance from this practice perhaps had more to do with a fear of it and of the threat of connection that it posed. It is to fail to recognise the importance of men changing themselves as an integral aspect of challenging the oppression of women. As men we cannot simply be spectators because we are individually involved with sustaining the relationships of power and subordination that are being questioned and challenged.

Traditionally, the Left has separated and compartmentalised 'personal' and 'political' issues. Thousands of people have 'been through' the organised Left since the late 1960s and emerged feeling uneasy and a little guilty that they are not active enough, but knowing that there is something deeply unsatisfactory about a politics that focuses exclusively on the abstraction of 'the class struggle' and has no space for the pressures and joys of everyday life. However, no systematic critique of the traditions that dominate the Left has emerged.

It is in this context that talk of men's politics is so threatening since it challenges the conventional separation of personal from political; but sexual politics has been important for many of us in renewing our political ideas, energy and language by firmly grounding our politics in our lived experience. It transforms our understanding of the workings of both modern capitalism and traditional politics and it also shifts our grasp of the connections between identity, power and consciousness as we are forced to rework the relations between class, race, ethnicity and gender. In order to illuminate some of these connections I need to share more about what can be learnt from the experience of men's consciousness-raising.

WHY CONSCIOUSNESS-RAISING?

It is easy for people to think of consciousness-raising as a 'stage' that women have to go through on their way to becoming 'political'. This is where women learn that their feelings of dependency and inadequacy are not their individual fault, but a condition that is socially and historically created, through the powerlessness of women in the larger society. So it is assumed that heterosexual men, in particular, do not need consciousness-raising, especially if they have learnt to pay deference to the women's movement. This reinforces a cultural split between public and private and a conception that consciousness-raising is talking about one's private individual experience and so cannot have much to do with the public realm of politics. So it becomes conceived of as a necessary activity for the politically naïve.

through feminism learnt masculine restrictions

This helps to institutionalise the liberal distinction between 'private' and 'public'. It is only in the public political realm that we are supposedly dealing with issues of power. So, in the 1980s, it was not unusual for men to treat an earlier phase of consciousness-raising by men in the 1970s as an example of 'personal' politics when men were supposedly concerned with personal and sexual issues rather than with the broader realm of politics. This can further fragment our understanding of women's oppression into the 'private' that has to do with consciousness-raising and 'personal relationships', and the 'public' institutionalised subordination of women that has to do with politics and the struggle for power. This denies both historical reality and the political significance of consciousness-raising.

Rather, it has partly been through consciousness-raising that we have asked new questions as we have begun to learn *how* the oppressive structures of the family, sexual stereotypes, work, guilt, morality, authority relationships and class relationships, work themselves out in our individual lives. This is no less true for men than for women, and it is not something that should be seen as limited to an earlier time, somehow of less relevance to men now. It has a different significance for men, but the ease with which we intellectualise and distance our experience as men gives it a continuing significance, if men are to create a different relationship to their power, emotional lives and relationships.

Men want to be men

I was brought up, like many other men, feeling anxious about whether I was a 'real man'. Masculinity is something we have got to live up to. Was I strong enough? Was I responsible enough to be a 'real man'? There was the fear and anxiety that I would let myself down – be called a 'sissy' or a 'weed'. I was scared of not being good enough at sports at school. I could not admit to others that I did not like football. I had to find ways of getting on with the boys who were good at sport because they had the power to put me down. I had to learn to please and ingratiate and to suppress my own feelings and responses, my own anger and frustration, so that I was liked by the others. I did not want to fail in the eyes of others, even if this meant sacrificing a sense of myself.

Many of us felt ambiguous, even oppressed by the image of masculinity we were forced to live up to. This image had an institutionalised power. Too often, feminist theory has identified men, as such, with the dominant form of masculinity, so making it almost impossible to explore the tension between the power men have within the larger society and the ways they might individually experience themselves as powerless. Obviously, our differing class, ethnic and racial backgrounds affect how we come to terms with our masculinity, but our grasp of class relationships can shift as we learn what conflicts and tensions we have shared with other men. We learn how to bring together issues of class and masculinity and of how we share a relationship to women which cuts across our different individual histories. We have been forced to make similar sacrifices in our emotionality. None of us wants to be thought of as 'soft'. Often we just do not know what it is we are feeling. We experience ourselves as locked firmly inside ourselves. We have learnt to grit our teeth so that we can get on in the work process.

We have done a great deal of damage to ourselves but we are barely conscious of this nor able to identify it, because we have learnt to identify 'happiness' with 'success'. If we are 'successful', then we think we must be happy. Or we can think that happiness does not matter in the world of individual achievement. The nature of our gendered identity as men is rendered invisible as we learn to speak in the universal language of reason. On the Left, we often reproduce these notions as we make these same sacrifices in the name of duty to the distant revolution, having limited our understanding and imagination through learning that it does not make sense to think about the nature of socialism, while living within the class relationships of a capitalist society. We inherit a rationalistic culture where what matters is that we have the 'right' analysis, regardless of what people are feeling. The distinction between reason and feeling is barely acknowledged as we assume that people establish the meaning of their lives by reason alone.

GUILT AND SELF-DENIAL

Bourgeois society brings us up with a strong sense of duty and obligation. We have to be ready to do what is required of us, regardless of what we are feeling. In this way, sacrifice in the name of career, family, state, larger society, becomes part of our 'second nature'. The Left has often built upon this structure of sentiments, rather than challenged them. This is hardly surprising since these very assumptions are reproduced in so much of our moral and philosophical inheritance. An awareness of the structures of class, racial and sexual oppression feeds our sense that we do not *deserve* to be happy. Our individual lives lose any meaning or significance, beyond the private sphere, in the face of the realities of 'class struggle'. Our choices, needs and wants cannot be given any importance. It is hard to maintain a sense of balance, far easier to feel disdainful towards others who are unprepared to make the same sacrifices.

This is not to underestimate the importance of routine political work, or to argue that it should all be enjoyable. But it is important to see that the contradictions we feel are not in our heads, or to be resolved at some ideological level, but exist inescapably in our lives, living as we do in a society of class, racial and sexual injustice. There is a sense in which the politics of self-denial on the Left reproduce the dominant emotional and social relationships of bourgeois society. This means that the Left does not speak to many people who have somehow questioned these assumptions through, say, youth culture, music, drugs, therapy and Growth movement.

Some of these influences can be seen in the early 'Men against Sexism' tendencies in the men's movement, which formed some of the earliest developments in the 1970s.[3] As men we often felt guilty for being oppressive to women. We were offered the idea that we could deal with this guilt if we struggled hard against sexism or put all our energies into supporting the women's movement. Some positive things happened, especially men learning to relate more to children, through organising various crèches. Sometimes this formed the seeds of new men's groups. But there was a general tendency to minimise the ways we can change within a capitalist society, reproducing a split between personal change and the political transformation of capitalism. It was as if the recognition of the oppressive role of men was merely a stage in being mobilised into what was taken to be an independent struggle against capital. Sometimes this went along with the feeling that it was 'bad' to be a man, especially a heterosexual man. In the London men's conference in 1975, there was a strong challenge from gay men arguing that men should make the political choice to be gay, since otherwise we were colluding in supporting the oppressive norm of heterosexuality.[4]

It was important to be reminded that we need broad and open discussion on the nature of heterosexuality, since it is not the fixed quality we are brought up to believe. But nor is our sexuality something we can make clear choices about, as if it is simply a matter of *choosing* to be gay because this is taken to be 'politically correct'. These arguments have caused a lot of pain and confusion. They have led many people to withdraw from sexual politics entirely, convinced that it is simply a luxury for the middle class. This is to miss the feminist challenges that have been made to traditional roles and relationships in both working-class and middle-class families. It is to overlook the tensions which overflow into violence in many families, the physical and emotional damage done to children and thousands of children who are being left in care. In terms of all these issues, feminism has opened the way to a renewal of a socialist theory that can connect to the realities of individual lives and it is crucial for men to be integral to this challenge although this is not without its difficulties.

Many men have felt stuck for years now in the condition of being a man, living in precarious relationships with women who have changed through the women's movement. They have learnt to be aware of the language they use, especially when women are around. They adopt a soft and unassuming manner, always ready to seek approval from women. Many men have been made uncomfortable with their masculinity, but do not see any possibilities of redefining it. Often they end up wishing that they were not men, or simply further withdrawing into themselves. In some strange way, men can cease to exist at all, as their sense of self has been so undermined they cannot be the way they used to be, nor do they know *how* they want to be. It is almost as if they cease to exist and find it difficult to define themselves. We are constantly challenged in our relationships with women to be more open and emotionally supportive, but often it is hard even to grasp what we are being asked to do. We wish we could be, but we do not know what to do.

The changes we have made can seem superficial. It is almost as if we have pretended, even to ourselves, that we can make ourselves different and that, for instance, we do not have sexist fantasies, even dreams. It is almost as if we want to believe that we can change through an act of will. I want to explore the historical and cultural sources for some of these deeply held masculine notions which leave us so little understanding of ourselves and how we can change.

Again, traditions in the broader culture make it hard to identify the predicament that many men find themselves in. The ease with which we still assume, especially on the Left, that 'individualism' and 'individuality' are bourgeois, while collectivity is essentially 'socialist', makes it hard to appreciate that socialist culture has to redefine the notion of masculinity for us to be able to live out of the strengths of our individuality. Otherwise the danger is that we further the processes illuminated in Orwell's 1984 vision of the very obliteration of individuality. This is something crucial that the women's movement recognises in practice. Women demanded to be treated *as people* in their own right, since they recognised the ways they were being undermined and ceased to exist as 'individuals' through the social forms of dependency, powerlessness and objectification. They also recognised the need for solidarity and support in struggling to realise a sense of themselves which is systematically negated by the structures of power and subordination.

For men, a similar process has to take place, within which we separate ourselves from the competitive and ego-centred notions of masculinity as we gain a fuller sense of our individual needs. This involves developing a critical relationship with what have traditionally been taken to be qualities of masculinity. So we become critical not of reason, but of the particular development of our rationalistic conception of rationality, partly because of the ways that our minds and understanding are separated from the rest of our emotional and bodily experience.[5] The abilities to organise, and the practical skills some men have, are not to be depreciated. It is only when they are used to put others down and to prove ourselves better than others, that we begin to be suspicious. We can appreciate our abilities to concentrate, but have to wonder when it means that we are 'cut off' from the situations we are in.

MEN AND MASCULINITY

An aspect of this critical relationship to masculinity will be a discovery of our own caring, gentleness and vulnerability, as well as our power, anger, resentment, love and understanding. In this way, we will be redefining our masculinity as we alter our vision and expectations of ourselves. We will become aware of the damage done to us, as well as the damage we continually do to ourselves as well as to others. We have been educated to put our careers and our jobs above our relationships. We organise our lives, especially within the middle class, to make sure we 'get on' in the capitalist world. Just think how most men's lives would have to change if they took their kids to school and picked them up at four o'clock. Capitalist society expects us to minimise our relationships with children, with friends, with lovers. We do it ourselves, at some level unaware of the choices we make without realising or understanding how our lives are being impoverished and how others are often being made to suffer.

A 'men's politics' has to challenge the forms of male socialisation while going beyond the notions of role theory which fail to illuminate the larger context of the social relations of power. Many people are beginning to wonder about why boys are not allowed to have emotions and feelings, acknowledge their weakness, or admit that a girl knows more than them or that they do not like sport. But people often fail to appreciate how deeply forms of masculinity are tied into the very organisation of production in both capitalist and socialist societies. It is possible to make some of these changes, particularly in primary schools, without challenging the larger structures of power in society. This shows up the inadequacy of talking about 'socialisation' without talking about the 'character forms' which are necessary for men to perform their tasks within capitalist society.[6]

A men's politics that challenges these aspects of male socialisation cannot avoid challenging the larger structures of power in society. At present, men are socialised in a way that equips them to function well within the capitalist productive system, but if men are able significantly to change the way they relate to one another, to their bodies, to their children, and to their emotional selves, that will profoundly alter the forms of their exploitation as workers. At the same time, the forms of controls are often built into the work processes themselves, so that particular developments in the work process might mean that capital does not need people to identify so strongly with the work they do. The traditional identification of men with 'men's work' and with the idea of a 'fair day's work for a fair day's pay' is being undermined through the restructuring of the labour processes of modern capitalism. This itself is provoking a crisis in masculinity for many men who are unprepared to deal with these changes.[7]

It is not that men are competitive or ambitious by nature. Rather, the institutions of capitalist society are essentially competitive and hierarchical, forcing men to be competitive to survive. Of course men are competitive and ambitious in other sorts of societies, but this is given a particular form and organisation within capitalist societies. Men have to show themselves to be competent and capable at their work in order to win promotion, even if they do not any longer identify so exclusively with work. This is not to say there is anything wrong with competence and ability, but these are developed in a context in which men cannot admit doubts, fears, anxieties.

Rather, these are all suppressed in the show of strength and self-control which is so closely identified with our very sense of masculine identity. The anxieties and frustrations are brought back to the home. The tensions are offloaded as one lays them on one's lover or wife. We are constantly seeking a confirmation and support for our decisions which we rarely get at work. We return next morning feeling that we were in the right all the time. Often this means being a 'strong adult' at work while being a little boy who wants to be cared for and protected at home.[8]

This fragmentation within masculine identity can create all kinds of tensions within relationships, which are forced to take on anger, tensions and frustrations originally created within production. But women are less prepared to support men emotionally through all this, realising that they have got enough to deal with themselves already, so we have to look to ourselves as men to find the support and understanding we have traditionally looked to women to provide. But often we discover that we do not have a language in which to identify what is happening to us, nor the friends to support us. We cannot just change by acts of will – because we have to learn to discriminate and identify our feelings and emotions and articulate them, rather than relying on women to intuit our needs and meet them without our having even identified them. We resent being left exposed in this situation. This is another aspect of a contemporary crisis in masculinity.

How should we live as socialists within a capitalist society? For some people this simply means having different 'ideas' and 'beliefs' to communicate. So for teachers it can simply mean teaching different ideas, not developing different relationships within which teaching and learning take place. But if we understand that sexual politics as a politics of process and identity is integral to a socialist vision, we are led to consider authority relations in society in different terms. This can help us become aware, for example, of the importance of pre-figurative work.

If, as a teacher, you encourage students to do co-operative work, they can either be accused of cheating or you are seen as challenging the system because students can no longer be individually assessed. Similarly, we have to negotiate different levels of contradiction as men aware and conscious of sexist institutions and relationships. These situations come together when I realise that, if I am to change within the context of the teaching I do, then I need the support of other men who are also redefining their masculinity in an open and public way. Otherwise, 'being anti-sexist' can be a very lonely activity, cutting us off from traditional male bonding and often suspected by women for claiming a supportive difference from other men.

As men become aware of the workings of patriarchy not only as it affects women, but also as it affects the lives of men and their relationships as partners, friends, lovers, fathers and workers, so it can be important carefully to consider and make demands for ending violence against women, ending the pervasiveness of pornographic and degrading images, for paternity leave, for time off to collect children from school, to end shift work and night work, for part-time work on full pay so we can be equally involved in the lives of our children. In this sense, we need more than consciousness-raising, or rather a consciousness-raising practice which helps us articulate and feel validated in these concretised demands. In some senses, we have got the options of whether we make changes, although these options are themselves set within social relationships of dominance and oppression.

But once we have begun changing, then others are bound to think of us as 'weird', 'funny', or 'threatening'. In some ways, we can become less capable of doing the work expected of us, if we are living in fuller contact with how we experience what we are doing, rather than simply cutting off from our emotional and somatic realities. In this situation, we are up against the structures of power, in a way that women, gay men and lesbians have experienced for a long time. We begin to experience the power of sexism for ourselves. This is when we will need the support and solidarity of others.

Understandably, many people have doubts about any idea of a men's politics, assuming that it is the oppressors organising themselves. In the end it is what people are prepared to do to change their lives and relationships which counts. It is important not to exaggerate the strength and power of the women's movement, and to recognise how entrenched the structures of patriarchy actually are. I know many women feel that very little has changed. People have learnt painfully that changing some of the structures of everyday life is not enough to change the powerlessness and dependency that women feel. Women have been forced to recognise how deeply internalised some of these feelings are. This is a moment of vulnerability in which women are still bound to be sceptical about men getting together.

It can become a further source of cynicism that when men have got together in organisations it has often been to defend rights which they see as threatened directly by feminism. It is important for men involved in sexual politics to grasp the significance of this. This does not mean that feminism can set an agenda for the development of men's politics, but men would be setting up a false parallelism if they did not recognise how women have for centuries been systematically oppressed and subordinated by men. It is crucial for men to support women's struggles while recognising that it is also crucial for them to take responsibility for themselves, which means engaging critically with those men who seek to defend what they take to be their rights, which they see as threatened by feminism. But these are issues, especially where they have to do with men's relationships with children, that cannot be settled by principle alone or by assuming that virtue or injury is on one side alone.

These issues are compounded by the realisation that emotions and feelings have been an area in which, as men, we have very much needed women. This has been one of the few areas of women's power, so that women can feel that if men are more into their feelings, they will need women less, and women will have even less power. I have heard this many times since publication of *Achilles' Heel*, the journal of men's politics in the mid-1970s. I am sure that it expresses a genuine fear. But I also know of many women who, over the fifteen years, have repeatedly said that they are sick and tired of supporting men in their efforts to change. This is what puts enormous tension and strain into relationships. Certainly, as men we have continually to reassess our relationship to feminism, but we also have to learn to take responsibility for our own changes as we develop a critical relationship to our own history and power. This is still a slow and faltering process, even if there is much greater awareness of the issues involved as we enter the 1990s.

We need different visions of ourselves but these have to be firmly grounded in a sense of the difficulties, hopes and pain of developing more equal relationships with women. We have to face issues about the relationship between men – between heterosexual and gay men – as well as raising a problematic about the relationship between gay men and lesbians. In all this, it is important to acknowledge the strengths of gay movement politics while recognising that it is important not to claim somehow to be speaking for gay men, but to allow space for different masculinities that each have to discover their own voice. Only if we learn to care, love and respect ourselves and other men, can we hope for more equal and loving relationships with other men and women. This has become all the more urgent in a time when AIDS has left many gay men feeling isolated and alone. As more men become involved in a collective practice of redefining our different masculinities, it becomes crucial to learn from each other.

3 Feminism

MEN AND THE WOMEN'S MOVEMENT

It is difficult to avoid generalisations when talking about heterosexual men's relationships to feminism, but it is a crucial issue if we are to face the challenges of feminism for men whilst also recognising the importance of men rediscovering and reworking their inherited forms of masculinity. This is in part something that men have to do for themselves and it is important to learn from history in this regard. It is bound to bring into focus men's relationships with each other and so inevitably the relationship of heterosexual with gay men.

Unless we are clear about the relationships of power involved, we will be in danger of invoking a false parallelism between the situation of women and men, or else we will talk generally about men, ignoring the specificities of sexual orientation, race, class and ethnicity. It is important to argue the case against prevailing notions of masculinity without seeking in any way to minimise the injustices perpetrated against women, gay men and lesbians. But it is also crucial for heterosexual men to take responsibility for their own masculinity which has remained invisible within the male-dominated universalist traditions of a liberal moral and political culture.

As men we have to learn to talk for ourselves. This is paradoxical since it might seem that we never stop talking for anyone else. But it is this appropriation of other voices that has obscured our incapacity to speak specifically out of our own experience. Nor can feminism be left for women to get on with, as if it does not affect or challenge us as men. To say that 'it has nothing to do with us' is a typical response of the socially powerful, who do not have to listen for they have the power to be heard. Strangely, we are still at the beginning of men's responses to feminism, but it is as well to learn from our history, for at some level it is a history which is still largely ignored. What is clear is that our lives as men have changed, even if we have been slow to recognise it or would wish it otherwise.

As men, we have responded to the women's movement in different ways. Some of us ignored it, thinking that it would disappear. Some of us felt that it was a dangerous distraction from the central issues of class politics. Some of us were simply excited by it, but we were all, in one way or another, threatened and confused by it, as soon as it touched the everyday reality of our relationships. Somehow politics was being brought home into the kitchen, the living room and the bedroom. All our assumptions about ourselves and about our relationships with women and with men, were being questioned and challenged. This has gone on now for more than twenty years. Our lives have changed. Our relationships have changed. Many men have been forced to recognise the centrality of women's oppression to the organisation of capitalist society. But how are we, as men, to respond to feminism?

I do not know that we are even asking the right questions at the moment, let alone being clear about answers. This is what makes me suspicious of the confidence with which some men have argued that it is all very well for men to get together in consciousness-raising situations, but anything calling itself a 'movement' is clearly to be rejected. For one thing, there are different kinds of movements, and people have not suggested there is the same basis of a shared experience of oppression for men getting together to redefine our masculinities and place within the larger society, as there is for women. The situation of men and women is clearly different.

But how are we to understand these differences and the consequences for the ways we live and organise ourselves as men? It has been easier to avoid these questions. We need to learn from women about the experience of feminism so that we can begin to work out what this means for our lives as men. This is not an attempt to reappropriate the experience of women, but is an attempt to take seriously the challenges made to our inherited conceptions of masculinity and the ways we are as men. Humility is needed as we appreciate how much we can learn. This itself is an important reversal since it is usually men who talk while women are supposed to listen.

WOMEN'S LIBERATION

In the United States in the late 1960s, women began rejecting the ways they had been subordinated within the anti-Vietnam war movement. They were no longer prepared to cook meals and look after children while men went to political meetings. Women demanded to be treated as people in their own right – thereby rediscovering a radical impulse in what was too easily dismissed as a liberal notion – and were no longer prepared to subordinate their own needs to the needs of men. This was the beginning of a powerful critique of the ways women had been brought up to find pleasure and happiness through servicing the needs of men and children. Women did not any longer see why men should not look after the house and children, so that they could have an equal chance of going to the anti-war meetings. They asserted the equal value of their lives, their needs, their desires, their time, as they challenged in practice the meaning of liberal notions of equality as equal respect. They were not prepared to allow that their husband or boyfriend's time was more important simply because he was doing waged work. Nor were they prepared to subordinate their relationships with other women, to be ready to meet the needs of their partners. But it was not always easy to reorganise relationships in order to accommodate these changes.

Through consciousness-raising groups, women realised they could not individually overcome feelings of insecurity, inadequacy and worthlessness without the support and solidarity of relationships with other women. Strength and understanding come from realising that you are not alone, but that other women have been brought up to think and feel in the same negative and self-destructive ways about themselves. This means you do not have simply to blame and punish yourself. Women understood how the expectations and treatment they received and largely accepted within the family, school and job, made them feel the way they did. So women realised that they were not going to feel differently about themselves and experience themselves differently, if they did not change the relationships they had with people.

It is misleading to say simply – as many men have tended to do – that in consciousness-raising people come to understand that the source of their individual feelings of inadequacy and insecurity, say, are not 'inner' but exist 'externally' in the ways that the social institutions of the family, school and work are organised. This is to pose too mechanistic an alternative that simply fails to illuminate the challenges presented to our rationalist traditions.

We certainly learn that we are up against the ways that society is organised and this does challenge how we are brought up in different ways as boys and girls to blame ourselves for the ways we are feeling, so that if we feel inadequate this somehow reflects a fault in ourselves. But this psychological reductionism, which is an integral part of the way liberal theory legitimates social inequalities, only leads us to punish ourselves more and feel even worse about ourselves. Consciousness-raising can challenge the ways we are brought up, especially within the middle class, to individualise our experience, to blame and condemn ourselves for the ways we feel. In this way, we can learn *how* we have come to feel the ways we do, by understanding how we were made to feel, say, by our parents and the organisation of family relationships. But there is nothing mechanistic in this.

There have been two inadequate ways of theorising consciousness-raising on the Left. Some of the Left groups have wanted to grasp it as a shift from 'psychology' to 'politics'. So it is seen as a way women can realise that the sources of their oppression are not 'inner' and therefore they do not simply have themselves to blame – as liberal moral theory would tempt us into thinking – but exist 'externally' in the ways social institutions are organised. In this way, consciousness-raising involves a short-term transition towards politics. This fits in neatly with assumptions of Leninist politics, which tends to see politics as a more 'advanced' form of consciousness. This leaves the nature and conception of politics untouched and unchanged by the experience of feminism and sexual politics. The Left organisations have nothing to learn, but everything to teach. The reality of women's oppression is conceded, but it is left to women to organise around it, so bringing more women into the organisations. The women's movement became a recruiting ground as the traditional ideologies of the Left reasserted themselves in the late 1970s. The 'material basis' of women's oppression can safely be talked about by one and all.[1]

The other argument, influenced by Althusser, has the same general drift. It talks about the 'individual' as an aspect of bourgeois ideology, so that, through the process of consciousness-raising, the 'individual' is dissolved into his or her class, sexual and racial determinants. Through consciousness-raising we are supposed to demystify the very category of the 'individual'. In this way, we are supposed to make the move from bourgeois 'psychology' to Marxist 'politics'. This tradition is less anxious to show the 'material basis' of women's oppression in a narrowly conceived notion of economic and work relationships, being more willing to recognise ideology as an autonomous level of social power.

But if structuralist Marxism can acknowledge patriarchy, it is only as something operating at an ideological level in capitalist society. This does mean it can more fully recognise the significance of ideological struggle; but this is done at the cost of isolating ideology into a sphere of its own, so that we never grasp the ways sexism exists not simply at the level of ideology and culture, but is structured into the very relationships at work. This preserves the 'economy' as an autonomous and independent sphere which can be tightly controlled by the party machine. In its own way, this helps explain why, for instance, the Communist Party has been able to give more space to sexual and cultural politics in the last few years. Althusserian Marxism has given a way of isolating feminism and sexual politics theoretically from 'more central' areas of political practice within industry. Economic relations tend to be technologically conceived rather than seen as part of an ongoing relationship of power and subordination which is contested at different levels.[2]

INDIVIDUALISM AND INDIVIDUALITY

There is an important difference between individualism and individuality, which consciousness-raising can help both men and women in their different ways appreciate in practice. There is a difference between liberal individualism as the moral and political theory of a liberal moral culture, and the struggle to express and live our individuality in our everyday lives. The fact that we come to understand how we have become who we are, through experiences in our families, schools and work, often changes our sense of ourselves as 'individuals'. We recognise, sometimes for the first time, the significance of our class and sexual experiences in the formation of our individualities and sense of self.

But we can also learn to redefine what we want for ourselves as individuals as we begin to separate ourselves from the conventional expectations of 'femininity' and 'masculinity'. We learn that what we are supposed to want for ourselves does not bring us the happiness we want, nor help us satisfy our needs. As men, we are taught to subordinate all our energies and desires to 'getting on' in a job or career. We are taught, especially in the middle class, that 'success' will bring 'happiness', and that 'success' comes with 'individual achievement'. We are automatically suspicious of other men, who are always potential competitors. We learn not to need anything from other men, because we fear this will give them power over us.

So I can begin to understand why it is threatening to acknowledge any need for closeness, love and understanding from other men. This threatens the ways I have been brought up to organise my life. I take it so much for granted that I rarely think about these issues at all. But in acknowledging my needs, I am redefining what I want and need for myself – I am redefining my 'individuality'. I am also moved to be more in touch with how lonely I can feel at work and how little I really expect from others. My relationships and the work situation would have to be reorganised and transformed if I were to get more of my needs fulfilled here.

This is to point to a dialectical relationship between my individual thoughts and feelings and my awareness of the structures of power and authority within which I live my life. Women's rediscovery of this dialectic through concretising it in the personal and political practice of consciousness-raising, then, has power and significance for men in the very ways it challenges the conventional liberal distinctions between 'psychology', 'experience' and 'social power'. My ideas, thoughts, desires and feelings are being constantly affected by the situations I find myself in. They do not simply come from inside of me. This gives people a firmer grasp and contact with their experience, as they redefine the formation of their individuality in the context of personal and social history. In our own generation, this is a way open to us to grasp the meaning of historical materialism, without falling for the kind of crude materialism Marx was anxious to combat.

Let us give an example to show how men have been challenged in their very sense of themselves through feminism. Susan had a relationship with John long before she got involved with the women's movement. She had always been very anxious about whether John liked her friends or not. She had always been ready to change whatever arrangements she had made to see her friends if it turned out that John did not have to work and they could go to the pictures. Her women's group made her question this. Why should she change arrangements she had made, when John was never prepared to do this himself? Anyway, she did not care any longer whether John liked her friends or not. They were not his friends. If John was not working, that was his own choice. He would just have to cook his own dinner and look after himself. She is no longer prepared to subordinate her own needs.

So Susan's desire to be treated as a person in her own right was already a challenge to the kind of relationship she had with John. The women's movement helped her to decide that she was not prepared to go on as before. Things had to change. Susan came to see some of the ways that the power relationship between her and John was implicit in the everyday organisation of the relationship. She did not see any longer why she should have to do any more housework or childcare than John. It is not good enough for John to say that he 'doesn't know how to cook', or that 'the kids prefer spending time with Susan'. Susan insists he learn to cook and change his relationship to the children, so they do not see him as such a remote and distant person. His relationship with the children is not fixed, nor does it simply reflect his individual qualities. It is created in particular conditions and it can change.

Mechanical interpretations of consciousness-raising which wish to separate the 'psychology' from the 'politics' of the situation can have damaging and painful consequences. In the 1960s it was this inherited vision of personal change that generated the idea that if you change the situation, then you would change these feelings. This involved a very simplistic psychology which said that our feelings were simply the product of our social conditioning. If we have learnt anything, we have learnt with the experience of the late 1960s and early 1970s how painful and difficult it can be to make these changes, even if we have the support and solidarity of others.

Our patterns and feelings do not only grow out of the social relationships of the present, so changing automatically when these relationships change, in the way that Marxists at the time of the Russian Revolution thought that sexual relations would change with the socialisation of property relations. Rather they also have a deep history in our past relationships and history. This does not mean we cannot radically change our relationships, so changing ourselves, but we cannot simply assume these changes will happen automatically, or that we can change simply through individual acts of will.

This helps explain why it is crucially important to understand people's personal and political experiences in the 1960s and 1970s, rather than simply dismiss them as 'naïve'. This is the way we can learn about the possibilities and processes of change, especially if we begin to appreciate the deeper cultural and philosophical assumptions which were taken for granted in this period of experimentation. This has far wider implications for what we mean by 'revolutionary transformation', as Reich was to face in *The Sexual Revolution*, when he recognised that once the means of production had been socialised in Russia after the revolution in 1917, the expected changes in the 'superstructure' did not occur automatically.[3]

At another level, it means that, though the women's movement is more than twenty years old, we should not overestimate its strength. Rather we should learn how very hard it has been to make and sustain these changes within a society so pervasively sexist and patriarchal. In the 1990s we live in a period in which some of the advances like safe abortions and childcare provision are being continually threatened. But this makes it only more critical for men to deepen our understanding of the challenges of feminism, both theoretically and practically.

Returning to our example, Susan might recognise how necessary it is now to make changes in her relationship with John. But at some level we have to realise this is scary for Susan, especially if it means she is giving up control of the children and kitchen. She knows how much of her own identity has been built around being a good cook and good mother, even though she realises how this has trapped her and prevented her developing parts of herself. The women's movement has made her aware and given her a language in which to identify how much she has sacrificed of herself over the years. She wants to regain her strength and individual power. But she knows that she can only exist as an individual in her own right if things really change in her relationship with John. She knows that it is not simply a matter of his changing his attitude towards her as the liberalism they used to share encouraged her to accept.

They have always tried to organise their relationship as an 'equal partnership' in which they do different things. But she has learnt through her own painful experience of being undermined both mentally and emotionally within the relationship that it has been partly this conception which has trapped her. These different realms have obscured her own experience of subordination. She is not going to carry on doing things for John any longer, so he is going to have to change. Susan wants to be treated like a person with her own needs, wants and interests. She wants John to recognise that she has a life of her own. She realises that a fuller development of her individuality involves both a personal and political challenge to the power John has always been able to assume in their relationship.

This has become a familiar moment of crisis in the lives of many relationships. It is also a moral and intellectual crisis for many men who discover the poverty of both a liberal and Marxist inheritance in helping them isolate the issues involved or in giving them a vision of how they can begin to change. Both traditions seem to deny the centrality of our emotional and personal relations until the damage is done and then leave us with no way of grasping why we cannot *do* anything to make things better.

LIBERATION, NEEDS AND IDENTITY

The women's rights movements fought for equality with men, but this was very much in terms of gaining the same legal and political rights *as men*. This was a struggle to give women equal access to public life, particularly the institutions of representative democracy. These rights were regarded as the rights which citizens could possess in the public realm, so that women could claim them without seeming to challenge the power of men in personal and sexual relationships. This was a particular challenge to the subordination of women and to the notion of male superiority.

This was an assertion of the rights of women, rather than a challenge to male power. Nor was it a challenge which necessarily touched the private realm of domesticity, or the division of duties and responsibilities between men and women. If women were able to pursue careers in the public realm, they had to fulfil all the duties and responsibilities of being a wife and mother too. This was limited in that it was primarily a challenge for access to the 'public sphere', although we should not underestimate its significance in transforming our conceptions of what men and women can do.

The women's movement in the late 1960s talked of liberation, not simply of rights. It extended the notion of the 'political', to show that the very organisation of the family involved relationships of power and subordination. Domestic structures were no longer safe within an ideology of the division of family responsibilities. The ideology of romantic love which said that women were working for love and that 'true fulfilment' comes through domesticity and motherhood, was to become a crucial issue. Problems in relationships could no longer automatically be put down to issues of personality and temperament. In the early days, these notions were all simply seen as 'ideologies' hiding the reality of women's subordination. These were the days in which 'the family', 'monogamy', 'jealousy' and 'possessiveness' all had to be 'smashed' as integral aspects of bourgeois ideology.

We have learnt that we cannot simply change through acts of will, so that we need a much richer and deeper psychological understanding than prevailing liberal and Marxist theory tend to offer. But we have also learnt through the harsher economic realities of the 1980s that the family is a much more contradictory institution for people.[4] For many women it is a place of comfort and love, if it is also a situation of subordination, even violence. We have to be careful that our theories can illuminate these contradictory feelings and experiences rather than force us to make false choices. But this is an integral aspect of a critique of moralism that seems to have as deep a hold over those who would question the personal and sexual relations of bourgeois society as those who would uphold these as ideals we should all be struggling to realise.

The women's movement has often actualised a critique of liberal conceptions of equality in practice. Women were often *told* that they were equal and that they had the same rights as men, even when they experienced subordination in their everyday lives. The language of liberalism was shown up as upholding purely formal notions of equality, as women came to realise that they did not exist as individuals in their own right. The assertion of 'individuality' and the demand 'to be treated like a person' challenged the different ways women had become objectified in consumer capitalism. The liberal language of 'equal rights' mystified the everyday reality of dependency and subordination, as the language of rationality and reason had systematically devalued the significance of much of women's experience.

Politics had come home as we were shown that it was not a matter of what 'attitudes' we took up as men towards women, but of what we were prepared to do to change our relationships. Equality was no longer a gift in our control as if we could make others equal through treating them with equal respect. We were no longer, as men, the undisputed authorities within our own homes. Our power was threatened. Freedom and equality were being given a different meaning as they now had to sustain the existence of women as independent human beings able to take control of their lives. Women had to be free to make their own lives, not live in relation to others. They demanded to be equal to men in being able to realise their capacities and hopes for themselves.

Women were no longer the passive objects we had been brought up to expect as men. Women were active in the world, defining their own individual needs and wants. Thinking back to my own male identity in the early 1960s, I found this scary and threatening. I remember how threatening it was, even to be asked to dance by a woman. It threw me completely, though I tried not to show it. Part of me felt she was now being 'too forward' and I felt uncomfortable. I realised how important it was for me to have control of any situation, even though I had barely faced this in myself because I had been able to take it so much for granted in my relationships. I also remember being challenged for interrupting while a woman was talking. My behaviour showed that I assumed women did not really have much to say, so that I did not really listen. We have been educated as men into these assumptions of superiority, and into feeling that if we do not have 'control' we are not being 'masculine'. This affects every area of our experience. At another level this created enormous confusion and made it difficult to respond to the challenges women made. Often it was easier to withdraw into an angry and bitter silence.

I want to say a little more about the emotional and sexual chaos which many of us lived through – and, at some level, are still living through. I want to introduce more of myself to make clear that I am not simply trying to generalise from a specific class and ethnic experience. I want to show the way I was personally confronted by these issues. I began to search for the moral and intellectual sources of a masculinity that was not only limiting my life, but denied me a language in which to grasp the nature of the feminist challenge, or a way of understanding how I could change.

I was brought up to be intellectual and rational. This was the way that I protected myself in the world. I had continually to prove that I was good enough to be a man. Because I was not big and strong, I became clever and quick. I could smell danger, and I was always ready and alert. I was not much in touch with my own anger and sexuality because I was too concerned with being accepted and liked by others. I had asserted considerable control over myself, which largely meant killing off my softer and warmer feelings, so that I could 'do well' at school. My identity was closely identified with 'getting on' in a situation that was alien to the refugee Jewish family I had grown up in.

I do not think I shared much with others because I did not want to acknowledge that I had deep needs for love and affection. I did not want to know about them. I wanted to be self-sufficient and independent like the other boys at school. I did not need anyone. In my early twenties, I had hardly any sustaining relationships with women. I longed for a relationship, but I was not open to having one. I think I had got stuck into the role of being 'understanding' – this was the way that I established a safe and unthreatening form of intimacy with people. But it was at the cost of my sexuality. For some time I became 'the friend that you are close to, but you don't want to spoil the friendship through sleeping with'. This was its own form of agony.

I think I was scared of getting really close to someone. I was scared of the intimacy. I found it nearly impossible to say to someone 'I love you.' This felt so final. I was holding myself back. For years, I had divided women into those that I despised and looked down upon, that I did not want to go out with, and those that I put on some kind of pedestal, and would never have wanted to go out with me. I was given to adulation. So I would crave people who did not even know that I cared about them. Lots of this happened in fantasy which, I think, was a way of retaining some kind of control over the whole situation. It meant that I did not have to risk rejection. I would usually manipulate the situation, so that I was very clear whether someone would want to go out with me, before I would make a move. I needed to have the control since I was terrified of rejection. I was anxious about doing things wrong. Yet at another level, it meant that I was always ready to subordinate my own needs, so that I was never really satisfied. I harboured my resentments. I think a tendency to be 'too eager to please' meant that, at some level, I could cease to exist for myself.

I think this experience of shrinking away from defining our wants or needs happened to many men in the · early years of the women's movement. We were left feeling guilty, almost because we existed as men. We did not want to be thought of as sexist, so we watched ourselves very carefully. Yet it is in part this very watchfulness that constitutes the problematic structure of masculine experience. Again we thought that we could change through will. We did not show our anger and resentment since this was only to pressure and dominate women more. We did not even admit it to ourselves. We tried to be sensitive and understanding to the needs of women. A sexuality of performance was often replaced by a focus upon whether I had been able to give a woman an orgasm. It was almost as if we had few needs ourselves. This was the other side of our egos in which sexuality becomes just another way of affirming our male identities.

At another level, it might have been much easier and healthier if we had owned up much more to our sexist thoughts and feelings. At least we would have owned these feelings as ours. We would have had to admit to all the ways we had been brought up to hate, despise and loathe women. We would have admitted more of our fears and anxieties about sexuality. We would have had to start by admitting the reality of our feelings rather than attempting to shape them into ideas we could intellectually justify, even if this meant we did not have the 'correct feelings'. Usually our feelings return to haunt us in a different guise.

We were brought up to kill our feelings at an early age, so that we could survive as men. Often this means that as men we do not know what we feel. We do not have the words to express what is happening to us, nor a sense of how our emotional and personal lives have been disorganised. We do not want to face the pain and hurt that has accumulated. At the same time, we do not want to feel guilty all the time. For many men the confusion has meant learning to be silent in the appropriate situations. We do things so that conflict can be avoided. We learn to give women space and time of their own, hoping that they will appreciate this enough to leave us alone to live our own lives. But often the idea that it is for women to define and organise their own struggles can be used to avoid the painful and difficult issues raised for men by feminist practice. It can also excuse an ignorance of feminist theory and practice.

OPPRESSION, POWER AND INSTITUTIONS

Capitalist society is organised in the interests of those who have wealth and power in the society. One facet of this is that it is organised in the interests of men, especially where relationships with women are concerned. Men are assumed to be the 'leaders' in society and the 'authorities' within the household. Women's subordination is structured into the iron heart of capitalist institutions. It is largely male doctors who have power over women's bodies and childbirth. Women often find themselves in a subordinate and servicing position at work. They are the nurses, not the doctors.

This is driven deep into the psyche of children at an early age. I remember playing with my six-year-old niece who refused to be a doctor because she thought that was for boys. She got upset when I suggested that things could be differently organised. Often women's jobs are extensions of the caring roles women are supposed to have within the family, or else it is women who do the most routine and monotonous assembly-line work. They do not even have the same kind of job security, let alone wages. The economic crisis of the 1980s showed that women are still treated as a kind of reserve army that can be moved in and out of production, according to the needs of the economy.

Traditionally, it has often been the wage that has expressed the institutionalised power that men have over women. The wage has often made women dependent upon men for their everyday needs. Men were the breadwinners and women the homemakers. This division of responsibilities was taken to be a 'natural' distinction based upon biological differences. So the assertion of 'natural differences' between men and women has often legitimated the power men have over women in a patriarchical capitalist society. This is no different in many socialist societies.[5] What is more, the law often asserts that women are the property of men, and so institutionalises the oppression of women.

For years, the heterosexual relationship has been an implicit property relationship. Men traditionally have had control over women's sexuality, a control conceptualised as his 'rights' which cannot easily be denied. The council house has traditionally been 'his' house, so that a woman cannot ask a man to leave even if she wants to, and if she wants to leave, there are still few places she can go. What is more, she has been brought up to subordinate her needs, to be a caring and loving wife. She learns to put his needs first, if she is not to be considered and consider herself a 'bad wife'. Of course, there are very significant class differences, but the subordination to men is shared. So are the sacrifices that women are encouraged to accept as 'natural' – of their autonomy, independence and assertiveness.

If women are also working outside the home, they often find that men have authority over them in the workplace, and often also in the structure and organisation of trade unions. The very organisation of authority and discipline in the work process is rooted in sexism and patriarchal power. This is not simply an issue of the values of individual men, but of the very organisation of power at work. The submissiveness for which women are trained becomes an integral part of the allocation of jobs and the kind of authority structures and sexual harassment they are submitted to.

So sexism is not simply an ideology that has to be challenged, through changing the ways people think and feel. Rather, it is an essential aspect of both capitalist and often socialist organisation of work. It is because women's oppression is institutionalised that it cannot be neatly separated from economic and industrial struggles, into an autonomous sphere of 'sexual politics'. As I shall argue later in the chapter on fascism, the fundamental reorganisation of the capitalist labour process in the early twentieth century, with the introduction of assembly-line production, already involved a transformation in practice of our traditional socialist distinctions between 'economic', that is, trade unionist, and 'political' struggles and consciousness. We have to learn from how people are struggling. The struggles against redundancies, lay-offs, night work and the regrading of women's work have long threatened our inherited political theories, though it has taken almost a generation for this crisis in socialist theory and practice to be acknowledged.

The women's movement has helped us understand the different ways women are oppressed as a sex. It has shown how this subordination and dependency exists in different forms for women with different class backgrounds.[6] But it has also been willing to recognise the difficulties of theorising the relationship between sex and class, as well as race and ethnicity. It has made us aware that these issues, along with the ecological and planetary crisis, have become central for any meaningful redefinition of socialism for the closing decade of the twentieth century. They are also tied in crucial ways to the issue of masculinity that has formed such a strong part of both a capitalist and socialist inheritance, and the distinction between 'public' and 'private' – the personal and the political – that they have in their different ways sustained.

MEN, FEMINISM AND OPPRESSION

I think it is important to ask whether men can be oppressed because it is a question that reveals our theoretical and political confusions. Many people feel the difficulty of talking of men as 'oppressed', since we are not oppressed as a sex, whilst women's oppression has a material basis and is institutionalised. We have recognised this, but many want it to carry the implication that women's oppression is therefore 'social and political', while men's lives, in contrast, might be distorted, damaged, limited, but their problems are merely 'psychological', to be dealt with privately in consciousness-raising groups. The point claimed here is that they cannot form the basis of any broader movement.

This has rapidly become a kind of common-sense orthodoxy on the Left, and if it has a strength it is that it argues the case against prevailing notions of masculinity without in any way seeking to minimise the injustices perpetuated against women. But it again insists upon a crude objectivism in which the 'material' is identified with the 'external' and the 'political'. The assumption is that because men are not oppressed, then masculinity is not a political issue. This fragments our understanding and does not help us grasp the nature of women's oppression, let alone the situation of men. It leaves us with a limited conception of what is political and it does not help us group the ways that we, as men, have power over women.

Many women and men will say that men as a sex are the 'oppressors', so it is absurd to talk about men as 'oppressed'. This means that we can easily end up feeling guilty for being men, since we cannot escape our situation as 'oppressors'. We can feel we have got no right to exist. Often this awareness can itself be crippling as it reduces men into a state of non- existence, a kind of silence as regards our masculinity. The only political role for men in sexual politics becomes that of servicing the women's movement. We cannot do anything in our own right, as men.

We are left with the guilt that arises from the recognition that we belong to an oppressive group and are therefore part of the oppression of women whatever efforts we make on our own behalf. At least this involves taking the demands and politics of the women's movement seriously, but this can create its own politics of guilt, as does the idea of conceiving of masculinity as some kind of privilege that accrues to all men. I do not think that 'privileged' is the best way of seeing men, for it so easily gets trapped into a form of utilitarianism which fails to take on board the ways in which we do not exist externally to our privilege, but rather have a constant and dialectical relationship to it.

This sense of guilt was quite strong in the original 'Men against Sexism' groups in the early 1970s. It tended to feed the kind of self-denial and self-hate that many of us are brought up with anyway within a Protestant culture. There was little we could do or create as men. We could not really discover our relationships with each other, though this could be welcomed by many women if it meant we did not make the same endless emotional demands upon women but discovered ways of giving emotional support to each other as men.

As might have been expected, this carried its own political implications. Somehow sexism came to be seen as some kind of 'abstract ideology' that we can organise against, rather than as a set of social relations we are involved in and live out in our everyday lives. This made it difficult to work out a political practice as anti-sexist men, because we only had a negative identity. We had little conception of the relationships and vision we were struggling for. Because sexism was grasped as 'ideological', rather than as built into social relations, it was easy to say it had no 'material basis' in the capitalist economy. This meant we could not hope really to challenge sexism within capitalism. This was to be politically 'naïve' – and who wants to own up to that?

So in the early years of 'Men against Sexism', we set out to make men aware of their 'sexism' and then recruit them into an organisation capable of taking on the struggle against capitalist society. Sexism was not grasped as an integral aspect of the day-to-day relationships. 'Capitalism' was seen as a kind of 'external enemy' which we could take on, when we had sufficient recruits. So we had a kind of 'goal' that we, as men, are used to dealing with. In time, this inevitably led to its own kind of frustration and disillusionment. It was too much a reproduction of a politics of guilt and sacrifice to sustain or nourish a movement.

Another common reason for asserting that men are not oppressed is the effort to demonstrate an abstract support for the women's movement. Since it is up to women to fight against sexism and women's oppression, support for the women's movement remains abstract. This fits in with the ways sexual politics could be conveniently marginalised in the Left in the 1970s. Women are left with their own space, as long as they do not challenge our sense of class politics. What is worth keeping in view is that one of the most concrete ways men can support the women's movement is through being ready to change ourselves, rather than thinking the issue has nothing to do with us. Thinking in terms of privilege can paradoxically make masculinity itself somewhat unproblematic. To say that men are oppressed does not mean that their relationship to that oppression is in any way similar to women's. As the Frankfurt School was at pains to draw out in its critical theory, what is at issue here are the sources of negation, and the specific constellations of these are historical.[7] This is another problem of thinking in terms of patriarchy as some kind of transhistorical structure.

Our political thinking is deeply influenced by the dominant modes of thinking and feeling in our society. This means that within a liberal moral culture, as I argue later, we more naturally think in terms of 'oppositions', rather than dialectically. So, for instance, we think we must either love someone or hate them, that we cannot love and hate them at the same time. Our experience is often more dialectical, if we know how to bring ourselves into fuller contact with it. But this is why people feel threatened when they begin to admit their resentments against their friends. We have been taught to think that 'if she's my friend, then I should like her, and shouldn't feel resentments towards her.' We can learn from experience the ways our relationships get limited to a more superficial level, because we refuse to admit resentments and so bring an unreality into our relationships. We very much want to think and feel the way we 'ought to' – the way we can intellectually justify – and we deny any feelings that interfere.

The moralism of our culture has deeply affected the Left. It has deeply marked our political understanding, though it is rarely investigated critically since it does so much to structure and organise our 'common sense' within a liberal moral culture.[8] We will consider its sources in the following chapters. It is a moralism which tends to structure our thinking dichotomously, so we think that, if women are oppressed by men, it can make no sense to say that men are also oppressed in capitalist society. But it is quite possible to admit that women are systematically more oppressed than men and that men have considerable power in their individual and social relationships with women, without denying the oppression of men in capitalist society. Nor does this mean that all men are equally oppressed, but that it is sometimes important and valid to analyse and understand the different situations of men in these terms.

TENSIONS AT WORK AND HOME

It has been quite inadequate to talk about the ways men have been 'socialised' into restrictive roles, forcing them to be competitive, ambitious and unfeeling, though in many ways this has in different forms provided the most influential account of men and masculinity. This can make us think that it is possible for us to change the ways we are, without challenging the relationships of power and subordination at work and at home. It is not simply a matter of psychology, of roles, of consciousness and willpower.

Through men's consciousness-raising, I have some idea of how isolating work is and how difficult it is even in a relatively liberal and open college if I get upset and show my feelings, say about ways women students are talked about. This would give other men a chance to put me down, and they would not lose much time doing it, at least before the issue of sexual harassment came into the open. I know it is not simply a matter of consciousness or making a moralistic challenge, but of the competitive and hierarchical ways the whole teaching institution is organised and the power teachers have. But the more in touch I am with my feelings, the harder it can be to operate in these day-to-day situations.

I am aware of the kind of institutional changes that would have to be made for me to feel more myself, and these have become a lot less likely in the 1980s and 1990s. The more time I give to creating different kinds of relationships with students, the more I am made aware that I am not being a 'proper teacher', just an overgrown student. And all this is in the relatively privileged sector of education. It is only when you begin to behave differently, that you are made aware of what you are up against. This is totally familiar for women and gay men, but it is an experience heterosexual men need to have for themselves.

When people say that 'men are not oppressed', especially hetero-sexual men, since they have power in a patriarchal capitalist society, not only do they forget the nature of class relations, but they also fail to ex-plore the power capitalist production routines and disciplines have over the lives of both working-class and middle-class families. A man is not even free to develop a closer relationship with his children, if he is forced into the routines of shift-work. The fact that men do not experience this as a fundamental lack of freedom and control should be seen as a central and critical point from which to contest market notions of freedom and equality which have reasserted themselves.

Often it is the factory which governs the kind of time and energy a father has for his children. Similarly, the constraints of the office, school and hospital control men's lives. In the 1980s, it was often struggles inside state bureaucracies and welfare institutions, such as the health service disputes and social work strikes, that were the most significant, because they were not just economistic, but concerned the quality of services. Since these struggles have not taken place in centres of industrial power, they have too often been dismissed or marginalised in a socialist tradition too tightly organised around the male white industrial worker.

We cannot separate our understanding of the family and sexual relationships from our understanding of work and production. These are not 'autonomous spheres', nor are they mechanically related to each other, and we need critically to explore traditions of thought which make it difficult, if not impossible, to theorise these connections as central to any viable social theory. We need to explore the experience of men working in factories, offices, schools and hospitals and the ways scientific management has brought tighter control and regulation. Marx certainly helps us grasp the nature of exploitation in the capitalist organisation of work, though his analysis is too often presented exclusively as a matter of the distribution of surplus value. We lose a sense that men are constantly being forced to take orders as they are forced to keep up with work schedules. Men are left exhausted and drained after work. This is a freedom Marx long ago contested in the *Economic and Philosophical Manuscripts* of 1844, realising how hard it is for men to 'choose' the kind of relationships they want to have. But this has rarely been explored in Marxist theory.[9]

Godard brings out the contradictions and tensions graphically in his film *Number 2*. He shows how the frustrations and tensions produced in men at work are taken out on wife and children. The anger and resentment spill over. It is the power men can assume over women that allows this, though this is in no way to excuse or legitimate it or to argue that they cannot control their sexual feelings. It shows the explosive situation many families find themselves in, increasingly isolated from any support in a broader community, trapped into a small and inadequate flat. The man's sexuality becomes completely reduced to a mechanical exercise of power. He fucks like a machine. He does not have any grasp of what is going on, nor support at work. Relationships with other men have been broken up in the large factories, and he does not have much communication with his wife. The situation is grim.

Women are not so ready to accept their subordination in the home, especially as more women are forced to work outside the home themselves as well as look after children. They are increasingly making demands upon men to share in the housework. This is creating its own kinds of tensions within many working-class and middle-class homes, as the culture fails to provide a way of helping men to a redefinition of their identity as men. Often men feel threatened by this new independence of women, feeling the need to reassert their own power and show 'who's boss'. Often much energy is taken up within these domestic struggles.

There is little emotional and mental preparation for the kind of changes that men have to make. The image of men being forced to give up their privileges can push men into a corner rather than help them to change. They often fear being ridiculed by their workmates and often if they lend a hand at home, they do not want others to know. The economic recession has forced the pace of change as many more unemployed men take on more domestic and childcare responsibilities, but there is still little public and political discussion within which masculinity can be redefined, and in which people are helped to grasp the pressures that the organisation of work puts on to people's domestic situations. It remains crucial to analyse the social processes which help shift conflicts and tensions into the 'private sphere' of family and personal and sexual relationships.[10]

MASCULINITY AND POWER

As men, we oppress women, but this does not mean we are not ourselves oppressed living within a capitalist society. There is a serious sense in which any man can feel 'superior' to any woman and have power as a man in relation to women, in the way he can evaluate her as 'pretty' or 'ugly'. Women can make similar judgements, but they do not have the same social power or weight. Men will often collude in these judgements and feel fearful challenging these objectifications, lest we be regarded as 'soft'. Anyway, we will be told that 'it's only a joke, so what are you taking it so seriously for?'

These objectifications are written into the media and have enormous power to govern relationships between men, as well as between men and women. This is one of the sources of power we have available as men – even as working-class men – and we are still regarded as 'odd' or 'funny' if we do not feel comfortable with it, or if we reject it. It is also invoked to cover over and soften class differences which exist between men. Patriarchy creates its own sense of common interests and reproduces its own sense of equality between men in relationship to women. Capitalist institutions play on this and exploit it deftly to their own advantage.

But many men have always had an ambiguous relationship towards this power we are supposed to inherit. Some men have never felt easy or comfortable with it. We can feel oppressed by the expectations of who we are supposed to be as men, or deeply inadequate if we have not been able to live up to or recognise ourselves in the images of masculinity in the way the culture demanded. Of course, struggling to live up to the kind of competitive, rational, ambitious, strong and independent man image is not a matter of simply struggling to be more effective in our oppressor roles. This is to deny the reality of a lot of our experience as men, which hinges on the deep feelings of inadequacy and inferiority many boys are made to suffer, and more generally, to deny and invalidate the damage done to boys in their attempts to live up to notions of masculinity which prevail in the culture.

Often this means, at the very least, distorting our sensibilities and killing off our emotions. It means turning our bodies into unfeeling machines that we can control. We have been trained since we were young to identify more closely than women with a capitalist work ethic for positions within the industrial work machine. We were taught to identify our own happiness and fulfilment with 'success', and so with the goals of the larger society. We systematically denied, within a culture which identifies masculinity with self-denial, whatever awareness we might have gained of our individual needs and wants. We were rewarded for the sacrifices we made, so that often we even became scared of pleasure, though we continued to joke and talk about it.

At some level we have become estranged from ourselves. We use language in an instrumental way to define our goals and ends but rarely to bring us into closer emotional contact with ourselves. Men sometimes voice this by admitting a prevailing sense of 'unreality', saying they 'don't feel in touch with themselves'. At school, we were trained to 'do well', whatever we were doing. We had been forced to sacrifice the content and meaning of our activities, as the intrinsic interest was drained away and they became so many different ways of proving ourselves. Especially within the middle class, we were increasingly being brought up to fit into a society of bureaucratic capitalism. The individual with his strong individual opinions and wants has increasingly become a liberal myth. Strong opinions and commitments were threatening.

Often we learnt to do what we were told, and 'getting on' meant pleasing others. School was effective at training us for this world of bureaucratic capitalism. In the 1950s and 1960s, this connected with the widespread sense that you only really existed for others, and that you are 'different' with different people. The problem of 'identity' had emerged forcibly. You 'are' what you 'seem to be'. This was the society of the spectacle.[11] The unreality of social life had become a constant theme.[12] An interest in Laing and in therapy generally was to emerge to focus and give voice to this situation.

Adorno and Marcuse had already realised in the 1930s that the 'individual' no longer existed in bureaucratic capitalism, in the way liberal theory had assumed.[13] The 'individual' had been increasingly fragmented between work life and home life and only existed in pieces, so, for instance, we only feel 'real' as others see us, or experience us. We are brought up to define ourselves *externally*, constantly anxious of whether we have done the 'right thing' and out of touch with our own feelings and reality. As individuals, we come to exist as functions of larger organisations, be it the school or the office. As men, we often carry a deep, if unacknowledged, fear that we have become 'mechanical'. It is not that we do not *want* to respond when we are asked what we are feeling in our relationships, but that we do not know *how* to respond. This shows some of the depths of the panic we can feel, though our prevailing modes of moral and social theory usually fail to identify this situation so that we are left assuming it is a personal and private predicament.

Often we respond aggressively and violently, because a raw nerve has been touched inside. Often the only thing we consciously realise is that we feel happier if we can be working or doing things but are tense and scared of being alone with ourselves. Structuralist Marxism has completely misunderstood the situation. It has attacked the 'individual' as essentially a bourgeois conception, and so has continued rather than questioned the cultural trend of *instrumentalising* our thinking and feeling.[14] Its influence remains tacit in many of the discussions around post-modernity, wherein identities are seen as in constant flux. The importance of the Frankfurt School was that it at least recognised the erosion of identity as a significant problem. As men, we can live in fear, losing touch with our individuality. We can fear moving so far out of touch with our 'selves' that we cannot find a way back. We lose a sense of connection with different aspects of our experience. But with so much social theory, the 'self' is treated as an essentialist fiction so that critical issues of identity can barely be recognised. This is part of the problem, as we are presented with false polarities between 'humanist' and 'structuralist' accounts. We need to develop a critical relationship to prevailing traditions of thought and feeling which would render these issues invisible.

I think one of the reasons that many men have felt both deeply jealous and drawn to the women's movement and personal politics, has been a sense that the instrumentalism of life had been cracked by women and, somehow, a sense of what is important in human life has been rediscovered in the questions the women's movement was asking. In redefining femininity, women were recovering their own strength and power, but they were also rediscovering the meaningfulness of collective life in the notions of sisterhood. Some of this is being threatened in harder days but it touches a deep yearning and need for many men. So, as men, we are hesitatingly redefining and rediscovering the possibilities, meaning, fears, anxieties, hopes and loves of masculinity, recognising how little meaning is often left in the public spheres of work and ambition where we had invested so much. Rather than simply withdrawing into a painful silence, we are finding a new kind of strength and a new weakness in asking basic questions that directly challenge the prevailing definitions of masculinity in society, about the loss of meaning and significance in life.[15]

In doing this, we are also searching for a different, more equal way of relating to men, women and children. This has to be public if we are to learn from each other, and it has to be oppositional to the prevailing structures of power which will often ridicule us, and even try to crush us, if they fail to incorporate us. As we regain a sense of our own power, we sharpen our resistance to a society that will often crush our life for its own unscrupulous ends. But this involves both a theoretical and practical endeavour. It means learning about the cultural and historical sources of a masculinity that has been so identified with reason itself that the self-denial it demands has been rendered invisible. It also means learning about the different ways we can change ourselves as men, honestly facing the difficulties we have had in giving up our power and control in struggling to live more equal relationships.

4   Self-denial

It might seem strange, in the light of our awareness of the institutionalised power of men in the larger society, to focus on self-denial; but I am going to be looking at how self-denial is a mode of existence in the world which is systematically generated within bourgeois culture and institutionalised within masculine identity. It is a significant *paradox* that men's self-denial is both a source of men's existential alienation *and* part of the infrastructure of men's power. This shows how complex power is, and how inadequate are the conceptions of the workings of power that we inherit within social and political theories.

This sense of power is something liberalism and the traditional Left have great difficulty in grasping. The point is that there are crucial, if largely unrecognised, asymmetries in men's and women's self-denial. Women can learn to experience themselves through relations with others, developing capacities for empathy and emotional connection, whilst men's self-denial is of a different sort, and, specifically, centres on the negation of these very capacities. I will be exploring facets of this structure, which characterise masculine experience and are forged within a particular moral context. It is in part the asymmetry in the form of self-denial that is built into men's and women's exprience that accounts for the implicit and often unacknowledged relationships of power in traditional forms of relationship between men and women.

IDEOLOGY AND EXPERIENCE

My investigation into the relationship between morality and self-denial touches our inherited conceptions of masculinity and the different ways that we live it out in our lives and relationships. It grows out of a dissatisfaction with seeing masculinity as an ideology, as a 'set of ideas', or as a social role defined by social expectations, feeling that it digs much deeper, into the very marrow of our experience, forming our 'character' and the nature of the relationships we have as men. This also gives meaning to a possible reformulation of historical materialism, which has to be dialectical in its recognition that, as Marx has it in *The German Ideology* (in Marx and Engels 1968), 'it is not consciousness which determines social being, but it is social being which determines consciousness'. I want to show what this insight means for an analysis of the relationship between morality and masculinity.

There is something crucial to learn from a Marxist conception of morality, if this is taken as a critique of the whole idea of 'morality' as something 'separate' and 'distinct' from our lived experience. The Leftist discussions which conceive of morality as characterising the experience of a particular class, as Lukàcs does, often think of replacing a 'bourgeois' morality with a 'socialist' morality. This framework of moral discussion is flawed, for it can often involve the same kind of self-denial and 'splitting' of the self that I investigate. At the same time, it can be important to scrutinise carefully the universal claims of morality and the Enlightenment project to provide a rational found-ation for a conception of morality which is identified with reason. It is important to recognise the relationship of morality to power, as well as some of the particular workings of 'morality' within capitalist society. This relationship operates not simply at the level of people's ideas and values, but also at the level of people's relationships with each other. It also concerns the formation of 'character' within the context of these social relationships of class, gender and racial power and subordination. So I want to show morality not simply as an issue of individual moral action, but as working out in the very structure of people's relationships, forming the very quality of our everyday experience.[1]

So to give an example, we can no longer assume, as we tend to do in liberal moral theory, that we exist automatically in Kantian terms as free and independent moral agents. Rather, if someone is struggling to be 'independent', this moral conception of the individual can make it hard for them to ask for what they need, even when this help is available. Within liberal moral theory we learn automatically to identify this 'help' with 'weakness', especially if we were taught as children that asking for help is a sign of weakness and dependency. If this was coupled with ridicule for feeling helpless and dependent, then often we will not be able to ask for help, even as adults, when it is available to us. We will discover ourselves feeling humiliated and ridiculed if we do not live up to this image of ourselves and, unconsciously, we will often choose relationships in which this pseudo-independence is admired and encouraged.

If I talk a lot about morality in terms of 'bourgeois ideology', while being aware of how often such language has been abused, it is in the hope of giving specific historical content to a particular framework of moral theory roughly set within the terms of Enlightenment modernity, that identifies morality with reason. Often it is hard to recognise ourselves within these descriptions, just because we are brought up to regard morality as an 'individual matter'. This makes it difficult to recognise that we *share* a morality with others, let alone that the character of our inherited morality, largely organised around questions of egoism and altruism, grows out of the structure of power within a liberal capitalist society. This is especially difficult if we have not begun to wonder about the gendered and ethnic character of our experience, or the ways our experience has been shaped through living in a class-divided society.

I want to open up ways of recognising ourselves, not simply as individuals who can determine our lives by reason alone as moral agents, but through coming to have a more critical sense of our 'identities' and 'experience' as gendered. I do this by giving accounts of an everyday masculine experience of self-denial so that men can begin to rediscover some of the sources of their gendered identities in a way that does not compromise their individuality but grounds it differently. The experience of men and women has developed in different ways because of the power men have in the larger society, so I have talked about men specifically to uncover a fuller sense of our experience as men than would otherwise be possible. I provide the beginnings of a philosophical grounding for men's changing lives, partly in relation to the challenges of feminism but also as part of a positive process of redefining our masculinity.

Once we have recognised certain features of our 'personal experience' as part of a masculine experience of self-denial, I go on to show how they develop out of features of moral culture. This brings out how our 'personal experience' has been formed within the context of moral culture, even our most intimate and private relationships. This undercuts the liberal distinction between 'private' and 'public' which can so easily mystify the everyday realities of our experience. So rather than 'society' or 'culture' being seen as something 'distant', we discover its reality and meaning in our everyday experience. This provides a broader context in which both women and men can understand their feelings and experiences while giving more sense of what is involved in changing ourselves.

This challenges our 'common-sense' understanding of the relationship between psychology and morality and shows how this distinction organises our experience, and the understanding we have of ourselves. We are encouraged to think that 'psychology' has to do with feelings and behaviour, while 'morality' has to do with values. It is these values which are supposed to control our individual behaviour, but not that an individual *as a person* is somehow formed within the prevailing relationships and practices of a moral culture. We are rarely allowed to see that the very formation of our characters, within the relationships we have, is deeply influenced by our inherited moral conceptions.

But this should not be so surprising if, with Marx, we see ideology as a social relation, not simply as a set of ideas. It becomes easier to see how we live out our ideology in the very form of our relationships. Feminism learnt that even our personal relationships are inevitably power relationships, forming the very structure of our experience. It is the workings of power in our relationships that feminism implicitly used to challenge the assumptions of liberal moral theory. Power forms so much of our everyday experience, though we remain largely unconscious of its workings in the organisation of our inherited conceptions of masculinity.

All this works to challenge liberal conceptions of morality which assume morality to be part of rationality, part of thought. Within liberalism, morality has to do with discrete actions and, in Kant's terms, the ways we individually work out what we ought to do. This is a central feature which helps to define morality as we inherit it within modernity. Within sexual politics, morality is no longer seen either in Kantian terms or, as it was within the classical liberalism of the nineteenth century, as forming our 'characters' and 'personalities', but rather as being part of who we are in a much fuller sense. Because of the ways that the rationalist terms of modernity were largely set in the image of a particular conception of masculinity, I am trying to illuminate our inherited masculinity through exploring the relationship between morality at the level of rationality and morality at the level of feelings and relationships.

I try to show these are necessarily connected, though liberal theory does its best to conceal the connections, making it so much harder to identify and understand the hidden *injuries* done to all of us, living out our lives within class, race and gender social relations.[2] We can end up undercutting the critical analysis of capitalist patriarchy, unable to explain why people should work to bring more equal relations into existence, if we lose sight of the ways that power relations enter the formation of our identity. It becomes difficult to uncover the anger people feel at the ways their lives are wasted and powers, capacities and potentials suppressed.

We have to understand where our morality comes from, and what difference it makes to our everyday experience and relationships. Sociology tends to understand morality in terms of sets of rules or of different 'values and beliefs', which characterise different classes, cultures and societies somehow *separated* from the formation of character, relationships and experience. Within the dominant Durkheimian or Weberian traditions, morality is grasped either as a matter of sanctions reflecting society as some higher moral authority, or else as a matter of the meanings that people freely give to their experience. Within both traditions, theory becomes powerless to think about the *hurt* or the *damage* being done to people in different class, sexual or racial situations of power and subordination.[3] We still require within sociology a kind of 'politics of experience' that opens up a space for morality to show the differences made to the quality of people's lives by forms of injustice, exploitation and oppression.

As part of this, we need to understand how liberal morality, for all its strengths, individualises and reproduces splits within our experience that mystify our personal reality and make it difficult to situate our individual lives within the context of society as a shared social and historical experience. This is true in the competing conceptions we have of 'morality'. We either see it as something imposed externally – very much as Durkheim does – reflecting the 'values and beliefs' of the society we live in, while our feelings are seen as essentially egoistic and selfish, arising out of ourselves or out of our family relationships, or we tend to identify learning morality with learning rules, learning to behave in the right way, so that you are a good person, deserving of love.[4]

Here, learning morality is presented as learning different stages of a cognitive task and so as another aspect of 'thinking'. So, through reproducing this cultural split between 'thought' and 'feelings', between 'morality' and our 'emotions and relationships', we are unable to rediscover the ways morality helps form the totality of our experience and relationships. In identifying morality with reason it is implicitly identified with prevailing masculinity. We lose a sense of how our character as men is formed and our experience shaped, often antagonistically, within the culture we are living in.

Through exploring the relationship between masculinity and self-denial, we learn to challenge the idea that the splits we inherit in our particular moral tradition are inevitable, or are part of human nature. We learn how they develop out of the particular features of liberal morality, growing out of the structure of power and subordination within a capitalist society. Our rationality and emotionality are divided and fragmented because we grow up in a culture that divides them, therefore leaving us divided against ourselves. This is part of uncovering the damage of rationality, which does not mean we are in any sense against reason – though it does mean it has to find a more modest place in our lives.

A rationalistic culture is always trying to turn our emotions against us – thereby estranging us as men from our emotional lives. We take this so much for granted that we do not realise how this undermines our sense of self and our sense of the 'reality' of our everyday experience. We also do not appreciate how this denies us the personal power we might otherwise have, if we did not denigrate our emotionality as an integral part of our masculinity, to challenge the structures of power and domination which form our everyday experience at work and in the family. Nor is this simply a matter of allowing men to extend the range of our emotional lives, as role theory has it, but of rediscovering the painful knowledge of ways our identities as men have been injured, contracted and distorted, along with our experience.

In this way we uncover that morality is a question of *power*, not simply of rules, or learning what is 'right' and what is 'wrong'. This was an important insight which feminism developed. It means we cannot divide off morality from the politics of our everyday experience as men, or from the realities of power in our relationships with other men and women, gay men and lesbians. In challenging the ways liberal morality leaves us divided against ourselves as men, mystified about the material conditions that shape our everyday experience as we identify male identity with individual success and ambition within the public realm, we have a chance of regaining parts of ourselves and developing different visions of masculinity.

Obviously there is a constant danger that I have generalised too much from my own experience, though in showing the depths at which some of these themes work I have tried to acknowledge relationships of power that exist between different men and different masculinities, gay and straight, black, white and Asian, Christian, Jewish and Muslim. I have also tried to show how ideas of masculinity are used to make working-class men identify with prevailing structures of power. But this will be an experience that others will have to illuminate.

I am trying to set down some of the implications of an identification with reason that at some level have guided western conceptions of masculinity since the seventeenth-century Scientific Revolutions. This needs to be given careful historical specificity in the class and ethnic experience of different generations of men, for it has often set the terms on which, for example, gay or black men – and women in general – have had to prove themselves if they are to be admitted into the magic circle of modernity. A critique of our inherited moral and political traditions of thought and feeling which have set the terms of an Enlightenment modernity is inescapable, since these have so often both sustained and rendered invisible contradictions and tensions in the lived experience of different masculinities. Liberal and Marxist traditions which stand opposed to each other in many ways have often served to block, in their different ways, a redefinition of masculinities.

INADEQUACY AND IDENTITY

Sometimes, reflecting upon a moment in our own experience can help us uncover the dialectical nature of processes working within our relationships. I remember, for instance, someone saying 'we can't love others, unless we have learnt to love ourselves.' Somehow this struck home. It said a lot to me, though I did not know how to integrate it into the ways I was brought up to think and feel about myself. I would not have thought that being able to love others had anything to do with how I felt about myself. But in those days also I did not really know *how* to think about how I felt about myself.

It was a slow and difficult process coming to terms with this idea. It seemed to challenge too much of my philosophical training, all at once. It hinted at a different way of thinking and feeling. But even if ideas strike us, it can take time, often many years, to develop a relationship with them, even longer to appreciate the different ways that they are at odds with how we have been brought up to think and feel about ourselves. It can take even longer if we never learn to expect that our education should be able to illuminate and clarify our everyday experience.

Feminism has challenged the universalism that characterises so much liberal moral theory.[5] Our gender has assumed a new significance. This is going to say different things to men and women, to gay men and lesbians. We have to find our own ways of recognising ourselves as gendered beings. The challenges of the women's movement have made it possible for us to recognise ourselves as 'men' and 'women'. This already promises us much more of an 'identity' than the notion of abstract bearer of rights that has been at the centre of liberal moral and political theory. It breaks through the abstract liberal notion that 'we are all individuals', and encourages us to locate ourselves within a structure of power that organises relationships between men and women. This gives us a way of recapturing some sense of 'reality' in our everyday lives. We are encouraged not simply to see ourselves as individuals free to make our own lives, but to ground our experience within the social relations of power.

The society can no longer simply be presented as a 'collection of free and equal individuals', because we have been forced to recognise that, at the very least, 'men' and 'women' have different power in the society, and to some extent share a different upbringing, history, experience and culture. Our experience is no longer isolated and individual but is shared by others. So when we, for instance, explore our own individual masculine experience, we are uncovering something that is shared and social. We are engaged, as Gramsci understood, in a process of self-knowledge which is at one and the same time a social and political investigation. It is a process in which we uncover sources of solidarity with others who have shared a similar experience so that we no longer have to feel so isolated and alone in our masculinity.

It can set us thinking, for instance, if we realise that we are not the only men who put ourselves down, but that other men do this as well. This is not simply a matter of inadequacy, weakness or individual personality, something we want to keep to ourselves. Rather it potentially reveals something about the kind of society and culture we are living in that we might otherwise take for granted. It need no longer be a matter of a private realm, of our private shame. Rather it is a hint of the ways we automatically seem to devalue and discount our own experience, if we put ourselves down or if we put down people we have relationships with. I have recognised how, for example, even someone's attraction or readiness to have a relationship with me can already *prove* their unworthiness. My estimation of them drops. I am sure that men and women experience this in different ways. Many heterosexual men have said they are only attracted to women when they are 'unavailable' – the excitement is in the chase. Since this seems to be quite a common feeling, it is bound to say something revealing about contemporary masculinities in our society.

It does not help to be told that we have got the 'wrong attitude'. We know this. This is why we have such difficulty admitting such feelings to ourselves, allowing them to become conscious. This presupposes that it is quite possible for us to change how we feel about others and about ourselves. This expresses the underlying conception which liberal society has of emotions and feelings as 'mental states', as if 'feeling unhappy' is a matter of being taken over by a certain mental state. So we might be told that it is wrong to put ourselves down, as if it is a matter of 'changing our minds' – something we are imagined to be always 'free' to do. It is like being told 'to pull ourselves together'. This only leaves us feeling the impossibility of admitting to ourselves the reality of what we feel.

We end up feeling ashamed, thinking that this 'does not have anything to do with anyone else'. So that, as Freud partially recognised when he developed psychoanalysis, the everyday reality of emotional life in capitalist society becomes hidden and suppressed in the individual consciousness and sense of shame. Of course, knowing this does not prevent us putting ourselves down all the time, though it could make possible an understanding of the sources of a masculinity which psychoanalytic theory too often takes for granted. In many ways Freud failed adequately to challenge a Kantian inheritance, with its stress on the necessary negation of our desires and wants, though he wanted to ease the burden it creates for us.

DEPENDENCY AND RELATIONSHIPS

It is very difficult for men to realise the different ways we put ourselves down. This is partly because we are brought up to feel that we must be 'independent' – we must 'achieve' things in the world. We must be 'strong' and prove that we can cope in any situation that presents itself. We always have to be proving ourselves and our masculinity to other men and to women. This is a constant strain and builds a lot of tension into men's experience. It also means we never learn *how* to be dependent on others, even women and men we are close to. Dependency is taken as a sign of weakness, so it is a need which we barely acknowledge even to ourselves. It is a challenge to our very sense of masculinity. It threatens us. We expect other people to be dependent upon us, but we do not expect to be dependent upon others. So we end up feeling that we do not *need* to be dependent. We do not really want to need other people. This all becomes identified with weakness. If we allow ourselves to cry with someone, we cannot help feeling that our very masculinity is at stake. There are moments when the only problem about dependency we can recognise as men is a problem about women when they become too dependent. We want to shy away. We begin to feel 'trapped'. We think that they want to have something from us. We immediately feel that our 'independence' is threatened. At the same time it is too simplistic to argue that the women's movement has encouraged women to become less dependent, while the struggle for men is to become more dependent. It is more a question about the *nature* and *character* of dependency. So it is not that women want to be *less* dependent, but that they want to change the character of their relationship with men, which is making them feel too dependent.[6]

There is also an implicit challenge to how we think about emotions, once it is recognised that 'dependency' is not simply a feeling that comes over women. Rather it is an experience of a lack of an independent sense of self women are made to feel because of the character of their relationship with men. Feminism has connected this above all to the power men retain, even if largely hidden, within relationships.[7] So it is not a problem for women – in the way we, as men, have often posed it – 'to change the ways they feel', but of men and women coming to terms with the ways our relationships create and sustain particular forms of dependency. This is the context in which we can begin to understand what we are feeling.

We need to understand the formation of the structure of emotions of both men and women as developing out of the relationships of domination and dependency that we have grown up in since childhood. Psychoanalysis can help with this task, though often it sets itself too narrow a framework within which to grasp these processes. But at least Freud helps us grasp that it is not simply a matter of recognising the apparent differences between men and women, say, for instance, the common idea that women are able to cry while men are not. This can only be understood in terms of our individual and gendered sexual histories. So we need to understand that many women get upset when they are 'really' feeling other things. Given the power relationship it is 'easier' for women to get upset than it is to get angry. Because this is a more acceptable form of emotional expression for women, a whole range of feelings will be narrowed into this form. Anger more readily challenges the balance of power. It involves a greater risk. A women might not want to be aware of her anger, especially if this is something she had been punished for as a child. Little girls are not supposed to have 'tempers'.

This is not simply a question of the 'expectations' society has of girls, but of the particular power which fathers have over their daughters.[8] It really matters at particular stages of sexual development if your father says he will not like you if you are 'an angry little girl'. You would not even want to recognise yourself in this description, so often you will not even let yourself know when it is anger you are feeling. Again, this challenges our common-sense conception of emotions within liberal society that theoretically hardly allows for the possibility of us not knowing, or being out of touch with, what we are feeling.

I am struck by how unfamiliar it still is to talk in terms of 'power' when we are thinking about our personal relationships. Within liberal society we are brought up to understand what happens in our relationships in terms of the individual personalities of the people involved. Any problems that emerge in our relationships are put down to differences in personalities. Obviously sometimes this does help us to understand what is going on, but it becomes mystifying when it becomes the general conception for our understanding of relationships. The significance of the power relationship between men and women gets submerged. Within a liberal democratic society, power has to do with politics and parliament, so that we really have to work against our common-sense understandings to gain a sense of how power enters our most intimate personal and sexual relationships.[9] All the sociological talk about the different 'roles' men and women have only serves to submerge the real issues of power and dependency and the ways they work themselves out in our relationships.[10]

EMOTIONS AND DEPENDENCY

We have little cultural sense of how our emotions have developed within the context of our relationships. So women are called 'emotional' in a way that is implicitly contrasted with being 'rational'. Men reason and follow arguments, while women supposedly follow their intuitions and emotions. This reflects a deep fragmentation in masculine experience, in which 'reason' is *separated* as an autonomous and independent faculty which has little connection with our wants, needs and emotional capacities.[11] What is more, as men we are superior because of our power to reason. This is a quality that men have appropriated to themselves since the Enlightenment. Men are encouraged to be detached and 'objective' about their experience. This is partly why we, as men, can be so threatened by becoming more in touch with our feelings and emotions. Our superiority and power is threatened. Instinctively we do not want to have anything to do with feelings and emotions.

What is more, our prevailing moral traditions fully support our inherited identification of masculinity with reason and our distancing ourselves from emotions and feelings. Since Kant, morality has fundamentally had to do with reason. Morality was made a matter of reason and intellect. Feelings and emotions are unwelcome distractions which can only make it harder for us to be truly 'moral'. The separation of 'reason' from emotions and feelings is what largely underpins male superiority within society. The identification of morality with reason gives our superiority a moral legitimacy which is difficult to question because of the supposedly universal character of morality and reason. So as men, we are brought up to despise emotions and feelings. They only signal weakness. It is partly because women are 'emotional' that they are the 'weaker' sex.

Dependency enters our relationships in all kinds of subtle ways. A woman might be talked into going to see a film she did not really want to see. She might, for instance, have known that her friend George really wanted to see it, so she thought she might as well go along. Typically, she did not really know whether she wanted to see the film or not. On its own as a single incident, there might be nothing to question in this desire, but this is part of a total situation. If it happens that, for example, George always has a much clearer idea of what he wants to do than Karen, different issues come into focus which are difficult to think about within liberal moral theory.

Karen used to think that this just reflected a difference in their personalities, but now she is beginning to think this says more about the differences between men and women. Along with this, Karen might realise that she finds it really hard to stick out for what she wants with George. They usually end up doing what he wants to do, even when they try and talk it out together. She also knows that now she is likely to sit through the film sulking and unsatisfied, though this is not what she used to feel. Her feelings seem to have changed along with her growing feminist awareness of the situation.

Karen recognises that this is a way she gets her own back, especially when they end up seeing something she does not really want to see. She sulks through the whole film, letting him know she is not enjoying it at all. She recognises that part of *her* power comes through being able to make him feel bad. She knows this gets him every time, because he always wants to feel that he can give her a 'good time'. A lot of George's sense of self and male identity comes from being able to feel that he really knows what is 'best' for them both, though of course he thinks they should talk about it 'rationally' together. This is what really irritates Karen, though she cannot really express it. He always presents himself as being reasonable and rational, as if their deliberations have to result in what is best for both of them. She is sick of men knowing better. It reminds her of her father who always knew what was 'best' for the whole family.

Even though Karen realises part of this, she finds it really difficult to get angry at George. She knows that this would really shake up the relationship. It would challenge the power George assumes in the relationship, though Karen does not really think about it in these terms. Though sometimes she thinks this is exactly what he deserves, she usually falls back into thinking that George is kind to her most of the time and does not really mean to boss her around. And she also knows that some part of her admires and still likes the fact that George is so masculine, knowing what he wants to do and being able to make decisions so easily. She also knows she is usually able to get what she wants in the relationship by crying and getting upset, because George just cannot stand that. So somehow, crying and sadness become her characteristic emotions in the relationship, which covers over whatever anger Karen might really be feeling. It becomes part of a *passive* exercise of power, very much exercised within the confines of power in the relationship.

But Karen also feels – though she does not express it in these terms – that getting angry would somehow challenge the pattern of dependency set up within the relationship and might end the whole thing. Hopefully this begins to provide a context for understanding *why* some emotions are so much easier and more acceptable for women to have within a relationship since they do not really challenge the terms in which it is set up. But again these issues are so taken for granted in traditional relationships that we barely conceive that power and domination are involved in how a personal relationship is structured.[12]

The ways we are brought up to think about personal relationships within liberal moral theory submerge issues of power. The notions of love and personal feelings are made to explain so much of our thinking and feeling about relationships that we can begin to feel 'ungrateful' or 'disloyal' if we challenge conventional morality. What is more, the areas of control women have in the family and home, which is talked of as an equal area of activity, make it hard to uncover the sense of women as 'powerless' within a relationship. It becomes tempting to think in the familiar terms of different 'roles', 'responsibilities' and 'duties', rather than to focus upon issues of power and subordination in relationships. Somehow this is tied to a whole cycle of gratitude women are often made to feel because it is men who go out to work to earn the money to 'support' the whole family. So within a conventional marriage, women have to feel 'grateful' for everything their husband is providing, which makes it more difficult to uncover the forms of dependency.

Women's work in the home has traditionally been seen as an act of love. It goes unrewarded, regardless of the labour women are forced to do, so that men are 'free' to do eight or ten hours every day. The wage is only regarded as payment for the labour men do. Women's work is unrecognised and unvalued.[13] It becomes difficult for women to assert its importance in the face of the paid work men do, even when so many women are working in the labour market themselves. This sets up a structure of economic dependence that influences the character of the emotional relationship. But we have to look beyond an explanation in terms of role and socialisation also to think about the psychodynamics of identity and sexual development.[14] Somehow everything a man does comes to have so much more 'importance' – as if it is the very fact that a man does it that seems to give it its importance.

Women are brought up from an early age to discover identity, meaning and satisfaction in serving others, so they become used to

discounting themselves and their own n...
almost second nature to define their own...
satisfaction of others. So in a deep sense a...
losing whatever sense she might have otherwi...
life of her own. So it is often easier for women ...
to challenge the power men have in a relationshi...
really difficult to imagine being able to make it...
especially with children. Feminism has demons...
marriages work to undermine whatever sense of ... ...,
identity and independent ability to make it alone a won...

INDEPENDENCE AND COMPETITION

Most men have grown up to treasure their 'independence'. We want to be 'free', which often means we want to be able to do whatever we want to do. We do not want to be 'trapped' by women. If we will feel a little threatened to discover that a woman is dependent upon us, this will also allow us to feel quite good about ourselves. Of course there are significant class differences in what we have been brought up to want and expect as men, but there are also important ideas and feelings that men will tend to share. Often a feeling of our own 'independence' allows us to feel superior to women in our relationships, though we will not acknowledge this. The influences are deeply set in our gender and sexual development. From an early age, going out with girls is a way of proving ourselves to other boys. We wanted them to know that we could do it. The possessive nature of our relationships is so deeply set in our sense of male identity that as adults it is still hard to see women in other terms.

Our relationships are all tied up with our egos – with a way of proving ourselves and establishing a sense of masculine identity. Somehow this dominates our character formation from a very early age since our masculinity is never something we can take for granted but continually has to be proved and reasserted. It is easier for us to be in touch with how we have proved ourselves – made the grade – in going out with someone, than with any intrinsic feelings that might develop within the relationship. It is as if we have the greatest difficulties in seeing beyond ourselves, though because we always think we are doing things for others, we rarely acknowledge this as selfishness. Freud usefully thinks about this as narcissism.[15]

From our earliest days as boys, we are in competition with others. This is almost our dominating social reality. It controls the conception of self we can develop. In some sense it is shared despite differences in temperament and personality between different men. What is

...at, as boys, we are brought up to feel good about ...men we do *better* than others. In this way my sense of self is ...alised, tied into comparisons with others. I cannot help ...mparing myself with others, feeling bad, for instance, about whatever bicycle I might have, because someone else has got a slightly bigger one. This structures so much of our masculine experience and is taken so much for granted it is difficult to uncover its deep and abiding influence. We seem to be trapped into constantly proving ourselves, comparing ourselves with other men – as if it is only in these comparisons that we can begin to feel easier about ourselves. This is a way we seem to keep our fear of rejection and being put down in check.

Because, as men, we are always proving ourselves, we always have a sense that we could do better. We have so absorbed these conceptions that we even discover ourselves proving ourselves to ourselves. This ideology so controls our experience that you often hear middle-class men talk about 'letting themselves down'. From an early age, 'happiness' becomes some kind of 'goal' that will be the reward for all our efforts. We will have to explore some of the sources of this conception in the history of our inherited moral culture. We grow up identifying 'happiness' with 'success', assuming that you can not expect to be happy if you are not a 'success'. So happiness becomes something that is aimed for, worked for, struggled for. Activities themselves are robbed of any intrinsic satisfaction and joy they could have otherwise given us. Very crudely, our culture seems to have worked to make us almost incapable of enjoying ourselves, of pleasure, of intrinsic satisfaction that has not been worked for and deserved.

Within a Protestant work ethic we should not be idle and lazy, but we should make something of ourselves.[16] Only 'work' would bring real satisfaction – we could only expect to be happy once we had really proved ourselves in this realm. This has parallels in other areas of our lives. Though it is an ethic that has been challenged, it is so tied into our inherited conceptions of masculinity and male identity that to challenge it is bound to create a deep social and cultural crisis of masculinity. The only thing that mattered was that we 'did well', not that we developed any kind of interest in what we were learning. These objectives are often antithetical, but school tended to identify them. I remember, for myself, how hard it was at school to develop any sense of what I was interested in, as the different subjects just became different ways of 'doing well'. They were ways of getting marks, thereby proving myself at school. Others who might not have identified with academic success at school still wanted to be respected for their masculinity. If boys cannot base it on anything else, they will base it on strength – forcing others to respect them.

The other side of this, within the middle class, is that we are brought up to feel that we can always do better. It might be at school-work, but it could just as well be at football. This is important in extending the context of family relationships within which so much psychoanalytic theory can get trapped. Freud stresses that we have grown up in families in which we are vulnerable to be hurt and abused as children, where there has been a tension between love and approval. As small children we all want and need the love of our parents. It is part of the power parents have that they can withhold love and approval. Parents use this power in different ways. It is pernicious when, in the middle-class family, love is used as a form of control. This means that, as children, we have often got little sense that we are unconditionally loved by our parents. Rather we are made to feel that love has to be *earned*.

As Freud argues in psychoanalytic theory, we are left constantly working for the *approval* of our parents and this is used to manipulate and control. This does a lot of damage in our formation – damage that we cannot easily recover from and which is able to mark our future relationships. It can leave a child, boy or girl, feeling that she's got to prove herself all the time, if she wants to have the love of her father. This is doubly frustrating if he always makes her feel that he could do it better, and that she should be able to. But often we need a broader social and historical framework within which to appreciate the workings of these processes than is usually provided by Freud in his focus on early family relationships.

Because we are often brought up in our competitive society and culture to feel that we can always do better, we end up *discounting* whatever it is that we have been able to do. This can leave us feeling that we have not done anything at all. We end up feeling that nothing we do is 'good enough', so we are robbed of any sense of achievement at all, let alone any intrinsic joy in what we do. So from an early age a child can be robbed of any basic sense that she is lovable *regardless* of what she does for others. Rather, she is left feeling that it is only if she does things for others all the time that her parents and others will have any 'reason' to love her. She feels that she has to *earn* this love by constantly being kind to people, doing things for them; yet there is bound to be an edge of disbelief in the feelings, because she can never completely allow herself to feel that people will love her, just because of what she *does* for them. Rather, she comes to live through a contradictory structure of emotions in which her efforts for others fail to find their proper place.

For men, this contradiction has a different shape. It is especially common for men to feel that we have constantly to be proving ourselves. This digs deep into our very sense of self. It can leave us badly damaged, somehow existing *outside* of our own experience. You can be moved into a position of beginning to feel an 'observer' in your own life, finding it increasingly difficult to get any kind of spontaneous joy out of what you are doing.[17] Any kind of spontaneity seems to have been killed off – though we have little grasp or understanding of the social and personal processes through which this has happened. This seems to be the price of our 'independence'. Anything that we do has to be done for a 'purpose' or 'aim'; all our action has to be purposive and rational. In some haunting sense we seem to have almost been turned into machines, incapable of feeling and experiencing our own lives.

This a situation men often recognise, but feel fearful of acknowledging. We cannot help feeling 'unreal' in our own experience, as we have been systematically cut off from our emotions and feelings. Somehow our rationality seems to have crippled us – we can feel 'superior' but very little else. It is difficult for us to give or take love in our relationships, though we continue to pay lip-service to this. Our language becomes increasingly formal and empty. This says something about the crisis of masculinity in our culture and the poverty of our inherited traditions of moral and political thought to give us any way of understanding what is happening to us as men.

5 Morality

REASON, MORALITY AND MASCULINITY

To understand the sources of masculine self-denial we have to explore the implicit connections that have been made between reason, morality and masculinity since the Enlightenment. This established a particular identification between modernity and masculinity. This world was to be a world of men and if women were to play any part, it was to be supportive. Feminism has challenged the patriarchal organisation of knowledge and power in the 'modern' world that was brought into being with the Enlightenment. It was this world that the 'masculinist philosophy' – as Bacon saw it – that became known as science was set to legitimate. It confirmed the impersonal and objective knowledge of science while invalidating and marginalising the subjective, emotional and personal.

The modern world was also a secular world but it fundamentally offered a secularised form of Protestant culture as the source for its universal conception of reason and agency. It was a world in which Christian, Jewish and Islamic cultures were no longer conceived as providing different visions of the natural and social worlds. Rather, the claims to modernity were the claims to a universalism that would marginalise and diminish as 'backward' and 'uncivilised' those who refused to accept the terms of the Enlightenment vision of freedom and emancipation. The challenges of the counter-Enlightenment – Herder's challenge to Kant – were soon forgotten as the world of reason, science and progress became the only possible world. It defined reality itself.

So it is that issues about the relationship of masculinity to morality – in particular the identification of reason with morality and masculinity – lie at the heart of our modernist culture. Even now it is a latent issue that separates the defenders of Enlightenment in the terms offered by Habermas in his recent work and the challenges of those who argue that we are moving towards a post-modern culture. But often these issues around the status of modernity are not clearly formulated because there is a peculiar silence that surrounds the whole issue of masculinity. It is these issues I begin to raise, through exploring some of the tensions and contradictions within our inherited moral and political traditions. We will then go on to investigate how these are lived out in everyday experience of different masculinities.

CAPITALISM, PROTESTANTISM AND MASCULINITY

Weber can be read as illuminating our experience of masculinity when he focused on the connections between Protestantism and the spirit of modern capitalism. He recognised it is not an issue simply of the background conditions for the development of capitalism, but of appreciating the depths to which a Christian culture influences our character formation within capitalist society. This is something that Erich Fromm attempted also to develop, without talking specifically about masculinity, in the early chapters of his still illuminating book *Fear of Freedom*.[1]

Obviously Christianity has played a different role in different periods of capitalist development, but it is important to investigate its place in the sources of individual experience as part of a recognition of the shared, social character of what we have been brought up to think of as private and individual. It also helps to begin to recognise the depths to which our 'character' – the very structure of our emotions and feelings – has been formed within the limits of a liberal moral culture.

Thinking too crudely in terms of a 'capitalist culture' too easily denies the historical contexting of our experience and the significant differences between different societies. At the same time, we are trying to explore our inherited conceptions of masculinity partly as features of the historical development and domination of a specific moral culture. It is misleading to think of this in terms of the domination of a 'set of ideas'. As I have argued, this does not help us understand the ways we *live out* ideology in our everyday lives at work and at home, as well as in the ways we experience ourselves. Ideology cannot be separated from the everyday reality of our lives, though there is bound to be a tension because of the ways bourgeois ideology will mystify people about the nature of capitalist domination.[2]

More specifically, the ways people are brought up to think and feel about themselves will systematically mystify them about the *sources* of their suffering and oppression within a capitalist society. This is not to argue that sexual, racial or ethnic oppression have their sources in capitalism, but that they assume a particular form and character within a capitalist society.[3] Hopefully this undercuts structuralist formulations of the relationship of patriarchy to capitalism which conceive them as autonomous and independent structures, the one ideological and the other economic, that can somehow be related to each other. The assumptions of such an analysis are misconceived and only make it more difficult to understand the relationship between class, sexual and racial oppression in a particular society.[4]

Christianity prepared notions of equality which proved useful for the developing liberalism's inability to illuminate injustice and oppression within a capitalist social reality. There had always been tension between ideas of 'equality before God' and the existence of social inequalities. The contradictions reached a pitch in the ideas of 'love thy neighbour', where it was deemed possible to 'love thy neighbour' regardless of the inequalities of wealth and power that separate us from our neighbours. Part of the historical role of Christianity has been systematically to teach us to *abstract* the differences in people's everyday lives, so that they are regarded as barely relevant when we talk in general ways about 'how people should be treated'. In creating ideas that a person's material and social situation does not matter to God, Christianity brought people up to *discount* these differences. The only thing that mattered was a person's spirituality. This was particularly clear in Protestantism where individuals were concerned to prove themselves to God, so that what mattered in life was salvation and the individual's relationship to God.[5]

What Weber crucially helps us understand is the connection between Protestantism and the systematic *denial* of everyday experience and social reality. The only thing that really matters is 'salvation', against which life on this earth is of little significance. So that our lives are a 'test' – a way of proving ourselves to God. With the decline of explicit religious belief, it becomes really difficult to understand how these conceptions have continued to have enormous influence on our sense of male identity and on our relationship to our own experience. It is important to understand how a liberal moral culture has depended on and developed some of these conceptions.

This is particularly so when we think about the importance of 'work' – the ways work becomes an end in itself – so that men are often undermined and lost without it. This resonates with what I have already said about the ways work becomes a way of 'proving ourselves' as men and how most things we do get turned into occasions for proving ourselves, making it really difficult to get intrinsic satisfaction. This affects our relationships with other men, whom we cannot help seeing as competitors. It becomes a struggle to make our relationships with other men meaningful to us, which is why so many men seem to say nowadays that they can talk more easily and openly with women.

The Protestant idea of proving ourselves in the eyes of God connects up with traditional notions of masculinity. If we are locked into proving ourselves against others, it becomes really difficult for other people really to *matter* to us. We can uncover the somewhat shocking realisation that we do not really care about anyone. We pay lip-service to our friendships, realising that we want to do things with other people because we do not want to be lonely. We realise how brittle our male friendships really are. Again, we might think this reflects something about our own individual inadequacy, rather than something about the fractured relations of masculinity we are locked into, which form our very sense of self.

This is what makes it plausible to think in such general and abstract terms in liberal moral theory about the 'right' ways to treat others, because, in some sense, other people do not really matter to us. In the Kantian idea of 'respect' for others, we pay lip-service to some abstract idea of 'humanity'.[6] Christianity prepared the way for this notion of humanity to play such a crucial role within a liberal consciousness. It 'makes sense' within a structure of social relationships in which, in competition with everyone else, we are trying to assert ourselves individually. It becomes plausible for us to think about our relationships in such general and abstract terms because we experience ourselves very much in individual isolation, protected within the family against the rest of the world. This is the clearest image of a capitalist social reality.

Liberal moral culture dissolves our social experience into individual experience. It isolates the individual as it produces loneliness. The individual – especially a man – is set to prove himself against the rest of the world. It is no accident that the issues of 'egoism' and 'altruism' dominate liberal moral theory, so that, for instance, we have to discover 'reasons' for doing things for others because we are so locked into taking for granted our own individual self-interest that it is assumed that we would not do things for others unless we had good reasons.[7] This is what makes it easy for us to think in such general terms about our relationships with others – about treating others with respect, say, while at another level really being oblivious and ignorant about the moral character of social relationships. So we become oblivious to the issues of power and domination in our relationships with others.

KANT, LIBERAL MORALITY AND MASCULINITY

Kant provides the clearest foundations for bourgeois morality. He helps articulate and confirm its implicit individualism. Salvation provides the centre and core of life and is a matter of the individual's relationship with God. Morality demands that we act out of a sense of duty, regardless of what we might want to do. Our relationships with others are automatically presented as 'threatening' since they potentially tempt us away from doing our 'duty'. Kant clearly identifies morality with an independent faculty of reasoning. It is through the use of our reason that we can come to know what the moral law requires of us. Somehow reason is our connection with the spiritual, sharply separated off from our 'animal natures' which are identified with our emotions and feelings, and which Kant thinks about generally as 'inclinations' that tempt us away from acting out of a sense of duty.

So as far as 'acting morally' is concerned, there is a systematic *denial* of our emotions, feelings, wants and desires. This becomes an integral part of the formation of our masculinity. Kant legitimates our feeling that doing something because of what we feel about a certain situation, or person, is bound to lessen the 'moral worth' of what we do; and since, as men, we are so taken up with having to prove ourselves to others, if not to God, we are bound to treat emotions and feelings as threatening. Our sense of male identity will develop along with a sense of the 'rightness' of what we are doing.

Kant's moral theory manufactures a strong sense of 'right' and 'wrong'. It legitimates our thinking that we should do what is 'right', regardless of what we might feel about doing it. This separates off a sphere of morality – of 'right' and 'wrong' – from the concrete social relations of everyday living. Morality comes to have an independence and autonomy of its own, which is prepared for in the religious underpinning of Kant's writings. Since God is ultimately the source of the moral law, morality exists independently of human experience. Whatever connection it has in other traditions, with living a certain kind of social life or with satisfying and fulfilling human needs and wants, gets severed. This is reflected in the ways people still think about 'principles' as somehow existing abstractly, somehow validated outside and beyond social experience and relations.

Kant legitimates the fragmentation of our masculine experience in liberal moral and political theory. He maintains the Christian split between the 'earthly' – the animal, our desires, wants, feelings and emotions – and the 'spiritual' – duty, reason, morality. What is important for Kant is that morality means acting *against* our inclinations, against our emotions and feelings. This means that 'salvation' involves the systematic denial of our emotions and feelings so that we are free to act out of a sense of duty. Our lives are completely divided. There is no point of contact. Morality comes to involve the systematic denial of emotions and feelings so that we can do our duty. This has profound implications for our inherited sense of masculine identity. Kant provides the foundation for thinking that a person with a strong sense of self is the person who is able to do his duty, to do what is expected of him, regardless of what he feels about it. This has been most clearly assimilated into the formation of masculinity. It helps explain the sense in which men are supposed to, and often do have, a strong 'sense of self'.

What becomes clear is that men are divided against themselves. Our morality and 'sense of self' have no connection with our natures, our desires and needs, our emotions and feelings. Our sense of self develops with our reason out of a sense of the rightness of what we are doing, but is systematically separated from any sense of our feelings and emotions. This becomes so taken for granted in our masculine character formation that we never think about its implications for our lives. Rather, we tend to define our lives in very much these terms.

So as men, we structure our lives in terms of the 'goals' or 'aims' we have set ourselves. If, for instance, a young middle-class boy wants to be a lawyer, he will be ready to sacrifice his time and energy to do whatever is involved. He is ready to do this because he *already discounts* the place his feelings and emotions, needs and desires might play in his experience, in giving quality or meaning to his life. Happiness automatically comes with the realisation of the 'goal', if he ever allows himself to appreciate it. The structure and organisation of our male identities become set so that we systematically discount our emotions and desires, oblivious to the hurt or damage being done. As men we learn to put up with things, proving our masculinity by showing that we can withstand whatever the world has to throw at us. It is yet another way of proving ourselves as men.

HUMAN DIGNITY

Within a liberal moral culture we often hear talk of human dignity. Often it sounds abstract, with little connection to the everyday reality of people's lives. Somehow it has often worked to legitimate male superiority through a tacit identification of reason with masculinity. It is almost as if people have 'dignity', in spite of the kind of lives they live, the kind of work they do in factories and their squalid housing conditions. Since dignity is somehow guaranteed to us, we fail to understand how it can be undermined.

Part of what we also need to understand is how people are ever sustained by this abstract talk of dignity, rather than simply dismissing it as blinding them to their material reality of injustice, subordination and oppression. Rather it has an important and real existence in liberal democratic societies. Sometimes it comes to have greater reality, just because it is a way for people to maintain a grasp and confidence in their humanity, *despite* the conditions of their everyday lives.

The notion of 'equality' was important to the period of the French Revolution to help provide a critique of feudal conditions of life. It challenged ideas of different 'orders' of society, and made it possible for people to compare themselves *as individuals*. Ideas of individual ability and of careers open to talent became important for the first time. Tocqueville helps us understand the significance of these changes.[8] With time, these very same notions, which tended to presuppose that people are independent and self-sufficient, have worked to mystify people's experience of relations of power and subordination. The reality of class, racial and gender domination has been legitimated in terms of the abilities and talents of individuals. If social inequalities exist, they are seen as growing quite properly out of the different endowments and abilities of individuals.

The contradictions in Kant's writings on human dignity have a particular significance for our inherited conceptions of masculinity where reason is identified with masculinity whilst also being a source of dignity.[9] When we talk about 'human dignity', we can be rediscovering a basic truth of human equality. Kant recognises capacities people share, and it is important that he asserts that people have an equal capacity for living moral lives. This could be an important basis for developing a sense of equality between the sexes, if it were not that Kant saw reason as overwhelmingly identified with men and so legitimating the subordination of women to men.

But this is also where his own thinking reaches a paradox since, when thinking about relationships between rich and poor, he is forced to recognise that the material conditions of a person's life can make it easier to live a moral life. Kant refuses to escape from this contradiction through falling back on a Christian conception that abstracts from the inequalities of social life, but still he does not see human dignity as coming from qualities or needs that people have. Rather it is seen as an inner quality that people can draw from, whatever the indignities of their conditions of life. While having this inner reference, the source of this dignity remains external in the moral law, which can somehow be seen through each individual's actions. So it is the moral law, somehow tacitly identified with God, and seen as external even if we have access to it through reason and in what we supposedly legislate for ourselves, that gives people 'dignity'. We have inherited this paradox in liberal moral theory, though we have lost touch with the religious antecedents which could have made its workings clearer to us.[10]

So Kant provides the secular moral foundations for the separation of dignity from anything to do with people's wants and needs in their everyday lives. Dignity is connected with reason and thus with the moral law. It renders invisible a fragmentation of human life at the same time as it also sustains a particular conception of masculinity. This is what allows dignity so easily to become an abstract notion, an abstract possession of people with little connection with their everyday lives. So as men we have often been able to assume that women are guaranteed dignity and self-respect without ever having to face up to how a woman can be undermined and invalidated within a relationship. This is reflected in the paradoxical character of Kant's notion that we should not treat people only as means, but always as ends in themselves. Kant originally connects this with the presence of God in each person, shown in the 'reason' each person has. He thereby separates what it means to treat people as ends from questions about human needs, since as moral agents it is only through acting out of a sense of duty that our actions gain any moral worth or dignity. Rather it just becomes another way that we learn to *discount* the everyday reality of people's experience, since people's needs and feelings have so little bearing upon their moral lives. If Kant helps to put limits on certain ways of mistreating people, his ethical theory does not really illuminate them for us.

For example, a factory-owner can talk about how he prides himself in treating all his workers with respect. This does not have to mean more than politeness. He might say that he tries not to talk down to them and tries to take their 'point of view' into account. This will say something about the character of his 'personal relationship' with them. In a not dissimilar way men might talk about the respect they have for their wives. It is important to recognise the way Kant's moral notions become limited to face-to-face personal relationships. This protects the factory owner from thinking about the conditions of work and the everyday realities of wage labour.[11] He does not have to think about the relationship of power and subordination with his workers. He only conceives it as a 'personal relationship with individual workers', not as a social relationship of employer to workers.

Somehow work experience, be it in the factory or at home – however dominating of everyday social reality – becomes denied as a moral relation as we learn to talk of the 'different jobs' people have. In this way, people are led to discount and deny their own experience. What becomes significant is only whether people are acting 'morally' or not, whether they have decided to act out of a sense of duty, which has a reference to a sphere all its own, beyond the experience of people's everyday relationships. It becomes a matter of individuals living up to abstract moral principles which they have supposedly freely legislated for themselves, regardless of the class, sexual or racial relationships of power and oppression. We find ourselves discounting the everyday reality of our lives, unable to think critically about it.

EXTERNALISING MASCULINE EXPERIENCE

Within liberal capitalist society, men especially are encouraged to 'get on'. This becomes the way that men validate themselves, think well of themselves. School is an important preparation and can illuminate more general social processes in the formation of a masculine identity. We might think well of ourselves if we 'do well' at school, and we are told that we should be 'happy', or at least satisfied, if we have done well. Or we are told that we have 'got nothing to be happy about', if we come home with a poor report. So we are brought up to identify 'happiness' with 'success', as if it is something that is automatically going to come to us if we have done well. Much of our experience is structured in the way we take this conception for granted. Our position in school, or later our job, somehow stands as *proof* of who we are. So we come to identify ourselves as men very much with what we *do*.

Within the middle class, we do whatever is expected of us to get on, and we expect others to do the same. We very much identify ourselves with what we are proving ourselves to be. Of course our class and ethnic situation are crucial in this. Men will relate to their work in different ways depending upon whether it be working on a Ford assembly line or entering a profession. The Ford worker might simply see it as a way of earning money, while the professional man sees it as a more complete identity and way of life. But what might be shared is the relationship work leaves us in with women. In either case, men can still expect women to be *grateful* for the work they supposedly do only for them and the family. Men still expect to be recognised and appreciated as the 'breadwinners', though this is obviously changing too.

Something missed, because it is so taken for granted, is the ways we, as men, easily *externalise* our experience and fall into treating ourselves as objects. We direct our energies towards a particular goal of 'getting on' and we are brought up to assume that the achievement of this goal will bring 'happiness'. But, from an early age, setting 'goals' is a mental process to do with working out what would be best for us and has involved the systematic denial of our emotions and feelings. This is already prepared for in the ways we, as men, identify ourselves with our 'rationality', treating any sign of emotion as weakness. The ground is thereby prepared for treating *ourselves* as objects. It is crucial to grasp how this happens and how our traditions of thought and feeling make it so hard to identify the costs to men that this involves.

From a very early age, our sense of self develops within a particular constellation of power and dependency within the family. The women's movement has illuminated this process for women, showing that girls are brought up to win the love and approval of others, especially their fathers. Girls grow up feeling the compulsion to conform to an externalised image of femininity, in fear of being rejected and left alone in a society that cruelly despises and puts down a woman who 'can't get a man'. Traditionally, the man is seen very much in contrast, as encouraged to go out and do what he wants to do, effective in the real world, active, powerful, self-willed.

The passive images of femininity are generally contrasted with the active images of masculinity. Along with this goes the general idea that men have a strong sense of self, whereas women supposedly have a weak sense of themselves, being ready to serve the needs of partners and children. This contrast oversimplifies, failing to reflect the personal reality of many men's lives. The ways that men are strong and determined are too easily confused with what it means to have a 'sense of self'. The ways that men so readily treat themselves as 'objects' have an important bearing upon what it means to have a 'sense of self'.

I need to write about this a little more openly and personally. It was not easy for me to establish a sense of self. This can be difficult to explore, for so much of our structuralist intellectual culture would diminish and deride these concerns, secure in, or possibly hiding behind, a sense that the 'self' is itself a social fiction for it is socially and historically constituted. There are no truths to be explored about our selves, no single history that can be laid bare. But even if there is no single history, no single narrative but a series of histories that bring different aspects of our experience into focus, it is still significant that we can feel able to contact feelings and experiences that we had long buried. I think that the quest for a more truthful, less rigid and more open, vulnerable and flexible relationship to the self remained powerfully motivating for Freud, even if we are in danger of losing aspects of this within Lacanian interpretations of his work.[12]

But, talking more personally now, my fragmented sense of self also had something to do with not being very strong physically, or at least thinking of myself as quite weak. Probably it had also to do with being Jewish and growing up in an isolated continental community where my family did not really speak English 'properly'. This gave me an acute sense of having to learn 'how to behave'. I could not assume that the feelings and relationships we had at home were going to be repeated outside. This connects with the ways morality appears as 'standards', for as a child it very much meant that I accepted the 'rules' that other people set. I got used to 'getting on' with people, very much on *their* terms.

I wanted to be 'English' so that I could 'belong' to the world I was living in. I did not want people to think I was 'different', so I felt very anxious about saying what I felt and needed. I could not know that my desires would not be strange to others, and I feared being exposed. So from an early age I got used to conforming to external standards, especially at school. I very much wanted to 'do well', but I only seemed to be able to do this by becoming strangely invisible to myself as if others could see straight through me. I wanted to make my family happy because, as refugees from Hitler's Germany, I was made aware of how much they had already suffered. At school this meant that I worked to 'do well', but never really developed a sense of what I liked doing or was really interested in. Somehow I felt I had to 'do well' regardless of what I might be drawn to. I could not afford to touch the resentments I felt for other boys at school, because I needed to be accepted too much. I assumed an easy and friendly manner, but did not reveal very much of myself. I was very much a 'good boy'.

At home I was conscious that my mother was carrying a heavy load bringing up four boys on her own. I knew that I had to feel grateful to her, which taught me – at some cost to myself – to put the interests or happiness of others, above my own. I learnt to discount myself, somehow feeling that it was more important to make others happy, or at least not to upset them, than it was to be in touch with my own needs. I did not really want to discover anything that would threaten my image of myself. In any case, I had learnt it was selfish only to think of yourself. Possibly it was this kind of background and the marginality of being Jewish within a Christian society that drew me to feminism. But this was still difficult for me to own in its own terms.

At the same time, this 'getting on' was something that happened almost independently of my sense of self, though I drew great satisfaction and felt proud when I did well. I was protecting myself by maintaining a sense of the 'real me that nobody else really understands or appreciates'.[13] Many children have a fantasy world they do not share. I had withdrawn into myself to find warmth and comfort. This was an important part of my survival, because it allowed me to withdraw and seem unaffected by the humiliations and indignities of school life, knowing it did not really touch me. I was safe and protected in my own space. Other people could not hurt me any more. I had learnt to treat myself as an object so that I could make myself invulnerable to the everyday competitiveness that is so much a part of boys' lives together.

But locked into myself, as are many boys, it was difficult for me to connect with others on anything but a superficial level. My life turned in on itself. I had learnt *not* to need others, especially other boys that I was competing with.

SELF-CONTROL AND ACHIEVEMENT

As small boys, we already know that we have got to have 'self-control'. We are told that without self-control we are not really boys and we will not get anywhere. This is especially powerful in the middle class. You have to decide rationally what you want to do, which already separates it from any consideration of what you want or need to do for yourself, and then make whatever sacrifices are necessary to achieve the goal. Implicit is a conception that this is the only way of getting 'real happiness', in contrast to any short-term happiness you might get doing what you want to do. This has to be understood within the context of the power which the middle class has in the organisation of the larger society. It affects the formation of a middle-class masculinity very deeply.

Self-control is often reached by killing whatever emotions and feelings we have, so we can always do what is required of us. This means we become wary of our own emotions, partly because we develop so little ongoing relationship to them. We fear that if we get angry we will be overcome completely and there will be nothing that stops us destroying others. If we get sad we will disappear into nothing. These fears are very pervasive. They encourage us as men to maintain a real distance from whatever we are feeling. We need to be able to think that the sacrifices in our desires and emotional lives are always worth making. This is only possible if we can always identify ourselves with our achievements.

Kant argues for the control of our emotions so we can do what is morally required of us. We are taught to distrust our emotions. They can only lead us astray. There is a complete separation between our emotionality and our morality. As Weber recognises, this prepares the ground for capitalism, which wants us always to be dissatisfied with what we have, so we will work harder to 'improve ourselves'. But it is partly because we have been cut off from our emotions and feelings that we have been cut off from the sources of knowing what we want for ourselves.

Capitalism replaces notions of 'self-fulfilment' with ideas of 'getting on' and 'proving yourself' which turn out to be endless tasks, because we are always proving ourselves against others. We can always do better. It is almost as if our capacity to enjoy ourselves has been destroyed, slowly but systematically. It has been replaced by a goal of endless work. Work becomes an end in itself – though men rarely feel so self-righteous about this these days – very much in the way that morality is separated from the rest of our lives. There is always more to be done. We can never really settle, never relax. Self-denial is involved in the very definition of our masculinity.

Competition is integral to capitalism. We form our sense of masculine identity in comparing ourselves with others. We constantly compare ourselves with others as the way we form our male conception of self. What counts is that we are doing 'better' than others, not what we are doing. In this way, we learn to discount our activities, undermining whatever intrinsic satisfaction we might otherwise get.[14] We gain little joy if we always have an eye on how well others are doing. We will find it hard to give importance to the different things we do without really understanding why. So, especially at school, we have a way of *abstracting* ourselves from the concrete activities themselves. We are left wondering what really matters to us. In the end, we discover that very little matters, because we have been doing things only to do 'well', never with much sense of what we really *want* to be doing. We are left as men with little chance of discovering what our own needs are. A language of need will be bereft of meaning for us and so it will be hardly surprising if we are drawn to structuralist traditions of work that discount its meaning altogether.

This kind of schooling can prepare us well for work. We do not expect to identify with work at the level of our own needs. So it is easy for men to learn that nothing that they do at work matters, only the wages they get. We learn not to expect much intrinsic satisfaction from work, because we have never got it from anything else. Given that our sense of masculine identity is formed within the context of these kinds of relationships, it is hardly surprising if we are left with little sense of our own emotions or wants. Education can so often leave people feeling inadequate as it reproduces a deep sense of failure. It can make boys feel that if they have not lived up to certain standards, they are 'worthless'. Because it connects us through competition with everyone else at school, it can leave us effectively isolated and lonely. Since other boys are simply occasions for proving ourselves individually, we never share much of ourselves with them, or even learn *how* to make ourselves vulnerable. So we easily find ourselves discounting our relationships, thinking that we can make it alone. We find ourselves with few friends and a deep sense of estrangement from our individual emotional lives.

Self-control is important for men, because we are brought up within a culture that still makes us believe we are basically evil and that our animal nature is constantly to be guarded against in our masculinity. This is very deep in the Protestant tradition. It partly explains why we cannot *trust* our feelings and emotions, especially as men. If we 'let go', people will discover what we are really like – and nobody will want to have anything to do with us. This is the vision which underlies Kant's influential discussions of duty and haunts our sense of male identity. Our reason allows us to act in accordance with the moral law, so becoming the way we can save ourselves *from ourselves*. It is only by *denying* ourselves that we stand any chance of living a moral life.

By ourselves we are worthless, so our sense of male identity is tied to the control and subordination of our natures. This is partly why nothing that we do with our desires and emotions can be valued. It is merely idleness, bound to lead us to no good. We only have a chance of 'making something of ourselves' if we keep ourselves busy *doing* things. Our only way of escaping from who we are is in what we *do*. This self-denial is the way we can escape our feelings of worthlessness and assume a sense of superiority first to women and then to other cultures whose domination is thereby legitimated. But it is hard to know how we have assimilated these conceptions, since they are so taken for granted as a part of the European culture we have grown up in. When imperial conquest was secured, notions of racial superiority which so often had a basis in ideas of reason, civilisation and progress in the Enlightenment could be replaced by much gentler ideas of liberal democracy and the development of the individual. Often this removed the contradictions in our experience to a deeper, less accessible, level until, for instance, they were questioned and challenged by feminism and movements for national liberation.

Within the work ethic of capitalist democracy, activity becomes a protection against loneliness for men. We do not know how to be with ourselves alone. We are often scared because of what we might discover about ourselves. This ties in with notions that we should find 'meaning' within our own individual achievements. Isolated from others through competition, we can only find solace in the individual family – but, even here, men are often now isolated and withdrawn as fathers. Happiness is always eluding us. We can always be more successful, so we cannot expect to be happy until we have really 'made it'. We never understand what our emotions and feelings could possibly have to do with our sense of self, even with happiness. Happiness is so closely tied in with success that it becomes self-evident that only self-control and self-sacrifice will enable us to succeed. Mill had glimpses of the damage this rationalism did to himself and his own capacities and powers in his *Autobiography*.[15] But he only partially develops this into a critique of liberal capitalist society.

FEELING WORTHLESS

Bourgeois morality has deeply religious foundations. Kantian ethics is central because it articulates a secular ethics that maintains the Protestant religious foundations. God is replaced by a conception of the 'moral law', and the awe we were to feel towards God, we are supposed now to feel for the moral law. Before the law, we can now feel our worthlessness. We are nothing before the moral law, even if it gives us a way of feeling 'equal' with all other people. As people, our experiences and feelings count for nothing before the moral law.

Rather, we grow up, learning all kinds of ways of discounting ourselves, so we can struggle to do what is 'right', regardless of what our feelings and experience tell us. Kant is clear that men somehow exist closer than women to reason and the moral law. It is only through the moral law, through acting out of a sense of duty, that men can begin to think well of ourselves. The moral law gives us our only chance of living worthwhile lives. But women are supposed, in Kant, to look to men for guidance and the light of reason, so have to subordinate themselves to men whose superiority is tacitly assumed.

The idea of the evilness of human nature lies deep in the Protestant tradition. It has become an integral part of bourgeois morality, though it is rarely talked about openly. The religious sources have been covered over. We only get glimpses of its hold in thinking that 'we can't expect to be happy' or 'we really aren't very nice, so it is very important to have self-control'. It is often the source of the feelings of emptiness that we have all experienced at some time. Because our 'natures' are basically evil, it is only in denying our natures, denying our emotions and desires, that we have a chance of living 'worthwhile' lives. This is the deep source of the self-hatred that exists within our inherited conceptions of masculinity.

It is because we grow up as men with such a deep, if unacknowledged, sense of self-hatred that we often do anything to escape ourselves. This becomes the spur to work and to the creation of a male identity that is so closely tied to achievements. It is connected to the ways our culture denigrates our bodies and sexuality, even when it talks about the naturalness of sexuality. We are all left struggling with feelings of guilt in our sexual feelings without any longer being able to understand why we should feel this way. This is so tied into the texture of our everyday experience as men that it is hard to recognise its deep historical and cultural sources.

This is especially so when everything is done to mystify us about the *shared* character of these feelings. Rather, we are left to assume we are the only ones to feel this way so it must reflect something about our individual personalities. We will want to keep our shame to ourselves. This is why consciousness-raising can be revelatory, helping us discover not only that other people feel much the same way about their bodies, but also how our feelings have grown out of our experience and relationships. So it is that we can begin to locate our own experience of masculinity in a social and historical context.

Our moral traditions have helped organise the social relations of masculinity and the ways we think and feel about ourselves as men. The Kantian influence makes us feel that our emotions will just interfere with our rational judgement, so that, especially as men, we should work to weaken their influence over our experience as much as possible. We will have to consider the costs in terms of integrity and self-respect of doing this – the damage we are doing to ourselves as men. But at the moment, it is enough to realise how it distances us from any sense of our needs and wants, so that men can have a strong sense of male identity in terms of goals and achievements, but little sense of our emotions and feelings or what we want for ourselves individually. Often it is easier for men to do what we 'ought' to do or what is expected of us than it is to know what we want to do.

John Stuart Mill noticed this sense of weak individuality in a liberal society that prided itself on its individualism in his essay *On Liberty*. He was aware of how a Calvinist inheritance weakens a sense of identity through turning people against themselves. He appreciated how morality brings us up to distrust ourselves, especially our feelings and emotions, but tended to think we could develop a different vision of ourselves without really challenging the social relations of power and subordination. As it is, we become plagued by a sense of worthlessness that threatens to come to the surface as soon as we stop 'achieving'. We lose any sense that individual fulfilment might have to do with identifying and satisfying our wants and needs. Rather, it becomes a moral notion that is implicitly tied to self-denial. It becomes yet another goal we have to sacrifice ourselves for, which is always in the future. Our masculinity becomes controlled by a sense of obligation. We find ourselves always doing things we 'ought to do', never sure of what we want to be doing. Occasionally we are open to realising that, despite a strong public identity, we have a weak sense of self.

REASON AND LOVE

Within Kantian conceptions of morality which maintain such a pervasive hold within a liberal moral culture, reason reigns. Reason is the source of all understanding and all truth. This cuts a deep split in our experience between what we 'know' through 'reason' and what we feel. The only thing that matters is what we can defend through reason, which very much affects the place we give to argument in working through problems in relationships. We take for granted that reason exists independently of our 'experience', of our emotional and somatic personal reality. This is a way morality helps define a conception of masculinity which *separates* us from contact and relationship with our own experience, in the end making us feel we are often 'observers' in our own lives, automatically deciding what would be most 'rational' to do. Reasons exist universally and so independently of us, in the way that it becomes 'rational' to send boys to boarding-school because it helps make them become 'independent'. It is the universal character of reason that has been such an ambiguous, though relatively unexplored, inheritance.[16]

So, for example, what Charlie feels about leaving home and being sent to boarding-school does not come into the argument because the family is trying to establish a 'general principle'. Only later will they go on to consider the particular situation of Charlie, but then only as an instance of an already established general principle. Somehow the whole procedure auomatically denies any sense of Charlie's personal needs, and must make him feel almost 'incidental' in the considerations going on. This is very much the feeling of being impersonalised. This illustrates more general social processes through which we are made to feel that our feelings do not really matter or count when it comes to reason and love. So Charlie might be told 'at this point we aren't interested in what you feel, but just in the arguments about the principle of boarding-schools'. So the only way he could enter the discussion to win some kind of approval from parents is to *discount* his own feelings.

We have been brought up, both as men and women, to 'control' our emotions and been made to feel that it is 'selfish' to do things for ourselves. From an early age, we have been told we have to consider the wellbeing of others. This has often meant that if we have known what we wanted ourselves, the only way of getting it was somehow to present it as in the interests of everyone. So, for example, if I wanted to go away for the day, it would be difficult to say 'I want to spend a day in the country', and easier to say 'the whole family needs some time off in the country.' We feel that it is 'selfish' to say 'I want' or 'I need'. Our inherited tradition of liberal moral rationalism means we feel easier working out the 'reasons' for doing something and then feeling we 'ought' to do what is 'required of us'. This is how a sense of obligation comes to dominate in everyday life.

So the whole structure of our moral experience becomes tied to doing what we 'ought' to do, regardless of what we feel ourselves. This means that, in some sense, our decisions are made for us in the neutral workings of the moral calculation. So again it becomes a matter of conforming to the 'authority' of reason. Even though liberals always talk about individual responsibility, in a sense this is exactly what is denied in the reality of experience in liberal culture. We have been separated off from our emotions and feelings, taught to regard what we 'ought to do' as somehow given independently of our own experience. Again this is a paradox which Mill notes in his essay *On Liberty*, without really exploring the sources of the conformism he saw everywhere around him. He recognised that the liberal ideology of individual responsibility was somehow really working to produce subservience and obedience.[17] This says something about an ongoing tension between the demands of liberal morality and its talk of developing our capacities, abilities and powers in our everyday experience.

It is a tension that can help illuminate contradictions in our sense of masculinity and in conditions created for love in our relationships with partners. We are brought up systematically to deny our emotions and feelings, yet we are brought up to expect love to give the central meaning to our experience. This connects deeply with our experience within the middle-class family where love is often used as a form of control. We are made to feel that love is something we have to *earn*, through what we *do* to prove ourselves. This leaves us with a formative experience of the conditional character of love. It also connects to an abiding suspicion created for us that we are not really lovable anyway. What is more, as boys, we are not in touch with our caring feelings for others, which we easily regard as 'soft' in the face of the hard realities of 'reason'. Often, as boys, we just cut off from whole areas of experience and need. If we never learn how to give of ourselves emotionally in our relationships with partners, it is hardly surprising when, as adults, we do not even understand what is being demanded of us.

We are made to feel that it is through success and individual achievement that we are going to earn the love of others, especially our parents. This leaves us with a weak sense of love, which often has little reality in our personal relationships. As boys, we are moved out of touch with our warm and caring feelings. We learn to desire and suppress these feelings, in order to be 'manly'. We do not like to think we are dependent, or that we need other people. It becomes painful to accept such needs, because they seem to compromise our sense of male identity. Dependence becomes a sign of weakness, a sign that we cannot make it on our own.

This means that we can grow up feeling quite distant from others, especially men, who are always potential competitors. We are locked into constantly 'proving ourselves', thinking this is the way to win 'love'. As middle-class children, this was the way we assured the love of our parents. We end up confusing 'love' with 'approval'. In some sense, this undermines our capacity to be close and intimate with others. We often fear intimacy as we feel trapped in our own sense of individuality. This becomes a prison. We find ourselves incapable of reaching out to others, even when we desperately want to. This is part of the tension built into our inherited masculinity, though we more readily witness it as a sign of personal inadequacy.

As men, we cannot help withholding our love. I know how I could not help treating it as some kind of 'valuable possession' that I had to give sparingly. I cannot give my love easily. I cannot help feeling that I am 'wasting a valuable product' and that I should hold tight to it. The denial of our emotions and feelings, which is such an integral part of a masculinity so tied to a morality of reason, weakens our capacity to love. The damage can be severe. We can feel so estranged from our own emotions and feelings, so much in control of them, that we do not really know what we feel. This often only strikes us in our loving relationships, when we are called upon to respond openly and lovingly towards another person.

We find ourselves automatically withholding our love, more or less as a way of asserting our control in relationships, making sure that others love us more openly than we can love them. Our diffidence becomes a source of power. This is deeply tied into the possessive character of our relationship with ourselves and with others. We can confidently feel we are doing everything that can be expected of us, so we do not know what a woman is asking of us when she says we are giving very little of ourselves in the relationship. We can be secure thinking that 'we cannot be expected to change the ways we feel', which only blinds us to the damage done to our capacity to feel and to love.

For men, this is connected to the inability to ground ourselves in our relationships. This produces within heterosexual relationships strong images of a search for the 'right woman'. Inevitably, the women we are relating to do not live up to the image we have of the woman 'I'm really going to love'. This becomes yet another standard that dominates our everyday experience. It becomes part of the ways we 'put down' women we are relating to, for not living up to a standard that, in reality, has nothing to do with them. Somehow it is always another woman – some fiction – who dominates our sense of what a woman 'should be like'. So we can make a woman feel bad in a relationship, because she is not well dressed enough, beautiful enough, independent enough, loving enough – because she is just not the fiction we have created for ourselves.

A consequence of systematically suppressing our emotions and feelings as we live up to images of masculinity, is a weakening of any individual sense of what we want for ourselves. This is part of what we mean by 'being out of touch with ourselves'. We are moved so out of touch with our own feelings that we turn our heterosexual relationships into areas of rational decisions, unable to act confidently out of our feelings. We find it hard to experience much reality in our everyday relationships, doing our best to sustain the idealised image of our partners. Our relationships with women will often be so shot through with 'standards' and 'ideals' that it will be difficult to appreciate even the good things happening in our relationships. We will find it hard to accept a woman as a 'person' with her own wants and needs.

This will all be part of the context within which we 'withhold' our loving feelings, so we have them ready for when our 'ideal' enters our lives. This will lead us to devalue our experience of the moment, always thinking that things could be 'so much better'. This puts us out of touch with the everyday reality of the relationship. Since we do not know how to accept ourselves, we are out of touch with our individual needs – a consequence itself of the denial of our emotions and feelings – and we often have little sense of how to love and enjoy our relationship. We find ourselves so controlled by the 'ideals' that we can never accept and settle into the reality of the relationship. Not only are we constantly judging our partners, but we are constantly judging ourselves for not living up to the goals we set ourselves. Often we are so taken with our own failings and sense of inadequacy that we cannot begin to accept and appreciate what our partners have to offer.

6 Emotional life

SELF-ESTRANGEMENT AND RELATIONSHIPS

As I have argued, Kant establishes the 'moral law' as *external* to our everyday lives and experience. We have to *aspire* to live moral lives, being ready to do what we 'ought to do', regardless of what we feel. In this way, we *separate* ourselves from developing a sense of our emotional needs and wants. As men, we develop very little relationship with these parts of ourselves. This becomes the source of self-estrangement that is taken for granted in our definitions of masculinity.

Morality supposedly offers us a 'fulfilment', which is supposedly deeper than anything we could possibly reach through fulfilling our needs and wants. So we inherit a feeling of the 'wrongness' of spending time with ourselves, of doing what we want. This becomes a form of 'self-indulgence'. We cannot help feeling that we should be doing something 'more worthwhile'. This only proves how evil we really are, that we are tempted into doing things for ourselves.

So being a man means being ready to sacrifice ourselves for 'something higher', something more worthwhile. This kind of self-sacrifice becomes central to the social relations of liberal capitalism. Of course, we do not think about it in terms of 'self-sacrifice' because it has become so automatic. We cannot identify the character of hurt and 'self-denial' this kind of identification involves. This is built in a different way into the experience of women, who are often forced to 'live through' other people, especially their children, discovering their own happiness in the success of others. But this, too, involves a deep estrangement from self. Women, according to feminist insights, are never given a chance of discovering what they want for themselves, of living *their own* lives.

As men, we are brought up to identify our very sense of masculinity with our rationality, with our understanding. This leaves us in a contradictory situation in relation to our emotional lives and sexuality.

Culture so often concedes the importance of sexuality, while destroying our ability to enjoy it. From an early age we are brought up to despise our bodies. Sexuality within a Protestant culture is deemed dirty and low. We should be concerning ourselves with 'higher' things if we want to assert our humanity *against* our animal nature. The same splits occur in our experience, where the contradictions operate at a less conscious level, since there is a significant rift between the language and consciousness of liberal attitudes towards sexuality and ways people are brought up to think and feel about themselves. We are ashamed of our bodies, of our sexuality, while 'attractiveness' has been made into an important commodity. We cannot help caring about whether others are attracted towards us and, objectifying ourselves, wanting to be desirable objects for others.

Treating ourselves as objects, though profoundly different from the way women are treated as sexual objects within a relation of power, is a mark of the ways men have been estranged from our emotional lives. As men, we are brought up to despise our sexuality, in the search for 'higher' things. We find ourselves denying our sexuality, while at the same time acknowledging it is at the centre of our experience. We are brought up to be ashamed of our sexual feelings, though at the same time often obsessed with them. This is part of the dynamic of repression that has been used as an integral part of social control.[1]

We can feel caught in a paradox. Within the middle class, men are made to feel their careers are *important*, while everything else can only bring fleeting satisfaction. We find ourselves continually asserting ourselves in competition with other men, so we often end up feeling isolated. We are locked into a competitiveness that can extend into the centre of our sexuality. So it is very easy for women to become 'objects' for us, ways of making us feel good about ourselves. It is as if relationships are essentially self-referring so we can go out with women who are 'attractive', because this allows us to feel good about ourselves. We get trapped into objectifying women, treating them as possessions that reflect back upon our own sense of 'achievement'.

Georg Lukàcs develops his notion of reification to help explain how, within bourgeois culture, possession becomes our basic orientation towards the world, including our relationships with others.[2] We get glimpses of this, for instance, in the ways women become 'attractive' to us because they are sought after by other men. Exchange value is recognised as the only source of value within a capitalist society and so dominates our experience. We find it hard to value women who are not found attractive by others, even if we pay lip-service to an idea that 'love is in the eyes of the beholder.' This is denied in the everyday reality of our experience, even if it is an experience we refuse to acknowledge in these terms. Possession becomes our *mode* of relating to others, even though we might be largely unaware of this and so deny any kind of responsibility for it.

Given the way a liberal moral culture individualises our experience, we fall into thinking of relationships as a matter of individual personalities hitting it off with each other. This has painful consequences. It strikes deep into the ways our emotions and feelings have been structured. Jo, for instance, might have been brought up to see his wife as 'mine', feeling deeply committed to *looking after her*, without ever realising this puts restrictions on her. So if he experiences his wife as 'part of him', this hints at the depths of hurt and jealousy he feels when she begins to feel attracted to other people, or discovers that other men find her attractive.

This goes totally against how Jo has been brought up as a man, and he cannot help feeling betrayed by her. He feels humiliated in her attraction towards other men. Within the ways his own morality connects to his inherited sense of masculinity, he has no way of understanding his own feelings. As far as he is concerned, 'she is my wife and that means she shouldn't be mucking around with other men.' He does not experience this simply as jealousy. He feels this deeply as an insult to his very masculinity. He finds the situation unbearable and has been given no cultural language and experience for preparing himself for it.

It does not help to say that he regards his wife as a 'possession', without developing an appreciation that goes beyond moralistic judgement to see how deeply embedded this is in his sense of male identity. He thinks of himself as a 'faithful husband', and in many ways he is. Partly because for many men their sense of individual identity is so tied up with their sense of masculine identity, they literally 'go to pieces' when their masculinity is challenged. This is not to justify unequal sexual relationships, but it helps us to appreciate the depth of issues we are dealing with, which are so often misleadingly set in the rationalistic terms of choice, will and determination.

Liberal morality often follows Kant in talking about the 'wrongness' of treating people as objects, almost as if it is simply a matter of 'attitude' we freely take up towards others. This is profoundly misleading, though deeply embedded in liberal conceptions of freedom, making us feel that we are free to have whatever relationship with people we want to have. This idea makes it difficult to identify and question social relations of oppression and domination within human relationships. It is built upon a very naïve psychology of self-interest that does not help us understand social forms of dependency and subordination. Its truth is questioned in feminist analysis of women's subordination, whose theory originally grows out of consciousness-raising based in the everyday realities of women's lives, rather than existing in an independent realm of its own.

When we say, as men, 'we can't help treating women as possessions', we might be refusing to change but we are at the same time trying to show that it is not simply a matter of an act of will that men are 'free' to make. What is at issue here is a restructuring of our relationships and experience. We are bringing out how the close relationship between our sense of ourselves as men and our sense of individual identity can make it hard especially for older generations of men to change themselves, and to relate to women and gay men in different ways. This is to question the ways identities are formed in the cultures we are living in.

The idea that 'we can relate to others in any way we wish' mystifies the realities of our everyday experience as heterosexual men and does not prepare us for the difficulties we all face in giving up a power and superiority we take so much for granted. This does not mean the need to change is not pressing, but we have to realise how much of our inherited conceptions of masculinity need to shift if we are to relate to women in equal ways and come to terms with a homophobia that is often deeply culturally and psychologically embedded. At least in challenging these notions we might develop a clearer sense of the significance of feminism and gay liberation rather than fool ourselves into thinking we can change ourselves simply as a matter of will.

SELF-DENIAL AND FANTASY

The control and domination of our feelings on which our sense of ourselves as masculine is built eventually weakens them. We end up feeling very little at all. This undermines the base of our experience, whether we are straight or gay, meaning that we are less *grounded* in our own experience. Now the self-understandings of bourgeois society can protect us from feeling this as any kind of 'problem'. Utilitarian culture has little room for emotions. If anything, they are regarded as 'inferior thoughts'. It is almost as if an ideal life would preclude the 'interference' of emotions and feelings. This sustains fundamentally the Kantian identification of our 'humanity' with 'rationality'. Emotions and feelings have no real place in the humanity of our lives, which is strictly defined in opposition to our animal nature. This is a source of élitism and superiority, because a 'human life' is always defined as being 'superior' to an 'animal life'. For Kant, our emotions and feelings are a part of our 'lower', animal selves.

In this way, modernity, as it is lived out in bourgeois morality, *undercuts* our experience. Utilitarianism shares this fundamental structure with Kantianism. It is this systematic denial of our emotionality, that is part of what *defines* morality as 'bourgeois'. Our experience is left inevitably fragmented, and we are left denying whatever feelings and emotions are emerging, so that we can live up to the ideal of ourselves as 'rational', never to be 'swayed' by any feelings. This denial makes it difficult for us, as men, to say what we want and need, because we do not want to talk out of our emotions and feelings. Already we regard emotional life as a sign of weakness. So, to give an example that illustrates the workings of these processes, Richard would never say that he was hurt because Susan had started a relationship with Tom. We have to find room in our understanding for the idea that Richard was not *allowing himself* to feel hurt. This does not mean that he does not feel hurt, but that he does not allow himself to feel his hurt or even his jealousy. This is not simply a question of 'mistaken' identity, nor is it a matter of Richard not knowing what he feels.

Richard might say that he objects to the relationship because he thinks that Tom is not a nice person, and is bound to be just leading Susan up the garden path. He finds himself giving all kinds of 'reasons' that are supposed to be 'objective', which could bring Susan to make a decision against the relationship. He wants her to conclude that it is 'irrational' for her to have the relationship, given what she knows about Tom. But all the time Richard refuses to say that he is 'hurt' and that is why Susan should give up the relationship. In this way, he denies his feelings, but also mystifies the reality of the relationship that exists between them, presenting it simply as Susan's decision.

He could think that his feelings do not have anything to do with it, because Susan is free to do whatever she wants to do. At the same time, he is providing 'objective reasons' for her ending the relationship. In this way, Richard *discounts* himself in the situation. He presents it 'impersonally' as a matter of 'reasons' that should be taken into account. We need to realise that this mystifies his personal reality. Whatever ideas of freedom and equality he is living up to, make it difficult for him to accept his feelings in this situation. His energy, as Freud understood, becomes taken up with suppressing his feelings. This is part of what creates a sense of 'unreality' in the situation, and means that Richard is cutting off from his own experience. This is part of the reality of self-denial.

This kind of emotional self-denial is often more familiar to men than it is to women, who are allowed to be more 'emotional', though they are put down for it. In some sense, this relates to the emotional unreality of male experience and goes some way to explain what we mean by saying that men are less *grounded* in our emotional reality, in our experience. This follows directly from the hold notions of 'rationality' have in organising our masculine experience. It is also related to the high level of 'fantasy' that exists in men's lives. It seems that, in some sense, men fantasise much more than women or have more visual fantasies, which seem to play a much larger role in their experience. Certainly, sexual images and fantasies become part of everyday experience, even a means of communication and contact between men. 'Do you see that bit walking along the pavement? I fancy a bit of her' – as men we are assumed to be all in the same 'club', living by the same rules of masculine behaviour.

Walter Mitty was bound to be a man. It is hard to accept the everyday grind of most of men's lives, if we think about the 'images' we have been brought up with since childhood. The more out of touch we are with our feelings about the situations we are in, the greater the hold of these 'images' upon us. Certainly, with the fragmentation of social life and the isolation of our experience, it is often easier to live *inside* our fantasies. Since we can be different people in the different 'spheres' of our lives, we are often left with a very loose sense of our own personal reality, partly because we do not want to identify with the different things we are forced to do. It has become increasingly important as work becomes less meaningful and fulfilling to manufacture fantasies to sustain men in their unreality. This is an integral part of consumerism in modern societies. As men, we end up feeling that we have only to be smoking our menthol cigarette, to be already sitting by a stream with a beautiful woman. The product delivers the fantasy. We do not even have to close our eyes. Of course, these fantasies enter our lives differently depending on our class, ethnic and racial experience, but, in a very real sense, we come to live in our fantasies, displaced in different ways from our emotional lives as men.

Psychoanalysis recognises a connection between the systematic suppression of emotions and the place of fantasy and 'ideals' in our lives.[3] But sometimes it does not help us understand how these 'idealisations' become so much a part of our lived experience that we often end up feeling discontented and dissatisfied with our relationships and experiences. We often want the situations and relationships we are in to be different from the way they are. We easily feel that other men are going out with women we somehow deserve ourselves, or that our sex would be better, if only we were with our fantasised woman. We are locked into comparing our experiences with others, and then with our fantasies.

It is little surprise that life never comes up to the expectations of men. Often we seem to get more from our fantasies and day-dreams than from the reality of our relations that can so often disappoint us. It is not unusual for some men to be happier in their isolation, than in having to work through the emotional difficulties of relating to people. As men, we often find it hard to admit what we are feeling, even to ourselves. We thereby block the way to being able to accept more of our experience. It is as if we are constantly falling back into an isolation within relationships, finding it difficult to sustain meaningful relationships with other men that might be able to be supportive and nourishing.

IDEALISATION AND RELATIONSHIPS

Self-hatred can be a deep feature in our inherited conceptions of masculinity. But we might be barely aware that it shapes our relationships with others and connects to difficulties men often have in self-acceptance. At some level, we are often unsure of why people are attracted to us, because we can be so down upon ourselves. This shows itself in a split between public confidence and private doubts which works to undermine our relationships with others, especially our ability to see women as people with their own independent lives and experience. The other side of self-hatred is the power of 'images' in our experience, so that when we relate to people, we are virtually relating to 'images' of them.

This is part of an ongoing polarity within masculine experience, between self-hatred and idealisation. Possibly, the more down upon ourselves we are, the more likely are our relationships to be 'idealised'. This also connects to our image of 'love' and the glimpse we sometimes get that 'people can be in love with love'. So we sometimes find that women we relate to, say, are transformed into images of love, without our really being aware this is happening. We can end up relating to the 'image', fighting any sense of engaging with the everyday reality of a woman as a person.

The more out of touch we are with our own needs and wants, the more self-denial will encourage 'idealisation'. We can find it hard to relate to people as they are, always wanting them to conform to images we have of them. Often these images take over and we deny those aspects of people which do not fit them. This also shows the strength of ideology within our experience, though it presumes an understanding that there is an ongoing tension between ideology and experience and so resists a structuralist notion that our experience, along with our individuality, is somehow constituted through our language.[4] We are always struggling to live up to standards, images of ways we 'ought' to be living, and this extends to our relationships with others. The years of tight control of our emotional lives and desires have made it easier to do what we 'ought' to do than what we want to do. But we barely sense the hurt we have done to ourselves or the destruction this does to our emotional powers and capacities, because we very much think of our lives in terms of individual achievement and success.

An example might make this a little clearer. Suppose Richard is going out with Susan and she starts a relationship with his friend Tom. Now, in conventional terms, this would be 'wrong' and Susan would be made to feel she has to make a choice between them. As a matter of principle, people might think it is 'wrong' to have a relationship with more than one person. Richard might say that it hurts his pride. He might say that it is not a question of 'jealousy' but he just thinks it is wrong of her to do this. His male consciousness is reflected in the way he almost automatically interprets it as an act of aggression against him. He might think less of Susan because of this, though he might feel a little ashamed of the feeling.

Within the challenge of feminism, Richard might find it hard to accept Susan's relationship with Tom, but feel it is wrong of him to treat her as a 'possession', denying her the possibility of whatever relationships she wants. He might think that it is 'wrong' to be jealous, because this only shows that he treats her as an object, though he also has a sense that jealousy is a difficult feeling to question. So Richard ends up feeling quite 'cool' about it, at least on the surface. Liberal theory tends to take it for granted that people know what they feel, because it tends to think of feelings as 'states' that come over you, almost involuntarily.

Reason is felt as superior partly because it allows you a control over your life. This is the context in which emotions are threatening to the control we assume it is important to have as men. This control often allows men to work, regardless of what they are feeling. Bourgeois discipline and morality was imposed on the working class at the end of the eighteenth century when it became necessary to get them to accept factory discipline, which meant working people had to accept a 'duty to work', regardless of what they might be feeling.[5] What had emerged historically as the Protestant morality of a particular class became an important instrument for disciplining emotional lives, legitimating a strong sense of duty and a systematic denial of emotions and feelings. The rootedness of masculine identity in the public world is crucial to this, as well as the emotional structure that it presupposes. As long as workers 'worked', few were interested in identifying the emotional harm or damage that was being done.

What is important is that both liberal and socialist moral traditions rest upon a notion of duty and involve a denial of the moral significance of feelings and emotions. So Richard is left feeling he would be 'giving in' if he allowed himself to be upset. He would experience this as some kind of defeat. He does not realise how he is still committing himself to a fundamentally Kantian structure of experience in his denial of his emotions. Richard finds it really difficult to say that he does not want them to have the relationship because he is too hurt by it. This would be to impose a restriction on her freedom, which Richard thinks he 'ought not to do', but, possibly more to the point, he would be 'failing' by standards he has set himself. He would be admitting 'weakness', which would compromise his notion of masculinity.

Richard is trying to live up to a certain image of himself. This image easily becomes another potential 'achievement', another part of the struggle. This is a sign of the ways competitiveness enters our relationship with ourselves. We would be 'letting ourselves down' if we did not live up to these standards. In this case, the image endorses our masculine need for 'independence' and makes it difficult to acknowledge our feelings for others. So it would be hard for Richard to admit how much he needs Susan and how hurt he is feeling. This is threatening because, in some sense, he feels it would be 'giving too much' to Susan to be honest with her – but he also does not want to put pressure on her. Again this is tied in with how we feel about ourselves as men and shows how the politics of sexuality operates at levels of our experience which are often unacknowledged.

Cut off from our emotions and feelings, we are left as men 'proving ourselves' by living up to the standards we have set ourselves. We find it hard to acknowledge our feelings, partly because we have so long denied the resentments and bad feelings we have had, living up to these very standards. So we get scared at even touching or contacting our feelings to discover all these bad feelings, which only seems to confirm the worst fears we have about how 'bad' we really are. As young boys, we often grow up with an image that boys are bad, which is difficult to shake off. In a way difficult to describe, this makes us feel 'unreal' about ourselves, as we feel tied to these notions of male identity, out of touch with the emotions and feelings that could give some sense of reality to our relationships.

AUTHORITY AND DENIAL

Kantian morality takes it for granted that there is a *radical separation* between fulfilling our needs, desires, and wants, and any idea of 'morality'. What is significant is that morality exists 'outside' and 'external' to people's everyday lives. This helps reinforce a notion of masculinity as something essentially external that we are always trying to 'live up to'. This means that 'morality' undermines whatever trust we might otherwise have had in our own feelings and thoughts, though it obscures these social processes through sustaining a notion of moral individuality somewhat paradoxically upheld in liberal notions of freedom, in the idea that every individual has to rediscover the moral law for himself or herself. But this also easily misleads us about the character of our freedom in relationships, since the moral law exists independently of people's experience, waiting to be rediscovered, through the autonomous workings of reason.

Since our masculine natures within a Protestant culture are deemed to be basically rotten and evil, they can only lead us astray. It is because we cannot trust ourselves that we need an 'authority', even if it is the moral law. It is fundamentally only through an obedience to an external authority that we can escape the fate of our own 'natures'. This expresses the paradoxical and contradictory character of liberal notions of 'freedom'. We are free to discover the moral law that exists independently of our experience, yet whatever trust we might have in our own abilities and feelings is undermined. We grow up distrusting ourselves, our own reactions and feelings in situations and relationships we are in. This is another sense in which we deny ourselves.

We distrust our own feelings because we have learnt that they can only lead us astray. Within a Kantian moral tradition, we end up with little relationship with our emotional lives. We cannot acknowledge them as sources of legitimate knowledge and allow them to help us to grasp what is happening to us. We are encouraged, in living up to cultural notions of masculinity which identify it with rationality, to undermine a confidence in ourselves which could otherwise be a resource for us. Our sense of our own needs and connection with our emotional lives weakens as we become focused upon doing what is 'right'. When the 'right' is established by reason alone, we develop a particular sense of identity which is weak and attenuated partly because it barely exists independently of a masculinity which is directly related to our denying the pull of our emotions, feelings and desires.[6]

Somehow we accept that morality – what is 'right' and 'wrong' – exists independently of our own wants and needs. We generalise from the situations in which this is true, to allow this picture to control and dominate our experience. In this way, masculinity in its different forms is identified with self-denial and we feel forced to judge ourselves by external standards which exist as norms of masculine behaviour. As we learn to live up to an external morality, a tacit identification of masculinity with a morality constituted through reason traps us into constantly proving ourselves as men. This becomes another way in which we objectify ourselves, losing any adequate way of thinking about the lives we are living. We become concerned with living up to standards, while our sense of our own emotional needs weakens. We find ourselves almost incapable as men of thinking about whether our individual needs are met in our lives. The standards we set become another focus for our individual achievement, another way of proving ourselves and sustaining our masculinity, regardless of the damage this does to our capacities for intimate relationships. This is partly why men can have a strong sense of self, in terms of a strong sense of morality, but a very weak and fractured sense of individual identity.

In some sense, as men, we do not know what is 'good for us'. The moral law knows 'better' than we can know ourselves, so we learn to identify with authorities. This says something about a masculine relationship to authority and helps to explain how a traditional father can so confidently take himself to know what is 'best' for the whole family. But in a very real sense, our individual sense of self is undermined, along with our capacity to make decisions for ourselves. We are left feeling that we have no basis on our own to take decisions for ourselves, because we cannot trust our emotions and feelings. Our 'sense of self' – as rational self – does not have anything to do with how in touch we are with our emotions and feelings, nor can liberal theory make much sense of such language.

Rather, the 'self' is identified with the will, with being able to make decisions, despite what we are feeling. So for many men, as we have argued, happiness comes from being able to 'do things', So the ego assumes a central place in liberal moral psychology and we are left bereft of a moral psychology to work out what it means to be 'out of touch with our feelings'. The language of feeling is dismissed since it does not make sense until we begin to recognise *experientially* as an issue how little we feel at all and question whether this is simply a feature of our individual personalities.

As men, we are brought up to value ourselves through our individual achievement, through proving we are 'better' than others. We might spend little time caring for ourselves or even looking after the rooms we live in, because we are so tied into proving ourselves. Often we are very *unaccepting* of ourselves and our emotional lives because we are pushing ourselves all the time. We barely sense the damage and strain this puts us under. We have to prove that we are 'exceptional' to value ourselves at all. This is a contradiction at the heart of so much male experience. So, for example, in everything that Lawrence of Arabia did, even putting out flames with his bare hands, he had to prove he was 'exceptional'. In the end, as the film has it, he is forced to face up to killing people and to a recognition that torture can make him talk as much as any man. This proves a revelation to him. He does not want to be exceptional any more, realising this is a trap. It leaves him estranged and isolated. Rather he wants to be 'like any other man'. He wants a share in a common humanity. In an extreme form, this expresses a contradiction often experienced by men.

We are brought up to feel 'different' from other men. We are brought up to believe in the uniqueness of our own experience. It is not simply a matter of being better than other men, it is also a matter of being 'different'. So we dwell upon the uniqueness of our individual experience. We have to be 'special', 'different' from others. This becomes the way we value ourselves. This undercuts our sense of what we might share with other men, in their different masculinities, as we feel increasingly isolated and alone in our experience. It comes almost as a revelation to discover that other men often experience the same unease and embarrassment in their lives. We assume that nobody experiences situations as we do. This is part of the isolation we are so often locked into as men.

We rarely learn that what we might share with other men can be a source of valuing ourselves in our emotional lives. This goes centrally against the individualism structured into dominant forms of masculinity. We are too locked into the importance of 'independence' to acknowledge we need the love and support of other men, and too deeply fearful of homosexual feeling. We have been competitors for so long that it is hard to relate to men in any other way. Certainly, it is hard to feel that we can have had a shared experience and that it might be possible to learn something from each other. We automatically assume other men want to put us down. We are always on guard.

We often feel too insecure in our achievements, and thereby in our sense of self, to be able to trust men. Men's lives are often precarious because they are always living out the dilemma between being 'exceptional' and being 'worthless'. These are two sides of the same experience. Both grow out of deep distrust and hatred of self, so that we cannot trust our natures or feel good about ourselves unless we know that we are 'successful'. It is only by keeping on proving ourselves that we avoid the feelings of worthlessness. This worthlessness seems always ready to break through into consciousness, though many men have built strong protective walls against feeling it. It becomes difficult to trust our partners in intimate relationships, for we can be haunted by feeling that if they knew more of what we experience, then they would have grounds to reject us. Often it is safer not to know ourselves.

Because we are competing with all other men, our sense of success is always insecure and fragile. There are always other men who are doing better. Our sense of achievement and belief in our own abilities can always be rocked. This insecurity in relation to self-esteem exists so widely because we are often so estranged from any sense of our abilities and needs. We are often living up to standards of work, which are not our own. It is as if we continually need the validation of others to feel good about ourselves. Our sense of achievement is reflected through the opinions of others, because it does not grow out of the recognition and fulfilment of our own emotional needs. In this way, our masculine sense of self remains precarious.

This can help explain how the power over women becomes so crucial. They become the captive witnesses of our achievements. We insist on having control over the responses they give because we fear that they might challenge a self-esteem that seems secure but is often brittle. We can only hear what we want to hear. This provides strength and confidence to carry on in the competition, even if we are at some level aware that we are living a lie. This domination over women is no less important for the salesman than it is for the company director. It is part of an unspoken tension that haunts many relationships. It is as if we can only trust those we are intimately related to if they are prepared to collude. Often this structures the relationship itself, which can be presented quite differently in public from the ways that it is lived and experienced from day to day. Feminism has been so frightening for many men because it threatens to break this collusion.

FREEDOM AND VALIDATION

Liberal theory can mystify our understanding of our experience partly by making us feel that we are *already* free and able to make whatever choices we want to make. If we are 'free', then whatever subordinations and dependencies we feel in our everyday lives 'must' reflect our individual inadequacies. Along with this goes a systematic denial of the forms of interdependence which exist in our relationships with each other, in the family and at work. Again we are misled about the character of power and domination in relationships, since we are made to feel 'free' to make whatever decisions we want.

If we turn to look at this for a moment in microcosm within the middle-class liberal family, each person is made to feel 'free' to do whatever they want to do. Parents are there to be consulted and give advice, but children have to take responsibility for decisions they make. This can serve to mystify children about the nature of the power parents have over them and the needs children feel to win the love and approval of parents. Neither will be publicly recognised in the ways the family thinks and talks about itself. The emphasis will be put on the 'freedom' each child has to do whatever they want to do.

This liberalism can make it hard for both parents and children to recognise the needs we have for other people, for love, caring and affection. Somehow it can become part of the atmosphere of the family that these 'feelings' are 'childish' and should not really be admitted to. Rather, everyone is supposed to be pleased because of the 'freedom' they have been given. This assumes, as I have already argued, that 'happiness' comes from the activities children and adults choose to do. But it denies quite systematically the need we feel to know how we are affecting other people, how we are cared for by them. In the name of 'freedom', most of these feelings will often be suppressed within the family. People will become wary of expressing any kind of open affection and love for each other, because they feel this can 'interfere' with the freedom someone has. Children are left alone to pursue their development as individuals, which is understood in the totally individualistic terms of being left alone to follow your interests.

Within this kind of family, people will often be systematically mystified about the character of their relationships. Freedom has become a fetish. As children you will grow up never really knowing whether your parents care for you or love you, because everything is expressed in terms of 'rules' or 'principles'. So, for instance, as we have seen, going to boarding-school will be discussed in terms of the benefits of this kind of education for children, while little will be said about what parents feel or what children feel about being sent away. Somehow the feelings in the situation come to seem 'very much beside the point', almost irrelevant in the situation. And somehow everything that goes on in relationships is *impersonalised* in this way, presented as a matter of principle.

If it is regarded as a 'good thing' for children to go to boarding-school because, say, it makes them independent, then there is no question that it is good for Charlie to go. Questions of what Charlie feels about leaving his parents, as we have already raised them, cannot come in till much later in the discussion when the issue has somehow been already settled in principle. At most, it will be recognised that 'Charlie is upset' about going to boarding-school, but this will be taken to be 'natural' for children of that age, something they will soon get over.

Relationships become depersonalised partly through the workings of morality. Charlie will be presented with the conclusions of the rational argument – which he is free to contest – that it is 'best' for children to go to boarding-school, and he might then be asked whether he wants to go. So he is presented with what he 'ought to do' – as something externally worked out and settled – and the issue is whether he is 'man enough' to do what is clearly 'the best thing for boys to do'. This is a paradox of liberal freedom. In one sense, he is told that he can choose to do whatever he wants to do, while, on the other, he is presented with what is 'best', given the logical reasons that could be taken into account. So that if he still says he just does not want to go, he will be considered irrational, and his parents are bound to think badly of him, even if they never say so openly. Charlie might feel he has no alternative, but at another level resent the way logic has rendered him powerless and invalidated his feelings.

Within this kind of family, it becomes difficult to acknowledge our feelings for others. There is no way of saying we need people, or that someone's love is important to us. Everyone can be so wary of encroaching on the 'freedom' of others, that the relationships people develop are almost 'accidental', a matter of individuals wanting to do similar things or sharing common interests. The notion of 'happiness' is conceived very individualistically and leaves no room for recognising and affirming the ways people are important to us. We can hardly acknowledge our feelings for others without feeling a little embarrassed about it. So feelings are quite systematically suppressed and relationships come to have an impersonal character.

This means, especially as boys, that you are only *validated* through what you do, how well you do at school, not through people recognising the individuality of your feelings and needs. Emotions are so generally put down against 'reason' and 'argument' that little room is left to validate and recognise the personal experience of individuals. At some level, you remain unnoticed and unacknowledged and you grow up expecting very little from others. A distance is maintained between people in the family and even later it becomes difficult to acknowledge the love and caring you need from others. Recognising a need for love is too easily interpreted as a sign of weakness and lack of independence.

Because we are told we are 'free' to do whatever we want to do, it is hard to recognise a lack of love and attention. This is not recognised as something that can cause us suffering, or something we really need. Somehow our needs for love and support are systematically denied. We are presented with the impression that we come to identify closely with our sense of masculinity, that the only thing we could 'really want' is to be left alone to get on with doing things. This is our 'freedom' and the source of happiness. It is not really conceivable to want anything else, so it becomes difficult for adults, let alone children, to be aware of needing the love and support of others. So the ways people are dependent upon each other in their everyday lives become systematically denied. Not only does this weaken our sense of personal reality, but makes it difficult to feel good about our needs for love and support. It is so easy for us to feel uneasy and embarrassed, as if it is an inadequacy to want and need the love of others. This has a continuing influence upon many men's continuing difficulties to commit themselves emotionally in relationships.

There are different ways we can be brought up to deny our emotional lives. At one level we can be brought up to discount our emotions and feelings, so that we can act 'rationally' or 'morally'. I have discussed how this expresses itself in a middle-class liberal family, so that you can be given every encouragement to do what you want to do, though there are implicit standards that can be terrifying just because they remain implicit. The more identified this leaves us with our rationality, the more it can leave us estranged from our feelings, so that we have difficulty grounding ourselves in our experience. This freedom in a family can be mystifying, especially if it makes it difficult to acknowledge and express our needs for others.

Having to be 'independent' can make us deny whatever sadness, fear or anger we feel, so others will think well of us. We are often unclear what others really feel about us, because they want to leave us our freedom. Paradoxically, this can leave us feeling tense and anxious in our relationships. It becomes hard to 'test out' our feelings with others, because there will often be a 'distance' if people do not want to 'encroach' on others. People will rarely confront each other emotionally. This can be subtly undermining, making it difficult to know how relationships, even with parents, are developing within a middle-class family. You are left 'alone' a lot of the time. This encourages a whole fantasy world and set of 'fictions' about, for instance, whether Dad is pissed off with you because you didn't come back to lunch yesterday. You know he will never come out and say 'I am upset that you weren't at lunch', nor will he show his anger. If there is never much feeling expressed in the family, you are often left alone to work everything out in your isolation. This can create all kinds of fantasies, since we are rarely able to work through to some sense of 'reality' of what is going on *between* people.

Within this kind of liberal family, people learn to deny, even despise, their feelings, experiencing themselves rather as proceeding by means of reasoned argument. They do not have to resort to emotions. People are often left with a feeling of 'unreality' about their relationships. This is partly because our sense of 'reality' is not simply built out of correct knowledge – out of knowing what others 'think of us'. We also need to have some experience of how others feel about us. We need to know we are loved and cared for, and that we matter to others. These are things we need confirmed in our everyday experience, especially within our families, otherwise we are left feeling 'unreal', never having really had a chance of working through our fantasies.[7] So, for years, I might think my father was angry at me though he would not let himself express it. This is a tension I can learn to live with in my relationship, but it is bound to leave an edge of 'distance', making it difficult to express whatever love and caring I feel.

DENIAL AND SELF-ESTEEM

Psychoanalysis helps us realise our relationships are not discrete as it challenges the naïve psychology of liberalism that simply talks about the 'interests' people share, or about 'liking' and 'disliking' people. We come to realise that there are 'patterns' repeated in our relationships. What is striking is how even years later in our close relationships we are continually 'reworking' the unresolved conflicts in our relationships with our parents. It is part of the significance of Freud and Klein that they recognised the influence of these early relationships.[8] Possibly it is the power and dependency in our early relationships that make us so vulnerable and give them such lasting effects on our ways of relating. So if we are wary with our parents, not really sure of what they felt, we are likely to be wary with others, finding it difficult to express warm and loving feelings.

We also have the stricter family that does not believe at all in the kind of freedom of middle-class liberal families. Children are likely to have less space to themselves. They will be subject to different forms of parental control and discipline. This is not supposed to be a clear articulation of class differences, nor is it a matter of assigning blame or responsibility to mothers, as is so often done; but it is an attempt to highlight different ways we are brought up to deny ourselves as men. I will give an example of Harold who was brought up in a strict family in which he was made to feel 'freedom' is 'idleness' and that he should always be finding himself something 'useful' to do. Often this meant doing things for his mother, like getting the shopping and helping to clean up the house.

From an early age, Harold was made to feel that he could not do anything right. Even if he went shopping and got what his mother wanted, she would tell him that he was an oaf, because he had got the wrong sizes, or that he should have remembered they also needed flour – 'Why am I the only person who can think about things around here?', she would scold him. Whatever he did to make his mother show affection towards him, he would be told he had done it 'all wrong'. Nothing he seemed to do was any good in her eyes. He was made to feel that he was 'worthless'. Sometimes his mother would say, when she got angry at him, 'I don't know why God brought you into this earth because you are so useless.'

This made it really difficult for Harold to feel any confidence in what he could do. She would tell him that even his friends were 'no good' and that he would become 'no good' if he hung around with them. She would block his every move and make him feel that he could not do anything that was 'all right'. This was all extremely undermining for Harold and left him with a weak sense of self-esteem. This made him scared of other people and shy of getting to know them. He assumed that others were much better than he was, and that if he let them know more about himself, they would only realise how 'useless' he was and they would not want to know him. He became very shy with others, not really letting them see very much of himself. He was anxious about taking any kind of risks with people, because he expected to be rejected. His mother had said that any 'good person' would reject him, if they knew how 'evil' he was.

There were a few times Harold got angry with his mother. He tried to say that she was unreasonable telling him off when he had got everything she had asked for from the shops. But she really laid into him, telling him that it is 'wrong' for him to get angry with his mother – did he realise what he was doing? His anger was *denied* by her, as she took it as yet further evidence that he did not have any 'self-control'. She said to him 'At least I thought you had some self-control.' Harold was paralysed. He did not know what to do with the anger welling up inside of him. He just stormed out of the house in a hateful mood. But this only made him feel worse about himself, because these 'hateful' feelings only seemed to confirm that he was a 'bad person'. This just made him feel hopeless.

Harold was left feeling that he did not have any 'self-control' and this only made him more scared of his feelings, thinking he did not know how to control them. This made him wary of getting into any kind of argument. He found himself backing away, because he unconsciously became scared of losing his temper with them. Many men will recognise this fear. Because we have been brought up within a Protestant culture to deny our feelings for so long, trying to prove we are superior 'rational' creatures, we have very little experience of our own feelings. We are dimly aware that we have suppressed our anger, even if in easier situations than Harold found himself in. We learn as men to be wary of the control that we have over these feelings. We become literally scared of our own emotions, having such little ongoing relationship with them.

Whatever confidence Harold could have in himself was shattered. He found it hard to value anything he wanted to do. He was left feeling that he 'wasn't as good' as other people, so he expected others would not want to have anything to do with him. He was really taken aback when anyone showed some kind of interest in him. He grew up assuming that he had continually to do things for people to make them like him, otherwise they would soon find out that he was 'useless'. This fear of being 'useless' or 'worthless' is familiar to most men. It relates to self-esteem and is the other side of having continually to prove ourselves. If this conception of masculinity is different from what we find described in some feminist writing that insists on seeing all men as self-confident and powerful beings, it is no less part of the truth. It is an aspect that it is important to explore because so many men experience a contradiction between their supposed public position of power, at least in relation to women, blacks and gays, and how powerless and confused they themselves often feel in their personal and emotional lives.

FEELINGS AND RATIONALITY

As boys, we are made to feel that feelings are 'soppy'. They are what girls have. We are told that we have to be strong and that we have to be ready to support others, even our mothers. We learn to discount and weaken our feelings through a long and painful process, eventually reaching a situation in which we feel very little about anything, though we might have 'opinions' about everything. The sources of this denial of our feelings reach back into the early relationships of the family. They are not much illuminated in sociological discussion about the 'roles' of boys and girls. Where this makes us sensitive to the very different expectations we have for boys and girls, almost from the moment of birth, it does not bring us to think about the *hidden injuries* or the *damage* done to our emotional lives. We have to face up to the destructive character of our inherited social relationships and the realities of class, gender and racial power and domination.

From an early age, we can be made to feel as boys that it is 'wrong' for us to have certain feelings. I shall give an example. As very young children, we could want our mothers' love and attention, more than we were getting it. This happens to Leo. He cries for his mother, but his mother will not come to him. When she finally comes, drawn away from doing the housework, she might be really angry at him. She might scream at Leo, staring him straight in the face. Therapy shows that such an incident can have a lasting effect on personality, even though the child is entirely unaware of this. We can only grasp the significance of early childhood if we are aware of the power relationships involved between parents and infants and the nature of the dependency which flows from this.

When Leo was a little older – about five – he might be told that he is a very 'demanding child'. This could be enough to make him feel that there is something 'wrong' with him. He might be told that he has to recognise that his mother has got more important things to do than to be spending all her time with him. This can make Leo feel guilty for wanting the love and attention of his mother, because he does not have any sense of how she could be feeling. This is an aspect of the power relationship which exists. But this can mean that Leo does not *allow* himself to feel this need. He tells himself that he is going to be 'strong', because this might be the way his mother gives him more love.

This is not to suggest that Leo's mother is particularly distant. This is simply the reality of having to do both domestic and waged work, which is what many women are forced to do. Psychologists focus upon the 'qualities of the mother' because their theory renders invisible the reality in which many women are forced out to work, often separating out our emotional lives as if they exist in an autonomous and separate inner realm. It could be that Leo's mother had to support the family on her own, possibly because her husband was ill, or because she had chosen to. Relationships are set within the context of the different demands made on a mother's time.

Leo does not allow himself to feel the aching need, let alone the *anger*. He can be made to feel that his anger is not *legitimate*, because he can understand that his mother has to work. So he might not even admit these feelings to himself. He has been told, 'don't be silly. She's working and *can't* be with you.' This is powerful, especially when boys are told that to grow up means that you dispense with your feelings. We are made to feel 'unreasonable' or 'irrational', even 'stupid', for having the feelings we have. It is as if knowing that your mother has to work is going to make a difference to your feelings of need and your anger that she cannot be with you when you need her. It is not simply a matter of intellectually 'realising' what the situation is. But parents also have the *power* to make boys feel 'stupid' because they have got feelings. This is the situation in which boys learn to suppress their feelings, because they do not want to be made to feel stupid in front of adults.

So, as boys, we were told that we *cannot* have these feelings because they are not 'rational'. So we cannot want our mothers to be with us, when we 'know' that they are out working, because this is to be 'unreasonable' or 'irrational'. We are made to feel that there is something 'wrong' with us if we persist in feeling this way. The balance of power in the situation can mean that Leo does not allow himself to miss his mother, to cry for her, especially if he thinks he is going to be punished. He might do everything to be 'strong' and 'reasonable'.

In this way, he learns to *deny* his feelings in the situation so that later it might seem as if he does not have feelings about it at all. Only years later it can be uncovered in therapy, how Leo continues to have these tears inside him, the tears he was never allowed to have for his mother. Similarly, this is anger he has never been able to express. Rather than simply seeing himself as a bundle of 'qualities' and 'interests', as liberal moral theory would have it, his shyness and his fear of asking for love reached back into the despair he had felt in relation to his mother.

Men, in particular, learn to be 'rational' and 'reasonable'. This is part of the process through which we learn to deny our feelings. We are almost made to feel that any feeling is irrational, because there are always ways of settling things through reason. The power adults have over us makes it easy for them to define what is 'rational' for us. We are brought up to value 'independence', which is not just a matter of individual preferences or orderings. What needs investigating is how such 'values' are lived out. With Leo, it means he cannot acknowledge his need for others. He is embarrassed by feelings of care and concern. Through such processes, men come to have less relationship to their emotional lives as their capacity to feel spontaneously becomes attenuated. We end up, as men, feeling very little, even for our friends. With our caring and warm feelings so suppressed, there is bound to be difficulty in feeling our love for others. Our notions of love become unreal and idealised.

FEELINGS AND KNOWLEDGE

As men, we learn to deny our feelings, seeing them as intrinsically of less importance than our 'thoughts' and 'ideas'. Embodying this is the way we prove our manhood, from the earliest years. Boys do not want to be cry-babies. We grow up being insensitive to what we are experiencing emotionally. We are rarely even *aware* of what we are feeling. What matters is our thoughts and reasoning, because this is the foundation of any action. We struggle to live up to an image of ourselves as 'rational', even if this means cutting down feelings emerging in us. The only way to value ourselves as men – to feel good about ourselves – is through our clear reasoning and the achievements this leads to. The insight that our emotions and feelings could be part of our identities as men and the foundation for our being able to create and maintain some enduring sense of individual reality, strikes a challenge to the self-conceptions we absorb as part of the dominant forms of masculinity.

Freud provides a new possibility for our understanding of ourselves and our relationships. He gives us ways of understanding the injuries we hold in silence, although in the end he justifies the repression necessary to conform to the prevailing 'civilisation'.[9] What is crucial is that Freud gives us a way of accepting our feelings and emotions without judging them prematurely. He helps us accept greater parts of ourselves as well as thereby helping us rediscover sources of our own power. But to do this, the hurt and the injury has to be faced as we re-live and re-experience our disregarded pasts. This helps us face up to the complexity of our experience, showing us the value of reworking our own histories if we are not to be trapped by them.

Freud promises an awareness of what we are feeling, allowing us to become more aware of what we want and need for ourselves. For men, it can have the power of revelation, when we first learn to accept our feelings and learn *how* to talk about what is going on in relationships. This gives us a new relationship to our experience, making us aware, sometimes for the first time, of the importance of our emotions. We become more in touch with how relationships are making us feel, rather than simply proving ourselves. We begin to question the 'standards' we had taken for granted as ways of 'proving ourselves', never really aware of what they made us feel about ourselves. We become more in touch with what *we* are getting for ourselves, so that we can begin to negotiate with some reality in our relationships, rather than simply doing what is expected of us and then feeling uneasy or frustrated without understanding why.

Let us think through an example again. Joel might have just dropped out of college where he was doing physics, because he realises it is not what he wants to do. It was what he was 'good at' at school, but never really got much out of doing it himself. He realised he was doing it to make his parents happy and to be a 'success' in the eyes of people he knew. He never even thought about what *he* wanted to do. This did not even occur to him, given the ways he was brought up. Strangely enough, he felt this was the first decision he had ever really taken in his life. His parents had made him feel he was 'free' to do whatever he wanted, but now he realises that this never really allowed him to make any decisions for himself. If he was truthful with himself, he had always wanted to be a carpenter, to use his hands. His parents, however, had made him feel that this was OK as a 'hobby', but he would be 'wasting his talents' if he did not go to university 'if he had half the chance'.

His parents had made him feel that he had to be 'aiming' for something in life, though it did not matter what it was. This conception deeply structured his expectations and experience, though he barely realised at the time. It meant that he had to be trying to be the 'best', whatever he was doing. This undermined whatever sense of freedom they might otherwise have given him. They might equally treat a daughter in a similar way, though in many families it is still thought that the primary meaning in a girl's life will come with marriage. With Joel they made him feel that being a carpenter was 'beneath him'. It proved that he had a 'lack of ambition' because he could do 'better'.

This reveals the hierarchy of 'talents' that often lies implicit beneath the liberal notion of 'freedom'. Some people are obviously more 'equal' than others. It would be all right for some people to be carpenters, but not for someone with his 'abilities' or 'background'. In this way, the career structure and relations of power within capitalist society is legitimated, even if it remains implicit. It controls our sense of what success is, and in *whose* terms it is important to succeed.

In this way, it becomes clear that success is not simply what an individual calls 'success', however liberalism wants to define it. This is denied in everyday experience when being a carpenter clearly is not counted as 'success'. In this way, ideas of success are gradually estranged from any concrete sense of our own capacities and wants, from our sense of what gives us fulfilment. Rather, as Joel discovered, it involved him giving up carpentry so that he could study his physics, even if he was not really interested in it. Success, in other words, was very much *defined for* Joel, in terms of 'getting on' in the institutionalised terms of society. He could be a banker or an architect, but he could not be a carpenter.

For a long time Joel did not expect to be happy, without really understanding why not. This made it easier to carry on with his physics. It was only through thinking about what made him happy that he realised how miserable he was. He realised that he could get a 'good job', but that would not make him happy, even if it did mean he was 'successful'. A whole range of questions was opening up, creating space for a different relationship with himself. He became more aware of what doing his physics made him feel, and allowed this to have more significance than he would have given it before, when he would have equated being miserable with 'not trying hard enough'. He realised that physics was not what *he* wanted to do, it was what other people wanted him to do.

We are brought up to think that 'our feelings are our own business'. They are part of our private affair. We learn to keep them to ourselves. One of the ways we are taught this is in ways we think that we cannot really learn from our feelings. They cannot really give us knowledge about situations we find ourselves in. So we are made to *separate* our feelings from the everyday lives we live. We are led to think that feelings reflect our own 'individual reaction' to situations, so that if anything they tell us something about ourselves, not anything objective about the situation. So it is that the power of emotions and feelings to help us learn about features of power and domination in situations is undercut by the ways our emotions are *individualised*.

In liberal culture, our emotions and feelings are derided as 'subjective' or 'personal', where the only 'real' knowledge is taken to be 'objective' and 'impersonal'. We are encouraged in our sense that 'this is how I might feel, but, of course, someone else might feel quite different.' This works to relativise our feelings, making us feel we are only making a comment about what is happening 'inside' of us; I can only make statements in terms of how a particular situation is making *me* feel. This makes us very wary, to say the least, about learning from our emotional responses to situations.

Our inherited cultures so often systematically deny a role to our emotions and feelings in helping us to be critical of situations. This becomes a powerful weapon to deter criticism of the institutions and forms of life of society. Such anger is even denied as a legitimate response to injustice or mistreatment as we are told – too often by psychotherapists too – that it reflects an emotional, and thereby somehow an invalid, response. This works to take the edge off criticism, turning it against the person, making him or her feel it says more about themselves than about the destructive power of the institution.

DEPENDENCE AND INDEPENDENCE

If we think about the feminist challenge to the ways women are made to feel 'dependent' because of the power men traditionally have in relationships, it helps us recognise the *character* of the relationships, within the broader social and political context, that is making women feel dependent. If we think, for instance, about Karen (see p. 59, chapter four), liberal theory always wants us to individualise our understanding of Karen's situation, making us think we are inevitably saying something about Karen's qualities as a person when we call her 'dependent', rather than anything about her situation. Rather, it is because she is a 'dependent' person that she ends up in that kind of relationship.

Somehow we are taught to *abstract* our feelings from the social situation we are in, by *internalising* them. So Karen can be made to feel that her feeling dependent is a problem about *her*, which she has to deal with through some act of will, learning how to deny these feelings whenever they 'come up' for her. Even this image misleads, suggesting as it does that feelings 'come up' from somewhere inside of us. Different feelings and emotions cannot always be thought about in the same way.

This becomes clear when we think about dependency and the different experiences of dependency that men and women have. If Karen individualises her experience of dependency, she is left feeling that she has to change in some way so that she feels less dependent on George. This confuses because it could simply lead her to make fewer demands on him and give him the 'independence' he is always asking for. George has the power in the relationship to make Karen feel that her feelings of dependency are *her* problem, almost that there is something wrong with her for feeling this way.

A liberal conception of feelings encourages us to think that there are two distinct feelings – one of dependence and the other of independence – that people might have 'inside'. These definitions become part of the assertion of male power. The question is falsely posed as a matter of a person's choosing whether to be 'dependent' or 'independent'. Again this sets up some kind of ideal or standard that we are supposed to aspire to, as individuals. This presumes a false conception, as we shall go on to show in the next chapter, of the ways people can change themselves. It is supposed that it is a matter of an act of will, an intellectual recognition that it is 'bad' to be 'dependent' so that we will not allow ourselves this feeling any more. This is to deny human realities in the name of some ideal that only moves us further away from understanding processes of change. It is possible to *disallow* any feelings of dependency, trying to be as 'independent' as we possibly can. But it will involve considerable energy being taken up with the denial of what we feel, and will not mean that we are changing.

Nor is it a matter simply of changing the relationships we have once we recognise how the ways we feel are largely determined by the character of our relationships. This maintains a false notion of causality. It sustains the view of our emotions as something happening 'inside' us.[10] Certainly, it is important to change the character of relationships, but we must also recognise the historical character of our feelings and how they have developed out of our childhood. At the same time, it is the character of Karen's relationship with George that makes her feel dependent. This is an integral aspect of the relationship they have with each other.

There is a danger of falling back into the same reified conceptions if we say that men have to learn to be more 'dependent' while women have to learn to be more 'independent'. This contains some truth, but it is important to see it in the context of realising how our feelings of dependency stretch back into our early years. We might have to 'regress' to re-work our experience in the past, if we want to relate differently to our partners in the present. Otherwise we can find ourselves locked into patterns of relating, without even being aware of them. This will be different for men and women. The process of change can be slow and difficult. It can involve re-living a lot of pain, hurt and sadness, but it can also bring new depths of love and joy.

So Karen can realise that it is not simply her 'problem of dependency', which *she* has to do something about. Rather, it is the character of the relationship she has with George that is making her feel dependent. So it is a matter of working out how the balance of power in the relationship works to make her feel more dependent than she might otherwise need to be. Both she and George have to explore the sources of dependency, working out how Karen can come to have more power in the relationship, and thus more sense of her own independent and autonomous life. This might not be possible without the strength and support of other women, because, as we argue against liberal theory, it is not simply a question of individual personalities.

This also concerns the structure of male power in the larger society, which gives George some of the power he has in the relationship, and so implies George struggling with his own fears of changing. He has to be ready to give up control within the relationship rather than simply discovering more subtle ways of sustaining it. He has to meet his own fears of dependency if there is to be some balance or mutuality within the relationship. This is to bring into question some of the deeper sources of masculine identity, for though we often say that we are ready to give up power, we fear that we will disintegrate as soon as we give up some elements of control.

7 Work

MEN, WORK AND EMOTIONAL LIFE

Morality can be an important form of disciplining our masculinity when it gets us into thinking and feeling that the moral law – doing what is 'right', or even what is 'expected of us' – is always more important than identifying and living out our own wants and needs. As I have argued, this is part of an identification of masculine fulfilment with self-denial. It connects up with how men are brought up to think and feel about 'work' within a Protestant culture. Work has always been a way of proving a man's individual worth and achievement. It has been a question of 'getting on' and 'making it' in the world.

Work was supposed to give a 'meaning' to life, particularly within a middle-class definition of masculinity, through providing the means for 'individual self-realisation'. More generally, men are brought up to identify themselves with their work, rather than with fulfilling personal needs and wants. So, for instance, it can be more 'important' to do school-work, because this can affect your eventual career, than to develop your musical or artistic talents. Within a utilitarian moral culture these are acceptable as hobbies, as long as you realise what is really 'important' in life.

Nearer to the core of the Protestant spirit, any kind of time for yourself tends to be regarded as 'idle' or 'wasted time'. Work was the means of individual salvation, because it allowed an *escape* from self – from the temptations of our evil natures, sexuality and desires. This shows itself – whatever liberal talk of sexuality abounds – in the fact that few men are really used to having time to themselves, without feeling uneasy and often creating some kind of panic they want to escape.

Working-class men are still forced to work in order simply to survive and get enough money to live on. The more skilled work is, the easier it is to turn this necessity into some kind of virtue. The routines and indignities of much work can become another way in which men can prove themselves, but the moral injuries and harm can also be reflected in the ways men 'split' their sense of themselves. With changes in the labour process, many men might be tempted to discount their experience at work, while trying to construct a sense of self within the confines of the family. Not only does this put a new kind of strain on the family, but it can undermine a man's sense of reality, which has traditionally been organised in relation to work, to be split against himself in this way.

The more men feel forced to deny different parts of themselves – starting with the ways traditional notions of masculinity bring us up to deny our emotions and feelings – the more undermined and attenuated can be a sense of self. This creates a condition in which men more often describe themselves as feeling 'unreal' – as if men increasingly feel themselves to exist 'outside' their own experience – without realising how the organisation of modern work is continually *undermining* their sense of reality. As long as prevailing intellectual and moral traditions deny the significance of creative work within people's lives, people are often left bereft of ways of illuminating the indignities and humiliations of their everyday lives at work. Often people diminish themselves in their own eyes as they learn to discount these experiences, for they learn to expect very little for themselves.

The conditions of modern capitalist production encourage working-class men increasingly to *discount* their experience at work, especially where it means being ordered around and subordinate all day. Often men feel they are 'doing it for the family and kids', otherwise they would not work in the place. With the destruction of working-class communities, young families have found themselves increasingly isolated. This restricts the closeness of people's relationships outside the immediate family and can leave men feeling tense and uneasy about relationships because they have so few models with which to compare themselves. Men often need more support and validation from their relationships within the family, without really knowing how to get it because they can be so trapped in their inherited sense of what men should be like. So, for example, men have assumed that the children are looked after by 'the wife', but now that she is in paid employment, men are called upon to have more of a relationship with their children. At first this is something they might do 'to help the wife out', but gradually it might give a man a chance to show different sides of himself.

With changes in the labour process, much work has become increasingly routinised, so that it can no longer provide the same sources of satisfaction and grounding for male identity. This can make it more important for men to identify with their private experience, with their families and children. Work becomes meaningful because it is *for* the family, so you cannot expect to get much for yourself from it. It becomes significant as a form of self-sacrifice, or as a way of providing consumer goods for yourself and the family. The media have become important in producing this image of people as consumers. TV helps men submerge any sense of their work lives, and helps create a different 'identity' for men as 'family men' within the home.

So men are encouraged to give very little *reality* to their time at work, even if it dominates their weekly lives. This can be undermining for men, because work makes up so much of our experience. It is almost like accepting that this is 'dead time' and that your life only begins 'outside'. This must make men's sense of reality a bit precarious, especially if they feel that they are not 'appreciated' when they get home. The tension moves to the home, especially if men feel they have to struggle to gain some recognition of themselves there.

The hurt and harm which the indignities of work can do to the very capacities, powers and abilities liberal society is supposed to protect and nourish can make it difficult to give much credence to liberal rhetoric. It seems to make most sense in its collusion in a silence about work, in its implicit assumption that it is some kind of necessary evil, and its promise of respect and equality in other contexts, in the marketplace to consumers, and with legal and political rights to citizens. The Protestant-inspired contrast between 'work' and 'idleness' makes it hard to recognise the limited 'choice' working- class people still have over the conditions of their work. The idea of the wage contract as a contract between equals freely entered into, as Marx showed, covers over the realities of class power and subordination. Working-class people in the economic crisis of the 1980s learnt to count themselves lucky to have work.[1] Within the disciplines of Thatcherism and Reaganomics, people have learnt to expect very little, often feeling that they can only be grateful to have a job at all when so many are unemployed.

But it is hard to accept that people are 'forced' to work when we know that people have choices about where to work, even if the conditions seem very much the same. The traditional connections between work and masculinity still show themselves in the feeling that it is 'wrong' to be 'idle', especially when this means other people have to do your work for you. All this makes it difficult to grasp the realities of capitalist domination, especially where things seem so much worse, say in Eastern Europe, where people have not enjoyed either the compensations of consumption or of democracy and civil rights. Our inherited socialist traditions have not illuminated these contradictions. If we are also to recognise that, say, the difference between a sympathetic and a harsh boss comes to mean a great deal if you have to contend with that person every day, we need to acknowledge the importance of respect and care within personal relationships as part of our political understanding, rather than simply to reduce them to 'mystifications'. The companionship people get at work, as well as the chances to test themselves in various ways, have also to be considered if we are to explore the complexities of the relations of men and work.

The realities of work are mystified within a liberal theory that says that 'everyone has to work', and that the different jobs people do simply reflect their individual talents and abilities. This dissolves the everyday realities of power and domination, as class, gender and ethnic relationships become reduced to individual differences. At the same time as we have to be aware of the class and racial experience of different men, we also have to recognise how masculinity can be used to soften the workings of class relations of power and subordination by creating particular forms of identification and solidarity between men in opposition, say, to women, lesbians, gays, blacks, Jews and Asians.

THE FRAGMENTATION OF EVERYDAY LIFE

Within the changing conditions of capitalist production, especially the deskilling of work that has been brought about with the domination of assembly-line production, generally known as Fordism, workers have tended to identify themselves much less with the work they do.[2] There has been an important shift in the ideology of work that is also part of a reorganisation of masculinity. Men more readily see work as just a way of getting money with few pretensions left that work can be 'satisfying' or 'meaningful'. Men see more clearly the naked relations of domination involved in capitalist production. They are often cynically aware that companies do not really care whether they live or die, as long as they are working on the line. Workers know that, if given the chance, most firms would suck the last drop of blood if it meant increasing their profits. If they are not careful, they could be left on some scrap heap as a new batch of young workers are brought in to take their place on the line.

This very much ties up with people's desire to separate off 'work' from the rest of their lives, so making more plausible liberal notions of people being equal as citizens or even as consumers. It also makes consumption so much more important than socialist theory has been able to acknowledge, firmly locked as that tradition has been in the notion that fulfilment can only come from productive work. People know that they are forced to work to earn enough money to live on, but often this is the last thing they want to think about. This is because the fragmentation of modern life makes it possible to maintain totally separate and independent worlds. So the liberal vision of life as lived between independent and autonomous spheres comes to have a new historical significance, as Thatcher in England and Reagan in the States were quick to realise.

As long as you dress properly, there is no way people know that you work, say, on Ford's assembly line. It is very possible in an urban world not to mix socially with people at work. So it becomes possible to maintain 'different identities' in the different parts of our lives. So it is that style and appearance became so critical in the 1980s. More concretely, if our lives are fragmented, a sense of identity is more readily conceived of as something not fixed and harmonious but as fractured and so as something that you manufacture for yourself through available objects, such as clothing, music and hairstyles. This creates problems for our inherited socialist theories that have tended to dismiss as superficial just these aspects of people's lives, which theories of post-modernity have focused upon.

But if it is possible for people to *discount* their experience at work, hardly ever wanting to bring it home with them, it can be misleading if social theories collude in refusing to acknowledge tensions and contradictions which exist beyond the level of appearances. People are not any less exhausted in their bodies and souls even if it has become easier to feel that we are a 'different person' outside of work, and that we are as 'good as everyone else', especially if we can afford to buy the same car or visit the same clubs. We can increasingly live in fictions of ourselves which the media in all their forms do their best to encourage. This cannot be dismissed as false gratification or 'consumerism', for it reflects much more pervasive historical and cultural changes. It opens up critical questions about the increasing importance of consumption in people's lives and whether we can sustain the idea that this is all 'compensatory' for lacks that people are barely aware of in their relationship to work.

The liberal idea that 'we are all people, each living out our own lives as equal citizens' plays an increasingly crucial role. Even though this idea of 'human equality' remains abstract, mystifying the everyday class, gender and ethnic relations of domination, it comes to have another life in the fragmented conditions of life in modern capitalism. Working-class people are encouraged to develop an independent identity outside the everyday realities of work. Social democracy encourages this in preparing all kinds of independent identities for us, as 'citizens', 'voters', 'consumers', 'car drivers', 'beer drinkers' that cut across the realities of class, sex and race. This is all the more tempting given the degradation of so many modern forms of work and the ways the organisation of industrial production splits people's lives into different spheres.

Work is less able to sustain a believable notion of masculinity. Men have to look elsewhere to discover new sources for their masculine identity. This creates its own emotional reality. When a man comes home, there is often a whole day of activity in the home to be caught up with, while his partner might have little sense of his conditions of work. This leaves it open for a man to 'assume an identity' at home that allows him to feel better about himself as a man, in the sphere made by his freedom to describe what happened to him at work. Often he can present himself as what he wants to be, since others often do not know better. In some real sense, it becomes more possible for men to create fantasies of themselves as they realise how the deskilling of work has undermined traditional conceptions of masculinity. But this is a hazardous task which can often leave men in crisis wanting to distance themselves from work but unable to feel at ease at home.

The split between the 'inner' and the 'outer' has deep roots in Protestant thought and experience. It has become part of our everyday experience of ourselves. The 'inner' is the 'real me' that remains untouched by the everyday realities of social life. A foreman can boss me around at work and force me to shift jobs, but he cannot force the 'inner me' to subordinate myself. This has proved a source of strength and resistance, but it has also hidden, even from themselves, the injuries that many men carry from the everyday indignities and humiliations of work and how they organise their experience.[3] The idea that, whatever the everyday conditions of domination, we are somehow left 'free', is at the heart of the liberal notion of freedom. It opens a way to conform to the relationships of power and subordination without feeling that they necessarily touch you. It allows people to make all kinds of compromises with injustice.

This fits with the fragmentation that is a feature of modern life. With the processes of deskilling, hard work and skill no longer guarantee that we 'get on', even if they remain integral to the ideology. Now it is often, especially within bureaucratic and state institutions, more intangible qualities of personality and 'image' that become important in promotion – being the 'right man for the job'. This calls for a deeper objectification of self which allows us to assume the 'personality' required for the job. So our identity becomes something we can manipulate and control. Goffman's book, *The Presentation of Self in Everyday Life*, reflects this attitude without really grasping how it shows the depths of alienation of self.[4]

In this way, our 'self' becomes something we construct, which is why social theories that talk in terms of the 'social construction' of the self have such a contemporary resonance. All we are concerned to do is to 'get on' in the firm because we are so identified with our individual 'achievement'. The self as such becomes a commodity, rather than simply the labour people have to sell. Capitalism comes to colonise deeper layers of the self, which are constructed in its image. This can leave a man feeling 'good' because of his 'success' in the office, while feeling totally estranged from himself. He feels very little about anything. This is not an uncommon predicament for men who dimly feel that there must be something wrong with their lives, but find it hard to identify what is going so badly wrong, when economically it might seem that they are doing so well.

WORK, FAMILIES AND VALIDATION

The family can provide protection and support for men. The stresses to which the family is put can depend on the character of work men are doing. Sometimes the family is the only place where a man can allow himself to relax and have softer feelings. But it is also the place he brings all the tensions and frustrations from a day at work. For working-class men, this means the frustrations that come from the everyday experience of subordination. Frustration is sometimes expressed directly at foreman or management, but most of it has to be held in.

If people expressed what they felt at work, they would be forced to leave their jobs. The structure of power in the work-place means that men have to suppress their feelings of anger and resentment. The management has the power to sack, so that they have to repress themselves. This frustration is often brought home with them and it is often easier to let go at wife and children for the bad day you have had. You can come home grumpy and annoyed, sick to the teeth of the foreman who has been on your back all day. Even if you keep all this to yourself, the atmosphere of tension can be oppressive, especially if children are told to keep out of the way for fear of what might befall them.

Sometimes talking out the day at work can be a way of working through some of these feelings, so the frustrations of everyday life can be mediated. But if this allows men's experience to be validated, it can put great pressure on a woman and children, especially when there is little space for the acknowledgement of the frustrations involved in a day of housework and childcare. The inequalities in the situation are often reproduced at an emotional level, reflecting the power men often have in families. Men can use their power to be listened to, and their wage can serve to substantiate that what they experience has somehow to matter to everyone else.

As an increasing number of jobs on the factory floor and in the office have become broken up and routinised as part of a process of rationalisation, people have been allowed less and less control over their work. So on an assembly line you are forced to work at the rate set by the machine, while in an office you have to type the letters placed in front of you. In both situations people rarely feel validated and recognised as individuals. You know that the firm does not care who does the job. You are constantly aware that you are replaceable, because increasingly anyone could do the job you do with a minimum of instruction.

This process of deskilling, which means that work is increasingly divided between those who understand the machine and those who simply know how to work it, means that working-class people more directly experience themselves as powerless. Fewer men have the power and identity which go with a definite 'skill'. People more easily experience themselves as replaceable units within the industrial machine. This is why ideas of citizenship and the freedom and equality that come with legal and political rights, as well as the sense of equality that can be sustained by consumerism itself, become so important. Capital needs people to believe that they count as individuals, despite people's everyday experience of powerlessness at work.

Work does not allow men to *validate* themselves as it did when skill was a larger component in production. Men cannot so easily feel valued and recognised within the conditions of mass assembly-line production. Increasingly in large plants, people only know a couple of others at work to talk to. Work is increasingly seen as a way of earning money, nothing more. This marks a shift with both men and women identifying themselves and creating their sense of identity in their social and family relationships. It is a pressure that is intensified for younger working-class couples who have sometimes chosen to live alone as a couple, separated from the context of the larger family, perhaps on a new housing estate.

In the 1990s, howerver, we need also to attend to the significance of the post-Fordist reorganisation of work which means newer, smaller units of production in which it might be easier to form more lasting relationships. Sometimes people choose to work for themselves, even where deregulation has meant that they lose all kinds of social benefits. We are forced to think more carefully about the nature of effective control over work, knowing that traditional conceptions of workers' control have often disappointed. They have left most workers in a similar situation of subordination, even if participation had allowed a few trade unionists to sit on the boards of companies. Again, it means reconsidering our inherited conceptions of individualism and control, as well as citizenship and freedom, so neatly exploited in the libertarian right in recent years.

If men are made to feel that they do not 'count' at work, then they might want to be more 'recognised' and 'appreciated' at home. If work does not give men a sense of having independence and self-respect, but simply of being ordered around as if they were still at school, they might look for more of this traditional male recognition in the family. This can work out in different ways. They might want their partners to tell them how strong and independent they are, and they might feel resentful if this is not forthcoming. All this is an aspect of the contradiction men face in the family. On the one hand, it is the 'refuge' where men can feel they do not have to be competing and proving themselves all the time. This could allow men to be softer and more relaxed, able to show that they need love and attention too. But, paradoxically, it might be even harder to do this, if the conditions of modern work leave men feeling bossed around and useless most of the time so that they can only feel respected if they can order people around in their families. This can lead to tension, even violence, if men do not get their way.

Whether the family has become more important in validating men's experience obviously depends on people's class situation. Men in professional and managerial positions have an experience of greater power and control through their work. But also living closer to the centre of industrial power gives them a strong sense of individual competition and achievement. This can build its own tensions into the family if men also expect their wives to make them feel like God's gift to the human race. The individualism bites deeply when it is brought into the relationship, producing different kinds of pressure. Men will want to feel the 'uniqueness' of their relationship, either needing to feel that they are great as lovers, or else that their relationship is the best thing since Anthony and Cleopatra. In any case, it has to allow them to feel 'exceptional'.

The male ego is often fragile, infused with self-doubt and fear that there is nothing behind the mask. This can make it all the more pressing to retain appearances. If women know different, they can often be threatened into silence, being told that they have everything to lose if the status quo is questioned. If they refuse to play the game any longer, there can be violence and abuse which often ends up in separation and divorce. This is no small part of the deep hostility many men feel to feminism and the sense of betrayal they can feel at men who would attempt to take its claims seriously.

WORK, POWER AND FEELINGS

Within a liberal moral culture, we often learn to turn our emotions against ourselves. Our anger is often delegitimated as a valid response to oppression and social injustice, even within much psychoanalytic theory and practice. We take this so much for granted that we do not realise how this denies us the power we might otherwise have to challenge the structures of power and domination forming our everyday experience. To give an example to bring out some of the issues, if Jack is working as a receptionist for a tax firm, he can think that if he does not like his job, this will mean something about him rather than his work situation. Obviously, sometimes it is a question of people just not liking the job, feeling they are not suited. The question, however, is how blaming ourselves can become the general mode of explanation. If I feel irritated and frustrated by my boss, the 'question' that emerges is 'why do *I* feel so frustrated?' There is an implicit assumption, built into the situation of power, that 'other people have worked perfectly well in the situation, so that there must be something wrong with you'.

On a small scale, this reflects the power bosses have within the organisational structure of power to *define* our understanding of the situation. Why do we so easily *assume* that it is going to say something about us, our individual character and inadequacies, if we feel frustrated at work? A similar assumption is revealed in the classroom, where people will often assume that if they do not understand what the teacher is saying, it is because they are individually 'thick', since they assume everyone else understands. Very rarely will pupils think that the teacher is being unclear, or even unintelligible. Again this reflects an imbalance of power in the situation, between 'teachers' and 'students'. Again we are uncovering implicit assumptions within a liberal moral culture, which we readily make, and which often remain invisible to us. As we reveal these processes at work, we extend our sense of sexual politics into the sphere of institutional relationships and practices.

Let us think more about Jack working as a receptionist. He might be led to think 'why is it that I always frustrate myelf, end up in jobs that I find frustrating?' The accompanying liberal assumption is that, 'because we have free choice, we never have to stay in situations we don't want to be in'. This 'freedom' has been drummed into him, ever since he was a small boy. This is partly what makes him think that his unhappiness and frustration say something about the kind of person he is, rather than anything about the situation at work. Jack is barely aware of how these ideas like 'you are free to do whatever you want to do' have come to *structure* so much of his interpretation of his experience, or how they connect to the fact that he is always blaming himself, thinking what this frustration says about the kind of person he is and how he is continually letting himself down.

So he automatically internalises his feelings, taking responsibility for his frustration – since these are 'his feelings', it seems only 'natural' to do this – on to himself, leaving the situation completely unchallenged. Our inherited moral traditions seem so invincible that they provide him with a reason for not allowing himself to know any different. Weber's social theory echoes liberal assumptions with its idea that we are free to assign whatever meanings to our experience we would want to. Jack never connects up his feelings of frustration with his situation of powerlessness in the office. Rather, he keeps these features firmly separated off from each other, in separate spheres. This ensures that people maintain their situation of powerlessness, be it in the office, school or factory. They are free to interpret their experience as they would, which makes the indignities and humiliations they suffer simply a subjective, personal matter. If they were only stronger in themselves, none of this would supposedly matter to them.

Liberal moral theory works to place the responsibility for our misery and unhappiness firmly on the shoulders of the individual. It is Jack's 'problem', and he has been brought up not to shirk problems when they come his way. He has to work out why he is staying in a job that frustrates him. I am not saying that there is not a real issue here, but the way that it is formulated as the only issue makes it difficult to deal with clearly. Therapy, too, will often assume that Jack has a 'problem' about relating to 'authority', which might go back to the unresolved feelings for his father. In bringing Jack to work through his unacknowledged personal history, the situation of power is often left intact, almost sanctified. There is rarely an issue of the nature and character of this authority and how it makes people feel powerless. So the question of how we might live within these contradictory relationships, recognising the limits of our individual power to transform these relationships by ourselves, is subverted.

We are uncovering some of the frameworks of understanding that are implicit in the common sense of liberal capitalist society. This makes visible how the structure of power and domination in the society remains untouched, while the individual learns to accept the frustrations that living in a subordinate and powerless position work into everyday experience. As men, we are often brought up to deny the very existence of these feelings of frustration, anxiety and fear. This becomes a way of proving masculinity. If we are forced to acknowledge these feelings, we can think there must be something 'wrong' or 'inadequate' with us. In any case, Protestant culture brings us up to expect the worst, knowing that underneath it all we are really 'rotten' anyway.[5] This is a 'discovery' we are constantly trying to hide from others, trying to be as friendly as we can be, afraid they might one day discover what we are 'really like'. This is a deeper level at which we take everything on ourselves, so that somehow it is our 'fault' if we feel bad, upset or simply frustrated.

This has been consolidated in the identification of masculinity with self-control, so that we are left feeling bad if we ever 'fly off the handle'. We do our best not to let others know what we are feeling, because we are brought up feeling anxious that the slightest show of emotions indicates we have no 'self-control'. This is a real fear for men. The culture digs deep into middle-class men, making us feel that we should always be ready to settle disagreements in a 'reasonable way'. The frustration Jacks feels working for his boss will be presented in rationalist terms, as a 'disagreement' which should be 'talked through'. This does not allow for there being anything frustrating in Jack's situation, in the social relation of boss and receptionist itself, but only a clash of personalities. This means that Jack cannot feel *legitimate* in the anger he feels at the ways he is treated within this relationship. Rather, the common sense of liberal morality makes him feel that his anger is bound to be illegitimate, simply reflecting his lack of 'self-control' and 'unreasonableness'.

The challenge comes in realising that your feelings are not merely 'your problem', simply saying something about your qualities as an individual or your subjective response to a situation, but are a *part* of the situation, of the structure of power and subordination. They are not simply 'subjective' responses to an otherwise independent and 'objective' situation.[6] Of course, there are always distinctions to be made. Jack can be frustrated because his boss treats him like a complete idiot whose every letter has to be checked. This is different from Jack feeling frustrated at having to take instructions and orders at all, so challenging the power defining the relationship between boss and secretary. It might be harder to put his feelings into words, when it is not a matter of personalities or particular mistreatment at the hands of his boss.

But in either case, it makes a real difference for Jack to understand his feelings as a *legitimate* response to the situation. It is because the structures of power, be they capitalist or socialist, can make us think that factories, schools, nurseries, hospitals have to be organised in the 'rational' way that they are, that we think there must be something 'wrong with us', if we are left feeling powerless and useless as we work. It is partly because it is so difficult to trust our individual feelings as sources of knowledge about how social institutions might be legitimately organised, that we learn to *discount* our feelings, thinking that individual action can make little difference. Again this brings out how morality exists, not simply as a set of abstract ideas that have to be 'combated', but as something we live through, and are partly controlled by, in our everyday experience. As we extend our vision of sexual politics, so we begin to transform our moral conceptions. Rather than becoming less important, it becomes crucial for individuals to learn to live out of a sense of their inner knowledge and experience.

As Jack challenges the way society sets him against himself, feeling legitimate in *externalising* his anger, he is brought to face a situation in which he can lose his job if he gets angry. He comes to face the realities of class power. So he cannot abstract his feelings from the situation. In the beginning it feels strange to think of the 'political' features of the situation he is in with his boss. It is only when Jack realises that if he expresses some of his angry feelings, he is bound to get the sack, that he recognises the power in the situation. This makes him aware of different ways power is usually hidden in the relationship. The boss has always talked about how the office was really like a 'family' with everyone working and having a part to play in the firm. This idea had attracted Jack, helping him to feel he was doing something 'useful', even though he spent most of his time typing boring letters and asking people to wait in the next room till the boss was ready to see them.

But this comfortable picture was beginning to crack. Jack was realising how since he was young he had been brought up to think of all relationships as if they were *personal relationships*, an outcome of 'personalities' of the two people involved. He always thought that any 'relationship' was simply a question of 'getting on with people', and if your personalities did not 'clash', you had a fair chance of getting on. This 'picture', which carried its own implicit sexual politics, guided Jack's vision of relationships. It very much dominated how he thought about himself and work. He saw work very much in terms of whether he would 'hit it off' with the boss.

Only later did he realise how this confused him about the realities of work. He was beginning to feel he had been conned, though he could not put his finger on any one person. His 'personal relationship' with his boss is also a relationship of power. He recognises that how he feels about his boss and the way his boss treats him, are not simply consequences of their 'personalities' or of the meanings that they each give to the situation, but are *shot through* with the power his boss has over him, even though it is not made explicit. It becomes hardly surprising that he rarely allows himself to express his annoyance to his boss, or express his disagreement with what he says. Even the anxiety and tension he often feels around him makes more sense when it is traced back to the relationship of power between them.

ANGER AND SUBORDINATION

The political character of our relationships with people is often covered over as our emotions are structured to reflect relations of dominance and subordination. We find ourselves personalising our relationships in a way that blinds us to how issues of power are continually affecting how we feel and relate to others. A liberal moral culture encourages us to *abstract* our relationships from their social situation to see them as relationships between two individual personalities. If we are not getting on with someone, we automatically assume that it must be something about their personality that we cannot get on with. The ways our relative powerlessness in the situation, say as a secretary, makes us feel insecure, deferential, nervous and hesitant, are submerged.

Rather, we are left thinking that this is simply a subjective or personal matter of the kind of person we are, of what our qualities are. This draws upon the same internalised conception of feelings as 'ours', saying something exclusively about us. Whatever sense we have that the way the boss treats us makes us feel nervous, rarely develops into a more general understanding. If a feeling ever comes into the open, the boss has the power to say 'I can't help it if you feel nervous, that's your problem.' He draws upon the common sense of a liberal moral culture to say this. He has the power to make it stick.

Even when Jack realises that he does not like the way the boss treats him, he can still find it hard to accept the legitimacy of his anger. For one thing, he might know that other bosses treat their secretaries even worse. This makes him think that he has nothing really to complain about, because others have got it a lot worse. Rather, he should feel lucky that he's got a job at all, since many bosses would not accept men to do this kind of work. This can make him feel 'unreasonable' in having the resentment and anger. It makes him feel he is a bit choosy or even vindictive. All this can work to undermine his belief in his own feelings, making him feel less sure about their legitimacy. This all works to sustain existing relationships of class, gender and racial relationships of power and subordination.

There are all kinds of ways of invalidating our feelings, especially the anger we feel at the subordination or oppression we are made to endure. So Jack can easily be made to feel 'you've got very little to get angry at, others have got it a lot worse', as if you have to be suffering the *most*, before you can feel legitimate in putting up any opposition. This idea cannot just be rebuffed intellectually unless we also uncover its deeper cultural and historical roots. It echoes Protestant conceptions of life as a 'test', in which we have to prove ourselves by putting up with whatever hardship comes our way. This makes it hard to struggle against conditions of oppression. 'Anger' appears as a 'threatening emotion', because it brings the possibility of challenging power. So Jack can be made to feel that because other people are putting up with a lot worse at work, he should, especially as a man who can take the pressure, be 'reasonable' and put up with his lot.

Another way Jack's anger can be invalidated is in beginning to understand the problems of his boss. So if his boss realises that Jack is frustrated and annoyed, he might say 'you have to realise the tension involved in running a large firm like this. It makes it difficult for me to be human all the time.' Jack is invited to see his boss as a 'fellow human being, having a hard time trying to hold things together'. He is made to feel that if he has problems putting up with his job, this is nothing when put against the frustration and anxiety his boss feels about his business. So the boss *personalises* the relationship, appealing for some understanding, from one person to another.

This can again make Jack 'unreasonable' if he refuses to try and understand the situation his boss is in, 'to get the other side of the picture', as it is said. Jack is supposed to feel that he should put up with whatever frustrations he feels in his job, realising this is an inevitable part of work that everyone has to put up with, even his boss. This makes him think that he is in the 'same situation' as everyone else working, whatever jobs they happen to have in the firm. There might well be 'frustrations' associated with different jobs, but then this is what work has always been like.

All these themes work to undermine feelings of anger at situations of subordination. They feed upon many different sources that have undermined our trust and confidence in our emotions, let alone the long years of masculine training in 'self-control'. This has all left its mark. It goes along with the pervasive tendency in a liberal moral culture for us to 'personalise' our relationships, recognising the 'problems' others have, even in positions of power. So we learn to overlook the question of the hours and conditions in which people work, the conditions of working-class housing, as we overlook issues about the holidays and clothes for children.

A liberal capitalist society so often uses the traditions of caring and understanding against working-class people themselves, expecting them to accommodate and accusing them of envy as soon as they complain. Class realities still mean that people live very different kinds of lives in

Kensington and Poplar. People leave work to go home to very different conditions and, even if we want to believe that children start with an equal chance in education, the reality is very different. Undermining Jack's sense of subordination and frustration in the office – getting him to feel that it is 'inevitable' or that 'other people endure worse' – works to undermine his sense of class relations in the larger society.

Jack's feelings of anger at his boss for the ways he is treated could generalise to anger at the ways people in a situation of subordination are treated. Jack might come to feel that people are more capable than they are allowed to be, in the jobs they do. So he might think that it is not a matter of his boss coming to treat him differently – being more understanding and letting him think more for himself – but of changing the ways offices are organised so that everyone can use their capacities and abilities. In some way, this would be to take the promises of liberalism more seriously than liberalism has itself tended to do. This is the point at which individual anger connects up with feelings of class anger at the ways power in the society is controlled.

So Jack becomes angry for all the ways he has been put down, at home, at school and at work, recognising how little power and control working-class people like himself ever seem to have within a democratic society. He recognises how deeply ingrained it has been to deflect and invalidate his feelings of anger, never really uncovering the source of what was making him feel powerless in his life. As he learns to value his anger, he also learns to take greater responsibility for himself, recognising that it can be equally false to externalise all his anger as if others are always to blame for his feelings and frustrations. He also learns to recognise other feelings that he has learnt to dismiss as 'unmasculine'.

He begins to find a place for feelings in his life, recognising that it is also important for him to change himself as he learns to take greater responsibility. This inevitably involves a challenge to prevailing conceptions of masculinity as it involves understanding the sources of personal power and vulnerability. It can also involve a challenge to traditional conceptions of socialist politics that have too readily taught that happiness and fulfilment can be delivered through political transformations alone. They have also failed to recognise that relationships of authority or issues of scarcity will not disappear but will have a different basis, as individuals take greater responsibility for their lives.

EMOTIONAL LIFE AND IDENTITIES

The idea of self-control is so powerful for inherited conceptions of masculinity that it makes us continually suppress our emotions and feelings. Our first response as men is often to deny whatever we are feeling, because the very fact that we are feeling anything is taken as a sign that we are not 'in control'. So it becomes difficult to legitimate whatever feelings we have, especially at work – where we can fear being exposed and ridiculed by other men. The distrust has been deeply established. In order to win approval in a rationalist culture, men learn to keep whatever feelings they have very much to themselves. We often feel embarrassed when they threaten to become 'public'. This varies with our class, racial and ethnic background, but we can often respond with anger, even violence, as a way of defending an otherwise threatened masculinity.

So, as men, we do not really allow ourselves *to have* our feelings, really to own them. We are brought up to think that it does not make any difference to us whether we express them or not. Supposedly, it does not limit or injure our expression or individuality. We believe that, in keeping them to ourselves, we are just allowing our reasoned thoughts and beliefs to dictate our behaviour. This fits the secondary importance given to emotions and feelings as sources of knowledge, as if they simply register how we, individually and subjectively, respond to situations or relationships. They do not relate fundamentally to *who* we are, or *how* we are to learn about the social world.

So, within a liberal moral culture, we are given no hint that in denying our feelings, we might be *undermining* our sense of self. We are made to feel that it does not really matter if we live very much out of touch with our emotions. At most, they are an incidental part of life. Work, not relationships, is supposedly the source of our masculine identity. We are never helped to understand or care about how systematically denying our emotions might undermine our relationships. Rather, relationships are assumed to be built upon what 'interests' we share in common with people. This gives them a supposed objective basis with little connection to the importance of *working through* the feelings and emotions we have for people. So, in the extreme form of liberal family, the fact that people are born of the same parents is not taken to signify that they have much in common. This says something about how 'differences' between people are conceived, but also about how 'abstract' is our inherited sense of human relationships.

Within liberalism, feelings are often regarded as interferences that get in the way of our developing relationships. The emotional reality of our relationships is denied, even within the family. We have explained how confusing this can be for men developing a sense of the 'reality' of others, because so little weight is put upon working through the emotional reality of relationships. We rarely identify the processes through which a liberal childhood can *undermine* a sense of reality because it discounts everything happening emotionally. We learn to have the emotions that are expected of us and, as children, we are often told that we cannot be angry because children are not supposed to feel this way.

As men, we learn to discount what is happening emotionally, and we find it difficult to ask for love and affection. It becomes hard to identify our feelings and own our experience because this is something that we have never learnt to do. Traditionally, it has been no part of education. Rather, we even feel embarrassed about the very existence of these emotional needs, feeling that they simply demonstrate weakness. We rarely understand the ways we are undermining our individuality through this process of emotional self-denial.

We simply grow up distrusting our feelings, automatically internalising whatever we feel. This itself tends to separate us as men, as it isolates us, and means that we never learn how to locate ourselves firmly within emotional realities. So, for instance, it can mean that Jack spends considerable energy trying to make himself feel that he 'really' likes working in the office because this is the way he thinks he 'should feel'. When he becomes more in touch with his frustration, he thinks of it as 'his' problem – as a sign of inadequacy that he had better keep to himself. This shows how difficult it can be for men to *ground* their feelings as a source of identity in their situation, or really feel themselves to be part of larger social relations.

If Jack spends his energy suppressing the frustration he feels working for his boss, this works to divide him against himself. It is likely to mean more day-dreaming and a greater sense of 'unreality' in his experience in the office. Denying our emotions in the ways men are brought up to do – especially at work where it would seem they have absolutely no space, especially if you are a subordinate – undermines our sense of 'reality', even if it is difficult to convey this clearly. It is akin to denying *part* of ourselves. Rediscovering that our emotions and feelings are not incidental, but are an integral part of establishing our sense of self, and also our sense of reality, identity and connectedness with our own experience, is to challenge central notions in the legitimation of authority and power within a liberal moral culture. It is to question a prevailing rationalism and to bring into focus different questions concerning the workings of ideology, power and subordination.[7]

Self-denial makes it hard for men to sense how feelings and emotions are an integral part of our individualities and relationships. They help our relationships to develop and deepen as we become more able to express not only what we think, but also what we feel. This is a condition for the development of friendship, and men have often paid dearly. Men often have very few male friends they can share themselves with, emotionally. In truth, as men, we have often been crippled by our upbringing in our capacity to make warm and close personal relationships. This is a source of the isolation so many men are forced to suffer, denying the significance of feelings in their experience. There is a considerable strain in maintaining this false conception of 'rationality' which has no place for our emotions. It often means that when men crack, they often do so suddenly with little warning. It also can mean considerable tension and unexpressed anxiety locked into the aura that surrounds men. It opens up a distinct gap between what men say and the ways in which they are feeling inside and behaving.[8]

Our emotions and feelings can play an important role in grounding us in our everyday experience. They should be central in defining new terms for an education into masculinity that allows men to acknowledge more of their experience without feeling shame or that they are thereby compromising themselves as men. In so many ways, we are denying our own power in denying our feelings. So if Jack is able to get in touch with the anger he feels at the way his boss treats him, he is in touch with an important part of his experience that would otherwise be suppressed. In expressing this anger, he would be in touch with a source of power and self-esteem that he would otherwise be forced to deny.

In denying our feelings, we undercut our sense of reality, because we are not allowing ourselves to make contact with our experience. We blind ourselves to the ways we are feeling and responding in situations. This makes it harder for us to accept ourselves or to feel good about ourselves, because we are unknowingly rejecting an integral part of our experience. In the end it cripples us and makes it hard for men to allow themselves feelings of love and comfort within relationships, even when sanctioned within the broader culture. We trap ourselves into constantly feeling there are things we 'should be doing', unable to feel very much. This does not simply concern how individual men happen to feel, but is a critique of the hidden injuries of masculinity.

As men, our lives are often dominated by extrinsic goals of 'success', so that we are never really able to feel good about the different things we do. Because we can always do 'better', it is hard to accept what we can do. So we find ourselves trapped into living externally, judging ourselves by standards not of our own making, but reinforcing a dominant conception of masculinity we might well feel estranged from. These standards come to be their own validation, in terms of which we judge our own lives and experience. The more out of touch we are with our own needs, especially at work, the easier it is to accept the 'objective' character of these 'standards'.

We have limited our experience in trying to live up to 'standards', so that we have often undermined our capacities critically to evaluate the kind of lives a capitalist or socialist society prepares for men. We have so internalised these 'standards' that it becomes really difficult to separate ourselves, to think about what we are getting for ourselves out of the kinds of jobs we do and the relationships we have. The circle has been closed, and these questions are in danger of no longer making any sense to us. All we know is that we are doing what is 'expected of us' as men, providing support for the family. Otherwise there is often a pained silence.

Often we are simply out of touch with what we have to cope with, day to day. Sometimes we do not even realise when we are tired or hungry because we are so used to pushing ourselves. Certainly, it can be frightening moving a little closer in touch with our feelings and emotions. We become aware of how we have neglected and negated them for so long and so undermined a sense of worth and identity. The society has brutalised and blinded us to the forms of our oppression, making us accomplices in our own emotional destruction as we identify power with aggression, trapped into regarding emotions as a form of weakness.

As men, the only 'rational' response to a society that is undermining the very trust that we can have in ourselves is anger and a determination to transform the conditions of life. Men have learnt to discount and invalidate their anger in this context, not wishing to bring undue attention to themselves or fearful that this will only prove their 'irrational' natures. As men, we often collude not only in our own emotional destruction, but in a society that oppresses and destroys the lives of people and nature. We are often haunted by a fear of failure and a sense of inadequacy which further serves to silence our resistances.

Part of the process of reclaiming emotions as part of establishing a sense of identity that is not built on reason alone, has to be engagement with those emotional expressions which currently emanate from a damaged experience of masculinity. One cannot get a handle on one's emotional life without understanding the emotional processes of displacement and denial that grow out of a particular rationalistic sense of self. This brings me to violence, which is often shrouded in silence as the shadow of our rationality, and which is wholly unexplained by the terms of liberal culture except as the action of an inherently 'bad' personality. If we do not wish to accept *in toto* the claim of some radical feminists that men have an inherent lust for power or domination of women, we nevertheless need to engage with the radical feminist critique of male violence at a level which opens up the question through an engagement with the processes of creation of masculine identities.

8 Violence

MASCULINITY AND VIOLENCE

As men, we often grow up to be strangers to ourselves. We experience little connection with our emotions and feelings. This is not the way we are born, nor is it a feature of our biological nature as men. As Anne-Marie Fearon has expressed it,

> I believe that all human beings, even male ones, are born (or are at any rate conceived) sensitive, loving, intelligent, open and real. We all know that they don't stay that way for very long and that males in particular tend to grow up arrogant, insensitive, alienated and, above all, violent.[1]

This is part of the price we have been forced to pay for being effective and competent in the world. This can make consciousness-raising a particularly threatening and difficult experience for men. It is often easier for us to talk about our experience in an intellectualised way than actually to express how we are feeling. This can be yet another way in which we retain a certain distance from ourselves. We can envy the access that women seem to have to their histories and experience, and, particularly with the development of the women's movement, the relationships they have with each other. This can make us more aware of lacks in our own lives.

Contact with feminist ideas can drive many men into a deeper silence about ourselves, guilty about our position within the relationships of power and subordination. The idea that 'all men are violent' or that 'all men are potential rapists' can deeply challenge our sense of our masculinity.[2] It can produce a sense of despair, guilt and a paralysing self-hatred. It leaves no room for us as men to change. In a strange way, it can leave many men untouched as they accept this judgement of themselves intellectually. We can find ourselves giving tokenistic or uncritical support to the women's movement. In this way, men can credit themselves with supporting the women's movement while not really having to challenge themselves.

I do not think we should underestimate the difficulties of changing ourselves. We each have our own histories. We need to be aware of the deeper pattern in our experience and relationships. Sometimes the men's movement has tended to concentrate on a change of manner in which we have wanted to identify with the softer qualities of warmth, emotionality, caring and kindness, but we need to be aware of the depth of the legacy of our socialisation and the ways this continues to influence our experiences and relationships. We cannot simply wish away our angry and violent impulses or our tendencies to control and dominate. It is important, however, for any men's movement which would seek to take the challenge of feminism seriously to engage critically and attend to the nature of these impulses. They have formed the ground on which certain powerful radical feminist claims have been built, to the effect that men's will to power is ultimately and finally irreconcilable with a sexual politics which aspires to freedom and fulfilment.

It is partly because of the ways in which we are made strangers to ourselves that our violence can erupt in such frightening ways. It can take us by surprise. Often for men, anger can be used to dispel feelings of vulnerability and need which are taken to be signs of weakness. I remember the constant anxiety of having to prove my masculinity. Because I was not tall or strong, I felt vulnerable at school to being called a 'weed', 'soft', or 'puny'. These were different ways of not being a 'proper man'. This creates constant anxiety and tension. We get so used to living with it that it comes to feel 'normal'.

Masculinity is never something you can feel at ease with. It is always something you have to be ready to defend and prove. You have to prove that you are as much a man as everyone else. Often this means putting others down, especially girls. It is because feelings of softness, vulnerability and need are so peculiarly threatening to our very sense of ourselves as men, that we fight them off so strongly, but this can also give us an ambiguous relation to our anger, especially if we do not feel the confidence of being able to defend ourselves physically. I was scared of getting involved in physical fights. This meant that I could not feel confident in my anger.

ANGER, FEAR AND VIOLENCE

I did not really want to know that I was angry because this was threatening. I learnt to suppress angry feelings, but I was constantly aware of the threat of physical violence. At school there was the constant fear of being 'bashed up'. This was an aspect of the relationships between children as much as it was an aspect of the authority and power of teachers. Competition was always combined with the threat of physical violence. Adorno is right to remind us that

> In fact, competition itself never was the law according to which middle class society operated. The true bond of bourgeois society had always been the threat of bodily violence... In the age of the concentration camp, castration is more characteristic of social reality than competitiveness...
>
> (quoted from 'Social Sciences and Sociological Tendencies in Psychoanalysis', *New Left Review*)[3]

As boys, we have to be constantly on the alert. We always have to be ready to defend ourselves, constantly on our guard. I think I felt this acutely because I could not be confident in defending myself physically.

This builds enormous tension and anxiety into the very organisation of our bodies. It makes it difficult to let go or relax, and fits with the ways in which we are encouraged to treat our bodies as efficient machines that we use. This deeply marks our sexuality. Often we have very little relationship with our bodies. We do not see them as a source of joy or satisfaction. We are estranged from our bodies. This makes it easier for us to use them in an unfeeling way. Sexuality becomes an issue of conquest. It becomes a question of how many women you can get off with and how many times you can screw them. In this sense, sexuality is closely identified with power. For men, it can become almost second nature. Often it becomes connected to violence. This is partly because this form of sexuality can leave us frustrated and unfulfilled, and it can be easier to take that out on others than to look at ourselves. The roots go very deep.

Anne-Marie Fearon shares how her son came home from nursery school one day with the information: 'Girls are soppies.' She points out that 'This did not emanate from the school which is consciously opposed to sexism; but the active members of the male "club" seem to say these things with such conviction that it only takes one or two of them to affect the whole class.' As a boy, you have to be ready to defend yourself. You cannot admit your fear. If someone challenges you, you cannot afford to be a 'scaredy-cat'. You have to learn to fight, or at least pretend to be ready to fight. You cannot afford to let others think of you as 'wet' or a 'drip'. This partly explains the symbolic importance of boxing within masculine culture. At school we were expected to do it, even if we hated it. Luckily we did not have to do it often. This becomes the training ground for masculinity. As Anne-Marie Fearon says:

You teach him to deny his fear and hurt. This is very hard and puts him under constant tension; so you give him a gun and a monster mask, and now whenever he feels that tension he can channel it into aggression and project his fears onto someone else ... But it doesn't do to feel it and discharge it by crying and trembling; and this is forbidden. So he is stuck with it; fear, tension and aggression become a way of life, and the only consolation is that the Club tells him: it's natural, that's what boys are meant to be like – now you're one of us!

(Fearon 1978)

I want to explore this theme through looking at certain scenes in Martin Scorsese's film, *Raging Bull*, and the discussion which this generated. I want to use this film to bring out issues in the relationship between masculinity and violence, rather than simply to offer a review of it as a film.[4]

Many people refused to see the film. There are moments when it seems to come all too close to a glorification of violence. The camera almost seems transfixed with certain brutal scenes in the boxing ring. The use of slow motion serves to romanticise. I do not want to defend any of this.

I want to use the film to illuminate different conceptions of the ways in which we can change as men. I do not want the contrast to be too crude. I want to suggest the importance of particular forms of therapy for men, ways in which we can explore our anger, resentments, fear, hurt and violence. This involves developing more contact and experience of ourselves, rather than simply denying these feelings as 'unacceptable'. If we repress these feelings, we will often act them out unknowingly in our relationships with others, often without realising how controlling we are being because we deny these very feelings in ourselves.

The film is about the life of Jake La Motta, the 1949 middleweight boxing champion. It is about life in the Italian community in the Bronx, New York, in the 1940s. It is about a world that is very different from the suburban Jewish middle class into which I grew up. But the film is about masculinity, male violence, frustration and pride. It hits home. In parts the violence is unbearable and out of control. But it did not estrange me. It was painful but understandable for most of the time.

I want to argue that our violence and anger cannot be denied. We have to learn to distinguish the different aspects of these feelings, rather than simply deny them. Therapy is important within this process, especially if it helps us grasp the ways in which our violence is a sign not just of our strength but of our impotence and frustration. Scorsese's *Raging Bull* helps us understand how male violence works, even if it leaves us with little sense of how men can change. He shows how masculinity can be used up. Jake is used up by the crowd. He is often incapable of expressing himself. He fights his way out of situations. In the end nobody wants to know him. He is imprisoned by his own masculinity.

Raging Bull can help us connect to an aspect of our masculinity that we too easily deny. It can put us back in touch with our own 'raging bull' – the desire to hit out and hit back. Scorsese himself is no tough guy. In an interview which Don Macpherson and Judith Williamson did with him for *Time Out*, he admits that 'I don't punch people in the face. I'm too short, and I can't run – and I've got asthma' (p. 20, 6 Feb 1981). The film can also help us face our rage and anger, rather than think that they will disappear if we feel uneasy and ashamed about them. Rather than keep these feelings to ourselves, it feels better to socialise them, to bring them into the open where they can be explored, possibly in a safe environment men create with each other.

This is to suggest a different conception of the ways in which people can change. Often if we deny our feelings, they simply reorganise themselves at a deeper level, expressing themselves in more spiteful and hidden ways. It can be through exploring our anger and rage that we come to be more familiar with these feelings, clearer about the different feelings of need and vulnerability which they sometimes cover and hide. This can give us more control of our emotional life. This will not be a control based on repression, but rather on an experience of connection. At the moment we often take out these fears and frustrations on those we are closest to, often the women and men we are sexually involved with. Sometimes this is the only situation in which we can feel safe enough to share them. Often our negative feelings and our resentments have a very different source, existing at a level of which we have little awareness. We can find ourselves hitting out blindly.

There is an early scene with Jake at home in his Bronx apartment. He is sitting at the table as his wife is standing cooking him a steak. He is impatient. He does not want to wait. He gets annoyed at his wife because the steak is not ready. He blames her. It is her fault. He wants it to be ready when *he* wants to eat it. She cannot take it any more. She gets angry and lets him have it as it is. She locks herself in their bedroom. She stands up to him. He hits her. He takes out his frustration on her. She will not take it. The relationship breaks up.

The film shows Jake developing a second relationship and eventually marrying Vikki, a young woman from the neighbourhood. He is infatuated with her, though he hardly knows her. He is introduced to her by his brother, who also likes her. His brother is brighter and more intelligent, but Jake is going to be the champion. There is a scene when

Jake gets his brother to hit him as hard as he can in the face. His brother thinks that this is stupid but Jake forces him to do it. Jake wants to prove that he can take anything that is given to him. In the final moments of his boxing career when he is eventually beaten for the championship, he stands there almost letting himself take whatever punishment is given to him. When he has finally lost, he goes up to Sugar Ray Robinson who has beaten him and, with blood pouring from his face, he says with stupid pride, 'I could take it. You never got me down.' Robinson just laughed. Jake seems to have proved something to himself. He has proved that he can take whatever the world has to throw at him. It is a difficult moment. I did not understand it completely.

This connects to another incident which takes place when Jake has won the championship. He has moved into a new house with Vikki. He has never been able to satisfy her in their sexual relationship and is suspicious that she is having relationships with other men. He is madly jealous. You witness some tenderness in their early sexual relationship, but even here he is always telling her what to do. He gives her a series of instructions. He will not allow her spontaneity. He is forced to withdraw to reassert his control of the situation. He always needs to have control; he cannot surrender to his desire.

In this later scene, Jake is watching TV in his living room with his brother. His wife Vikki is upstairs. As he messes with the faulty set, Jake's huge, powerful body is useless, and his pent-up frustration builds at this thing he cannot make work by hitting – like his home life. Confronted with something too complex to be bent to his will in the only way that he knows, Jake goes berserk on a quite different tack. His suspicions rise to an accusation of his brother: 'You fucked my wife? You fucked my wife?' 'You ask me that, your own brother? You expect me to answer that?' Both are outraged with a sentimental pride that is peculiarly masculine. Jake goes upstairs to his wife. His insane jealousy takes the form of both physical obsession with what he imagines to have happened – 'You sucked his cock?' – and of physical revenge. In the culmination of the episode, he beats up both his wife and his brother.

The success of *Raging Bull* lies in *not* just showing more male violence, but in the fact that the TV set build-up is inseparable from the whole sequence, and creates, not the sense of Jake's strength, but of his impotence. This is also made clear when in another scene, Vikki observes idly that a young contender has a pretty face. Jake cannot rest until he has knocked the boy's nose halfway to his ear, in one of the film's most brutal boxing scenes: 'He ain't pretty no more'; but again, instead of power, we feel the inadequacy of using the ring to work out a paranoid personal obsession.

Jake takes out his anger and frustration on this young contender. In this way, he thinks that he is getting even with Vikki, or even proving something to her. But this is not even something that she knows about, or could guess about. This is a kind of acting-out of emotions and feelings that is less familiar within a middle-class masculine experience. Jake's emotions and feelings are much nearer to the surface. He has less control over them. We gain little sense of his ongoing relationship with Vikki. We simply learn of the restrictions that he places upon her freedom and the intensity of his jealousy whenever she makes contact with other men. We have little sense of his need in the relationship, of his vulnerability. It is this sense of 'self-sufficiency' that is deeply related to masculinity. This is often what makes our relationships difficult. We are brought up to feel that needing things from others is a sign of weakness. We grow fearful of acknowledging and getting to know these needs, lest they have grown to such proportions that they threaten to overwhelm us.

CONTROL, FRUSTRATION AND VIOLENCE

Within a middle-class setting, our bull is less likely to rage. It is too firmly controlled. We are more likely to be cynical and spiteful. We are brought up to use language to control and moderate our emotions. We are likely to be greater strangers to our violence. This does not make it any the less threatening for being veiled. It does not necessarily mean that we are more capable of asking for what we need in our relationships, but it becomes easier to feel self-sufficient, to feel that we do not really need things for ourselves. We can pride ourselves on our reliability and our dependability.

This does not mean that we do not expect women to cook and clean for us and that we do not get irritated when things do not go our way. It is our invulnerability that can block us from deepening the relationships we have, since it is hard for us to recognise the kinds of needs we bring into a relationship. Rather, we often expect women to be able to interpret our needs for us. It is tempting to feel that we do not want to have to ask for what we need, but want people who love us to have some kind of intuitive grasp of what we need. Often this is an avoidance. It means that we do not have to take the risk of asking. It means that we do not have to accept the pain of rejection. I remember the difficulty of asking girls to dance at the local youth club when I was fourteen. I would find a way of asking without really asking. In this way I would never have to feel rejected.

If Scorsese is right that 'You have to claw your way through . . . the "negative" aspects' because you come to a point in your life when you cannot any longer deny them, we have to be sensitive to the differences in our class and racial backgrounds. This means coming to terms with our individual histories, with the experiences that have shaped our masculinity. This has been part of the importance of consciousness-raising for men, but it has also shown the needs for different kinds of therapy since, especially for middle-class men, talking can be a way of avoiding facing difficulties in our experience. We need to find ways of coming to know and explore the broader extent and depths of our feelings and emotions, not judging them too early and too easily.

This involves acknowledging the full range and force of our emotions and feelings, often resentful, painful and spiteful feelings that we would prefer not to acknowledge. Therapy understands the importance of expressing these feelings, not simply talking about them, and thereby promises to give us a fuller contact with ourselves. Sometimes we will learn how our feelings and experiences are shared by others. This itself can be a form of liberation as we are often brought up to assume that our fears and inhibitions are completely private and individual. We learn the significance of class and ethnic differences, but also what we have been brought up to share in our experience of masculinity.

Some of this became clearer to me in our *Achilles' Heel* collective discussions.[5] It showed that Scorsese had expressed something of more general significance. When Tony asked a friend whether she saw him as violent, she first said 'no', and then she said, 'Well, yeah. I think in some ways you are. My experience of your violence is always in relation to things going wrong, and frustration with machinery and with inanimate things which frustrate you.' This helped Tony understand that it is when arrangements go wrong which seem important to him at the time, when, for example, the car does not work, that his anger and frustration are brought out. He also realised that

> the thing is that the only person who kind of sees that very much is actually S, and it often happens when I'm with her. It's got a lot to do with our relationship. And that's partly to do with a feeling of licence that I can let things out. That she knows me that well that I can let things out.

At a more complex level, Tony explained,

> it's also something else as well. I can let things out but at the same time I feel that somehow exposing myself to her means I have less power or something. It means I feel vulnerable. And that makes it worse. It means I feel more frustrated and more angry about it and

end up being increasingly uptight. I don't feel that angry when things go wrong with other people. It's something about taking it out on her in a kind of oblique way.

I know how I can avoid feelings of vulnerability in a similar way. It is not easy even to know when we are doing this. Often we need the help and support of others to recognise these patterns, which sometimes have deeper sources in our earlier relationships. This is something therapy can help us with. It is also something that consciousness-raising can help us to develop different patterns about.

Sharing this experience reminds Andy of a similar pattern:

'I haven't cleaned up and the place is a mess and I feel depressed with that. She comes and says the place is in a mess, and that reminds me I feel depressed and I'm immediately hostile and angry with myself because she's kind of exposed me to myself, I suppose. And I feel frustrated with myself that I haven't got things together for myself. . . I feel frustrated that it takes her to remind me that the place is in a mess. I don't want to be reminded and . . . oh . . . it's really painful. And so I get all gritty faced.'

Often we do not thank people for putting us more in touch with ourselves, even when it is women or men we are particularly close to. It is easy to feel exposed, found out. Sometimes we can feel that we are doing reasonably well and it only takes the presence of someone else to make us realise we are feeling bad. It can be difficult to accept this in a straightforward way, often easier to hit out. This can connect to an impulsive feeling to reject the support and help others are ready to offer us, even when this is exactly what we need. Again it can be difficult to acknowledge this need and vulnerability because at some level we continue to feel this as a form of weakness and defeat, even if we have consciously rejected these notions of self-sufficient masculinity.

Often these patterns have deep sources. As men, we are often brought up to get our way. We can find it hard to accept changes, even if we want them intellectually. Sometimes we can retain control in our relationships through the very unspoken sanction of our tempers. This can create fear and uncertainty in others. It can give us power within the relationship as others find it difficult to challenge us directly. This can only change slowly. It involves a different process of transformation for men and women, which has to happen at different levels.[6]

Sometimes, for men, it is through coming to acknowledge and accept our vulnerability, pain, longing and fear, that we can escape from the need to respond so immediately with anger and violence. This can help us to a different kind of control of ourselves as we do this emotional work for ourselves, rather than relying upon the women and men in our close relationships. This involves taking a different kind of responsibility for ourselves as we learn to gain more support and understanding from other men. It is partly through coming to more understanding and experience of our own 'raging bulls' that we can begin to re-evaluate what matters to us in our lives and what kind of relationships we want to have with others. This will mean learning to ask more directly for what we need but also accepting we will not always get it.

MEN, RESPONSIBILITY AND VIOLENCE

At another level, this remains a totally inadequate response to male violence, especially when it is taken out on women and gay people. Nothing can justify this violence. Individual men have to be held responsible for their verbal and physical violence. It is up to all of us to say that this behaviour is unacceptable, whether it is going on within a relationship or not. Often we collude in silence. We are brought up within liberal society to think that it is a 'private concern' that we should not interfere with. Often we remain silent rather than challenge friends who are involved in violent relationships, or people we see harassing women in the street.

Until we experience this sort of behaviour not simply as a violation of others, but also as a violation of our own humanity, we are likely to collude. Often it is difficult when a man responds to us saying, 'I'm only having a bit of fun – why are you taking it so seriously?' We can easily feel that we open ourselves for ridicule if we intervene. These are situations we need to confront openly and directly. We are surrounded by them most of the time. It is easy to collude in denying the significance of the pain and violation that is taking place.

Andrea Medea and Kathleen Thompson, in an article 'Little Rapes', talk about the gradual effects on women of having to endure walking down a city street at night, or even during the day:

> If you are subjected to this kind of violation every day, a gradual erosion begins – an erosion of your self-respect and privacy. You lose a little when you are shaken out of your day-dreams by the whistles and comments of the construction workers you have to pass. You lose a little when a junior executive looks down your blouse or gives you a familiar pat at work . . . In themselves these incidents are disgusting, repellant – in fact, intolerable. Acceptance of them as normal is dangerous . . . Learning to avoid being hassled in the street is as much a

part of living in the city as learning to cope with public transport. To see a black person subjected to this kind of abuse would make one sick. It would be painful to watch them lower their head and try to get past a group of whites unmolested. Today black people are no longer expected to 'know their place', although deliberate humiliation and discrimination against them still exists. But women face this kind of badgering and taunting and accept it. They have come to think of it as an unavoidable part of life.

(Peace News, 22 April 1977)

At the same time as it is important for us to be able to identify with other men in the ways they behave towards women, understanding the frustration out of which they sometimes respond, it is important to know that this behaviour is completely unacceptable. This very much has to do with the relationships of men with each other. Too often the Left has limited understanding of the women's movement to a support of demands and campaigns which have then been left to women to organise. This has been a comfortable tactic since it has meant that the Left has not had to challenge the sexist practices which are often deeply endemic, for example, within the trade union movement.[7] If we are not to fall into a moralistic position, we need much deeper discussion of the experience of masculinity. This has been slow and uneven in development.

Partly because as men we often do not have a language in which to identify and express our experience, we may feel uneasy and nervous in personal discussions and often have little sense that there is much to be gained from this kind of exploration. We feel confident enough in the public language we have been brought up to use. At some level, we often feel guilty for the ways we treat others and do not want to be reminded of this. We have been brought up to expect that women will do our cooking, cleaning and emotional servicing for us and it can be difficult for men to accept that this has to change.

We often hurt those we feel closest to as we take out our tensions and frustrations on them. As men, we often have little confidence that things could change if we were ready to talk our feelings through. Often we lock them tightly within ourselves until they explode or we tend to disappear into ourselves. Somehow we need to connect the frustrations that are generated through the indignities and subordination people have to endure at work with the strains and tensions in our closer relationships. This involves developing a socialist theory and practice that does not divide work from other areas of our lives. This has been one of the significant contributions of feminism.

With the strains of a more intensive work life and the frustrations of unemployment that have dominated the 1980s and look set to dominate the 1990s, we are often finding the family a locus of violence, tension and abuse.[8] Often people are left in isolation to work things out, though there is increasing recognition that issues of physical and sexual violence and abuse cannot be exclusively considered as issues of communication within the family unless they are also connected to issues of masculinity. This is a difficult insight for practitioners of family therapy to integrate because issues of gender are often left implicit. Through sharing our different experiences of masculinity, isolation can be challenged and new ways of working with men developed.[9]

But this involves the development of different forms of socialist politics which refuse to marginalise these issues as 'personal', recognising how they emerge out of central tensions within culture and society. It has been an enduring influence of radical feminist work to place issues of male violence at the centre of an understanding of social relations, although often this has been done in a way that forecloses the possibilities of men to change. In this context, it is crucial not to treat masculinity as a unified and homogeneous category, fixed within particular relations of power, but to explore the emergence and experience of different masculinities. This has to be done in a way that can recognise the centrality of masculinity within an Enlightenment vision of modernity that has largely been cast in its image.

9 Fascism

FASCISM, RACISM AND ANTI-SEMITISM

Fascism is the most blatant institutionalised form of violence. We cannot begin to understand it unless we grasp that the indignities and subordination people suffer grow out of changing social relations. Relatedly, to understand the rise of the New Right and authoritarian politics is to engage with the form of these power relations in the particular historical context out of which they grow. It is to think about the dialectical interrelation between forms of institutionalised power, including masculine power, and people's experienced needs and the negation of those needs. Deskilling and what it does to masculine identity, traditionally organised around work, is a facet of this.

Developing a different kind of socialist politics means understanding what allows right-wing politics, in whatever form, to make sense to people – how they can experience this kind of politics as somehow alleviating, or giving a space to express, existential pain that arises in relationships of dominance and subordination. This it to take seriously Marx's problematic of ideology, understanding that 'ideas' cannot be separated off into an autonomous realm but rather provide the terms of reference for, and thereby shape, the experience of conscious existence.

The Left has tended to dismiss many of the concerns of ordinary men and women either as some form of false consciousness or as the result of consumerist brainwashing, thereby leaving the way clear for a New Right to tap these fears and anxieties. Probably the best example in recent years is the way the Right has orchestrated public anxiety about law and order to justify a massive extension of policing, and managed to portray the Left as anti-police and so as pro-mugging, burglary and violence. The Left has only slowly learnt to validate as reasonable people's fear of mugging and women's fears of assault on the streets at night and so grasp people's felt need for a policing strategy that could be more effective.

The 1970s saw the emergence of a fascist movement in England, for the first time since the 1930s. If its electoral popularity has seen a demise in the immediately recent past, this has to be seen in the context of the eleventh year of an aggressively right-wing government and the ongoing popularity of the Right in general. What are the conditions for the growth and development of authoritarian politics? We have to learn the lessons of the 1930s and to understand that historical experience, but we have to be careful of drawing lessons too mechanically, sustaining an awareness of the need to distinguish between different forms of right-wing politics. We cannot relive the victories of the past; nor can we remake the past, through giving it different endings in the present.[1]

More personally, I have lived with the experience of the Nazi concentration camps, having been born out of its suffering and its fear. This is not a history that I own easily. At one level, it is a source of shame and difficulty. I wanted to leave this history behind, in the search for acceptance and the security of an 'English identity'. I did not want to be different from the other kids at school. I wanted to be like them. In so many ways, this feeling persists. Like so many others, I do not want to identify myself as 'Jewish'. This makes me nervous. For so many years I have not had to face these issues, secure in my identity as a socialist; but at another level, this feels like a disowning, even a weakening, of some part of myself. I still feel a little ashamed of my Jewish identity, unsure of how to live it out in my relationships. I feel scared that people are going to laugh. This shows me how deeply affected I must have been in our early relationships at school.

I felt scared in the late 1970s at the development and growth of the National Front, especially in strong working-class areas, as I now do with the re-emergence of anti-Semitism and racism in Eastern Europe and the Soviet Union. I cannot experience fascism as a weak movement, because at some level I carry the fears and anxieties of my parents. The fear of the knock at the door in the middle of the night. The fear of being pointed at and ridiculed as a Jew. These fears are all the more pressing because I have not faced them directly. I keep pretending that it will all go away. I do not feel well prepared to face the present.

Our parents did not educate us clearly about the realities of the war against the Nazis. They did not know how to talk about it. The experience was too enormous and involved too much loss. If anything, the fear and the anxiety were passed on. I was told that, as I was Jewish, I should not involve myself in politics. It was 'dangerous'. We had to be inconspicuous. We had to be careful that other people did not notice us. We should not stick out. You had to be watchful and careful. If 'being Jewish' was something that you could be proud of at home, it was something to be careful about 'in public'. This created a pervasive split in the consciousness of those growing up in the Jewish community after the war. We learnt, in our different ways, how to be 'accepted' by others. We conformed to the expectations of others and needed the approval of others, to be able to feel good about ourselves. Often, 'getting on' in the society meant an insecure hold on our own sense of individual identity.

The emergence of the National Front and the British Movement forced me to face issues I wanted to put aside. I cannot simply offer an analysis which says that it was the Jews in the 1930s and then the blacks in the 1970s and 1980s. The reemergence of anti-Semitism in the early 1990s belies such assertions. Rather, I have to own my experience, however muted, to understand something about the relationship of anti-Semitism and racism to fascism, and, more recently, the displacement of racism into right-wing liberal democratic politics, which should not be taken to guarantee the atrophy of fascist consciousness. Originally, I intended to write a purely 'objective analysis' of these issues, knowing that this would be more acceptable in terms of orthodox Marxist theory, but also that it would be easier for me to keep myself firmly and securely hidden. My experience in the men's movement has taught me that I only cripple my understanding by imposing too firm a split between 'objective analysis' and 'subjective experience'.

Reich understood this in the 1930s, forcing us to recognise that the appeal to suppressed emotionality and an identification with leadership were terribly powerful material forces.[2] The Left could only identify 'material forces' within the realm of the 'economy', so that it could never grasp the nature of social power within the society. The Nazis had a more powerful understanding of this. Somehow, in the Germany of the 1930s, fascism became deeply psychically embedded as it was able to capture the emotional sentiments of everyday life. As Reich says:

> While we presented the masses with superb historical analyses and economic treatises on the contradictions of imperialism, Hitler stirred the deepest roots of their emotional being. As Marx would have put it, we left the praxis of the subjective factor to the idealists; we acted like mechanistic economistic materialists.
>
> (What is Class Consciousness? in Reich (1972))

Reich points out that, despite the intense spirit of rebelliousness among the German people, 'socialism' never became a concrete vision for them.[3]

WE ARE NOT LIVING IN THE THIRTIES

Capitalism was in a period of crisis in the late 1970s and early 1980s, as it was in the 1930s. We have experienced a period of mass unemployment as capitalism has sought to restructure and reorganise itself. There has been a definite shift towards the Right as Thatcherism has consolidated a decade of power. But even to understand this, we have to come to terms with the changes in the organisation and structure of capitalist society. It will not do simply to identify the National Front or the British Movement with the Nazis and call them 'scum', however important it is to challenge the image of respectability which the Front sought to create.

Nor is it enough to focus in on the history of fascist organisation, showing the Nazi background of its leadership. We have to be aware of the continuities across forms of authoritarian politics, and wary of being made to think that any fuller analysis and critical thinking is a cop-out, as if all we need to do is draw our political lessons from a study of Hitler's own words. This can too easily encourage a kind of blind machismo militarism, in which the 'forces' of the Left are set against the Front.

Our confrontations with right-wing politics need to be informed by a fuller understanding of the conditions for the emergence of the right-wing groups in this period. What is of significance here is not simply a matter of a refusal to think critically about the changed conditions of life in capitalist society, but of the domination of a Trotskyist tradition within the British Left which has generally insisted that we are in the same 'epoch' as the thirties, so that we do not need an understanding of the changed conditions. In many ways, the disillusionment with the sixties led many people back into established traditions, before they abandoned identification with politics completely, rather than forward through a theorisation of the practice in which many of us were involved. This could have yielded important insights into broader changes that have taken place in capitalist society, especially since 1945.

In thinking about the post-war era, many of us are trying to grasp a period in which we have grown up ourselves. We are forced to reflect upon institutions we have experienced ourselves. We have lived through the demise of England as a colonial power and we have experienced an education in which we were taught to assume our 'superiority' over others. In thinking more personally we can hope to understand what kinds of crisis in the lives of people encourage them to support the growth of authoritarian politics. Our traditional conceptualisations have to be rethought, as we realise that many traditional working-class Labour voters now provide at least tacit support for the New Right, and that more recently in Central and Eastern Europe with the sudden demise of the power of the Soviet Union, racist and anti-Semitic movements develop with intensified support alongside populist revolutions focused upon freedom from state domination.

THE CHANGING ORGANISATION OF WORK

So it is not enough to adopt the political understandings of the 1930s and apply them mechanically to the rise of a fascist movement in the 1970s or 1990s. It is quite misleading to think of fascism as necessarily a 'petit bourgeois' movement. We need to confront the reality of many working-class people who were formerly active Labour Party supporters and later came to support the National Front. In some East London furniture factories in the late 1970s, the National Front provided the only viable political organisation within work. I shall be saying something about the connection between work and masculinity, hopefully to illuminate older white working-class support for the National Front, as well as the younger recruitment of 16-20 year olds. I shall say very little about the relationship of women to the Right.[4]

These ideas are presented speculatively, in order to provoke broader discussion on the Left. They are written out of a conviction that we can apply neither Trotsky nor Reich to the changed situation of the 1970s, 1980s or 1990s, but need to develop our politics so that we can grasp a developing social and historical reality. This proceeds from Marx's realisation that:

> The presuppositions with which we begin are not arbitrary presuppositions; they are not dogmas; they are real presuppositions from which one can abstract only in fancy. They are the actual individuals, their actions and the material conditions of their lives, those already existing as well as those produced by action.
>
> (*The German Ideology* in Marx and Engels 1968)

Since the 1920s there has been an accelerated transformation of the labour process with an increase in assembly-line production. This has been part of a longer process of the reassertion of control over the workplace, using the techniques of scientific management initially worked out by Taylor. In this attack on the autonomy of skilled work, the machine has come to dominate the very movements of people, depriving work of whatever degree of skill it used to have. This has become part of a systematic programme with the workings of scientific management. It is generally known as Fordism because of its initial association with Henry Ford's car plants. Management has learnt to use science in the very control of work and has found an important way of reasserting its power and control.[5] If the introduction of some machinery has brought with it new areas of skill, this is overlaid on a more general trend for workers to be increasingly controlled in the very details of their movements. The very pace of work is dictated by the management through control they have over the speed of the line.

Large-scale factory production was generally organised in this way until the reassertion of trade union and workers' industrial power in the late 1960s and early 1970s encouraged a further restructuring of the labour process using new technology and robotics to break the bottlenecks in industrial production that had been used as sources of workers' power to shut down whole lines of production. Harry Braverman in his *Labor and Monopoly Capital* (1974) has shown how principles of 'rationalisation', involving the detailed control of workers' lives at work extend into the reorganisation of hospitals, offices, services, and schools.[6] Telephone engineers, for instance, are 'timed' for the jobs that they do and will be expected to complete so many jobs in a day. In this way, it is not the job itself that dictates the time and attention that people can give to it, but rather, the control has been *externalised* and workers are expected to complete so many jobs in the time allotted, otherwise they have to explain themselves. So it is that workers have less and less power to affect the outcome and organisation of their work.

Even nurses complain that they are expected to carry through certain 'standard procedures' with each patient on the ward. They are only allotted a certain time to do this, so they often experience a contradiction between the care and attention they want to be able to give to patients and the criteria which the administration dictates for doing a 'good job'. These contradictions are submerged in the professional ideology, which does its best to say that a 'professional nurse' does not get emotionally involved with the patients. This pushes many nurses into treating patients 'impersonally', even though they feel there is something wrong with doing this. At the same time, the nurses are under such pressure of work that it is difficult for them to relate any differently. In this way, patients get 'objectified' and the nurses themselves have to cut off from their feelings.

At one level, these processes of rationalisation have made work so much more monotonous, boring and routine. This is not just a product of greater mechanisation, but also of the growth in the 1960s and 1970s in the scale of the organisations in which people work, be they multinational manufacturing industries or municipal bureaucracies. So many more people seem to complain of their work being 'meaningless' and experience themselves getting very little from their work. This has happened in whole areas of professional and service work, for instance teaching and social work, where people have traditionally sought a certain amount of 'meaning' and 'purpose' for themselves in their work. It has often been within these sectors that the Left has developed recently.

Certainly, we have only just begun to develop a politics of these sectors, or an understanding of their changed role and significance within corporate capitalism. Work has become split into routine areas of responsibility, within very large organisations. Young people get easily frustrated and disappointed. Work is defined by a set of rules, which define the nature of the job. Increasingly, people feel 'replaceable' in the work that they do. The frustrations and problems of teachers and social workers are also rooted in larger structural changes and tensions in the wider society, in mass unemployment, poverty and continuing inner-city decline, as well as the low status and pay they receive while being blamed for whatever 'goes wrong' in society.

WORK AND MALE IDENTITY

Within capitalist society, work has always been an essential aspect of male identity. As men, we inherit an image of ourselves as 'breadwinners' looking after and providing for others in our family. Even if we have been encouraged to engage critically with this 'role' through the emergence of the women's movement and women discovering a sense of their own independent identity, this conception, often unconsciously, still governs so much of our lives. We rediscover it in an abiding sense of responsibility, in the ease with which we can look after others but can barely look after ourselves. We find it in the ways we assume superiority over others, without even thinking about it.

This is an aspect of patriarchal power, which affects men in different ways depending upon our class and ethnic background and experience. Men's sense of potency and superiority used to be strongly reinforced by work. It has been through work that men have traditionally validated themselves and have been able to sustain a positive psychological image of themselves. The tradition of skilled work within the working class allowed for a sense of pride and identity with the work done. This went along with a certain sense of male community that was built around work, especially around traditional industries – coal, steel, shipbuilding and others. Without work, men often experience themselves as worthless.

With the processes of deskilling which have affected all these industries in different ways, this sense of identity and identification has been undermined. But, as Cynthia Cockburn has pointed out in her investigation into the print industry in *Brothers*, deskilling and new technology do not inevitably challenge male élitism and power within the labour force because of the pervasiveness of established gender expectations at work. This was highlighted in the machinists' strike at Ford in the mid-1980s when it became clear that if men did the work, it would be classified as skilled, but because women did it, it was not.

At the same time, with rationalisation, men have experienced themselves as increasingly controlled and subordinated at work, divided off and against each other. Men's sense of pride and identification has been challenged. This has created a 'crisis of identity' for an older generation of white workers who have been brought up to believe in a 'fair day's work for a fair day's wage'. They believe in doing a 'man's job' and expect to do 'hard work', so that it is a big insult to be thought of as a 'slacker' or as 'work-shy'. In part, this structure of masculine identity makes possible the whole attempt to underpin the work ethic by labelling welfare recipients as 'scroungers'.

At the same time, contradiction is opening up between feeling that 'you should work hard and deserve every penny you make' and a growing awareness of the meaninglessness of work with such a small component of skill. This goes along with a realisation that the management has organised work to get as much out of labour as it possibly can, while giving as little as it can in return. The logic of capitalist production is becoming clearer, but this does not make it clearer how people fit in, or how they should respond to it.

Older white workers were brought up to accept work as second nature. As men, they are brought up to sacrifice themselves for the wellbeing of their families. It is through sacrifice that one will be rewarded with the good things of life. In the 1950s this looked possible. The intensification of labour had increased since the war, but the over-time meant that people could earn higher wages. People felt secure in the feeling that they were living in a way that their parents could never have imagined, with the full employment and plentiful overtime of the post-war years and a growing range of new and inexpensive consumer goods.

Men were often prepared to overlook what was happening at work while the vision of owning their own house full of labour-saving devices seemed attainable. Working-class people had TVs and could have holidays abroad. Even if they had to work hard for it, people often had a sense that 'they'd never had it so good'. Sometimes it was even possible for working-class people to afford a mortgage on a house. This was a sentiment that Thatcherism was able to build on as it promised working-class people the opportunity to buy their own houses. In areas such as the outer boroughs of East London, this guaranteed electoral success for the Tories. It allowed Thatcherism to consolidate its claim to offer freedom and possessions to working people.

Even though work was less satisfying, people felt they were earning the money. This made it easier to accept that work was simply a means of getting a wage, nothing more. This shift in the ideology of work had become clearly established since the war. People did not expect to identify with work, or to feel the same kind of pride as an earlier generation. Increasingly people were forced to regard it purely instrumentally, as a means of gaining a wage. There was a shift in identification as men found it harder to draw meaning from work, and from relationships at work. This is not just an issue about attitudes to work but about consumer culture, fuelled by TV in particular, which is far more a part of the experience of young people. Consumption became significant in a new way. All kinds of expectations were created through TV and hire purchase.

So much of this was suddenly undercut with the inflation and mass unemployment of the early 1970s and the economic crisis that stretched into the 1980s. Men had already done the work, so they could now feel cheated of the rewards. Their hard-earned savings were not worth as much. People had to get reconciled into living in the same flats. At the same time, this opened up all kinds of tensions and divisions. The consumerist vision was rudely undercut at the same time that men's traditional reliance on their work for a sense of worth came under attack by rising unemployment on the one hand and a new wave of feminism on the other.

There seems to be a generational split at work. People born after the war were not brought up within the same culture of self-sacrifice. Younger people were brought up to expect more from life. They did not feel grateful simply for having a job. They had not lived through the experience of the thirties and could not make sense of it in the sixties. If work was not interesting, they did not see why they should do it. Young workers did not think anything of taking days off work, though this was unthinkable to their fathers. If a young man did not like the work he was doing, he might give it up. The older generation did not expect to like work. They thought you should simply do it, regardless of what you felt about it. They had often lived through the mass unemployment of the 1930s, when there was virtually no welfare system. A day off work could mean the loss of your job and threaten starvation for the family.

The older generation can easily feel threatened by a younger generation, which does not have the 'right attitude' to work. It is hard when younger people do not seem prepared to make the same kind of sacrifices and do not even respect the sacrifices which their fathers have made. Younger people do not care about work in the same way. Young men in the 1960s and 1970s had never known that desperate poverty and unemployment, and if they lost their job there was a whole network of dole and social security to fall back on until you got another one. A different ethic has grown up through these changed conditions. You are forced to work to get money, so that you can *live* outside of work and relate to a whole culture of music, drink and clothes. Young people spend the money they earn, in a way which is incomprehensible to their parents. They want to have a good time out of life.

The older generation can react in a *defensive* way to feeling threatened. They assert more strongly the traditional values of hard work to their kids. They will want to isolate their kids, by demarcating them, thinking that it is young West Indians who are 'lazy' and 'good for nothing', always being ready to stop working at the smallest excuse. In this assertion of racism, they will want to be saying something to their children. They will want to say 'you aren't like them', as a way of forging a connection and subverting their own confusion, even though they fear that black and white young people share similar attitudes towards work. It will be important for men to assert these traditional values of 'hard work' and 'self-sacrifice' so that they can be assured of the respect of their children. This is just one of the things that has been brought into question by some of these changes in the organisation of work. Rather than accepting differences between themselves and their own children, people may externalise them as racial differences. So it can more comfortably be said that blacks are 'lazy' and do not want to work than that this is true of your own children.[7]

A reassertion of traditional values of work is a way of regaining the control that fathers had within the family. If men feel threatened at work by the attitudes of younger workers, they also feel threatened in their homes when this is fought out with their own children. This prepared the ground for Thatcherism's espousal of traditional Victorian values. It struck a chord for many people who felt threatened by the changes in social relations wrought by the 1960s and by the growing independence of women and young people.

In different forms, this 'crisis of authority' is being worked out in West Indian families, where the older generation of workers had much more traditional values than their children born in this country. It is not simply that the younger generation has different values, but is a question of the ways they undermine the authority and respect which an older generation of men have been led to expect. When this respect is not forthcoming, men often think it can be demanded. The New Right has understood some of these contradictions. In some ways, it gives older men a way of validating their ideas and values of work, through identifying the 'blacks' as the threatening force.

THREATS IN THE FAMILY

Prior to these developments, there was far more continuity between generations, particularly through the ideology of work. In many industries fathers could guarantee their sons a job. This gave men a feeling of power and control within the family, particularly over their sons. It did not really matter how well a child did in school, because you could guarantee him a future. But it is no longer possible to pass on a tradition of skill; deskilled work calls for very little training. This has also undermined the power of the father within the home. He is forced to acknowledge the power of state intervention, through education; it is up to the school to determine his son's future.

This is often an area in which men will feel particularly vulnerable because they did not do well at school. They will find even their younger children surpassing the maths that they did at school. It is threatening in its own way to have to admit that you cannot help, or that you cannot answer the questions your son is putting to you, and so fathers might well feel undermined by the very process of schooling. So not only do men not have a future to give to their children, but they feel powerless to help them at school. Men will deal with this situation in different ways. It is also not uncommon for working-class children, having gone through school and possibly higher education, to despise their fathers' demeaning work, not wanting to have anything to do with it.

Some men will further withdraw in the family, taking an even less active part in the life of the family. They will feel defeated. This itself is connected to a process of deskilling and the increased intensification of work. This has undermined the sources of male pride. Men cannot feel so good about themselves, especially if they have to work subordinated to the discipline of the machine. They come home exhausted and blanked out. So men will withdraw into themselves, feeling that they have much less to offer their children. Finding themselves unable to help with homework, men might further withdraw into themselves, feeling an intensified sense of worthlessness and thinking that all they can do is bring home the money. This becomes a source of tension just because men are not getting the kind of support and validation they need from work, so that they are looking more to the family and their sense of themselves as 'consumers' to give them this.

While some men withdraw, others will deal with a similar contradiction by asserting their power more in the family. They will want all the attention and power they can get, because they can no longer get this at work. All the frustration and anxiety generated through subordination at work will be taken out at home, so that if a son stays in bed one day 'just 'cos he doesn't fancy going to work', this might provoke an enormous row. A father may take this to be an affront to his authority in the family – 'who does he bloody well think he is anyway?' – as a lack of respect towards him.

It is only against a background of understanding of all the sacrifices the father has had to make over the years that we can have an inkling of the emotionally explosive situation. The father might have little sense of why his son staying in bed makes him feel so mad, nor the son why his father seems so upset. This is the reality of repression. It does not simply operate at a rational level. The fact that it does not always surface into open family conflict does not mean that it is not important to develop a politics which can grasp its reality and significance.[8]

With the destruction of working-class communities, with the war and the rehousing programmes, the family does not exist within the same kind of community. There has been a destruction of the street community, into which many children, even in the 1950s, used to be integrated. Young children were involved in a whole set of social relationships, looking after younger children and spending time with grandparents. They would be disciplined by any adult in the street. Younger people tended to grow up and exist within the community.

With the post-war rehousing, children are less likely to be involved in a whole set of social relations with people who have known them since they were very young. With little space for them in the flats, they are left to discover themselves within their own youth cultures. Within the families, the tensions with adults are more focused on the individual relationship with parents. There is no longer such a strong supporting community. And if young adults find themselves within their own youth culture largely in opposition to the culture of their parents, they have to work this out with their own parents, often alone.

In the 1930s, the Frankfurt School identified a weakening of the central role of the strong patriarchal father in maintaining authoritarianism in the family. The strong and powerful father who ruled over the family, demanding unquestioning respect from wife and children, was being undermined by changes in the labour process. This changed the character of familial relations, altering the terms of ego development, so making difficult any genuine individuality. So it was that psychoanalysis did not see 'authoritarianism' as a set of 'values' or 'attitudes', into which generations are 'socialised'.

Critical theory helps to undercut this kind of understanding.[9] It shows the effects of the actual structure of power and dominance within social relationships and recognises social relationships as relationships of power and dominance. It also has a sense of the depths to which we are controlled and influenced by these familial relationships, even if we think we are not. Critical theory does not simply talk about how the structures of capitalist society are reproduced within the unconscious, but understands how the very formation of identities within patriarchal families affects the structure of our needs and desires.

The destruction of working-class communities since the war has meant that working-class families exist in greater isolation than they used to. As men have less of a community around work, they put more of their energies and frustrations into the home, where they may feel increasingly powerless. The family comes to be more of a centre of emotional conflict. Men worked really hard after the war, in the hope of a higher standard of living, and it was as a provider of consumer goods that men sought to maintain their power within the families, since it was harder to do this through the significance and meaning of work. But with the inflation and unemployment of the 1970s and 1980s, men could feel powerless and cheated of the rewards of their labour. They realised they were going to have to stay on the East London estates they thought they would be able to leave. Often now they find themselves unable to afford the mortgage rates for the homes and flats that Thatcherism had made to seem so attractive. They cannot even provide housing for their married kids because of the housing shortage.

In this situation, resentment can take racist forms and get turned on to immigrant communities, especially when there are large immigrant communities within the most depressed and embittered white communities such as Hoxton, Handsworth and Toxteth. It becomes possible to explain how immigrants become structurally convenient scapegoats for people to project their anxieties and frustrations on to. But the anxieties and frustrations are real and their displacement into racism has real consequences. In some cases, these communities were the sites of the urban uprisings that took place in the 1980s as blacks responded to the intimidations of the police. In the white community, immigrants come to be seen as taking away the houses and the jobs. These used to be the symbols of male power within the family. They were part of the future men could promise their children.

While fathers often dominate the activities and organisation of families, they are at the same time often emotionally absent, withdrawn into themselves and into their own worlds, so that it is difficult to set up a close personal relationship with one's father. As work becomes more routinised, there is less room for individual initiative, more pressure just to follow the rules. This shows itself within relationships within the family, since we are talking about the same men as 'workers' and 'fathers'. We are talking about people in the different areas of their lives, bringing out how the pressures and frustrations will carry over, but also influence the sense people have of themselves. We are seeing how it is that the dispossession of control at work comes to feed a particular political vision, because changes in our emotional experience at work are fundamentally connected to the ways we relate to those we care for.

Structuralists will argue that we have not shown the 'mediations' between the organisation of labour and the organisation of the family. But this only shows the *externality* of their understanding. They are trapped into looking at two institutional spheres from outside. This kind of 'false objectivism' limits our grasp. We have to realise that it is the same people who are now at work and now at home, so that deskilling is not simply a process that occurs within the organisation of production which will have certain 'effects' on character formation. This is too mechanical, though it is the dominant way in which we conceptualise the relationship between 'objective structures' and 'subjective experience'.

Our grasp has to be dialectical. Deskilling is not simply a technical process which means that work has become 'less skilful', but is a matter of the *control* management has asserted through the very organisation of production. This can only be grasped in the context of the relationships of *power* between workers and capital. Capital is using science and technology systematically to subordinate workers to the machine.

Fathers are the same men who come home after a day on the Ford assembly line. This is the situation I am thinking about most directly, though I think 'Fordisation' reflects a more general process. People need to recover some sense of themselves individually, after the obliteration of their individuality that takes place within these conditions of work. This makes a difference to who you are at home, to the ways you feel about yourself, to the needs to reassert yourself with your wife and children. If men are coming home hating the work they do, they are not going to want their children to be 'like them'. The father will no longer provide a secure authority against whom to define yourself as a boy, especially if your father does not want you to 'follow in his footsteps'. This sets up a distance between father and son.

It might well be that a father needs the loving respect of his son, while the son feels that his father does not have any sense of the world he is living in. The son might well feel that his father has been beaten down at work, so that he wants something 'better' for himself. At least he does not want to 'end up like him'. At some level, this can create a kind of suppressed rage, at the ways in which a man has been worn down at work, or let himself be worn out. This is a difficult set of feelings, which emerges as unspoken hostility when you are a teenager able to compare your father with other men.

But this can further distance young people as they are left feeling they have to make a life of their own. There is less space for them within the narrower family space. Often the conflict is more focused. Fathers can no longer promise a future, but they want their kids to have the same feelings for work, even though at some level fathers must feel ambiguous about this themselves. At least they expect to get respect and deference, even though the sources of a lot of this respect between fathers and sons have been undermined.

Young people no longer find a place within working-class culture. They can often feel estranged from the values of their fathers. At one level, the media create all kinds of promises and expectations. It becomes tempting to 'live through' the lives on the screen, because they come to have a reality and excitement that does not exist on the bleak conditions of the housing estate. At the same time, there has been growing disillusionment since the mid-1970s with all the promises of the 1960s. Nothing has been fulfilled. Unemployment was the bleak reality for so many people leaving school in the 1980s. Deskilling and mass unemployment both worked to undermine traditional sources of male identity.

At one level, this can create intense cynicism with all authorities, including the media. So much of the liberal ideology that people were given turns out to be lies and hypocrisy. For so many people, it turns out to be a 'load of rubbish'. Nothing seems worth believing in. There is a negation of all values, which, while in a sense being the negation of capitalist values, also leads to the brutality of the Clockwork Orange. It arguably explains in part the mass support for a Thatcherite right-wing government which throughout the 1980s asserted a rigid ideology combining a reassertion of traditionalism with an articulation of this very meaninglessness.

Our conceptions of socialism have been too dominated by struggles around work. This is equally true of an orthodox Marxist tradition that insists on work as the exclusive source of creativity and self-realisation. It is as if it is only at work that we can really know or experience ourselves. Socialism is too concerned with issues of control of a workplace where people feel deeply estranged. The experience of the 1975 occupation of Ford Dagenham shows that workers want to use their power to spend more time at home or with friends, rather than occupying their place of work. If we continue to think that it is a 'lack of consciousness' that explains this, we will fail to transform our politics so that it can express and articulate a changed historical experience. Our understanding will no longer be liberating and clarifying.

We have instead to grasp the concrete experience of different generations of men and women. So much energy, experience and frustration is being worked out in the family, which used to have different means of expression. This does not contest the significance of wage struggles, but places them in a different kind of context. The experience of the 'Cowley wives', who organised to get their men back to work, so undermining a strike at British Leyland, rather than being an 'aberration' becomes something we need to reflect upon, to grasp a new emerging social reality.

It is a bitter moment when, as a boy, you no longer feel proud of your father. This can develop along with anger and resentment at the ways that your father has been worn out and wasted by work. On the Left we have too easily denied the importance of pride, identifying it too readily with self-assertion or narrow chauvinism. We fail to make vital distinctions between different sources of pride. There is nothing wrong in feeling proud of one's father, or one's football team. This pride does not have to go along with a feeling of superiority or exclusiveness. Nor is it wrong for people to feel pride in their country.[10]

This is not necessarily incompatible with an appreciation of other cultures or with internationalism. A richer sense of internationalism might grow more from an appreciation of the historical nature of different cultures than from abstract conceptions of humanity. Certainly the Left has never fully grasped issues of nationalism and this has left it open for the Right to identify itself with love of one's country. In a similar way, the Right has been more in tune with the crises for an older generation of skilled workers who want to feel a pride in their work. This used itself to be the heart of so much socialist politics.

MEN AND WOMEN, HUSBANDS AND WIVES

Traditionally, men have been thought of as the 'breadwinners' in the family. This has operated as a justification of their power. It used to be a source of pride in sections of the working class for men, that their wives did not have to go out to work. For years, this source of male power has been undermined, as an increasing number of women go outside the home to work, and as it becomes really difficult to manage a household on a single wage. So at a time that men have been looking to the home for recognition and support they used to be able to get at work, they also find themselves threatened in the home. Women want to live more independent lives and are less prepared to service the needs of their families, if it means totally subordinating their own needs. If they work, they are more likely to demand that men become more involved with housework and childcare. So the distribution of work within the home becomes another source of tension. Men feel threatened.

As men, we are not brought up to understand situations of emotional conflict. When we feel threatened, we often get defensive. We assert the rightness of our own position and we stop listening. This is an experience which is profoundly affected by one's class experience but there are certain shared features, which partly grow out of a shared relationship of power in relationship to women. I am thinking of the ways we, as men, identify so readily with our reason and rationality, thinking that women are being 'emotional' or trying to get at us. We are brought up to control our emotions and feelings, so that they do not get the better of us. We rarely learn the cost of this.

Often it means that we are out of touch with what we are feeling and experiencing. We easily discount, divert or displace the feelings we have, especially when they are feelings of hurt, loneliness, isolation and sadness. We would prefer not to feel this way. Often we simply do not know *how* to articulate and give meaning to what is happening inside of us. We are mute, even though we do not want to be. The very struggle to maintain 'control' over the self has robbed us of a means of expression. It has made it easier for us to repress whatever feelings are coming up. This makes us mechanical, even though part of us remains aware of all the feelings which are simmering beneath the surface of everyday experience.

Reich helps us understand the ways that the Nazis learnt to appeal to the repressed life. They learnt how to manipulate people's deep fears, anxieties and hopes and developed a whole politics of the irrational. This is particularly significant in understanding the relationship between masculinity and fascism, because so much of male experience is unavailable even to ourselves. Our experience often exists only as 'public' and 'impersonal', otherwise it is hidden in poetry. As men, we are masters of indirect speech and the bottle. So much goes on beneath the surface and seems to be locked away. Often when we are threatened, we see this as a naked struggle for power, as we act inconsistently, abruptly, even violently. Within the middle class, often more in control of our physical responses, we will act nastily. If we do not have a language to express our feelings directly, we at least learn how to use language as a weapon for both defence and attack.

When a man comes home expecting to find a meal on the table, only to find that it has not been cooked, he can act violently. At one level he can know that his wife has had her hands full looking after the kids, but at a deeper level he can feel threatened. He feels that he has as much right as his father to expect his meals cooked for him. One part of him will feel that it is a matter of asserting himself, showing who is boss and who is wearing the trousers in the family. He may react violently, if he feels that she is trying to get one over on him. He cannot really deal with the emotions that are coming up, and he might even hit her, without really wanting to. She is denying him what he has grown up to expect 'if he's a real man'.

Somehow his very masculinity is at stake, though this in no way justifies or excuses such abusive and violent behaviour. As men, we are often selfish and self-centred, often having been brought up by our mothers with a sense of entitlement to the emotional services of women. This is not to suggest that this obnoxious and misogynistic behaviour always springs from psychic pain, and it would be ridiculous to suggest that every time a man is being sexist, patronising or unreasonable, it is because he feels his masculinity is threatened. But the level of the self out of which aggression is generated is often not accessible to men.

At school we learn that our masculinity can be put at issue at any moment so that we always have to be ready to defend ourselves. In any confrontation, our 'masculinity' is immediately at stake. So it may be hard for a man to understand that his wife is not testing him or trying to make a fool of him, when she gets him to do more housework. He has got no language within which to express the contradictions that he is feeling. But this is something that men can learn about and it is part of what is meant by taking more responsibility for our emotional lives and personal relationships. Often we start hitting out, because the tension is too great inside of us. Typically, men have dealt with these situations by drinking, but some men are learning to identify this as an evasion and cop-out. This makes it easier to talk and feel easier about what is happening. It can also provide an excuse to be 'unreasonable' or violent whilst avoiding responsibility for this kind of behaviour. Often it is a way men can bond with other men, without really having to ask for connection directly.

We are led astray if we see these tensions too bluntly in terms of an opposition between men and women. The issues are generational and historical as well. In the 1920s and 1930s, women were brought up to see themselves as guardians of sexual morality. They were responsible for the 'moral virtue' of their children. Often this meant conforming to a clear code of moral duties, which did not educate people to articulate conflicts and close feelings. What is more, it would largely be the women who would be blamed if their daughters got pregnant. People did not talk about sexuality openly. So often it is also middle-aged working-class women who feel they cannot really cope with an easier permissive sexual morality. They feel powerless to help their daughters, who are growing up into such a different world and sometimes wish that the world would return to the days of a strong and well-defined morality. This would give them more control within their families.

Often it is these women who feel threatened by ideas of women's liberation and the freedom which they see younger women fighting for. They feel that they have a certain amount of power in the home, over the way the house is organised, the children and holidays. They feel that this security is going to be threatened by these new ideas of women's liberation. The New Right has understood the force of some of these anxieties and is looking to defend traditional conceptions of the family.

In this way it legitimises the traditional male position, but also gives women a clear position within the family. It allows a woman to feel valid as a 'mother' and does not make her feel she should be 'unhappy' or that she should be doing something else. The early conceptions of the women's movement had little to offer women of this generation. Often they will feel an appeal to the Right even if it involves their subordination, if it promises a 'simpler morality' with which they can maintain, even reassert, control over the children. This is why the Right does so much to present itself as part of the family, encouraging whole families to be involved in its activities.[11]

Unless the contradictions are faced, recognised and worked through, people will defend themselves against these changes and reassert traditional values. A socialism which focuses too narrowly upon production operates within the same kind of conspiracy of silence. Our socialism has to articulate a new vision of human relationships, between men and women, adults and children, which helps people recognise the difficulties they face not simply as 'individual' and 'private', but as public and social. This has been one aspect of the potential Marxist transformation of theory or the women's movement. At last we can begin to give a voice to the anxieties and conflicts that people experience, in social and political terms, even if it means abandoning the traditional ways that we have conceived of politics in terms of 'Left' and 'Right', since these categories are in danger of losing all power to illuminate the realities that we face in everyday life.

This does not mean a naïve reductionism which says that individual problems of meaning, sexuality, identity, pride, dignity and self-expression have to be re-described as problems of class struggle. I do not accept that problems of masculinity and patriarchy are a product of capitalist development, nor do I argue that the oppressive character of gender relations has necessarily intensified simply because of deskilling and decreased job satisfaction. In its own way this would be to deny people's experience. We need a way of recognising the reality of the conflicts we face and a language within which these genuine anxieties can be recognised and met. A revitalised socialism needs to provide us with a way of both identifying and meeting the anxieties created through the material changes in our lives.

We need different visions of 'masculinity' and 'femininity' which are grounded in the concrete reality of people's needs and experience. We do not need abstract appeals to ideals, moralistically asserted. We need, for instance, to recognise the importance to men of feeling some kind of pride in themselves, or the importance to women of having children, without legislating that it is 'illegitimate' for people to want these things for themselves. We must recognise that these feelings can be expressions of fundamental needs people have to express their creativity, even if they can be formed in restricted and distorting ways in both capitalist and state socialist societies. Rather than setting up alternative ideals against which we are to compare ourselves, we need to begin our analysis with 'the actual individuals, their actions and the material conditions of their lives, those already existing as well as those produced by action' (*The German Ideology* in Marx and Engels 1968). So we need to begin with the conflicts and contradictions that people face in their everyday experience.

The New Right in both America and Europe has recognised the reality of these conflicts which are felt by so many people. On the Left we too often invalidate people's experience as 'subjective' or 'idealistic'. We have to find ways of giving ourselves strength and confidence to ask racial questions as we help to create a different vision of life in society. We have to show that we have learnt the lessons of the past in both Western and Eastern Europe, so that we can recognise the reality of people's experience. We need to understand how a language of socialism has been degraded in the authoritarian regimes of the Soviet Union, and to take seriously the challenges of feminism and sexual politics to the traditional forms of social democratic politics that have largely been identified with socialism in the capitalist democracies. As men, this means recognising a 'crisis of masculinity' but also developing collectively a different sense of the ways that men can relate to each other.

In this way we have to concretise our vision of politics and personal life, as part of our striving for a more humane and decent life. We need to be clear that our learning to take fascism and the New Right seriously in the different forms in which it emerges in Europe in no way precludes their moral condemnation. This is not simply a matter of the ascendancy of a particular discourse that articulates an altered subjectivity, as post-structuralist theory might have it, but rather must be addressed in terms that fully express our moral outrage.

This means recognising that the social relations of power and subordination, giving rise as they do to the *experience* of powerlessness, are the soil out of which grows both fascist consciousness and our own consciousness. To imagine that anyone is magically immune from the structures of identity these relations underpin, is to lapse into a liberal theory of society as a set of inherently good and bad people. At the same time it is all-important to recognise that some individuals resist, as in Nazi Germany, and can foretell the developments that are coming into being. It is because of this that our social and political theory cannot simply take up an externalised critique of prevailing relations but must necessarily involve a critical relation to self.

This is part of taking greater responsibility for our lives and resisting the tendency to see our lives as completely at the mercy of external forces that we cannot resist. In this sense, a liberalism that leaves individuals feeling that alone they are powerless to effect changes in their lives, is a recipe for moral compromise and accommodation to an unjust and immoral situation. In this regard it is crucial to learn from the accommodation of the professions to Hitler's rise to power.

It is in understanding these crucial issues of responsibility and empowerment that therapy can become vital. This is an arena in which we can learn of the different ways that we have learnt to forsake responsibility for our emotional lives and personal relationships, a point at which identity meets politics. So it is that reclaiming identity through politics can be part of the grounding for a re-visioning of socialism.

10 Therapy

IDENTITIES AND DESIRES

Why do we need to bring therapy and politics into relationship with each other? This is an issue that has been with us in different forms ever since the attempts of Wilhelm Reich and the Frankfurt School to bring together the writings of Marx and Freud. The issue is both theoretical and practical. For Reich in *The Sexual Revolution*, it emerged out of a recognition that the experience of the Russian Revolution had threatened the orthodox Marxist idea that the socialisation of the means of production would automatically bring about a transformation in the form of moral, sexual and personal relations of power and subordination.[1] This called for a fundamental reworking of the basic premises of orthodox Marxism.

Marxism could no longer be presented as a form of economic determinism. The relationship between 'base' and 'superstructure', as conceived in the Marxism of the Second International, had to be fundamentally reworked with the historical experience of the Russian Revolution. Reich recognised this need even if he could not achieve the task. He could not resolve the relationship between psychoanalysis and Marxism which in his work remained mechanically related to each other.[2] But he did at least identify some of the important issues which we have tended to ignore as his writings have been marginalised within a structuralist tradition that has been too keen to dismiss his work as a form of biologism.[3] His recognition of the importance of bodily experience offers a crucial challenge to a tradition of Enlightenment modernity which Lukàcs identifies with 'the antimonies of bourgeois thought'.[4] As it is, Marxist theory, even in its structuralist reinterpretation, has often remained trapped within the rationalist dualism of 'subjectivity' and 'objectivity'.

In the 1920s, different critiques of orthodox Marxism were developed. It is still important to learn from them. In the writings of Lukàcs, Gramsci and Korsch we find a recovery of the dialectical relation between history and consciousness and the continuing importance of Hegel for an understanding of Marx's development.[5] But a tradition which recognises the importance of Hegel does not necessarily prepare us to value individual experience or the meaningfulness of individual lives. This was an issue the Frankfurt School, working within a Hegelian tradition, could only partially come to terms with.[6]

Marcuse recognised the continuing importance of moral traditions which dwelt upon happiness and the satisfaction of individual desire. He investigated the depths to which bourgeois culture was infused with notions of self-denial which involved the automatic sacrifice of individual wants and desires for something higher.[7] The notion of the 'autonomy of morality', in identifying morality with an independent faculty of reason, had effectively separated questions of duty and obligation from a consideration of wants, needs, desires and emotions.

If Kant had helped prepare a liberal notion of the autonomous individual, this had been done at the cost of identifying our 'individuality' with our 'reason' and so separating it from any consideration of our needs and desires. So we can easily grow up priding ourselves on the ease with which we have sacrificed our wants and desires to fulfil goals we have set ourselves through reason alone. While this can show a certain strength of character, it unwittingly encourages a morality of self-denial, as we have seen. We strongly identify our sense of masculine identity with the goals and purposes we have set ourselves, whether this be doing well at school or making lots of money. It becomes easy to feel morally self-righteous because of the sacrifices we have made.

Within a middle-class masculine culture, this is strongly tied to notions of guilt and responsibility. We are left with a strong sense of what we 'ought' to think and feel. We often do our best to mould ourselves within this image. Paradoxically, this can leave us with a relatively weak sense of individual identity – of what we want and desire individually. This is something that is all the more surprising because of the ease with which we continue talking as men about our individual wants, needs and desires. The talk so easily becomes empty. This was something Marcuse recognised in his desire to keep alive traditions of thought and feeling which could focus these issues for us, even if they tended to be egoistic. This could possibly help explain the ability of Marcuse to appreciate the theoretical and practical significance of the women's movement in the last years of his life.[8]

But it was Adorno, a colleague of Marcuse in the Frankfurt School, who wrote most acutely of the ways individual lives are 'damaged' within capitalist society.[9] He was sceptical about the very notion of 'individual experience'. He saw this as one of the powerful myths of bourgeois society. Long before the insights of post-structuralism, he saw the individual as irredeemably fragmented. This was a reality of individual existence in modern society, that a social theory wedded to assumptions of individual choice and decision was incapable of perceiving. In a strange way this finds echoes in the post-structuralist theory that became fashionable in the 1980s, although, since this often continues this very fragmentation within a theoretical realm, it often becomes part of the problem. Our fragmentation is presented as inevitable, to be accepted almost as a matter of fate. To think that we might be able to heal ourselves is supposedly only to show our naïvety.[10]

In the 1970s and 1980s these were to become powerful theoretical and personal issues. Often it was difficult for Marxist theory to conceive their importance and recognise their nature because they tended to be seen as 'subjective'; if these issues were to help challenge the dominant economistic interpretations of Marxism, they were never to be illuminated fully in their own right. The rediscovery of Reich's writings and the regained influence of the Frankfurt School barely helped to focus attention. These writings were often abstract and difficult. Reich was often misread in the early 1970s, making it seem that the path to personal change simply involved the rejection of all forms of repression.[11] This was a period of frantic activity and experimentation but the analysis often did not go deep enough. Often the writings could not illuminate the predicament many people faced in the post-war world.

Issues of personal identity had become central and not only for the middle class. With the breakdown of many working-class communities, men and women had to find a new identity. They could not rely upon the same kind of support from those around them. Women were often earning and did not want to accept traditional subordination in the home so that relations between the sexes were being redefined. There seemed to be more of a cultural break between generations that left many people confused in their sense of self.

This was particularly clear for a younger generation growing up in the 1950s and 1960s. The experience of liberal education often worked to individualise people's sense of themselves. Equality of opportunity had become a central notion in the organisation of schooling and in the relationship between social classes and ethnic groups. Often it worked to make people feel that it was their responsibility to find a place in the world and that they only had themselves to blame if they could not make a 'success' of themselves. If this could at another level confirm people in their sense that they had as much right as everyone else to have a good life, a sense of class and ethnic solidarity and loyalty was often weakened.

Men often became less inclined to identify themselves so strongly with the work ethic. Often the job was just a way of earning money. Men did not expect to find the same dignity and self-respect in the work they were doing. They knew that, with changes in the labour process, work was likely to be boring and routine. Young people looked for more sense of themselves in music, clothes and friendships. There was the sharpening of generations as the development of a specific youth culture gave young people an independent identity. They came to live much more in their own world, a world which was not any longer shared by their parents. Often there was hostility. Sometimes it was a culture shared with other people of the same age, regardless of their class backgrounds. Marxism was slow to recognise the importance and significance of these generational differences. They did not fit the theory.[12]

MORALITY AND IDENTITY

There was relatively little understanding of the workings of moral culture in the radical politics of the 1960s and 1970s. Often it was taken for granted. There was some sense of the workings of 'possessive individualism' but this often led to a rejection of individualism in general as inherently bourgeois. This could help people understand the ease with which we slipped into possessive relationships, for instance, in the ways men are brought up to see women, but it could be difficult to understand how we could learn to relate more equally. This was an issue which was sharply formulated with the growth of the women's movement.

In the early 1960s, the issues of identity were more keenly focused in the writings of Laing, especially in *The Divided Self*. This seemed to resonate with the common experience, that people felt themselves to be quite different when with different people. This connected with the disorganisation of working-class and ethnic identities encouraged within the ideology of equality of opportunity. It could seem that people existed as a series of discrete identities. Laing could recognise this as a dilemma. He could help people acknowledge the 'reality' of their different experiences.

If this encouraged a form of relativism, it at least helped people acknowledge the existence of 'different realities'. This was encouraged in the wider use of drugs. It helped many people to broaden their vision of what was possible and to acknowledge that people lived in very different 'worlds'. More generally, it helped people realise that others had to be understood in their own terms, rather than simply judged according to purely external standards. This was an integral aspect of Laing's important critique of objectification, of the ways mental patients were so easily treated as objects. This was not simply a consequence of the evil intentions of doctors, but had to do with the positivist theory they had learnt to take for granted.[13]

Laing knew that it was wrong simply to fit people into categories, without understanding their experience. We threaten to invalidate people's experience if we do not take people seriously on their own terms. This involves a recognition that people need their experience to be validated. This does not mean we need people to agree with us. Rather, we need people to acknowledge and confirm the truth of our experience. We have often been subtly dispossessed of this awareness within a liberal moral culture which sees experience in individual and personal terms. We fail to recognise that we need others to affirm our experience.

We also grow up to deny important aspects of our own experience. We do not want to acknowledge what we think and feel to ourselves, especially when our resentments or negative feelings seem to reflect badly on the image we have of ourselves. Either we do not want to feel this way, or else we find these thoughts and feelings unacceptable to us. We prefer not to acknowledge these aspects of our experience. This is especially severe within a culture which denies our sexual and bodily experience, and shows the importance of Freud's recognition that we are sexual beings. In this sense Freud was deeply challenging prevailing moral traditions and inherited conceptions of masculinity which, in identifying with rationality, have no place for the emotional lives of men.

As I have discussed it, the relationship between Protestantism and capitalist culture sets masculinity as divided against itself. As men, we are brought up to identify with our reason. This has to be the source of identity and knowledge. Our emotions and feelings can only lead us astray. They are not sources of knowledge. They connect us to an animal experience we should be doing our best to distance ourselves from. This is an essentially dualistic vision. In part it was an image Freud never really challenged. He found a way of identifying and learning about the conflicts this leaves people with and developed a practice within which these conflicts could be handled. This involved a partial reconciliation with aspects of our emotional experience. He could accept that it was 'normal' or 'natural' for both men and women to harbour deep resentments and jealousies towards their parents. He also recognised that it did not help people to keep this all to themselves.

Repressed and unacknowledged feelings would continue to affect the ways we could relate to others. We would continue to be trapped by patterns we remained largely unaware of. The fact that we are unaware of them does not mean for Freud that they do not have consequences for the ways we relate. But he also recognised that it was not easy to gain this understanding of ourselves. Rather than, as an Enlightenment tradition would have it, being people who seek knowledge, Freud understood how much effort we put into avoiding the truth about ourselves and our relationships. This knowledge often involves pain and difficulty. It is not simply an intellectual achievement. It involves accepting difficult feelings and emotions.

Freud also understood how deeply individuals are affected in their close personal relationships. They can cause enormous suffering and misery which is too often minimised through being identified as 'personal' or 'subjective'. But as men brought up to identify with the goals we set for ourselves through reason alone, it can be difficult to value these aspects of our experience. Within a Protestant culture we learn to take whatever injuries or humiliations we suffer as if they are signs of our manliness. Often this makes it hard to identify the abuse we have suffered, say as children, for what it was. We constantly take personal life for granted, having learnt to identify ourselves with achievements in the public world. This is not simply an issue of individual attitude but of the inherited culture of masculinity.

Marx also acknowledged the ways capitalist society subordinates people's relationships with each other. It fostered an ethic of individual ambition and success that tempts us into feeling that people do not really need each other. It is in the struggle for individual achievement, rather than in meaningful work, that men in particular were to find individual realisation. This could encourage people to mistreat each other, to use each other as means. This is partly what made it necessary within a capitalist culture to develop an ethic which encouraged people to feel that it was always possible to choose to relate to others, not merely as means, but also as ends in themselves. This partly explains the crucial position of Kantian ethics within bourgeois moral theory.

This ethic worked to legitimate the relations of capitalist production within which people were used as wage labour. Marx understood how working-class people often only existed as a cost of production within the capitalist firm. If firms could no longer make profit out of production then they would close down, regardless of the dedication and sacrifices of working people. These relationships of power and subordination were mystified as long as people could feel equally free to relate to others with equal dignity and respect.

Marx also understood how working people were estranged from themselves through the workings of capitalist production. This was integral to Marx's analysis of alienation in the *Paris Manuscripts*. Within the material conditions of capitalist production, people are rarely able to express their individual talents and abilities in work. For only a few does work involve a realisation of self. Marx had a deep belief in creative and productive activity as the source of our humanity, so that if we are deprived of meaningful work our humanity is violated. He tended to think that work could be restored to this centrally important position in people's lives with the socialisation of the means of production. As far as Marx was concerned, work should not have to involve a denial or sacrifice of self.

This was something that the Frankfurt School, particularly Adorno and Benjamin, were more sceptical of. They thought that Marx's emphasis on work had tied the socialist tradition too closely to an ideology of work. Orthodox Marxism had too readily identified creative expression with work – and with waged work at that – so it had often involved confusion with a capitalist ideology which stressed that human dignity and self-respect could only come through work. This is crucial for inherited conceptions of masculinity that are so closely tied to work. It easily drifts into a utilitarian ethic in which people are treated as 'useless' if they cannot work or do not work.

Resonating with a Protestant ethic, Marxism too often became incapable of challenging it as people could be treated as 'scroungers' or 'good-for-nothings'. There are depressing parallels with Soviet Marxism on this very point. If Marx meant much more by his emphasis on creative expression as the wellspring of humanity, this has proved historically difficult to sustain. The importance of estrangement was rediscovered through a very different existentialist literature. Some of the crucial connections are still to be made though the revolutions in Eastern Europe in the 1990s have discredited Marxism in a way that makes it harder to take seriously Marx's disavowals of Marxism in his own lifetime.

With the changes in the capitalist labour process, the rationalisation of work and the spread of assembly-line technology, young people are less hopeful about receiving satisfaction and meaning from work, if they can get work at all in a period of mass unemployment. This potentially undermines traditional notions of masculinity so closely tied to work. If men are more interested in finding satisfaction and realisation in other areas of their lives, this is not easy to do. Often men do not have the physical and mental space to develop meaningful relationships, though there are signs within a culture of unemployment that young men and women have sometimes been able to sustain different kinds of relationships, not without considerable threat and challenge from the state. This was an issue that Reich faced in the 1920s, particularly in his pamphlet entitled 'The Sexual Struggles of Youth'.

This shift also threatens the individual ambitions that men are brought up to identify with. Often, men, unable to prove themselves at work, will take their frustration and bitterness out in violence. The culture does not help men develop different notions of masculinity. It can be hard for men to accept the satisfaction they could discover in their relations with others. Often men are too locked into competitive relationships in which they have to prove themselves individually, in a capitalist culture that, increasingly in the 1980s and 1990s, only recognises wealth and achievement as sources of moral worth.

CHANGE, ACHIEVEMENT AND IDENTITY

How are people to change? Often it is difficult to realise the ways we inherit conceptions of personal change within the moral culture we grow up to take very much for granted. Growing up in the middle-class world of the 1950s, you were made to feel that happiness was a prize that you had to work for. It became easy to feel that if you had not struggled for something, then it could not be worth having. This can go along with an idea that you can always achieve more, that you should never be satisfied but should always reach for more. This is a central aspect of the capitalist ethic. In its own way it can undermine our sources of individual satisfaction and achievement. There is always the next mountain to climb.

This is deeply related to prevailing notions of masculinity. It can reproduce a continuing sense of dissatisfaction in men, and make men blind to their own capacities. It can fill our days with a series of activities and events as we are constantly pushing ourselves. We can easily feel that we can always pack more in, often having little sense of our own limits, of what we are capable of taking in and absorbing. This is part of a possessive relationship to our masculine experience. We can feel greedy for different experiences. Our sensitivity to the processes through which we integrate our experience is undermined as we easily become gluttons for experience. This has become an integral aspect of a capitalist culture which often leaves us, as men, feeling that we have never got enough or achieved enough.

If, as men, we ask the simple question, 'what gives us satisfaction?', we are encouraged possibly for the first time to organise differently the activities we are involved in. It is easy for this question to feel unfamiliar or even self-indulgent. We are not used to thinking about what we are getting out of our activities or relationships. Probably this question has a different meaning for men and women. It is often for men a matter of recognising that 'nothing really matters to me', when we have learnt to identify our masculinity with independence and self-sufficiency. If people and situations matter to us, then we can be hurt. Often it is easier for men not to acknowledge this vulnerability, even to ourselves. We can be so focused upon the goals we have set ourselves that it is easier not to let things matter to us. This kind of thinking can easily be dismissed as 'selfish', as if I am only involved in different activities and relationships for what I can get out of them. But the question remains important.

A competitive culture encourages us to be continually striving for more. It tempts us into being continually dissatisfied with ourselves. We can feel continually threatened by feelings of worthlessness, knowing that we could always achieve more or fearing that others are better than we are. It leaves us feeling as men that we continually have to prove ourselves. There is a pervasive feeling of fear about being alone or isolated. Often our need for others can be desperate and grasping. It is because our emotions and feelings, our desires and needs, are accepted as an aspect of an 'animal nature' that we have to escape from, that we are brought up to distance ourselves from them. It is not easy for men to learn a way back into relating to them more directly. It is not easy to accept them as the sources of knowledge they can be.

For this involves learning to trust emotions and feelings from which we have become completely estranged. We have learnt to be suspicious of them. We often fear they will make us less effective in the world where we have to struggle to prove ourselves. This is part of an estrangement from self that has become part of our masculine inheritance, and that is so taken for granted that its injuries are rendered invisible. This is something men have had to reconsider in the challenges made to our inherited conceptions of masculinity through the women's movement.[14]

Within a liberal moral culture it is easy to assume that men can change through acts of will. Often this is equally taken for granted within conceptions of socialist morality. Change has often been conceived in terms of replacing the ideals of a capitalist morality with the ideals of a socialist morality. The implicit framework within which we conceive morality and relate it to everyday experience and relationships remains largely unquestioned. It is rare to consider whether social transformation would involve a different relationship between will, reason and emotion. Rather, these assumptions have been part of the hidden history of a socialism firmly established within a rationalistic tradition, with reason and self-control as centrally organising notions. It is a strength of ecological politics to raise issues about relationships to our inner natures, for traditionally there has been little room for emotions and desires, which were taken to be inherently chaotic. In contrast to the supposed anarchy of the capitalist market, socialism would bring reason, order and control.

Within the dominant socialist traditions, personal change was often

considered as a consequence of larger social and political transformation or else as an act of individual will and determination. In many
senses these are the different sides of the same coin. The problematic
remains firmly within the dichotomy established in Kant. It rarely comes
to terms with some of the deeper assumptions of bourgeois moral culture largely because it embodies similar patterns in its relationship to
nature and emotional life. This is as true with conceptions of socialist
duty as it is for the political voluntarism that was a feature of a Leninist
tradition. Marx's insight into the ways morality is so often an expression
of particular class interests has paradoxically made it harder to develop
a fuller understanding of the importance of moral and political
culture.[15]

It became too easy to present socialism in terms of a morality which
asserted higher principles than the notions of individual selfishness and
egoism that characterised capitalist morality. This could equally confirm
socialism as a morality of self-denial in which individuals had to be prepared to sacrifice their own individual needs, wants and desires for
something higher. It was to make it harder to conceive of socialism as
involving the fulfilment and realisation of people, because it became
difficult to give weight to individual needs and wants. This kind of talk
was left to liberalism. Rather, socialism consciously became something
individuals had to be ready to sacrifice themselves for. It was to discover
its basis in the objectivism of reason and science. This inheritance is
something it has rarely escaped.

POLITICS, EMOTION AND CHANGE

These strands were given a new life and form in the political revival of
the 1960s. Politics was again to involve individual commitment and
moral concern. This was one of the strengths of the political movements
of the time. If there was a protest against notions of hierarchy and
competitiveness, this was because of the ways they were seen as
undermining people's capacities and desires to learn. Learning had to
be relevant to the kind of lives people live. Learning also had to
illuminate the contradictions of the larger society, such as imperialist
relations of power in the Vietnam war. There was also a pervasive desire
to develop different, more equal, relationships.

But there was a limited vision and understanding of how people can
change. There was a strong sense of moralism which encouraged people
to feel that it was 'wrong' to be 'jealous', 'possessive', even 'monogamous'. These feelings were treated as unacceptable and people often
did their best to conceal them, as if they were to be ashamed of

acknowledging them. It was felt that these feelings were produced within us because of the social relations of capitalist society. There was nothing 'inherent' or 'natural' about them. If we began to relate differently, we would begin to notice the ways our feelings changed. This did not challenge the form of relationship we were brought up to have with our feelings and emotions. It just promised a different rationalist reconstruction. It did not bring us into more contact with them. We still focused on the correct ways of behaving towards others.

Our feelings and emotions were still generally regarded as threatening or as self-indulgent. In a similar way to how Kant had educated bourgeois society to discount their emotions and feelings as 'inclinations' so that people could behave in ways dictated by their reason, so socialist morality recast itself within this image. It inherited a similar tradition. At the very moment at which people often thought they were challenging repression and forming new kinds of relationships, they were invoking a new form of moralism. This is not to underestimate the importance of social and personal experimentation, which is important to dwell upon and learn from. Experience gained in collective living has generally been too little valued and shared.

The experience of this period is often dismissed as 'naïve' rather than learnt from. This is understandable. Many people had been deeply hurt. There was little understanding of the sources of the pain or recognition of how it could be dealt with. At the same time, a recognition grew that the Left needed more psychological theory and understanding, and that Freud needed to be re-evaluated. Sometimes this developed as a theoretical interest. Sadly, it encouraged a false rejection of Reich, who was identified with this earlier period and who was crudely to be rejected for being 'biologistic'.

This was part of the more general dismissal that was one of the worst features of the dominance of Althusserian Marxism. A structuralist tradition did not make it easy to learn and reflect upon the earlier experience and practice, especially as it brought the very category of 'experience' into disrepute. This was not its concern. This history was to be left as a form of youthful embarrassment. Theory and practice were sadly separated, as theory was to be firmly established as 'theoretical practice'. If this did not last for long, its inheritance is still with us in post-structuralism.[16]

This is not to dismiss the lessons that have been learnt from a recognition of the importance of Freud and Lacan.[17] I still feel ready to learn about Lacan's contribution, though I am sceptical about the ways the French critique of this tradition in the writings of Deleuze and Guattari tend to be ignored.[18] Our importation tends to be very selective, as it was with the writings of Althusser. Often this has helped the Left towards what seems like a theoretically radical critique, but one which very much remains within the unquestioned confines of a rationalist tradition. It gives us a different language to interpret our experience, but says little about the *difficulties* people face living differently within class, ethnic and gender relations of power and dominance.

Part of its strength is in offering a way of thinking and validating different forms of sexuality and challenging the dominance of heterosexual norms, helping people think about how sexuality is socially and historically constituted. But it does not help people seek a different relationship between their reason, emotions, feelings, needs and desires. It does not give people ways of working with these tensions and contradictions in their experience. This is something the women's movement was coming to terms with in consciousness-raising groups and was later developed in the practice of feminist therapy.[19]

I want to share some of the experience of Red Therapy as it relates to issues of masculinity and politics. This grew out of the experience of a group involved in community and industrial politics in East London in the early and mid-1970s. We came to therapy not simply as an intellectual interest, but out of a need to develop a way of dealing with the different conflicts we faced in living our everyday lives. We also wanted to discover the relevance of this experience for people with a different class, ethnic and racial background. Some of us had had an experience of psychoanalytic therapy and felt the need for something different. We naturally looked to Reich as someone who, in an earlier generation, had attempted to relate therapy and politics, even if he had been blind to more recent concerns of sexual politics.

We recognised that we operated in a very different situation, but he helped us feel the validity of what we were doing. We also learnt from the ways his work had been developed in different forms of bodily orientated therapies such as bioenergetics, under the influence of Alexander Lowen.[20] This had been connected in an eclectic way with *Gestalt* theory developed by Fritz Perls and Encounter by Will Schutz and Carl Rogers.[21] These were all part of new movements that worked with the tensions in present experience and relationships that had developed in critical relationship to the historical focus of psychoanalysis in what was called the 'Growth Movement'.

We were familiar with the critiques of these techniques and methods and aware of the ways they implicitly carried certain individualistic conceptions of what people are like and what matters to people. This did not worry us too much. We thought these techniques could be appropriated and redefined within a socialist context. We recognised the validity of what they offered in our own individual and group processes through our participation in different groups in the different London growth centres. Sometimes we would consciously go to different groups to learn techniques and methods which would be useful in developing our own practice. For a couple of years we used to meet every Friday night in a large room off the Bethnal Green Road as well as organising longer intensives for ourselves. We learnt from each other. We developed a sense of what is possible in a self-help context. It continually renewed our sense of the importance of therapy both theoretically and practically for a renewal of socialist politics.

There is often a radical disjunction between the theory and practice of socialist politics. We spend time talking grandly and hopefully about a different kind of society and we find ourselves spending time knocking on people's doors, giving out leaflets, selling newspapers, to people who are often less than sympathetic to what we are doing. People involved in different kinds of activist politics have to live with this disjunction. It is not easy. Different traditions have coped with it in different ways. Many find consolation in the role Lenin prepared for generations of Leftists in his influential *What is to be done?* It provides a clear and unambiguous role for socialists to bring a political consciousness that would otherwise be lacking to working people.

This can give a sense of 'rightness' and legitimacy to what one is doing, regardless of the difficulties of connecting to the everyday realities of working people's lives. Our confidence and security come to rest in our theory and political principles. This has been an important bulwark, especially in periods in which the Left has been small and hopelessly isolated. Within this context, it is easy, especially for men brought up to pride themselves on their self-denial, to see oneself as a 'political militant', ready to make all the necessary sacrifices for a revolutionary struggle. This picture still has a powerful hold, even if it is in deep crisis as is the conception of Leninist politics that sustains it. The revolutions in Eastern Europe in 1989 have brought a Leninist tradition into question.[22]

MEN, POLITICS AND THERAPY

We need a different conception of politics which can sustain a different vision of masculinity. This involves understanding the deeper challenge of feminism. This is difficult for men because it involves understanding how we can change ourselves. This is threatening. We were brought up to feel comfortable with tasks which could be tackled with hard work and resolution. It is easy for us to turn everything into a task. We feel safer. We measure ourselves, even gain a sense of identity, through achieving the tasks or goals we have set ourselves. In this way our experience becomes *externalised*. We can cope as long as we can organise the different tasks that we have to tackle. This form of instrumentalism has a deep connection with masculinity. It makes us feel capable in the public sphere.

It is more difficult when the personal is claimed by feminism to be 'political'. This is something we can often only cope with if the personal itself is redefined as a series of externalised demands and obligations involving so many hours of housecare and childcare. We can *barely* cope with this. It is so easy to continue feeling that women should be there for us and available on our terms. It is harder to learn how to gain more support in our relationships with other men, knowing women will no longer do all the emotional work in relationships. This shifts the terms of relationships, both with ourselves and with others. Women have increasingly made demands that men take more emotional responsibility as well as involve themselves in housework and childcare. This has precipitated a crisis in traditional forms of masculinity, requiring men to discover different resources within themselves that we might never have learnt to value.

Our group shared a theoretical commitment to sexual politics. We knew how important this was in connecting us to the concerns, fears, anxieties and hopes of working-class people. At the same time we often felt pulled to pieces by the demands of the political lives we had chosen. The demands of political work in the mid-1970s, whether it was doing agitational work at Ford or organising a food co-op on a local estate, seemed all-important. We were so aware of how much needed to be done. 'Political work' came to seem so much more important and significant than our individual needs and wants. Our sense of individual needs gradually atrophied. We tended to lose a sense of self, of our needs and desires. This was an issue we could name and confront in therapy. It meant confronting difficult feelings and exploring some of the sources of our political ideas in our early experiences in our families. This involved honest exploration, often difficult and painful, not a simplistic reductionism.

It also meant coming to terms with what we expected of ourselves. This is especially strong for men who have been brought up to feel that we *should* be able to cope with anything the world throws at us. These were just different opportunities to prove ourselves. Therapy did not invalidate the importance of what we were doing, but helped bring into focus what we were doing to ourselves in the process. What was clear was that we were rarely in touch with what this life was doing to us or how it made us feel about ourselves, partly because we often obliterated any sense of personal life through our very level of activity. This is also a common experience for men. We did not realise how many conventional masculine expectations we were living out. We were constantly involved in activities. I can still remember how lost and uneasy I felt when I did not have something urgent that I needed to do. It was difficult to spend much time with myself. I lost the ability to do so.

As men, we often grow up learning to hide our vulnerability and need. We are left continually to prove that we are 'real men'. Our masculinity is constantly at risk. It is not something that we can be assured of. It is something we always have to prove and be ready to defend. This is something we can share as men, despite important differences in our class or ethnic backgrounds. It is hardly surprising that we learn to hide our vulnerability even from ourselves. Vulnerability either as sadness or fear might be something we respond to with anger, hitting out at the first person around or at someone we feel close to, as if they are to blame, or else something we learn automatically to swallow and ignore. The ways we learn to deal with our emotions and feelings will be deeply affected by our class and ethnic backgrounds but also by the particular relationships we have had with our parents and siblings. This is something we have to learn through gaining a different kind of experience of ourselves.

This is a difficult experience to share. I think that some of the expressive methods of the Growth Movement have been important because of the prevailing intellectualist culture. Within the middle class especially, it can be easier to talk about our feelings than to share them. We learn to intellectualise our feelings. This gives us a way of controlling them. We learn to talk our way out of situations. This has sometimes created difficulties for men's consciousness-raising groups. It has been difficult for heterosexual men to move closer to other men, to share more and feel deeper contact. In an important sense, our language has become estranged. It threatens to become empty and rhetorical. For others this is different and language can be a way of developing deeper contact with others. Again it is difficult to generalise, but it can make us suspicious of theories of language that do not appreciate this.[23]

A strong emphasis upon emotional expression as in the early years of the Growth Movement connected to people's desire to escape an intellectuality that had become second nature. This was important for a while, for it helped both men and women connect more deeply with feelings of anger, sadness, disgust and fear that sometimes we had barely come into close contact with in their lives. This could extend our emotional range, making it easier to respond appropriately in situations. When someone is in conflict, it can help to express it directly, rather than avoid it constantly.

In its own way, this could help people build a new kind of trust in their emotions and feelings as sources of knowledge which had been devalued and denigrated within a rationalist culture. People could validate themselves, gaining a deeper sense of self. This was a challenge to a culture which constantly invalidated people's emotional experience making us feel there is little to learn from it. The re-evaluation of experience as a source of knowledge was a crucial link between the politics of experience that developed in the 1970s and feminist and alternative therapies as they developed in the 1980s.

Therapy could be an important practice for men brought up to identify so strongly with their reason and intellect. We make ourselves feel in the 'right way' – the way that we can defend rationally – and we feel threatened by any signs of 'irrationality'. It can be harder to acknowledge how I feel, regardless of its 'rationality', recognising that emotions follow their own logic and reality rather than simply being subordinated to 'a logic of reason'. It is easier for us to flee difficult feelings into activities. So, for instance, it can be harder for me to stay with my feelings of sadness and loss because a relationship has ended, rather than to busy myself with different kinds of activities. We do anything to escape our feelings. We find it easy as men to believe that doing things and keeping ourselves busy will make things better. This is a deep cultural tendency.

In this way we can avoid the 'reality' of our experience. We do not face up to the feeling of sadness and loss. We do not want to recognise that we might be missing someone who has left us, especially if we know that it is right that the relationship ended. This is to admit our vulnerability. We can easily feel as men that this means someone has got one 'over' on us, that somehow we have been beaten, since life is a never-ending competitive contest. We would not want others to know how deeply we are affected, because this would be a defeat. But in this way we betray ourselves. We fail to acknowledge what we are feeling. We avoid our experience rather than live through it.

IDENTITY, THERAPY AND EMOTIONAL LIFE

Therapy can help us to a recognition of the centrality of our emotions and feelings within our experience. This is to challenge prevailing conceptions of personal identity and social theories that promise us control of our experience by saying that experience is a 'mental construction'. I might begin to realise how different it was for me to learn to stay with my feelings of loss and missing, rather than move into some activity. This is often a new experience for men. It means experiencing my feelings of loss and sadness, possibly for the first time. I can realise how much energy is taken up in avoiding these feelings.

I might have been telling myself that it did not matter to me that we had split up, that it was all for the best in the long run. I might think that if it was the right thing for us to do, why am I feeling such loss? This is the way we *invalidate* our experience and learn constantly to invalidate others'. We tell ourselves it is 'irrational' to feel the way we do. This encourages us to control emotions as quickly as possible. This is also to deny the significance of feeling. It is hard to learn that in suppressing these feelings we are supressing ourselves. We are making ourselves less than we need be. This is something a rationalist tradition has great difficulties with.

What matters to us? This is an important question. It is not a question we are encouraged to ask within a Protestant culture. But it is crucial for men as we realise that more is being demanded of us as men in our relationships. This is a matter of the domestic division of labour, but it also concerns the emotional work and labour that goes into a relationship. Women are no longer prepared to do all the emotional work. This also means acknowledging how few skills we have learnt as men in this area of our lives. Rather than the conventional notion of a man with a clear sense of himself, able to define his individual needs and wants, we often find that men define themselves emotionally in relation to women. If men get angry at women for not defining themselves, this is sometimes because of their dependency on women to provide clarity in the relationship.

Again we expect women to do this work for us. We blame them for being unsure of what they want and need when often we are unsure ourselves. Part of the power that men have traditionally had in relationships is the power to blame others and make them somehow feel responsible for our unhappiness or frustration with ourselves. Often men are relatively incapable in their private and emotional lives. We can exist as strangers to ourselves, having been estranged within a culture that refuses us emotional knowledge of ourselves. This is often the source of our deepest rage.

The Left has been slow to understand these insights. They are too threatening to its own structures of power. It does not realise how generalised this crisis in masculinity has become. It wants men to continue to identify with their roles at work because this is the area of their lives in which they have industrial power. It fails to come to terms with the changes in the labour process and the bitterness that many working-class people feel at the kind of work they have to do. This rigidity makes people cynical about the Left, especially of people who do not work in these conditions themselves. Often men are taken up with concerns in their relationships but feel uneasy in sharing these because they have been brought up to consider them 'private'. Men feel the need for a language to identify and name their frustrations, hurts, joys and pains. Men also yearn for ways of learning how to relate to these lost parts of themselves. There is a growing awareness that, if you suppress these parts of yourself, they do not just go away as a rationalist culture suggests, but will fester and continue to affect who you are with yourself and with others. If it is not just work that is a means of creative identity for men, it becomes important to look at the difficulties of the culture and institutions of a capitalist democracy to give full value to personal relationships, sexuality and children. This involves a recognition that society does not help us give value to these experiences as men. In this sense, it disorganises our sense of ourselves as men and makes it hard for us to value what matters to us in our lives, as we subordinate our sexuality and relationships to seek a worthwhile identity in achievement in work alone.

MORALITY AND RESPONSIBILITY

Eileen Fairweather's article in *Spare Rib* on abortion entitled 'The feelings behind the slogans' shows the importance of developing a politics that is in touch with the emotional realities of people's lives. This involves challenging the rationalist moral traditions we so often reproduce within sexual politics and within the Left more generally. She points out that:

> The women's movement was still very young when abortion first became a political football. We duly kicked back and, faced with the opposition's set of slogans, defensively came up with our own. In our rush to do that, the complexity of abortion and its emotional significance for women somehow got lost.
>
> (*Spare Rib* 87, Oct 1979)

She recognises the need to face these painful and difficult issues. This takes a different kind of strength.[24]

It involves challenging the notion that if a woman has made a 'rational decision' to have an abortion, this means she has no reason for all the difficult feelings of shame, regret, anger, longing and sadness that might emerge. This is the way in which a woman's experience is invalidated. Often, as men, we do not want to see these feelings. They are too threatening. They force us to face ourselves and our involvement in the situation. Often we do not find it easy to live through these difficult emotions with someone, let alone face our own. The article rightly challenges men, saying that 'The (relative) enthusiasm with which the male Left adopted the slogan "abortion on demand" may well be because abortion can mean men avoid any responsibility for the less pleasant consequences of sexuality.'

Recognition of the emotions and feelings people have is an integral aspect of validating their experience. This is a way of bringing us closer to the everyday experience of people. Acknowledging all the difficult and 'unacceptable' feelings we carry and do our best to dismiss and ignore can help us into a deeper contact and relationship with our own personal and collective history. It can also deepen a sense of what we share, at some human level, with people who have had very different backgrounds and experience. This is something we can learn for ourselves from therapy.

It can make an enormous difference to our understanding and grasp of what matters to people, rather than what we think *should* matter to them given our theoretical understanding. It can be humbling to share an experience of exploration through which someone is coming to identify his or her own needs. This is something that people have to explore for themselves rather than being legislated for them by reason alone. It is a deeply democratic process. It promises to give a more realistic basis to our politics.

I remember working in the Ford group and often encouraging workers to come to meetings we had arranged. Sometimes they would feel guilty at not coming and find it difficult to tell us they wanted the time with their families. They did not want to let us down. This was a situation we helped create since we wanted them to feel that organising in the plant was the most important thing for them and so they should be ready to sacrifice time and energy. It took time to appreciate the realities of people's lives. This is not to say that politics did not matter to them, but it mattered in a different way. In time, some people learnt to talk more openly with us.

Often they were more concerned with working out difficulties in their personal relationships. They wanted a chance to talk this out with other men. This need for communication is rarely appreciated on the Left, partly because we get trapped into proving ourselves as 'militant'. This can mean separating ourselves from our own backgrounds and histories, feeling ashamed of our own middle-class backgrounds. We can become even more moralistic in our politics. Since we are closed to our own histories and experience, it is hard to expect us to be open to others.

We lose a sense of what it means to talk about the contradictions in people's experience since our political traditions are too closely tied to notions of 'correct principles' and 'being right' for us to understand this. We easily reproduce a rationalist moral culture which derides and devalues a learning from experience, in which we are concerned to do the 'right thing' regardless of our emotions, desires, feelings and wants. This becomes the way we can prove ourselves. There is a strong sense of duty which has for long characterised both Leninist and libertarian politics. It becomes easy to dismiss therapy as a form of self-indulgence and experience as unreliable as a source of values, on the grounds that it is socially and historically constructed. It has often separated a sense of politics from the concerns and experiences of many people and has often made socialist politics in both Eastern and Western Europe abstract and moralistic.

It remains important to develop different kinds of political practice which give people the authority and legitimacy to discern their own needs, rather than having these legislated for them by an all-knowing reason or an all-powerful state party. It necessarily means becoming aware of traditions of self-denial. If we lose touch with the desires and needs of people, our socialism comes to lack vision and imagination and its language becomes discredited, as the revolutions in Eastern Europe have shown. It also lacks any basis in what matters to people, and a sense of how a capitalist democracy makes it hard to value ourselves and our relationships. As Felix Guattari expresses it in an interview in *Time Out*:

> It's also significant that capitalism excludes and ignores more and more forms of social 'valorisation'. By valorisation I mean how we choose an order of priorities, and decide what something is *worth*. Think of all the work done by women, and by children, think of all the use-values and desires that make up everyday life – relegated by capitalism as worthless.
>
> (*Time Out*, March 27, 1981)

Eileen Fairweather helps us focus some of these issues in thinking about abortion. She touches the shame and difficulty. As she says,

> What we seem to forget is that women in their thousands won't come flocking to our demos when so many have never even *talked* to anyone of their own experience. The Antis have 'God and right' on their side; we have a legacy of shame and secrecy, and often pain which goes so deep you can't even bear to think about it – much less fight back.
>
> (*Spare Rib* 87, Oct 1979)

The very ways that people are consoled with the assurance that this was the 'right decision' can make it harder to understand what is involved.

Often the issues of responsibility are far more complex than we allow for in socialist discussion.

We lose a sense of the individuality of the experience, the need for each person to work through the experience in their own way with the support and understanding of others. This can involve acknowledging the contradictions of responsibility. Sometimes our feelings are much more ambiguous. The issues are more complex. As Linda Bird Francke has written,

> Some women experience nothing but relief after abortion. Others only feel guilty because they *don't* feel guilty. But for many women, it's not so simple: 'I love children so much. It makes it even harder when you already have a child. This time I couldn't help thinking it was a human being. If you asked me how I felt about abortion, I would say I was against it. I feel very hypocritical.'
>
> (Francke 1979, p.99)

How are we to learn about how people change? Socialist theory has too often been restricted through notions of 'material self-interest'. In this way, it has reproduced the common sense of a utilitarian moral culture rather than help challenge it. It is rarely in touch with the deeper desires and needs of people and the ways these are woven into their everyday lives. Socialist theory as it has developed in both Eastern and Western Europe is often blocked by a crude distinction between narrow self-interest supposed to characterise the moral motivation in capitalist society, and notions of altruism and moral duty which supposedly come into their own within a socialist society. The movements against state parties in 1989 in Poland, Hungary, Czechoslovakia and East Germany have set the terms for freedom and democracy in different terms, if there is to be a valid alternative vision to capitalist market notions.[25]

The ways in which we are encouraged to identify socialism with collective and communal goals can blunt our recognition of the individuality of people's experience. This has been all the more tragic in Eastern Europe since people have been systematically denied a sense of human dignity and respect within everyday relationships of subordination. They recognise that the exploitation working people have to endure within capitalist society often goes together with consumer goods and a sense of political freedom that is unknown in the East. This is seen, at least, as a compensation for a shared feeling that people count for very little, especially at work. They know that they are replaceable and that the firm only wants them as labour.

In the West, it has been possible for people to be more identified with whatever sense of equality and respect can be guaranteed through their legal and political rights. The Left barely appreciates this, and it often derides these as 'bourgeois freedoms', falsely assuming that they do not themselves correspond to real needs like food, clothing and housing which are supposedly set apart as being 'material'. Working people have much more sense of the historical struggles through which freedom and representative democracy were secured. They know, as did people in Eastern Europe, that things can be much worse without them.

MEN, INDIVIDUALITY AND EXPERIENCE

This makes it important for us to learn *how* to validate the individuality of experience. People need to feel the validity of their emotions and feelings. People have a right to feel angry, hurt, sad, upset, disappointed, happy. Yet it has been made a struggle within a duty-bound rationalist moral culture for us to feel the *validity* of our feelings, rather than simply to judge ourselves lacking, worthless or inadequate because of them. Men can be made to feel that it is 'soft' to be upset and vulnerable so that it is a sign of weakness if we allow ourselves to feel this way. We judge ourselves critically before others have a chance to, so as to maintain control of the situation. We limit our lives and curtail our experience. Women can similarly be made to feel that it is wrong for them to feel angry, almost as if they have no right to this particular emotion.

These emotions are organised through the sexual relations of power and subordination which make different forms of emotional expression acceptable for men and women. Both men and women, then, need to learn to extend their range of emotional expression. This is not to live up to some abstract or idealised image of ourselves or to feel that we can change through acts of will alone. It is to acknowledge as a first step the importance of discovering what it is that we are feeling, to accept the reality of our experience. This has not been made easy.

There is a deep historical connection between masculinity and some idea of self-sufficiency.[26] Boys are brought up to pride themselves in their independence. Needing others is a sign of weakness. Often there is a difference between the self-control and definition that men achieve in their public lives and the needs for dependency we experience in private. In our relationships with friends and lovers, it can be harder to define a clear sense of ourselves, of our needs and wants. It is easier for us to feel responsible for providing the shoulder that supports others. Often we know little of ourselves emotionally. We are often displaced from our emotional selves with relatively little self-knowledge.

This can make it harder for men to connect with people more emotionally in a personal relationship. We feel easier *doing* things. I know more personally that I often do not make demands in my emotional and sexual relationship. I am challenged for not giving enough within the relationship. I know that I will tend to put up with things as if content with relatively little so that I do not initiate the conflicts which help us work through issues. I tend to put my energies into my work so that little of myself is focused on what is really happening in the relationship. I have got more understanding of what has made me this way. Therapy has helped me recognise how this has been affected through relationships in my family of origin. Even if I am impatient with some of these patterns, it can be difficult to change them. I think it is quite common for men to be challenged for being detached and unavailable. This is something we can learn to change but only once we have experienced how it blocks our own satisfaction in the relationship. It is part of learning to engage in a more equal relationship.

Sometimes, in response to feminism, men have been affected by a deep sense of guilt at our situations within the sexual relations of power. Men have often taken a supportive relationship to the women's movement, which has been damaging, while men have been left feeling that their masculinity is irredeemable, as if they have to reject themselves as men to be able to change. Sometimes this has only provided a hidden layer of suppressed rage and anger. Therapy can sometimes help us acknowledge and work through these difficult feelings. It can help us take more responsibility for ourselves as we understand the different levels at which we are feeling affected by feminist challenges.

It is important to explore what is happening on both sides of a relationship rather than just assume that men have to be responsible for all the suffering and misery. This is to continue to take on a responsibility that is not ours alone, as if the private realm is also now to be taken over. It can also help us own our own anger. We can learn to share our vulnerability with other men and learn to get support. We can no longer expect women to take the strain of our emotional lives, especially when we are so unclear about the kind of demands we are making. This is emotional work that we have to learn to do for ourselves.

As men, we are often brought up to expect others to serve us and to provide us with happiness and joy. We are very externally motivated because we are brought up to have an active relationship with the world and very little relationship with ourselves. If something is going wrong in a relationship, it is easy to blame the woman or man we are having a relationship with. We think it is bound to be different with someone else. This is especially easy to feel in our twenties. It is only later when we are forced to recognise that similar issues seem to crop up in different relationships that we begin to wonder about these patterns. This forces us to take more responsibility for ourselves. This can be especially difficult on the Left, in which it has become almost second nature to blame all personal misery and unhappiness on social conditions. Of course, it is important to challenge the ways society encourages us always to blame ourselves. Within a Protestant moral culture, we absorb a self-critical identity that encourages us to think we are always at fault for our misery and unhappiness, thinking things would be different if we had only worked harder at school, for instance. But, at another level, it is also important to realise how we might unwittingly be reproducing other cultural assumptions.

As men, it can be an important realisation to appreciate how we expect to receive everything from outside ourselves. We have little sense of what we can give to ourselves, of the ways we can nourish and enjoy ourselves. This is connected at a deep level with the disgust and estrangement we are brought up to feel within a westernised Christian culture for our bodies. We discover that we know our bodies very little. We have little relationship with them. Learning to connect to our emotional and somatic lives can give us a different sense of ourselves. It can help us take more responsibility for our lives.

It can make us realise how much we project on others, how easily we blame others for our own miseries. If the different techniques we can learn from the Growth Movement often contain simplistic notions of our relationship to the social world and so a false sense of the sources of our misery, they can also help us to a sharpened sense of individual responsibility. We are forced to learn of the different ways we are individually complicit in situations and relationships. We learn how we also continually reproduce situations that frustrate us.

IDENTITIES, INJURIES AND THERAPY

Therapy can bring us into deeper contact with ourselves. It can give us a more historical sense of ourselves, learning how we continually reproduce certain patterns which have been established in childhood. Often the ways we were brought up estrange us from our childhood, from the inner child that we continue to carry inside of ourselves. Sometimes we can discover how we continually give to others the very things that we want for ourselves. I have learnt the different ways I was affected by my father dying when I was still very young. This meant that I had to become adult before my time. It meant that I never had a full enough chance fully to live out my childhood. These needs remain unrecognised with me. It can mean that I get continually confused between my adult and my child needs. This is something I can learn to be clear about. I can learn about the different ways I can acknowledge and nourish these different needs.

This exploration gives a different sense of the complexities of such notions as 'fulfilment' and 'realisation', which, within an orthodox Marxist tradition, have been too exclusively identified with human labour and so with paid work. It gives a fuller sense of the scope and depth of human needs. This does not mean that these needs are fixed or ahistorical. Rather, they have a particularity and individuality of their own. This is something that therapy can help me learn about. In this way, it also challenges the false sense of fulfilment and happiness which a market capitalist society fosters when it talks exclusively of individual success and achievement.

It can help validate a different sense of what is important in human life, which extends to a recognition of love and relationships. This is not simply an intellectual knowledge. It is also a felt and experienced knowledge. It deepens our sense of human fulfilment and makes us aware of the costs of living within the competitive and hierarchical relations of a capitalist society. These connections are not always made, especially in many traditional forms of psychotherapy. Often quite conservative conclusions are drawn.

This is what makes it necessary to engage theoretically with the different traditions of thought and practice that have developed rather than simply with psychoanalytic theory alone. Feminist psychotherapy is beginning to work in this way.[27] This is what men are also going to have to learn to do. In the last few years, there has been more experience in the different forms of therapy than there have been careful evaluations. This is partly because we have often reached for these therapies, not out of intellectual curiosity, but from a deep sense of personal need and crisis.

Therapy inevitably challenges our sense of the importance of our early childhood experiences in our lives. I think it is quite common for this to be reassessed when people are in their thirties. When people have children this often initiates it, because feelings that have been long buried seem to find a way to the surface of our lives. This helps challenge the notions of agelessness that seemed to be an aspect of the politics of the 1960s and which went along with a naïve sense of progressivism. This illusion was rudely shattered with the economic crisis of the mid-1970s and the long years of Thatcherism. It encouraged us to be more specific about our generational experience as later generations were more prepared to identify with the goods and aspirations of the capitalist market economy.

We need to be far clearer about what was actually learnt in the struggles of the 1960s and 1970s about the restructuring of capitalist society and the possibilities of freedom and justice that it fostered. It is clear that the issues of gender and personal life have become important in a new way, as have ecological concerns as we become aware of the injuries that we do to nature and to the planet. With the advent of AIDS, new issues have been opened up and made sexuality an area of increasing tension and difficulty. In general, it seems much harder to establish sustaining sexual relationships with people. This is partly because so many more women have changed under the influence of the women's movement than men seem to have changed. Women demand much more from relationships than they used to and are more ready to live satisfying lives on their own.

The suspicions that women have often had about the changes that heterosexual men would make if they organised collectively, and the fears that men have had in giving up powers that they had long assumed to be their own, have kept a men's movement relatively weak.[28] This has been a pity. I do not think it had to develop in a way which would mean men regaining power that had been conceded to women, though this has happened with a large men's rights movement in the United States. There are more fruitful possibilities. But, certainly, if it has been difficult to raise issues of men's consciousness and experience within the Left, it has been far harder to take therapeutic theory and practice seriously. Therapy was a practice we could barely mention in the Big Flame of the mid-1970s. It was difficult enough to get people to take our men's group seriously.

If therapy draws us back into an involving relationship with ourselves and our individual histories, it also promises a much deeper sense of what is important in human life. For a time, at least it can encourage people to withdraw from activist politics. I do not think this is always a bad thing. I think we need times when we are more in touch with our inner lives. This is important work we have to do for ourselves to deepen our contact with ourselves. It confronts us with difficult moments, especially when we work through our relationships with our parents. This can be awkward, especially when it means relating to a class and ethnic experience we have done our best to disown.

But therapy does not have to foster a deterministic theory in which we are destined to live out these patterns established in our early relations. In reality, we are more likely to live out these unacknowledged familial patterns when we have refused to face them or dismissed this form of work as 'navel-gazing' or 'self-indulgence'. It does give us more of a sense of the ways in which our present is deeply informed by these earlier relations.

This certainly complicates our sense of our lives and a sense of male identity that is identified with achievement, and questions the naïve rationalism that is so current in cultural explanations of our behaviour. It broadens our sense of reason and rationality as we learn to integrate our emotions and feelings with it. It can also help us learn from our dreams and unconscious life. It can help us re-evaluate what matters to us, as we learn to appreciate our friends and relationships as much as our work. Our life can become fuller. This can give us more sense of the depths of human experience.

It also gives us a sharper sense of the ways in which people are hurt and their dignity abused. We all carry these scars with us. These are not only inflicted by our parents, but also by the everyday humiliations and degradations of class, race and gender experience. We have a very different understanding of exploitation as we see it not exclusively as a matter of surplus value, but as a moral and political issue of abuse, respect and humiliation.[29] This can also deepen our understanding of the workings of society as it bears on individual lives and so sharpen our resistance to the indignities and miseries that people suffer.

Therapy can also give us a different sense of what is involved in having more control of our lives. We are forced to realise the ways we often project and 'act out' in our relations with others. We learn of the ways we are still influenced by the unacknowledged expectations of our parents and the sharply self-critical sense of self we inherit, even if these are carried through in a realm of political activity they would barely have recognised. In a very real sense, we have to learn to separate from these relationships, but this can only be done by facing them. This is not done through ignoring them or wishing them away. We have to learn to face them and live through the difficult experiences they present us with. We have to learn to acknowledge their role in our lives not only intellectually, but experientially.

Different kinds of therapy help us to do this in different ways. It is often a disorientating experience within a liberal moral culture that has taught us to believe in mind over matter, and that if we turn away from painful experience it will go away. Therapy does not leave our images of ourselves untouched. This involves a clearer connection with the process and experience of our everyday lives. In many ways this involves facing ourselves as we recognise how few of our rationalistic moral and political traditions support us in doing this.

I think it is important to have moments in which we stop and look at our lives – to re-evaluate what matters to us and what freedom and expression we are struggling for. There are moments when we have to experience the reality of our misery rather than run away from it. For years, people on the Left have sought the private support of different forms of psychotherapy. Sometimes this has been connected to a theoretical task of bringing Freud and Marx closer to each other. This is a new task for each generation. But there is more to be learnt from the theory and practice of therapy, both for ourselves and also for the transformation of our vision of politics. We do not only learn about the processes of 'the other', we also always learn about ourselves. This was part of Freud's discovery. It is not easy to relate this understanding to our politics, for it raised difficult questions about the place of illusions in our conceptions of both personal and political changes. It can create confusions of its own. We are tempted, particularly under the influence of Freud, to limit our hopes for change and even to be critical of our attempts to do so.

I do not think that therapy relates to an autonomous inner realm which is exclusively its own, as many have been tempted into thinking in different ways with Lacan and Klein. I think the connections between the inner and the outer are more direct but also more difficult. We have barely begun to isolate the crucial questions which could relate therapy to the public sphere.[30] At another level, therapy teaches its own humility. It gives a lasting sense of the depths and joys of human life. It makes us aware of our individualities, but also of the depths to which we share our individual social experience with others.

Therapy has the potential to deepen our sense of injustice and to enrich our sense of politics as we recognise the different ways people are hurt and damaged. It complicates our sense of human freedom, showing how much more is involved in gaining control over our lives than we are accustomed to assume. It limts our sense of politics as we learn to expect less from political changes. As we learn to take greater responsibility for our emotional lives, it encourages us to rethink the relations between the 'personal' and the 'political'. It also shows the depths to which we can be involved and enriched in our relations with others. It can help us to treasure individuality while keeping sight of the importance of transforming relations of power and subordination.

11 Politics

MORALISM, EXPERIENCE AND POLITICS

The crisis in the mid-1970s and the abilities of Thatcherism in the 1980s to take a moral and political initiative have brought much rethinking and openness on the Left. People are beginning to talk to each other. There is less of the sectarian grip. People are more openly confused about how Thatcherism has managed to construct such a lasting political hegemony while the Left had seemed blind to the implications of widespread structural changes. Somehow people are ready to ask more basic questions, especially under the influence of the women's, gay, lesbian and ecology movements. It is when people find themselves in a 'political situation', like a conference, that the old sectarian reflexes seem to operate.

At a broader level, people seem most stuck around issues of political organisation and of the relationship of movements to political parties. There is a widespread questioning of the limits of politics, as if we have placed too many hopes in political transformations and not considered the relationship of politics to everyday life. Somehow these have become crucial matters, especially with the dramatic changes in Eastern Europe which have raised fundamental questions about the relationship of socialism to democracy. They bring into question inherited moral and political traditions on the Left which have reinforced statist visions and failed to validate the importance of democratic institutions and relationships.[1]

The events of 1968 marked a watershed in world politics and consciousness. It did not simply 'politicise' a new generation, but it redefined the very nature of 'politics'. A new kind of politics emerged which did not seem to fit the inherited traditions of the Left. Suddenly, there was new energy and new life, as new visions of freedom, equality and justice came into focus. New movements were emerging, which showed that capitalist society had changed in fundamental ways since the 1930s. There was enormous vitality in the student movement, which threatened the very foundations of the Fifth Republic in France, and was the spearhead for the movement that emerged in the United States against America's war in Vietnam and Indo-China. There was the emergence of a strong Black movement in the United States, and the early beginnings of the women's movement. These developments were echoed the world over. A new generation had emerged into political consciousness and activity.[2]

There was the growth of a broadly 'anti-authoritarian' politics which refused to identify socialism with a centralised state and developed a democratic critique and practice in areas as diverse as education, industry, medicine, community work, mental illness, the arts and the media. These broadly Libertarian movements redefined the relationship between state and civil society as they insisted that equality was not simply a matter of access to state resources, but that people had to control the different areas of their lives. More recently, we have been brought to realise that, if capitalism had undergone profound changes, Thatcher's victory showed that we barely had a grasp of the significance of these changes theoretically and politically. Marcuse and some of the Situationist work in France had suggested new insights into the place of consumerism and the media as influences on the making of identities, but little was done to develop these ideas systematically.[3]

In the early 1990s, some of this can appear strangely romantic and naïve, in the face of widespread hardships suffered through years of crisis. At the same time, these writings can remain strangely haunting as we own up to the inadequacies of our prevailing moral and political traditions to understand and grasp the broad social changes we live in. This is not to underestimate some of the theoretical advances that have been made, but it is to introduce a note of scepticism about the extent to which they have deepened our understanding and political practice.

France 1968 was deemed a failure. It can be hard to discern its continuing importance in a changed world twenty years later. For many people, the anti-authoritarian and libertarian traditions of the late 1960s seemed a failure too, so that it can be difficult to reinstate them, especially in a period when the idea of libertarianism seems to have been so firmly appropriated by the Right. Somehow there is a deep feeling on the Left, which mirrors a broader cultural feeling, that we should not have anything to do with 'failures'. The Russian Revolution mesmerised generations on the Left, for it was for so long deemed a 'success'. There is a fear that failure can infect us. We do not want to be associated with it, which is disempowering in a period of Eastern European revolutions which bring home the hollowness and injuries of an orthodox Marxism to which market capitalism seems the only viable alternative.

Many people are tempted into proving that they never really believed these things anyway. This is not an altogether unhealthy response, for it is part of a recognition of the ways that the world has changed. The personal and sexual politics of the 1970s also carried with it its own moralism which many people want to distance themselves from, remembering that somehow it had been held 'wrong' to be 'possessive', 'jealous' and 'competitive'. These feelings had somehow to be dug out of us, if we would admit them to ourselves at all. It was thought that we could change through acts of will and determination alone. This moralism had left its own inheritance of guilt that could often only be assuaged by abandoning a sense of political involvement.

Because the 'new politics' had politicised our everyday experience, it had come much closer to us. Politics was not simply a matter of our political convictions, nor simply of our commitment to a political group or party that we might support or vote for. Rather, activist politics had become a matter of the ways we live. As socialists, we expected ourselves to live differently and to challenge the prevailing structures of capitalist life which said that people were only worthy of respect if they were materially successful. As men, we expected a lot of ourselves, possibly far too much as we identified ourselves with individual ambition and success. We had little experience and understanding of human psychology, which, on the Left in the 1970s, tended to be dismissed as 'bourgeois'. We thought that we could change ourselves through acts of will and that there were no limits to what we could do as long as we applied ourselves.

We constantly tested ourselves, as men, against the limits of tiredness and exhaustion, assuming that others would be there to look after us. Often our best energies were drained in the public world of work where male identities are formed. These structures, which are deeply set within a Protestant moral culture, were often reproduced on the Left as politics became the proving ground for male identities. Many people got hurt. It was all too easy to replace bourgeois notions of 'correctness' with alternative socialist notions, reversing the Protestant framework rather than questioning its assumptions. Many people were left feeling that somehow it was wrong to be 'monogamous' or that they should be struggling to be less 'possessive' in their relationships, hoping to be able to reshape their emotional lives before they had really learnt how to identify their emotions and feelings. As Freud understood, this could simply be to turn the screw of repression even tighter. Often people got disappointed as the ideals that they had set themselves had little reality in their lived experience, and they had no way of working through the pain.

Somehow, too much was being demanded on the assumption that, if people pushed a little harder, the world was on the edge of a revolutionary transformation. Politics on the Left seemed to be a matter of 'everything' or 'nothing' and many people understandably withdrew. Unfortunately, there was often a turning-away from people's experience, rather than a critical learning from it. Surprisingly little has been written and learnt about this period. It is partly that people carry a feeling of shame, of letting themselves down. It has been easier to reject and to turn aside than to learn. Learning too often involves living through difficult memories again and this can be too painful. There has been a turning towards more theoretical work and a reassessment of traditional forms of politics. This seems to make more sense in the changed political climate of Thatcherism, as the Left has learnt to recognise the place of media and cultural politics.[4]

In many ways, it is right to criticise the anti-theoretical stance of 1960s politics, while also grasping the significance of its emphasis on a 'politics of experience' and the importance of organising with people on more of a basis of equality with them. For example, housing struggles in the 1970s often grew out of the fact that ex-students shared similar housing needs and were prepared to risk themselves in the same way as other people they were working with. We might have been guilty of a form of self-deception, blind to the fact that when squatting was made difficult, it was possible for many to draw on middle-class connections to acquire mortgages. The Labour Party was to learn the lessons of hypocrisy when Thatcher's government took the initiative in offering working-class people the opportunity of owning their own houses. But there were many important lessons learnt about the nature of housing struggles.

If it is important to gain a firm theoretical grounding for our politics, we must also ensure that our theory extends our grasp of the new forms of struggle that are emerging against class, racial and sexual oppression. Otherwise, our theory can lead us to condemn people for struggling for things that the middle class takes for granted so that our theory is in danger of being an end in itself. This is especially true for a younger generation on the Left who have not lived through an intense period of class confrontation but have come to 'politics' through 'theory'. This can make people falsely self-assured, with everything to teach and nothing to learn. This was a problem of coming to Marx through the writings of Althusser which all too often presented Marxism as an objective set of tenets rather than a mode of illuminating theoretically our lived and contradictory experience.[5]

THEORY AND POLITICS

Let us learn from the experience of Ford again. Let us suppose that
workers do not want to strike, but have chosen to put pressure on the
management in their fight for a new manning agreement by slowing up
the line. This might be because workers do not want to lose money
through strike action, but prefer to limit production, knowing that this
screws up management production schedules. People do not want to
hurt themselves if they can help it. They might think that it is stupid to
strike because this only means they hurt themselves, even if they are told
by the political group that this is the 'correct weapon' because this uses
their power as industrial workers. Workers can become cynical about
Leftist groups who are so willing to sacrifice their pay. It can seem as if
they must want the strike for their own ends. So little trust is developed,
just an atmosphere of mutual suspicion. Little is learnt by the Left.

At the same time, the idea of a 'correct theory' gives a certain amount
of security to the militant, especially to an ex-student militant. It allows
him or her to feel that he or she has something important to give. We
should not underestimate the contribution that a theoretical grasp and
understanding can make, but often it is just this kind of broader
understanding that the 'militant' does not offer. This connects to a
deeper problem. Often in these contexts, ex-students will be ashamed of
their own class backgrounds. They will do their best to hide them, so
minimising any differences that might draw attention to themselves, but
this is a dishonest strategy and it means impersonalising your
experience. I remember this experience in Big Flame. There is a particular male style of the black leather jacket and the jaunty walk. You learn
to talk differently and you fall into despising other middle-class people
who are not prepared to make the same sacrifices.

This does not mean that it is not important for people with middle-
class backgrounds to recognise the narrowness of their class experience
and to learn how to talk openly, honestly and straightforwardly to
working-class people. This should not be a private process but part of a
process of political discussion and education on the Left. It is important
for people to gain a different class, ethnic and racial experience and to
be involved with people in concrete struggles, but there are different
ways of doing this. Often, attempts at 'proletarianising' ourselves end up
as false and patronising, for we are not being true to ourselves but are
choosing to live a lie. People can see through these attempts in an
instant. This creates its own anxieties about being 'found out'. One's
own history and experience are denied and, rather than being an open

and truthful basis upon which we learn to share ourselves with others, it becomes something we remain ashamed about.

Often it means that we have an insecure grasp of why *we* are struggling against the oppressions and exploitations of a capitalist society. We can slip into thinking and feeling that we are doing it for others who are less fortunate than ourselves. But if this is so, our resentment often grows at a deeper level, because we are making all the effort to liberate people who do not seem to be working so hard themselves. Part of us still feels the need for recognition and appreciation for all the 'good work' that we are doing. Often it means we remain unclear about our own motivation. In Big Flame we created a situation once, where workers made excuses to us about why they could not come to meetings about Ford. They did not want to 'let us down' because we seemed to be working so hard. They thought we should take it a little easier ourselves. We did not seem to enjoy ourselves very much and this surely compromised our politics in their eyes.

The Left has tended to dismiss these issues as 'personal' and therefore of no political importance. This is one of the reasons for an enormous circulation of people through political groups since the available models of political militancy seem to involve a total dedication. If you are involved, it is very difficult not to feel deeply and genuinely that the 'class struggle' is so much more important than any needs or wants that individuals could have themselves.[6] You do not have to think and feel this consciously to slip into it. The significance of our own individual lives seems to disappear as we work harder and harder. It is part of a Protestant ethic that the Left has made uncritically its own.

I remember feeling this so clearly about people working at Ford. I used to be able to go back and sleep after we gave out leaflets to the early morning shift, but the people working on the line had no escape. The disparity became almost insufferable. I recognise how I lost a sense of my own individual wants and needs, even though we tended to talk about the importance of our personal and sexual lives. This language became increasingly rhetorical. We were exhausted as we fell into bed late at night, knowing that we had a meeting the next morning. I came near to losing a sense of myself. This was connected to living out a particular conception of masculinity in which politics as work had become an end in itself.

This is not unfamiliar to men, for we often learn that our male identities are secured in the public arena of work and that there are no limits to how hard we should work. Exhaustion becomes a sign of virility as all our best energies are used up and we come home empty and drained. As politics becomes work, these patterns of masculinity only seem to get reinforced. I lost a sense of what kind of revolution I wanted or why changing the society was so deeply important for me to be able to live a human life. At Ford people often asked what we were doing, thinking that we must be 'students'. Often people were genuinely interested in what motivated us, because we showed so much dedication. They had to get up in the morning, but we did not have to – so why did we? In the early days, we had things to say, but as it went on it was hard to maintain a sense of what we were struggling for.

This kind of politics does not create a more open, human and loving culture and consciousness to set against the way that capitalist society reduces, wastes, destroys and undermines so many lives. If anything, it tends to build, as I have tried to argue in earlier chapters, upon a moral psychology of self-denial that is created within the Protestant heart of capitalist culture, as Max Weber seemed to acknowledge. From an early age, we are taught as boys to sacrifice our individual wants and needs for something 'bigger' – school exams, the career, 'success' at work. There is always something for which we have to sacrifice our wants, needs and desires, if they conflict. We are brought up into a culture which identifies masculinity with 'self-denial'. It becomes second nature, so that we do not realise we are doing it.

We have so identified our male 'selves' with individual 'success', that we end up externalising our feelings, believing that we 'must be happy' because we have been given a salary rise. In a similar way, a woman is supposed to be happy because she has got such a wonderful husband and home. If she is unhappy, she is made to feel that there must be something wrong with her. She is made to feel ungrateful and often she blames herself more harshly than would others. In a not too dissimilar way, the 'class struggle' becomes a kind of 'end' that we are ready to sacrifice for, and against which our individual lives have little value or meaning. Whatever meaning our lives have comes from whatever efforts we have put into this struggle. It is an endless process as we become ceaselessly active. We cannot stop ourselves. Weber recognises the way that work can become an end in itself within a Protestant moral culture. For men, it becomes easy to take personal and family life for granted, for they slip into the background, whatever lip-service we might pay to them verbally.

SOCIALIST THEORY AND SEXUAL POLITICS

I think that this can also help us grasp some of the resistance to sexual politics within the Left, especially as it touches directly and personally on the experience of men. With the level of commitment and sacrifice that is called for in 'political work' – and it has the same structure in our lives as 'work', somehow opposed to play, love or joy – it becomes difficult to feel oneself personally. This is especially true if one is doing one's best to suppress one's personal family and class history. Sexual politics becomes acceptable only as it concerns the situation of women and if it does not threaten the power men have built up within the Left.

There is also enormous awareness of the personal sacrifices people have made 'for the struggle', which so easily turns into malice if one's power is going to be threatened. Feminism creates a very difficult psychological situation for men, and it will be important to watch the influence of feminism as it develops in Eastern Europe, so becoming part of the discussion on the nature of reform, freedom, democracy and social justice; for crucially it is the feminist notion that 'the personal is political' that can bring into question the rationalism, instrumentality and impersonalism of so much socialist politics.

This partly explains the level of feeling around the oppositions of 'experience'/'theory' and 'personal'/'political'. Theory is very much set against, and superior to, 'experience' as a 'higher' form of consciousness. This is held on to tightly since it has become the source of so much of male identity. The 'personal' is very much identified with 'self-indulgence' and 'selfishness'. The 'political' has to do with a sense of duty. So it makes some sense to see theory as 'rational' and therefore as 'superior' to experience and to the personal. This becomes a re-statement in a different form of the Enlightenment idea that men are 'rational' and thereby superior to women, who are 'emotional' and thereby taken to be 'irrational'.

Of course, men would strenuously resist this identification, especially since people on the Left have struggled to get the 'right line' on the women's movement. Yet it is precisely this effort to establish a correct line, and to experience our politics as operationalising a formula, that draws on a deep structure of people's thoughts and feelings in capitalist society. The tradition remains so tightly wedged in the role of 'correct theory' and 'correct principles', even if it is now about sexual relation-ships, and thereby fails to engage with the potential that sexual politics has for challenging these rationalistic structures themselves.

Edward Thompson has reminded us of the priority of the notion of class struggle in Marx's writings, although unfortunately he does not direct us to the significance of the Black and women's movements in transforming our inherited sense of politics over the last twenty years. Nevertheless, he reminds us of something important in his *Leveller* interview:

Class struggle is the central concept in my work. It is the most important concept of the Marxist tradition. It is prior to the concept of classes. Class struggle does not happen because of the existence of classes but, on the contrary, it is because people commence to struggle in a class way that then one can begin to talk about class formations. This is not to say that there aren't objective reasons within production relations why people define their interests in class ways. But that class formation is the result and consequence of struggle, and not the other way round.

(Jan 1978: p. 21)

This means that we have to take seriously who is struggling and what they are struggling for. This becomes the basis for our analysis of new forms of struggle and new social movements. A strength of the Italian Marxist tradition in the 1970s was its focus on the issue of 'who is the working class?'. It did not see the working class as some kind of fixed and ahistorical category, but as a developing historical reality. This meant, for example, taking seriously the urban and community struggles in Turin in 1969, as well as the industrial struggles at Fiat.

The richness of this experience, however it was to develop, initially grew out of the fact that the student struggles connected in a very real and concrete way with the industrial struggles of the Hot Summer of 1969. This is something that never really happened in England where the student movement was relatively isolated, though people gained enormous experience in community and housing struggles. There was a deep suspicion of 'intervention' in the libertarian Left which kept most people away from an ongoing relationship with industrial struggles. This meant that once the initial energy and initiative began to wane in the mid-1970s, the traditional Left organisations, particularly the Trotskyist Left in Eng- land, could reassert themselves. This happened in an even sharper way in France.

In France, the disillusionment after 1968 was enormous and there was a reaction. For many this meant the discovery of Trotskyism, since the failure was grasped as a failure of 'organisation'. Somehow the strength of the reaction is related to the depths of rationalism in French culture, even on the Left, and the rationalist tendency to seek a correct formula for political orientation which can then be applied to historically contingent situations. So 'spontaneity' had been rejected as a 'false idea' that had been tried and had failed, rather than something that had to be grasped as a response to the administration and bureaucratisation of life in the social and historical conditions of post-war France. This historically dismissal was fed by a Trotskyist tradition which already had a ready-made critique of 'spontaneity'. This was assumed to be very much the same 'entity' as Lenin had struggled against.

The fact that the new social movements had developed in a totally different social and historical situation could not come into the picture. Rather, 'spontaneity' existed as some kind of ahistorical sin that had to be struggled against through discovering the virtues of an equally ahistorical conception of 'party organisation'. This has particularly deep roots in a Leninist tradition which assumes that the political party, guided by a rationalist form of theory, can appropriate the truth to itself and so legislate for civil society.

It is partly this vision of socialist orthodoxy that is challenged in the movements in Eastern Europe that have broken with the leading role of the Communist Party. Truth is no longer the possession of a political party, nor can it be claimed by any single group within civil society. This reflects a pervasive Enlightenment tendency to think in terms of 'oppositions', which makes Hegel and a tradition of dialectical thought so hard to grasp. But, at another level, this Hegelian tradition has also been brought into question since it has fostered a notion that freedom and reason can be realised through a historical process in a particular state formation. So it is that the revolutions in Eastern Europe have posed questions about the relationship of truth and politics in quite different terms. It has seemed vital for individuals to learn how to be true to themselves and in part this means being true to their experience. In opening up again issues of how truth is related to experience, they have brought into question traditions of secular rationalism that have centrally constituted our inherited sense of Enlightenment modernity.

DUALISM AND EXPERIENCE

Thinking in terms of oppositions has deep roots in bourgeois culture and thought. We are brought up to think quite easily and naturally that you are either 'good' or 'bad', 'well-behaved' or 'naughty', 'successful' or a 'failure', 'adequate' or 'inadequate', 'worth something' or 'worthless'. These oppositions govern so much more of our experience. Dualistic modes of thought form a common sense, particularly within a Protestant moral culture. At one level we are stuggling to be 'good', 'well behaved', 'clean', because at another level we are left feeling that our natures are 'bad', 'naughty' and 'dirty'. So we are struggling to be 'other' than what our 'natures' would be, which are radically evil within a Protestant culture that continues to shape so much of our secular experience of modernity. These struggles leave deep scars in our experience.

We are torn between these oppositions and come to feel that if we behave badly, this only proves what our parents and teachers have known all along, and what we have ourselves suspected. One slip and we are made to feel that we are irredeemably 'bad', 'evil', 'naughty'. This builds a constant tension and anxiety into our lived experience because at some level we are left feeling that we simply cannot win. We are bound to be defeated. This is why we struggle against the sexual fantasy or feeling, experiencing this as part of an animal nature which proves our wretchedness and worthlessness.

These fears haunt long after much more polite and easier manners have been allowed. They move to a deeper level, from which they continue to determine inherited forms of masculinities. We learn to disown our fears, for these are emotions that men supposedly do not have, so we never learn to identify our fear for what it is. It is as if these aspects of our experience are eradicated but in reality they often assume a different form. We just have to get someone in a bad mood, and we discover the feelings of resentment and frustration they have been harbouring. We realise that there is another reality from the way that men present themselves in polite society. It is a reality that we learn to shut away out of a fear of rejection if others saw this side of us.

Men and women are affected in different ways. Society has different expectations of us which are in turn cut across by class. To be born masculine in the middle class often means to be brought up to be a 'success' and to be haunted by a deep feeling of inadequacy and worthlessness. It is as if the final judgement is announced each time we hear our exam results. All the energy and all the effort seems to go into sustaining ourselves and protecting our 'egos' against inevitable crashes.

As children, we grow up deeply believing that we are *either* 'good' *or* 'bad'. We cannot be good and bad at the same time; this simply does not make sense within traditional logic, though it is the essence of grasping the meaning of the dialectic as a challenge to everyday ways of thinking and feeling in a Protestant moral culture. Sometimes children are angry. But it is difficult to be angry if we are told that it is 'naughty'. We learn to repress our anger. We have to pretend that it is not happening, that this is not the way we are feeling.7 We do not want to be rejected. This will confirm so many of our fears. It is possible to be angry at someone and still like them, but we get scared that if we are angry or feel resentful this means that we *cannot* like someone, that our friendship is cracking.

These ways of thinking and feeling operate in the everyday organisation of our relationships. We can seem trapped into thinking in terms of oppositions. Our relationships can be limited as a result, for we learn to withhold so much of what we experience from others lest this affect the judgements that they would make of us. The truth might be that we can both be angry and love someone at the same time. It might be misleading to see these as predicates which exclude each other. More dialectically, our anger and our readiness to share our resentment might be an expression of our love and caring, of our seriousness within a relationship, so helping us to feel that we can be more ourselves. This might allow the relationship to deepen and so give us a chance to experience the reality of our feelings for others.[8]

What is at issue here, then, is not simply a matter of the ways we think. Rather, these grow out of, and can limit, the character of the social relationships we have. We need to recognise that we are not posing two different 'ways of thinking' against each other. We are contrasting different conceptions of life and opening out different possibilities in our relationships. We are also declaring that a more dialectical under-standing allows our relationship to deepen. It does not fix us and thereby limit our relationships. Rather, it can help us grasp what is keeping a relationship at a more superficial level than it needs to be, and to understand what is blocking the contact and intimacy that might otherwise be able to flow between us. In this way it offers us more truth. None of this should be alien to Marx, though he would probably have had little sympathy for these ideas since he was often trapped by a dismissive attitude to the personal. The recovery of a dialectic of emotional, personal life and social theory is rather part of the heart and meaningfulness of a reformulated historical understanding, as it allows us a substantive grasp of our relationships rather than a relationship to them which is built on a reified sense of our emotions.

Thinking in terms of oppositions seems to exist right at the heart of a Leninist and Trotskyist politics and so has shaped traditions of socialist theory and practice. It is one of the fundamental weaknesses of that tradition, at least in limiting its power to engage critically with a Protestant moral culture and its ability to legitimate capitalist social relationships. Rather than giving us a critical understanding of the ways a historical dialectic works in both the private and public spheres of life, it tends to write us more deeply into dualistic patterns of thought and feeling. This makes it difficult to develop any sustained critique of everyday moral relationships within a capitalist culture. It also makes it difficult to escape from an abstract conception of history and is bound to produce a limited version of historical materialism. It works to establish quite misleading oppositions between socialism and capitalism before we have begun to grasp how they both carry the marks of an Enlightenment modernity.

In Leninist politics we find 'spontaneity' and 'organisation' opposed to each other as abstract categories. Somehow this is connected with the ways socialist politics is presented to us as 'a matter of principle' to make some kind of clear choice. This is part of a crisis of Marxism in both Western and Eastern Europe. A number of these abstract oppositions still seem to dominate inherited socialist political tradition:

'reformist'	'revolutionary'
'anarchy'	'discipline'
'spontaneity'	'organisation'
'frivolous'	'serious'
'bourgeois'	'proletarian'
'particularism'	'universalism'

In place of thought, we are trained into a language of abstract categories. This has undermined the independence of thought and practice in the Soviet Union and Eastern Europe. So being 'political' often means being initiated into thinking and speaking in terms of these primary oppositions. This is taken to be a sign of 'advanced political consciousness'; the 'revolutionary' is felt to be in a strong position to look down on lesser mortals who are stumbling towards these insights. Somehow these categories come to define the very limits and meaning of political debate. So different regimes are assessed as to whether they are 'reformist' or not. This becomes the crucial issue of loyalty to be settled. Often we lose touch with what is specific and particular in the history of a particular society when the Communist Party appropriates to itself the monopoly of truth and wisdom.

The party as the source of truth has the power to transform the lie into truth, for it is the embodiment of progress and universalism. It is only sectional interests that can never challenge the monopoly of the party. For example, from 1968 in Czechoslovakia until the 1989 revolution, people had to accept the lie that the Prague Spring was a counter- revolutionary movement, if they wanted to stay in public life. There is a dreadful predictability in the accounts one reads, say of what has happened to socialism in Eastern Europe.[9] Somehow the crucial questions rarely get raised as the party insists that the answers have been discovered a long time ago by Lenin. People only have to accept the authority of the state, for to question is to be subversive. This has served to discredit the very language of socialism, which has been used to sustain party privilege and corruption. Against this, only the moral authority of the individual could be trusted, the personal integrity and dignity, which cost spells in jail, of a Václav Havel in Czechoslovakia or an Adam Michnik in Poland.

There is a promise of enormous security in the notion that history and progress is working on the side of the working class and in the feelings of rigour, precision and clarity that the scientific formulation of

Marxism allows. But it is something which many of us have learnt to distrust with time and experience. Gramsci recognised the way that it pacifies people, so undermining their sense of freedom. We become wary of what the sources of this 'correctness' really are. So we become unsettled at a form of analysis which claims that if the workers at Ford refuse to come out on a strike, say in support of the nurses, this is because they are 'backward'.

A Leninist tradition fosters the notion that it is still important to call for strike action and, in time, the workers will appreciate the 'correctness' of the positions that have been put. Somehow the party 'knows best' and has little to learn, whatever lip-service is paid to 'learning from the class'. This is confirmed theoretically within a Leninist tradition since workers are only capable of reaching 'trade unionist consciousness', so there is a clear task for militants to bring 'political consciousness' into the situation. This establishes a fundamental psychology that the party and the militants 'know best'. They have everything to teach and little to learn.

It is the arrogance of a tradition that said that the 'truth' was whatever served the needs of the revolution that has been widely rejected in Eastern Europe. It left morality as a tool of the party and it served to denigrate both morality and politics. Somehow the very notions of 'economistic' and 'political' consciousness exist as abstract categories, not as developing and changing historical realities. For example, it might well be that many of the black and Asian workers at Ford find it hard to identify with the union in the plant and develop a deep distrust of it. They come to work with particular histories and traditions. Somehow none of this really matters within a Trotskyist paradigm, since these are assumed to be the same 'limits' in their 'consciousness'. It might also be that there have been fundamental shifts in the relationships of people to their work, brought about by assembly-line production, so that the very meanings of 'economistic' and 'trade union' consciousness have to be rediscovered and rethought in this new class situation.

This is not 'empiricist', but involves being sensitive to the changing nature and meaning of class struggle, which, for many, has moved further into a period of post-Fordism in which mass production is less important. The point is that the Left inherits a political theory that can make learning about social restructuring extremely difficult. It can also make it disdainful to issues of feminism and ecology which are deemed marginal when issues of class relations are raised. These are dismissed as sectional or particularistic because it is only the working class that supposedly carries universal hopes. It is the hold of an Enlightenment universality that has for so long trapped orthodox Marxism, if not Marx himself.

In turning again to theory after the disappointments of the 1960s politics of experience, the Left has fallen victim to another set of false polarities, the opposition of 'theory' to 'experience'. Typically, any attempt to engage critically with the work, for example, of Althusser, is dismissed as 'anti-theoretical' and not taken seriously. The insights of an earlier generation in the Hegelian-Marxist tradition – Lukàcs, Korsch, Gramsci, Horkheimer or the different critiques to be found in Benjamin and Adorno, are lumped together and dismissed. Marcuse is rarely discussed and Reich is disregarded as 'biologistic'. This is creating its own forms of rigorous ignorance. If the terms of discussion have shifted with the theoretical move towards Foucault and post-structuralism, this has grown out of a shared antagonism to what is loosely called 'essentialism'. Individuality, like experience, is taken to be socially and historically constituted.

Socialism too often develops a broadly 'rationalistic' critique which sees 'reason' as an independent faculty inherently 'superior' to the wants, desires, needs, emotions and feelings which broadly make up our experience. Rationalism is an important critical tradition that can make us aware of what we take for granted unthinkingly, in our everyday experience. So, for instance, the concept of 'class' can give us a grip over differences that we might never have been able to name or really to understand when we were young. However, we need to be wary of the rationalistic and ahistorical assumption that there is an underlying structure of 'laws' which will somehow explain how it is that our experience takes the form that it does. This threatens to undermine our grasp of the significance of our everyday experience.

Admittedly this is simplistic. Althusser would certainly have resisted being included within a 'rationalist' tradition, and would see himself within a tradition of 'scientific Marxism'. But this might not be such a different bag. We might wonder why it is that the Althusserian tradition and the broadly Trotskyist traditions both seem to invoke such general concepts and categories, even if they take themselves to be very much opposed to each other. They both seem to involve a notion of socialism as a 'politics of principles'.

This is not to assert that there are no significant differences. Althusser's influence encouraged an important critique of economic determinism on the Left. He prepared the ground for taking issues of culture, identity and gender seriously, without feeling the need to reduce them too quickly. This has enabled people to take seriously important areas of sexual and cultural politics. But it has also limited, for instance, the kind of analysis that could be made of the state, the media, mass communications and education. It brings with it a strong sense of what such an analysis should look like. Often this inhibits a grasp of the changing structure of these social practices. So this freedom of analysis, while refreshing in relation to orthodox Marxism, also carries with it its own limitations. The conception of 'historical materialism' the theory carries still has a strong resonance in contemporary theoretical work long after people have consciously broken with Althusser's work. This means that these different institutions and social practices can only be grasped as 'legitimations', that is, seen as existing in a realm of 'ideology' placed in opposition to a realm of 'economy'.

This carries with it its own political implications. Positively, it means that 'patriarchy', for instance, can be recognised as a particular structure of relationships, that do not have to be immediately reduced to class relationships. In this sense a structuralist Marxist analysis gives much more freedom than the traditional Trotskyist analysis which, whilst challenging the notion that women's oppression can be explained purely in terms of psychology, tends to equate a 'material analysis of women's oppression' with an economic analysis. The Trotskyist analysis wants to argue that women's oppression and women's feelings of powerlessness and inadequacy have a material basis because women's oppression is institutionalised. It is limited by its tendency to identify 'material' with 'economic' so it tends to focus upon women's situation at work, or else to focus upon 'domestic labour', when thinking about the family. Giving 'patriarchy' some autonomy as an independent structure of relationships of power and dependency, as an Althusserian analysis has done, allows a much fuller exploration of the situation of women within contemporary capitalism.[10]

The theoretical 'autonomy' which Althusser prepares, allows for a certain kind of political autonomy within the Communist Party which gives people greater freedom to take issues of sexuality and culture seriously. On the other hand, patriarchy is seen as 'ideology' operating at a particular level. So the struggle against 'patriarchy' is seen very much as an ideological struggle, a necessary prerequisite to weaken the grip of capital in society. It tends to operate at the level of legitimations, where identities or subjectivities are said to be constituted rather than as part of a structure of material relationships. So it is taken seriously at the cost of being isolated from the level of the 'economy' which is preserved by the party as the real locus of 'class struggle'.

We often tend to find a technological conception of production, rather than one which recognises Marx's emphasis on the social relations of production.[11] This means, politically, that the 'level' of economic struggle can be more tightly controlled by the party, while people can be given 'relative autonomy' in these other areas, just because they do not threaten the development of the fundamental class struggle. This means that issues of family, sexuality and childcare are separated from issues around work. So, paradoxically, the very weakness of narrower economistic understanding of the Trotskyist groups does at least allow us to think about the significance of the relationship of work to the family and sexuality. We can think, for example, about the ways that shift-work controls people's sexuality and determines whatever relationships people can develop with each other in the family. The fact that children have to be kept quiet because dad is working nights, for example, can crucially shape children's relationship with their parents and with themselves.

Both traditions are left with an unreal sense of history. They do not prepare us to learn from people's concrete struggles against oppression and suffering. They want to judge history before they learn from it. So the Trotskyist wants to bring 'principles' *to* history. Lenin recognised this in Trotsky: 'In all his theses he looks at the questions from the angle of general principles. . . .' (Lenin 1972, Vol. 38). Trotskyism recognises this, though some commentators do not have much theoretical grasp of their sources.

Regis Debray is aware that the problems are much deeper. This is what he says in his Prison Writings:

> . . . the fact that he (the Trotskyist) rejects every concrete embodiment of socialism from his theoretical circle of pure forms, he is actually expelling himself from the reality of history. The wheel always comes full circle: the Trotskyist is always right.
>
> (Debray 1970)

The commitment to principles can be an important protection, when others around are expediently adjusting to the prevailing realities of power. It can give enormous moral strength and courage in the face of a crushing social reality. But this strength is gained at enormous theoretical costs.

Principles do not exist outside and beyond history, in some kind of timeless realm. This is essentially an Enlightenment notion. This was one idea Hegel was struggling against in his critique of Kant. Marx was to recognise that there are no points outside history, where some idea of eternal 'truth' can be preserved and rediscovered. But this does not have to mean that truth is thereby relative or simply the outcome of a particular history, class or culture. Our sense of what we are struggling for is an internal part of a historical struggle, which is not to say that it can be reduced to being an aspect of such a historical process. People are continually redefining what they need for themselves to live equal and human lives in a constantly changing capitalist society, as new sources of oppression and injustice are revealed.

Feminism, for instance, has forced us to rethink the meaning of 'equality' beween men and women, as we have recognised the damage of dependency. We have realised how feelings of inadequacy and worthlessness are reproduced within unequal gender relationships, even when people think they are treating each other 'equally'. We are left wondering how housework and childcare can be equally shared, not simply as tasks but as areas of concern and responsibility. This seems to be one of the material conditions for an equal relationship, so that it is not simply a matter of men helping out with duties that we have no real responsibility for. So we are rediscovering 'principles' within history, as the 'public' and the 'private' can no longer be neatly separated from each other. As this changes our visions of identity, equality and responsibility, so it transforms our sense of politics. Freedom and exploitation can no longer be seen exclusively as features of the public world of men.

MEN, EXPERIENCE AND SEXUAL POLITICS

A starting point for many people's involvement in sexual politics is the insight that the sexual divisions between men and women are not 'natural' in the ways that we are brought up to believe. They do not follow directly from biological differences, but are produced through the ways we are brought up to be, as 'men' and 'women' within culture and society. This realisation has meant acknowledging that there are deep divisions of sex and gender, which cut across the class, race and ethnic divisions of capitalist society. How are we to understand the relationship between sex and class? A few years ago, the Left clearly thought that the 'basic contradiction' is that created through the ownership and control of the means of production, that is, class divisions. This meant that any focus on the autonomous struggle of women to liberate themselves from the relationships of power and dominance from which they suffer, was automatically seen as a 'diversion'.

Some groups on the Left still believe this, but most people have been forced to learn from the idea that 'there can be no revolution without women's liberation'. In its own way, this has provided a critique of Marxism as a form of economic determinism which said that once the means of production had been socialised, then other forms of social, racial and ethnic oppression and subordination would 'wither away' because they were 'superstructural'. The revolution would supposedly offer real freedom and equality as opposed to the merely formal freedoms of a capitalist democracy. But the experience has been different and many had suffered at the hands of the communists, who had seemingly been relieved of liberal scruples in matters of justice by the intellectual framework of an orthodox Marxism which had contempt for bourgeois legality and which confidently felt that history itself would absolve them of any actions that they took to secure a proletarian revolution. The revolutions in Eastern Europe in 1989 have profoundly rejected the Communist Party's centralised vision of authority and call for a different vision of freedom and democracy.

The Left has been wary, envious and suspicious of an autonomous women's movement and the idea that it could help create a different vision of freedom, respect and equality. This is hardly surprising, since it challenged some of the deeply held assumptions of socialist theory and practice. The Left has tended to learn selectively. It has been forced to learn about consciousness-raising because it has been such a deep experience for so many women, gays and lesbians, but it has tended to give the experience a particular interpretation.[12] It is seen as a way for people to learn that they should not blame themselves because the sources of their misery and powerlessness do not lie on their own shoulders, but are part of a situation shared by others. This condition is not to be changed through individual personal change, but through collective social and political action.

This tends to contrast and oppose 'individual change' to 'social and political change' in a way that can distort the reality of the experience. It conforms with political assumptions which are dismissive of individual change, growth and development. Within the women's movement, reworking the relationship between the 'personal' and the 'political', the 'individual' and the 'collective', has grown out of a deep respect for the value and integrity of each person's experience. There is a different vision of freedom, equality and democracy within the idea that each woman has had an equally valid experience and has a voice to express it.

This is different from the prevailing liberal conceptions of respect for individual experience, which necessitates a certain distance from others. The ways in which each individual's experience is *validated* within a consciousness-raising group gave me, for instance, a way of recognising how much of my individual experience as a man was formed in the relationships with my parents, school and, later, at work. I recognised how much I *shared* with others, as men, and how much I had been limited and made to suffer through the expectations the society had of who I should be. I had learnt constantly to squeeze myself into the prevailing images of men, feeling that there must be something wrong with me if I felt at odds with this process. A sense of solidarity was created through this sharing, which was at once both uniquely individual and intensely social, as we learnt to explore our individual shapes rather than coerce each other to conform to values and relationships that were not of our own making. We refused to collude, even if this put us in a challenging relationship to what was traditionally expected of us, as men.

In fact, one of the things I learnt was how my understanding gets limited through this false opposition between the 'individual' and the 'social'. Not only did this leave me isolated, but also powerless to know what I wanted to change in how I relate to others to live a fuller life myself. I did not want to continue making the kind of sacrifices of my emotions, sexuality and feelings which the society implicitly demanded as the price of growing up to be an independent and self-sufficient man who supposedly has no needs of his own. I was regaining power over my understanding in challenging this prevailing sociological distinction between the 'individual' and the 'social', recognising how much I came to be who I am through the context of relationships of power and authority, often mystified as love and caring.

Within the men's group, I learnt, for instance, about some of the sources of my fear of authority. I had tried to pretend that this fear did not exist and that if I was strong-willed enough these feelings would go away. I learnt about some of the deeper sources of this fear and in so doing learnt something valuable about how people can change. I learnt more of what I can expect of myself and of the processes of coming to terms and facing my experience rather than rejecting and denying any feelings that did not seem to fit, so that I can live up to a particular ideal of masculinity. I learnt something of what people have to go through in order to change. This learning is crucial if we are to talk realistically about larger social and political changes that deeply affect people's everyday lives.

As a man, I very much felt that I *should* be able to do anything, if I only put my mind to it. More than that, I felt that I should be able to do it well. I *should* be able to cope with meetings every night and I should not get tired or exhausted. I did not want to admit my 'weakness', so I felt that I should be able to do a job, and organise politically, and have equal relationships with people. I put enormous demands upon myself, though I did not recognise this at all. All these things were 'important' to do. I felt I should be able to do them all. This aspect of my masculine upbringing was extended within a Leftist political culture which left me suspicious of specialisation as a source of hierarchy and false authority, feeling that I had to be able to do everything from printing to plumbing. I was left feeling that I should be developing all these abilities and skills *all* the time. I made ludicrous demands upon myself, yet I always felt that I was not 'doing enough'. I had no sense of my own limits or boundaries.

Often these connections have to be emotionally explored within the context of consciousness-raising before we can assert them theoretically. In this crucial sense, reason does not operate independently of our emotions, and an Enlightenment rationalism which would pull them apart into separate spheres makes it hard to illuminate the mode of learning in either consciousness-raising or therapy. My own sense of authority might be connected with not having a strong sense of who I felt myself to be, so that I tend to be adaptive, what others expect me to be. This, in turn, at a deeper level, probably relates to not having had a father to relate to in critical years when I needed to learn 'how to be a man'.

In less acute forms, a sense of the absent father is experienced by many children as they grow up, as men are often unavailable, either being tied up at work or else being emotionally inaccessible.[13] But it also relates to a schooling within which 'doing well' meant doing what was expected of you and conforming to rules that were externally set. In this way, the rules of the school exist as a microcosm of the rules of the larger society which dictate their own notion of 'normality'. As men, we have often built strong 'egos' around individual achievement and success, but, paradoxically, we can be left with a relatively weak sense of 'identity'. It is hard to generalise, but, at some level, we are taught to *do*, not to *be*. So we often develop a weakened sense of what we want and need individually. If anything, we often tend to be scared of pleasure, of getting what we need from others in our relationships. At some level, this can leave us feeling resentful, because we have never learnt how to ask for what we need.

Rather, as men, we are brought up to be 'independent' and 'self-sufficient', which means that we should not really want anything from others. Of course, these patterns vary enormously between different masculinities, but particular aspects also resonate across, so it is not enough simply to describe different masculinities. So for a particular style of adaptive masculinity, we tend to do what others expect of us, thinking that others should not grumble or complain since we are doing what they want. This makes us feel easier with a Leftist theory that does not touch us too personally and that is ready to externalise all our feelings and thoughts. This does not help us grow or develop individually but we do not really learn to care about this. Other things are more important and we have to be ready to 'get on with them'.

As I learn to value my own experience, I am more open to learning from others. I am aware of different masculinities and of the different ways that they have dealt with authority at home and at school. Some of us challenge this authority directly. Others of us feel easier avoiding it, pretending that it is not there. Some of us feel very insecure if it is not there, though we complain about it a lot. Often these patterns reproduce themselves within political groups. I also grasped the different ways we have been forced to limit and compromise our 'individuality', in order to be what others expected of us. These are different ways we have sacrificed our personal power and limited ourselves.

I often fear that if I let people know what I am 'really like', then they would see what a nasty, resentful and revengeful person I am. This is part of a Protestant inheritance. Sometimes we do not want to take the risk of showing more of ourselves. We do not want to be hurt again. So we 'present ourselves' in a way that is acceptable to others, creating some kind of 'inner space' within which 'I can truly be myself'. We take this disjunction between 'inner' and 'outer' so much for granted that we do not expect to be able to express our inner selves, or recognise that this could be a path of development. In different ways, we have learnt not to expect much from life. We have learnt to protect ourselves so that we keep what is precious to us hidden, often even to ourselves. It is difficult to escape the notion, as men, that others would put us down and prove themselves at our expense if our guard were down and we gave them half a chance. But we can also lose a sense of what we are struggling for and how we want and need to change.

In its own way, consciousness-raising is a dialectical process, suited to a period in which so much of our personal reality and experience is manipulated and mystified through the media and education. When it creates an atmosphere of acceptance, it can encourage us to admit more of the reality of what we feel and experience and so question the idea that we simply construct our identities out of the objects and images that have been made culturally available to us. We do not have to keep pretending, nor do we have to struggle to live up to the abstract ideals of masculinity we set ourselves. We can contact some of the fear and the pain we usually hide from others, for fear of their judgements of us.

In a competitive period in which individuals have learnt that success on the market is what matters so that subordination and control have been built into the very structure of our emotions and feelings, we can be brought to accept more of what we are feeling. An experience of consciousness-raising can help us grasp just how moralistic and ideological our conceptions of what we 'should be' or 'ought to be' are. Rather than, for instance, thinking that only individual ambition and success matter to us, we can explore what these notions mean to us and possibly accept ways that we have denied ourselves, say out of a certain fear of being successful. This does not have to mean compromising with prevailing notions of success, but working out what matters to us both individually and collectively. It can mean questioning a culture of self-denial and a sense that it is only in denying ourselves that we can prove that we are serious about the wellbeing of others. This can be part of discovering a different conception of moral psychology. Often this remained implicit in the practice of consciousness-raising and has a different significance for men and women.

MEN, SELF-DENIAL AND MORALISM

Often, as men, we have been brought up to be very hard on ourselves. As I have shown, we redefine the nature of happiness, so that we relate to happiness as if it is some kind of 'reward' for reaching goals that we have set for ourselves. As Freud knew, we have little sense of the sacrifices in terms of our sexuality and emotional lives that the culture has forced us to make. The culture has moved us out of touch with our feelings and emotions so that we have difficulty connecting with what we are feeling and experiencing. We tend to locate ourselves through our rationality and intellectual understanding, keeping ourselves, as men, emotionally distant and uninvolved.

Often this means that we are really 'living in our heads', unable to respond directly and emotionally, even when we want to. We are not magically different once the bedroom door closes. We discover ourselves trapped in our intellectuality, especially as middle-class men, brought up to identify our 'selves' so closely with our rationality. For so long, we have been brought up within a capitalist moral culture that reproduces a secularised form of Protestantism, despises weakness and dependency and identifies with 'independence' and 'self-sufficiency', that we become scared of acknowledging our needs for others. Some part of us is afraid that our emotional needs are so overwhelming that, if they were given even modified expression, they would simply crush any relationship we are in. This is scary. We prefer to be slightly aloof and distant, making sure that we can rationally defend our emotions before we can allow ourselves to acknowledge them, even though this makes it difficult for our relationships to deepen.

As men, we have been very deeply socialised into a capitalist culture of self-denial and individual ambition, from a very early age. We are competing from the very beginning in the womb. There are all kinds of dreams and expectations laid upon us about who we should be, or who we should become. We continually have to prove ourselves, for masculinity is something that cannot be taken for granted. Within a Protestant ethic, we learn that our natures are 'rotten' or 'bad', so that we continually have to prove that we are 'other' than our natures dictate. We have to cope with incessant parental voices, that have become part of our unconscious, saying, 'I always knew that you would end up as a nothing'; 'I always knew that you were a worthless good-for-nothing'; 'I always knew that you weren't as good as your brother'. Whatever we do, we seem plagued by a feeling of worthlessness. We think that we are not good enough and, beneath the surface, it seems difficult to sustain our self-esteem.

At one level, this seems different from the strong and self-confident male able to cope with every situation. It is the other side of the coin that is constantly pushing us on, making us feel that we are never doing enough and that whatever we achieve could somehow be better done by others. The idea that 'if it isn't excellent, then it isn't worth doing' operates as another way of poisoning our creativity and expression. We are continually scared of the judgements of others and sometimes we put ourselves down as a pre-emptive move before they have a chance. Sometimes we compete hard, closing off ourselves and our sensitivity so we can handle the situation and make ourselves invulnerable. At others, we refuse to compete and we are constantly putting others down and hiding our resentments of them. We are plagued by often unacknowledged jealousies, by the fear that others are better than us. Often our personal identities are brittle, as they are not built upon very firm foundations. If we remain aware of the underside of our experience, often we do not want to share it because this will reflect back upon the images of ourselves we are seeking to sustain in public. If we wish to share more, often we only feel easy enough with a couple of pints inside of us.

Self-denial goes along with a strong strain of masochism in the formation of male identity within a secularised Protestant moral culture. We constantly punish ourselves for not being good enough, not doing enough. With the early feminist challenges to sexual relationships, it was easy as men to punish ourselves for not even feeling enough, or feeling the wrong things. We found it difficult to deal with our feelings of jealousy and possessiveness and competitiveness, believing we should not be having these feelings at all. This did its own damage. In its own way, this just turned the screw even tighter. One way out was to feel even less. This did more damage to our experience.

Somehow the 'socialist morality' of 'equal relationships' shared fundamentally the same Protestant form as the capitalist morality it was challenging. This can teach us something of fundamental importance, since the parallel has been emphatically drawn in the Soviet Union and Eastern Europe, where notions of 'duty' and 'self-sacrifice' were supposedly turned towards more universal socialist 'goals' so that notions of equality became detached from people's actual experience. Obviously, we have to be sensitive to the histories and cultures of different societies, though the dominating conceptions of 'abstract universalism' within socialism block our developing this sensitivity. This has deep roots in Marx's relationship to Enlightenment modernity, particularly in his sense of universalism, history and progress.

The idea in the 1970s that we 'should not be jealous' or that we 'ought not to be possessive' in our relationships grew out of a significant challenge to prevailing personal and sexual relationships in our society. Because we were brought up to think of our personal relationships in terms of love and caring, it had been difficult to recognise the ways that power and possessiveness operated in our relationship. In the culture I grew up in in the 1950s, boys would express this in language like: 'she's mine and I don't want her talking to any other boys', or 'I want her to "act properly".' Girls existed in relation to us, as boys. They sat around the dance hall, waiting to be asked to dance. We were blind to our power because the situation was more than a little scary for us; we could always be rejected or refused. Once we asked someone 'to be my girlfriend', then the contract was sealed. This fundamentally denied autonomy and independence to women, who had to be submissive if they wanted to be liked. The strength of the politics of the late 1960s was in helping to develop a critique of 'personal relationships', showing how they were, at a fundamental level, relationships of power broadly institutionalised in the society. This challenged a liberal split between public and private life for we recognised the ways that power operated in a private sphere, so that the terms of relationship between 'private' and 'public' had to be reworked. This division was reproduced within a Marxist tradition.

But, not surprisingly, the critique carried the marks of the society in which it developed. The prevailing anti-intellectualism of the 1960s made it difficult to recognise how much of a Kantian morality we were implicitly accepting and living out. Gramsci has been one of the few Marxist writers to recognise the importance of a moral critique of our 'common sense', if we are not persistently to replicate the hegemonic forms of the dominant culture.[14] The new ideals of the 1960s were posed in fundamentally the same moralistic form as those of bourgeois morality, as a set of 'ideals' that we ought to live up to. They, too, became ways of proving our moral worth. We were left feeling that if we did not change the ways we felt, then we only had ourselves to blame. This showed how inadequate we really were, but this time as socialists. This new 'moralism' created its own forms of competition and put-downs. We were quickly establishing a new set of ideals that we could fail to live up to and so ways of feeling bad about ourselves. The original purpose and intention of the critique of possessive personal relationships tended to get lost because of the moralistic form it took. We were too ready to judge each other and not ready to accept what we felt and experienced as a basis for change. Sometimes we lost touch with the structures of power and dominance within the larger society. These were to intensify with the emergence of Thatcherism and its reduction of human worth to the amount of money people earned.

The 'unreality' of Left politics was unable to meet the moral and political initiatives of a libertarian conservatism that recognised freedom as a matter of individual choice. Thatcherism resonated with the frustration that many felt at bureaucratic state controls and at forms of welfare provision that appropriated control rather than giving people the chance to set their own terms. Fed by our 'moralism', the Left became a place in which we were continuously proving ourselves through what we were 'doing' and in which it became difficult to set new terms for the different vision of freedom, justice and equality.

This helps set the ground upon which we can appreciate the significance of consciousness-raising. It helped us accept more of the reality of what we were experiencing and living through. I am talking of men's consciousness-raising, as I think it is important to be specific; the power and meaning of the experience depends very much upon the particular historical and personal situation of people, specifically because we, as men, find it difficult to escape from intellectuality and to begin to talk more personally and openly with each other. This also helps explain why it can be so difficult for men to get into consciousness-raising. We can still be plagued by a feeling that this is 'self-indulgent'.

The experience can be frustrating, even self-defeating; but it can also make us aware of the dialectical formation of our individuality, perhaps, for example, helping us to recognise some of the inner compromises we were forced to make to win the love and approval of parents and teachers. We can rediscover the painful process of collusion and accommodation through which the society forced us to compromise our integrity and inner knowledge, to give up our power and mould ourselves in the dominant images of 'masculinity' and 'success'. We become aware of how the structures of power and authority within the society are built into the formation of our individuality.

We might gradually realise how we have learnt to do only those things that we thought we would be really good at and to be able to compete well with others. For example, I have never really learnt to appreciate music or to sing. I never really learnt carpentry. These were not things I was good at, or they were things I was brought up to look down upon. It was OK as a hobby but I should not be 'wasting myself' doing carpentry. I could make something 'more' of myself. It is not simply that these were values I was brought up to believe. Rather, they were built into the very organisation of relationships within the family and the school. It can be difficult to recognise the different levels at which contradictions in our lived experience operate.

So, for instance, I was told by my parents that I 'could do whatever I wanted to do, as long as it would make me happy', whilst, in reality, I felt that I would be sadly disappointing them if I had decided not to stay on at school. I carried the full weight of their hopes and expectations, though this was never acknowledged openly. This was a powerful reality that was felt in the situation. I was carrying much more on my shoulders whenever I did an exam than was ever publicly acknowledged. The power and expectations were always hidden. They were neatly transferred on to our shoulders, without our ever being aware of it. I was left feeling that I would only be 'letting myself down' if I did not do well. The realities of power had been internalised. They existed inside of me and I was not even aware of it.

INDIVIDUALITY AND POLITICS

The reality of the dialectic between the 'internal' and the 'external' is much more subtle than the Left has generally acknowledged. Often it distorts the reality of consciousness-raising by presenting it as if it were a matter of our discovering that the sources of our individual unhappiness, frustration and inadequacy are not 'personal' and 'psychological', but are 'external' structures of social and political power. This sets up its own form of reductionism whereby our 'individual experience' is reduced to a form of social and historical conditions. Rather than grasping the dialectical formation of individuality within these structures of power and authority, we are left with a mechanical form of reductionism which makes us feel that it is only in the struggle to transform the social and historical reality that we are going to liberate ourselves.

The links between psychology and politics are broken and we are presented with an irreversible shift from 'psychology' to 'politics' as a sign of political consciousness and understanding.[15] At worst, this is to reproduce, rather than challenge, an assumption of positivist sociology that people are simply passive creatures moulded by social forces. This also characterised the positivist Marxism of the Second International.

At best, this leads people to invalidate aspects of their integrity and the experiences they have had within consciousness-raising, defining them as part of a necessary stage of immaturity, before they involved themselves in the 'realities of political work'.

The mechanical dissolution of 'individuality' into its social and historical components leaves us with no hope for change and transformation within the prevailing society. At one level, in seeing people as products of societies, it may be a resistance to a bourgeois society that brings us up to turn all our anger and resentment *against* ourselves, so that we continually blame ourselves for the sources of our frustration and unhappiness. From an early age, we are divided against ourselves. So it can be a great liberation to recognise that our anger should not be turned in against ourselves, but that there is a legitimate focus for our anger in the social and political institutions of an oppressive society.

Nevertheless, there are different ways of conceiving this. The mechanical conception dissolves our very notion of 'individuality', which makes it harder to appreciate the strength that we have gained *as* individuals, often through the very processes of consciousness-raising. This externalises capitalism as a discrete set of social and historical institutions. Capitalism becomes the external enemy that has to be fought. It is simply a matter of marshalling sufficient troops for the final assault. Our 'inner lives' are seen simply as a reflection of external structures. So any ideas of 'individuality' and 'subjectivity' are taken to be 'bourgeois myths'. Even if they have a reality in our lives, we have learnt that they are reducible to 'social and material conditions'. We discover the same kind of passivity in the pervasive idea within the human sciences that the individual is socially and historically constructed. The only change that becomes possible is the complete overthrow of an unjust society.

The dominant Left traditions inherit an Enlightenment mode of thought, which thinks in terms of 'oppositions'. This is the other side of the coin of mechanical materialism, wherein the mechanical reduction of history to predefined stages of class struggle operates to allocate a pre-evaluated significance to people's experiences. So we are caught within undialectical formations which do not help us grasp how our experience can be 'individual' and 'social', 'personal' and 'political', at the same time. It does not help us articulate, for instance, the contradictions we live out as socialists within a capitalist society, as blacks within a white society, as Jews within a Christian society or as gays or lesbians within a heterosexist society. With regard to the state socialist societies of Eastern Europe, it tends to present socialism and capitalism as if they exhaust the choices available. It fosters the idea that freedom and individual dignity can only be achieved within a market capitalist society.

It is a strength of feminist theory and practice to challenge some of these prevailing dualisms as well as provide a sense of autonomy, integrity and dignity that breaks with the universalism of Enlightenment modernity. Women have to have their experience as women validated, as well as their values and ideas legitimated. In many respects, they may share a different experience of relationships and institutions which helps bring forward different insights and understandings. At the same time, differences of class, race and ethnicity between women have to be acknowledged so that we are not left with a homogeneous and romanticised conception of feminism. But, crucially, as women identify themselves with a shared experience of subordination and oppression, they are not weakened as individuals but strengthened and more clearly defined in their individual integrity and identity.

DISCOVERING CONTRADICTIONS

As men, we are brought up to live up to certain ideals of ourselves. Often this means there is a strong sense of fantasy in our lives, as we do everything to avoid some of the realities of our everyday lives. We very much live in our images of ourselves, as 'capable', 'successful', 'intelligent', 'hard-working' men. We do not want people to force us to face a different reality. There is a strong streak of vanity. We want people to tell us what we *want* to believe about ourselves. There is a deep structure of this in bourgeois society, where we are taught to deny our wants, feelings and desires, so that we can focus upon our 'ends' or 'achievements'. As I have argued, this is most clearly articulated in the philosophy of Kant.[16] At one level, we are brought up to despise our wants and desires. They simply distract and threaten us.

We are brought up to identify our 'selves' with the 'goals' we set ourselves, and we pride ourselves and gain moral worth because of the sacrifices we make towards achieving them. It is because we have been brought up to deny our desires, wants and feelings that we recognise only parts of our experience. These suppressed desires and needs assert themselves in all kinds of indirect ways. They refuse to be killed off. This is a very different kind of sacrifice from the one that women are forced to make in their subordination and service to men, but it is no less real for being unrecognised.

It was partly in the crises that these 'ideals' provoked that men's consciousness-raising became important. Not only did we become aware of how these ideals were tearing us to pieces, we had to admit to one another what we were thinking and feeling. We became conscious of how the very 'living up to ideals' was itself part of the same tyranny. It had become something else 'to work at'. The supportive situation helped us acknowledge the reality and experience of what was happening to us, even when it was not the 'ideal'. We discovered that others were struggling with the same contradictions. We realised that we could not simply change through acts of will but rather that this was still very much the conception we were brought up with. Suppose, for example, that I realise that I do not take much responsibility for contraception. I might have told myself a number of times to be more 'responsible', but might suspect deeper causes that relate more generally to my feelings about sexuality. This becomes something to investigate and explore with other men.

It might have to do with difficulties in accepting my own sexuality, let alone someone else's. This could be related to ways I had been brought up to deny sexuality and treat my body as if it were a machine.[17] I realised that accepting more of my own experience was an integral aspect of 'working it through'. This involves a different kind of moral psychology. I had to be ready to 'work through' the reality of my experiences with others, not pretend to myself and others that they are what they 'ought to be'. There is enormous shame, difficulty and fear that we hide as men, for fear of being judged. We have different ways of hiding. Some of us have the ability to 'cut off' and 'withdraw'. Others hide in humour or drink.

Suppose that I am going out with Kathy and she wants to have a relationship with someone else. I might feel very hurt by this but tell myself that 'I shouldn't be jealous', because this is to treat her as a possession. I might then do my best to hide my jealous feelings from her, hoping that they will ease, feeling that she 'should' have this other relationship if this is what she wants. We should be able to 'work it out' anyway; 'it's good for us' to struggle this through. At some level I might feel suspicious because I detect how often I have felt that I 'ought' to suffer; I might even suspect that I feel easier when I am suffering because I am so used to it. This is an enormously difficult situation that many people have struggled with. There are no easy answers.

But it might be important for me to realise that, as a man, my withholding my feelings about the situation might be yet another way of my controlling Kathy. I might develop a sense of the complexity of the situation, feeling at one level that if I told her how badly I felt, this would be bound to influence her. On the other hand, I might realise how typical it is of me to work out what is 'best' in the situation, to have some sense of overall control. It is almost as if it is easier for me to work out what is 'morally best' than to work out what I am feeling. This absurdity is almost second nature to me. At another level, others might help me realise that I am scared at a deeper level that if I tell Kathy how hurt and jealous I feel, then she will still decide to have this new relationship.[18] The way that I had thought we 'should work the situation out together' was a way of hiding my vulnerability from her and myself.

The fear comes in acknowledging that 'I really love you and don't want you to have this relationship.' This is to accept the *reality* of what I'm feeling. This means that Kathy at least knows where she stands with me. I might feel terribly scared to be so exposed, to admit so openly what I want and need. It might make me realise how hard it is for me to admit what I want and need for myself – almost as if I feel that I should not deserve anything for myself. But then Kathy is free to decide whether or not to have this new relationship. This is only the beginning.

This is to acknowledge a crucial contradiction between 'the way I feel' and 'the ways I want to feel or ought to feel'. It shows the importance of learning to acknowledge what we feel and experience. In this way, we can begin to situate more of what we feel in the contradictions of our situations, rather than denying large chunks of our everyday reality. We acknowledge more of what we experience, in our material situations, rather than setting up certain 'ideals' to live up to. This gives a more realistic grasp of the changes that people can make in their lives and gives us more sense of the *processes* of these changes. It makes us wary of abstract theorising. We became more conscious of our difficulties as men, in defining our own wants and needs.

Within this dialectical conception, we deepen a sense of how our 'individuality' has been formed within a particular kind of family, schooling, media and work experience. We have a deepened understanding of the power of these institutions, but we also gain a sense of *how* they need to be transformed and changed. Slowly we gain a stronger sense of ourselves and our individual needs, and a recognition of the ways these have been displaced, distorted and subverted. We locate ourselves *within* this society and its life. Capitalism, like socialism, is no longer just a set of external institutions that we can observe objectively. We are struggling to regain a sense of our power, integrity, vitality, dignity, emotions, experience and creativity, that have all in different ways been subverted and reproduced, within the dominant social images.

This is profoundly to reject the Left's idea that the women's movement and men's movement have only to do with 'personal change'. It is radically to challenge inherited visions of socialism and to argue that they have to be transformed through the insights of feminism. The Left often does its best to subvert the experience of consciousness-raising, perhaps unwittingly, through reintroducing an Enlightenment split between the 'personal' and the 'political'. It wants to identify an awareness that women's oppression is institutionalised with a recognition that 'political organisations' are uniquely qualified to take action at this level. So the Left wants to present the move from the women's movement to a political organisation as a 'progression'. This is in line with the assumption that some women have more 'advanced political consciousness' with which they can recruit their less forward sisters. This assumption is set within a Leninist tradition.

It undermines one of the basic egalitarian understandings of the women's movement, which found a way of equally respecting and validating each woman's experience without thereby accepting it uncritically within its own terms, and thereby tapped something deep and non-mechanical in the socialist tradition. In contrast, a Leninist tradition has too readily identified socialism with the state, centralisation and industrialisation. It has shared with capitalism a belief in economic growth and the idea that progress can be identified with the domination of nature. This is a notion that Marx never clearly breaks with. More recently, ecology has begun to challenge this vision of nature as well as Marx's core idea that fulfilment and self-realisation can only come through creative labour. It helps to respect our relationship to nature as well as helping to see ourselves as part of a broader vision of nature and, by implication, to see our emotions and feelings as an aspect of this vision. In so doing, it helps us also to recognise the importance of love, intimacy and relationship as potential sources of joy and fulfilment.

FEMINISM, SOCIALISM AND EQUALITY

The Leninist tradition has done a lot of damage to socialist conceptions of morality, freedom and equality. Althusser has done different damage in his misleading critiques of 'humanism'. We are in danger of learning very little from the experience of the Russian Revolution. Until recent events in Eastern Europe, the Bolshevik tradition still dominated Leftist thought as a 'success story' which dazzles and blinds our understanding. The Left has been wary of any fundamental critique of the Soviet experience, as the revolutions in Eastern Europe in 1989 have so clearly demonstrated. Too much of our thinking has been limited around the issues of 'organisation' and 'taking power', so that it has been important for a discourse of anti-politics to emerge. For too long the Left has been blinded by notions of revolutionary practice.

Yet the deeper reality is that we have lost any sense of what kind of revolution we want to make, partly because we have lost a sense of individual fulfilment and integrity, of the ways to think out the relationship between individual and collective. The dominant traditions on the Left rarely give people a vision of what society would be like and what changes would be brought into people's lives. The vision of socialism as a better society, organised in accordance with people's need in the full sense, has been very weakened. For many people, socialism means an increased involvement of the state, and they are rightly suspicious. Some of the anarchist critiques of the increasing power of the state seem more pertinent as ways of keeping alive a libertarian socialist tradition that seems in danger of being lost to history.

One of the strengths of the women's movement has been to give a new vision of equal human relationships. It has challenged the mechanical conceptions of equality and has rediscovered the meaning of equality, at the core of a creative individuality. Individual dignity and integrity are founded on the value of each person's experience, grounded in the very sharing of pain and suffering and the recovery of its social and material sources.[19] Feminism has also challenged formalistic notions of liberal equality and shown up the reality of power and dependency which they too often hide in the institutionalised distinction between private and public spheres of life. It has moved us to a point of recognising the kinds of reorganisation of domestic labour, childcare and paid work that are needed if this equality is to be realised. This exploration of experience is subverted in the reintroduction of the split between the 'personal' and the 'political' that the Left is anxious to reimpose. The analysis becomes formalistic and undialectical if it is detached from an exploration of the sources of personal pain and suffering.

It was through consciousness-raising that women became aware, as they shared their individual experience and feelings, of the institutional structures of oppression and subordination. The significance of these patriarchal structures were grasped and the Left was forced to acknowledge their power in the organisation and legitimation of a capitalist social reality. But it is very misleading to suggest that it was through the 'psychological' explorations of consciousness-raising that women came to understand the structures of power that the Left understood all the time, as if it was women who were 'waking up' to what the Left already knew and understood. The reality is that our inherited understanding of class, family, sexuality and relationships of power has had to be rethought and reworked under the influence of feminism.

The women's movement shows that structures of dependency and subordination in both private and public life have to be challenged if 'equality' is to be realised. It is not enough to give women equal access to work in the public sphere. Sexism is built into the very authority structures at work so that the very workings of the industrialised mode of production are profoundly challenged. These are not simply structures which affect the situation of women in society; rather, they affect our understanding of the organisation of power and authority in society.

Politics, then, is not simply a matter of political parties and representative democracy, but enters into the very institutional and personal relationships of people. This is an insight that is recognised in the anti-politics that has developed in Eastern Europe as part of a challenge to state authorities.[20] This focuses on the ways in which 'politics' enters the ways we live our lives day to day and the kinds of relationships we want to develop with people. So it is that it centrally concerns the truthfulness and integrity with which we live our everyday lives.

Feminism can deepen our sense of what is involved in an equal relationship with people and develop our sense of the kind of institutional transformations necessary if people are to live in freedom and equality. It recognises that freedom is not simply a matter of extending the range of market choices that are available to people as consumers, however significant this can also be in specific contexts. It recognises that equality does not simply concern issues of allocation and distribution, but has also to concern equal integrity and dignity. In this sense, freedom is a human need that has long been diminished and denied within a Leninist tradition that too often ridiculed it in thinking it was somehow unimportant because it was not 'material' in some doctrinal sense.

Truth and dignity are primary needs that have been crucially asserted against the lies of the state in the recent revolutions in Eastern Europe. In this sense at least, they are not 'relative', so that the human sciences which have readily considered truth at least to be relative to a particular culture, morality or discourse, have to reconsider their assumptions in the face of this recent historical experience. It also means that the liberal state does not have to consider itself to be neutral when it comes to the ends of life that are freely chosen by its citizens. Democracy does not have to assume relativism when it comes to moral values.[21]

DEMOCRACY, LANGUAGE AND SUBORDINATION

The analysis of power and dependency developed within the women's movement challenged our understanding of formal democracy and the conceptions of freedom and equality which are so often taken for granted within a liberal language of rights. The institutions of formal democracy on the Left, tied as they have so often been to notions of democratic centralism, had little understanding of the connections between power and language, so no relationship to the experience of fear and anxiety many people experience at the thought of speaking in public. People were made to feel that if they remained silent, it was their own 'fault'. The platform was there and you were 'free' to get up and talk. So many women blamed themselves for their 'silence', recognising that, in any case, if they dared to speak, they were forced to talk in a language that did not express and articulate their values or experience.[22]

Somehow the 'formal' language of democracy was something that they had to 'learn', but which they felt estranged them from themselves even further. It certainly did not help them explain to themselves the sources of their oppression and silence. It was only with consciousness-raising in the women's movement that women began to realise the political character of language and the concealed structures of subordination and power, which were built into the structure of formal institutions. Women recognised that they were not 'free' to participate in the discussion, even though the men said they were. They brought into question the *terms* on which they were supposed to participate. They showed these linguistic structures and the terms of discussion were not 'neutral' and that they would have to be organised in a different way if people were to be able to participate on free and equal terms.

So the women's movement created its own structures in which women could speak, but also in which others wanted to listen. This expressed the realisation that we can learn from the experience of others, that our experience is not simply 'individual' and 'personal', but can teach us, if we are ready to listen and to learn, about a shared social and historical experience. This is something that the Left is still slow to grasp, for it has been dominated by formal conceptions of organisation which continue to reduce and discount both theoretically and practically the worth and significance of people's individual experience.

Feminism promises a different vision of democracy and representation for it recognises the time, attention and effort that is involved in people discerning what they need or want for themselves. It challenges a utilitarian conception of preferences, which assumes that people can automatically express what they want in a form that can easily be made part of a maximising equation. It exposes the rationalistic vision of reason, which says that if women do not immediately know what they want for themselves, then this can only be because they are confused, that so often underpins these conceptions.

Too often within the Left speech is an aspect of individual self-assertion, for, as men, we grow up to assume that reason is our unique possession, able to deliver truth as within our control. Men as the rational gender have everything to teach, for we appropriate reason as our own and so can assume that we always know best. Often we are too impatient for our chance to speak to listen to others. We are simply winding ourselves up so we can be ready to speak, hoping that we are not going to make fools of ourselves. Much of the language is rhetorical and does not illuminate the realities of our experience for it tends to present language as a feature of an autonomous conception of reason. It can be strangely abstracted and can seem to have a life of its own. It tends to be a mechanical rehearsal of 'principles' against which some rendering of the present reality is being compared.[23]

The most important concepts are often ahistorical and brought *to* the situation rather than generated through developing personal and historical realities. The philosophy of the later Wittgenstein can be read as a challenge to these dominating rationalistic traditions, as it seeks to reconnect language to an experience that has often been seen as separate. But since his work is so often interpreted in a way that treats language as autonomous and able to constitute social reality through the categories that it provides, its significance is lost and it is made to support a cultural and historical relativism in the human sciences that it could challenge.[24]

Women recognised the need for their own solidarity and sisterhood within which they could listen and learn from each other's experience as they built their own self-confidence and power. It took time for the prevailing traditions of the Left to be challenged, and a situation emerged in which it is still tempting for women to feel that they can 'prove themselves' by making it in the male Left world. In this way, feminist insights into the workings of power and authority so easily get lost as it seems that the institutions of representative democracy are treated as neutral and independent. Women are encouraged to put themselves forward for elections with the notion that if some women can do it, the rest should be able to. This argument became pervasive in the 1980s and it silenced crucial issues about the terms upon which women, blacks and Asians were being asked to participate.

In so many ways, the Left reproduces the structure of dominant institutions. For instance, it is harder to challenge the social relations of teaching and learning than it is to accommodate to the same repressive relations in school. There is a 'job to be done' and the Left is organised to do its job well; it does not matter what you feel about it. It is a bit like the schoolteacher who is quite clear that it is her job to get these children two GCSEs, even though they are sixteen years old and are unlikely to be any better off on the job market. She has decided that 'it is best for them' and so she treats them as if they were five year olds, subjecting them to the same patronising discipline. Her politics does not have anything to do with her teaching but is separated out, say, in her union work.

This contrasts with another teacher who, as a socialist, wants to treat her pupils as responsible adults able to make decisions for themselves and able to formulate their own wishes and demands. This means they have to take much more individual responsibility, but this itself is acknowledged as really worth learning about. It gives them some experience of themselves as autonomous and free individuals, and they can come to expect to be treated this way by others.

Often the Left does not appreciate the politics of teaching and learning, or draw the appropriate lessons for the ways that it organises itself. It has a sense of 'discipline' that is drawn from a strong sense of Protestant ethic and a critique of 'individualism' as essentially 'bourgeois', which makes it hard to grasp the injuries to dignity, confidence and self-respect that are made. It undermines people's sense of self-worth because it so often discourages people from thinking things out for themselves within a Leninist tradition that takes the truth to be the exclusive possession of the political party.

It also corrupts people's moral sense in the way that it teaches people to despise morality as a 'bourgeois' concern and to treat anything that brings a revolution closer as conforming to a 'higher' morality. Everything is legitimated in terms of an abstract notion of 'class struggle' and the 'needs of the class'. People are so used to receiving these kinds of justifications that they have stopped thinking about what they might mean. It was women who developed in the early 1970s a critique which grasped that the ways they felt diminished and put down within the Left were related to the structure of Left organisations. Feminism provided the basis for a different vision of self-worth, autonomy and democracy.[25]

The Left had hidden behind the rules of formal democracy, as much as other bureaucratic organisations. The lived reality of this experience was one of subordination and powerlessness for many people. This is evidenced in Eastern Europe where, since the 1989 revolutions, an explosion of anger at party privileges has been voiced. It was part of what brought traditional distinctions between Left and Right into question, as Thatcherism was able to appropriate libertarianism as its own. The Left libertarian and sexual-political critique which had developed into a *substantial* critique of the hierarchy and authoritarianism which often existed as the hidden reality of democracy, was lost in the 1980s. It needs to be recovered, for this was not simply a critique in principle; rather, it was set in terms of the ways relationships of power and subordination distort people's emotional and intellectual lives.

An anti-authoritarian tradition has been rediscovered in the anti-politics of the Eastern European revolutions which have recognised the crucial need to talk of truth and dignity as challenges to administered state authoritarian regimes that had for so long lied with impunity to their citizens. It becomes crucial to identify the lie for what it is and to explode for ever the idea that a lie can somehow transform itself into the truth when it is in the 'service of history or progress'. It was not simply Stalinism but Leninism that was the problem. It was also important to acknowledge that Marx had bequeathed a contradictory inheritance that was crucially flawed when it came to issues of freedom and democracy.[26]

Within a politics of principles, it is very easy to see democracy itself as a 'principle', not as a lived structure of relationships. People often lose a sense of why democracy is *important*. It comes to be presented as one principle competing with others. It was a strength of the women's movement to develop a critique of 'abstract principles', to investigate the hidden structures of power and dependency within relationships and the injuries they wrought. This was the lived reality in terms of which we have to make sense of 'principles'.

Women connected the ways they felt diminished and denied on the Left with the inadequacies of formal democracy. These issues could not be dealt with separately as personal or emotional problems but had to be grasped as aspects of institutional practices and relationships. The usual political discussions on the Left, of democratic centralism versus various forms of federalism, are often unreal, taking place in some kind of historical vacuum completely unrelated to the needs for organisation that people feel. Nothing shows this more acutely than the movements in Eastern Europe for greater freedom and democracy.

In the crisis that Thatcherism and Reaganomics provided in the 1980s, the Left has been prepared to grant a certain autonomy to women, but it has not really learnt the lessons. It has made concessions, as long as women do not bring their critiques of identity, empowerment, citizenship and democracy into the heart of Left organisations. But the implicit critique of formal democracy remains crucial. Uncovering the gender, racial and ethnic realities of subordination and oppression behind the liberal language of democracy, human rights and equality, has also fostered an important discussion of rights, citizenship and democracy.

It has been important not to forsake the gains of liberalism while learning to reconnect with a tradition of socialist equality, freedom and democracy. If we recognise the flaws within a liberal tradition, it is easier to see that market capitalism is not the only alternative to state socialism. As there have been different traditions of liberalism, so there have also been different traditions of socialism. New life and new possibilities are brought into focus as a Bolshevik tradition is broadly rejected and we begin to recognise the importance of rethinking different traditions of libertarian socialism. It is in relation to feminism and ecology that a vision of socialism, too long identified with centralised state authority, can be renewed.

12 Conclusion

Recreating politics – socialism, feminism and ecology

TRUTH, ECOLOGY AND POLITICS

While it has become important in both Western and Eastern Europe to reconsider the place of the market within the economy so that people are no longer faced with the choice between a command administered economy and free market economics, it is important to learn from the different historical experiences. In Eastern Europe, in the wake of the 1989 revolutions, it may be difficult to reclaim a language of socialism since it has for so long been debased. In both Eastern and Western Europeans have for so long been presented with stark choices between socialism and capitalism, between Left and Right. But this has often proved to be a false choice and, as Simone Weil grasped, our political traditions seem powerless to illuminate the new historical realities that we face.[1]

Our moral and political traditions seem to reflect a historical reality that has long passed, yet, at the same time, a language of truth and dignity seems indispensable as a challenge to the authoritarian regimes in Eastern Europe. At the same time, there is a risk that people could be blinded with the idea that individual dignity, human worth and freedom can only be guaranteed or sustained within a liberal capitalist market economy.

In Eastern Europe, it seems as if many people are ready to accept the exploitation of a capitalist economy, for it seems to promise consumer goods that they have never had as well as freedom and human rights to a degree that they have not known.[2] The socialism that they had experienced seemed to offer as much exploitation and privilege without the compensations that capitalism seemed able to provide. The state had lied with impunity and there was no free press to challenge it, or the right of association that would allow people to develop new forms of collective expression. These authoritarian regimes used fear as a weapon to silence civil society.

As Walter Schwartz has written,

> Before the 1989 revolutions, green values were coming to be seen in the West as offering a way out of an impasse. Socialism was dying and capitalism was discredited by its moral and ecological contradictions.[3]
>
> (*The Guardian*, 3 Jan 1990)

He asks whether the Eastern Europeans, having been offered less than the minimum of goods and services for decent living, will not 'lurch towards the other extreme, a new and subtler subservience in which open-ended, artificial "needs" are "satisfied" at incalculable costs? Has the revolution nothing better to offer?' He recognises that the new Europe will not necessarily be capitalist in ideology but, as he says, 'social democrats, too, worship on the altar of economic growth.'

It is easy to pay lip-service to the ecological movement without recognising the basic challenge it makes to our relationship to nature and to ourselves. It challenges a utilitarian tradition that identifies well-being with wealth and which respects people in terms of what they *own* rather than who they *are*. In this sense it resonates with a libertarian sexual politics that challenges the possessive character of personal relationships and which argued that the fulfilment and meaning in life was to come in large part from the quality of our personal and collective relationships and quality of our relationship with ourselves. But whilst in one sense this presented a challenge to capitalist moral values, at another level it could be contained within their structures.

Despite crucial differences, there are also significant resonances between the politics of truth and dignity that have emerged, say in Czechoslovakia in the recent revolution, and some of the libertarian insights that informed sexual politics in the West. There is a shared scepticism of traditional socialist politics and a sense of the significance of the ways minds changed in the generations of the late 1960s and after. Reflecting in 1968 on the differences between himself and communists of the older generation, the young playwright Václav Havel said:

> They seem to approach reality by way of certain abstract categories, which seem to them to have a lot of meaning and to reflect concrete experience. . ., [whereas] members of my generation tend to use as a starting point reality as it exists at the moment. They form general concepts on the basis of this reality and they disregard categories which seem to have lost their relevance and to function more as incantations than as concepts.
>
> (quoted by W.L. Webb, *The Guardian*, 30/1 Dec 1989)

As W.L. Webb reports, making use of this earlier interview, in 'The Rule of Truth', (*The Guardian*, 30/1 Dec 1989) Havel talks about how people younger than he 'not only reject all *a priori* ideological filters, just as I do, but . . . refuse to have anything to do with people who use those filters. Their attraction to concrete reality is very much more radical' (p. 6). Similar insights were available in the ideas of a politics of experience, which, in sexual politics, when it was not blighted by its own moralism, could open up ways for an investigation and exploration of lived experience.

In part this has been developed in forms of therapy that questioned the ways that a psychoanalytic discourse had historically closed itself off from the open exploration of experience at its different levels, when it insisted on analysing and interpreting this experience within the given terms of its theory.[4] This does not happen when it is done with sensitivity, but often this takes it beyond the framework that it has established for itself. It is the richness of experience that it demands to form its own expression and to shape language that is resonant with it.

Like the new politics all over Europe, as Webb reports,

> They are passionately ecological, inevitably in a region where the dragon's breath of unchecked industrialisation has scorched great tracts of lately rural land, sickening trees and children indiscriminately.
>
> (*The Guardian*, 30/1 Dec 1989, p. 6)

With a sense of people's destructive exploration of the natural world goes a rejection of the corrupted language and thought of the old politics. Havel is painfully aware of how, in Czechoslovakia at least,

> Socialism . . . was transformed long ago into just an ordinary truncheon used by certain cynical, privileged bureaucrats to bludgeon their liberal-minded fellow citizens from morning till night, labelling them 'enemies of socialism' and 'anti-socialist forces'.
>
> (quoted by W.L. Webb, *The Guardian*, 30/1 Dec 1989)

As he says, 'in my country, for ages now, socialism has been no more than an incantation that should be avoided if one does not wish to appear suspect' (quoted by W.L. Webb, *The Guardian*, 30/1 Dec 1989, p. 6).

If a language of socialism is to be renewed and revitalised, it will probably only be through its relationship to feminism and ecology. Somehow it needs to reconnect with the realities of people's everyday experience in a way that can illuminate the truth and dignity of that experience. Václav Havel as the new President of Czechoslovakia is being forced to answer for himself the words of an interview he gave in Prague in 1968 where he declared that the culture of art

> is concerned with truth, it tries to show reality as it is. Politics wishes to change reality, it requires power, and thus is it primarily in the service of power. . . It is an open question whether intellectuals can ever play an active role in political life without becoming unfaithful to their main goal, which is the truth.
>
> (quoted by W.L. Webb, *The Guardian*, 30/1 Dec 1989)

Havel has struggled to 'live in truth' and his example has proved potent. The difficulties of living in truth – of learning to be honest with ourselves and with others – has also been a central moral theme within sexual politics and psychotherapy. This helps us recognise that it involves more than will and determination. To show our weakness and vulnerability is a particular kind of strength, but one which we have rarely learnt to appreciate as men. It is also out of step with the dominant traditions within Western intellectual life which have in large part been suspicious of any claims to the truth. We have learnt to think of the truth as relative and, within a post-structuralist tradition, to regard it as the effect of particular discourses.

The events in East Germany, Hungary and Czechoslovakia in the closing weeks of the 1980s reawaken us to the central importance of a moral language of truth, dignity and respect. In part this has been a movement that has been mobilised against the lies of the state. The Czechs and Slovaks had been required by the Politburocracy to 'live lies' since the popular movement of 1968 because the truth did not fit the pseudo-history that supposedly legitimated Brezhnev's appointed leadership. People had lived a lie for a whole generation and they knew the way that 'truth' could be manipulated to serve the interests of the ruling groups. But the degradation of the truth made it all the more pressing for individuals to learn to speak the truth that was in their hearts. To compromise with the truth was to collude and was to play one's own part in sustaining the regime. For as Havel points out, by not protesting against it, people

> *live within a lie.* They need not accept the lie. It is enough for them to have accepted their life with it and in it. For by this very fact, individuals confirm the system, fulfil the system, make the system, *are* the system.

> ('Does Central Europe Exist?' in Ash 1989, p. 173).[5]

As Timothy Garton Ash explains it in his probing essay, 'Does Central Europe Exist?', the 'line of conflict' does 'not run simply between victim-people and oppressor state, as in the conventional image' (p. 173). 'In the post-totalitarian system,' as Havel puts it, 'this line runs *de facto* through each person, for everyone in his or her own way is both a victim and a supporter of the system.' Except, that is, for the few who have decided to 'live in truth'. The popular movements that have brought about the revolutions in Eastern Europe show the way that these ideas have grown over the years in the restructuring of civil society, for, until recently, people rejected the idea of seeking power in the state, having been 'taught by history'; as Adam Michnik wrote (1985) in his 'Letter from the Gdansk Prison', 'we suspect that by using force to storm the existing Bastilles we shall unwittingly build new ones'.

In place of the old divisions between Left and Right, as Garton Ash puts it, they offer us the even older division between right and wrong. These moral categories provide the truly operative distinction for those living under these Stalinist regimes. But it can be misleading to say, as Garton Ash does, that this is to

> reassert the fundamental premises of Judaeo-Christian individualism. Reversing the traditional priorities of socialism, they begin not with the state or society, but with the individual human being: his conscience, his 'subjectivity', his duty to live in truth, and his right to live in dignity.
>
> ('Does Central Europe exist?' in Ash 1989, p. 172)

Even if this masculinist language captures something important, it also shows difficulties we inherit within a tradition of liberal individualism to grasp the developing relationships between individual and civil society. Garton Ash recognises that if 'first change thyself' might stand as some sort of motto, these writers all insist that the attempt to live in truth and dignity 'does not merely have profound implications for the individual, it can slowly make a substantial impact on the communist state'. For as Havel puts it, 'the main pillar of the system is living a lie' (in Ash 1989, p.172). History has proved them right.

FEMINISM, POLITICS AND INDIVIDUALITY

Feminist theory and sexual politics can help illuminate the terms of this discussion, for they challenge the duality between 'individual' and 'society', between individuals changing themselves and having an influence on the state. A socialist tradition forged within the terms of an orthodox Marxism has too often reduced individuality and individual experience. It is a strength of the feminist notion that the 'personal is political' both to recognise that the personal realm of love and emotion is also a realm of power and to reinstate the idea that justice does not only have to do with the distribution of resources within the public realm, but also with the just treatment of people in our personal relations with them.[6]

It is important to recognise that this is not to reduce or banish private life as if it has become part of a seamless discourse of power and politics. If anything, it is to reinstate the importance of personal life and sexual relationships which have traditionally been marginalised and taken for granted within a liberal theory that has insisted that freedom, equality and justice are exclusively concerns for the public realm of politics. This had the effect of diminishing the injuries and pain that women often endure in being taken for granted and subordinated within the private realm. This suffering has largely been ignored as 'merely personal' when set against the political and public concerns of justice and equality. This diminishing of the private sphere was fundamentally challenged by Freud and psychoanalytic theory which, in a somewhat paradoxical way, argued for the reality of this misery and suffering. The fact that it had its source within emotional life did not make it any the less real and intense.[7]

The traditions of sexual politics were significant in showing that these feelings of inadequacy and worthlessness did not have their exclusive sources in the history of familial relationships. This tempered a psychoanalytic theory which had slipped into accepting the autonomy and independence of an 'inner life' which had to be comprehended in its own symbols and language. It took time for feminist theory to come to terms with insights of psychoanalysis and it is still very much an open question how this should be done.[8] But a deep impulse of feminism was to show how the ways that individual women felt diminished, reduced and worthless was connected to the subordination and oppression that women in general suffered within a patriarchal society.

Feminism amounted in part to a challenge to a liberal moral theory that held that respect was a matter of attitude and that there was no reason in principle why equality should not reign in the private sphere as long as women were given equal rights also to participate in the public sphere. This language of respect and rights was challenged by a language of oppression that insisted that it was not a matter simply of attitudes but of what men and women actually did and how they communicated with each other in their everyday lives. It was not simply a matter of what men thought, but of who men are – of the masculinities that they had learnt to identify with.[9]

Crucial in this is the Enlightenment distinction between public and private life which insisted that masculine identities were to be fixed within the public arena of work. It is work that continues to matter when issues of identity are at stake. This allows men to take relationships for granted, whatever they might say. So it is that we inherit a tradition in which the public world is appropriated by men as their own so that they assume the right to set the terms on which 'others' can enter. The public world is also the world of power and politics. Within a liberal framework, morality was a matter of individual conscience and opinion while politics was a matter of the distribution of power and resources within the public realm.

But, in this regard, feminism has challenged the pervasive Enlighten-ment distinction of private and public as well as the demarcation of morality and politics that follow from it. In some respects, feminism provides another basis for an anti-politics, for it challenges the notion that politics has to do exclusively with gaining power in the state. This remains the dominant framework for both conservative and social democratic politics. It is only as a movement for women's rights, rather than the liberation of women from oppression, that feminism can be integrated in a non-threatening way into these dominant frameworks. Otherwise its insights are marginalised as it is deemed to exist beyond the pale.

Feminism provides a crucial challenge to modernity and to the notions of morality and politics which have flowed from an Enlightenment modernity. It refuses to think that morality can be organised around the Kantian question 'what ought I to do?', with the assumption that a solution can be provided by reason alone. It fundamentally challenges the pervasive distinction between reason and emotion. It also recognises the need for the support and understanding of others if we are to learn to relate differently and form different, more equal and meaningful, relationships. It forms a connection between morality and the form and character of relationships, for it is only with others that we can live differently.

Feminism recognises a need for people to explore the meaning that they can draw from relationships, recognising how this connects with the feelings we have for others. It suggests the importance of honesty in relationships and so challenges a utilitarian notion that, for instance, could suggest that our partners will only be hurt if they get to know about other sexual involvements. If they do not get to know, then no damage has been done. But feminism, along with humanistic forms of therapy, can suggest that distances are created in relationships as people withhold from each other; as people conceal, so their integrity is compromised.

But we also grasp that we cannot simply learn as an act of will to share the truth that is in our hearts. For too long we have learnt not to listen to ourselves and to discount what we hear when it does not fit the abstract images and ideals we have set for ourselves. As men identified with particular forms of reason, we often construe our experience as we would want it to be, somehow getting ourselves to believe that that is the way it is. It takes attention and time to recognise the different ways that we are untruthful – the different ways that we live out lies about ourselves.

Bob Dylan has expressed some of this searching in a recent song entitled 'Oh Mercy'. It might be useful to set out some of the words:

> If I shut myself off
> so I can't hear you cry
> what good am I?
>
> What good am I
> if I know and don't do
> if I see and don't say
> if I look right through you?
> . . .
> What good am I?

Individuality is construed in different ways that challenge the abiding possessivism of liberal moral and political theory, within a feminism that denies that people can be treated as possessions.[10] It is crucial to question Locke's assumption that people have a fundamentally possessive relationship to the self so that freedom becomes a matter of doing whatever we will with that which is our possession. There are no moral limits in the way that we can treat our bodies, for our freedom lies in our being able to dispose of our possessions in any way that we might choose.[11]

It is important to recognise that within this tradition, which remains the source for so much of our thinking about liberal individualism, is the implicit notion that women and children are fundamentally the property of men. This has underpinned the idea that there could be no such thing as rape in marriage. It was as if the only moment of freedom and choice is the moment of contract, but, after the marriage contract has been sealed, women cease to exist, if they ever had, as persons in their own right.

Liberal theory often seeks to extend the freedoms appropriated by men through guaranteeing particular rights to women. But this is to leave the assumptions of possessive individualism unchallenged, as if they do not carry fundamentally oppressive assumptions themselves. It has taken the women's movement to challenge the idea that women are merely sexual objects. Objectification is a denial of women's dignity and integrity as human beings. Women do not exist simply as sexual possessions of men or merely in relation to men and children, but as persons in their own right. This provides an important challenge to utilitarian assumptions which underpin the notion that, if a woman is well provided for by her husband, then she has nothing to complain about but rather, if she persists in her complaints, this only proves that there is something wrong or inadequate with her individually. Traditionally, psychoanalysis has often been used to accommodate women to their accepted positions of subordination within society.

Feminism asserted that these were not merely 'individual' issues, while still seeking to validate the reality of individual women's feelings of worthlessness and inadequacy. It recognised the ways that women are often brought up to turn their feelings against themselves so that it is easy to blame themselves rather than the situation in which they find themselves. This is reinforced, for instance, if they are being told that they should be grateful to find a husband who provides so well for them. The women's movement potentially suggests a different, more complex, relation between 'inner' feelings and 'outer' experience which, in the end, fosters a critical engagement with therapeutic theory and practice.

It suggests that our feelings cannot be separated from our behaviour and that we need the support and understanding of others to take the risks to change our present behaviour and relationships. If a woman feels that she is betraying something inside of her when she lives solely in relation to others, her sense of self has been undermined and she no longer exists as a person in her own right. It is not simply a matter of what she has or owns, in utilitarian terms, but of who she is. This relates to her integrity as a person. Gradually, as she learns to voice her own experience, she feels empowered as she ceases to live only in the shadow of others but begins to learn how also to live *for herself*. This raises fundamental issues of values, for it involves considering what brings fulfilment to a person, which could challenge not only a narrow utilitarianism, but all forms of theory which would locate politics externally to experience and identity.

CAPITALISM, FEMINISM AND ECOLOGY

As people learn to value their integrity, they can appreciate how much they have lost when they have lived a lie. But it is important to recognise how hard capitalist market relations can make it for you to live in truth, for often it means turning away from the poverty and suffering of others. We learn to focus on our individual wellbeing, closing our eyes to the plight of others. Within the revolutions of Eastern Europe it can be important not to assume that capitalism is the only alternative to state socialism, as if capitalism can be a guarantee of freedom and individual dignity. This is to blind ourselves to the class relations of power that capitalism produces.

A useful example of capitalist development is provided by the Docklands Development in East London, which has marginalised the old East End as development has changed the area's character irrevocably. As *The Guardian* (3 Jan 1990) reports,

An 18-foot brick wall separates a new Docklands housing development from the West Ferry Estate, a complex of soulless flats built in the 1930s by the London County Council. The wall was supposed to be six feet high, but the builders say they made a mistake. Its presence, according to Ms. Yve Amor, the chairwoman of the West Ferry Tenants' Association, is symbolic: 'It is a border line; this is yours, this is ours – don't cross the line. The Berlin wall has nothing on this.'

(p. 3)

It is also to blind us to how destructive capitalism has been to nature and the environment. If capitalism is working hard to come to terms with the challenges of the Greens, it can only do this by applying conventional economist's yardsticks to cost environmental 'benefits' like clean air and green fields. But, as Walter Schwartz acknowledges, if this is better than the nihilism that preceded it, 'it is based on the fallacy that the environment is a luxury. The environment is what makes life worth living.' Even if the worst stains of industrial pollution are removed in Eastern Europe, he warns us that, 'if the automatic pilot is set on endless growth, the filth will surely creep back again over the years' (*The Guardian*, 3 Jan 1990).

It is a strength of Green politics that it has questioned the morality and economics of endless growth and capitalist consumerism. It has also raised fundamental questions of moral value both about our relationship to nature and also about our relationship to our inner natures and to others. In this way, it has brought back into focus some of the concerns of libertarian socialist politics that always contested the form of Marxism established in Eastern Europe.

More specifically, it has also opened up issues about the relationship of the Protestant ethic to capitalism, for it has questioned a Protestant inheritance premised on a sense of our inadequate human natures which are endlessly acquisitive in order to fill a black void we carry within ourselves. In raising questions about spiritual values, it has opened up a discussion about fulfilment and satisfaction that challenges utilitarian assumptions embedded within our social and political theories to the effect that our needs are insatiable and infinite. For if as human beings we can know fulfilment, then we do not always have constantly to extend ourselves in our endless activity. We can learn to respect the place of peace and silence within ourselves.

With feminism, ecology recognises the importance of connection and the ways that we can find fulfilment in our relationships with others. Feminism taught women not to discount their relationships with other women and to learn to appreciate their own wisdom and understanding.

In so doing, it also recognised the *difficulties* of being honest and truthful in our relationships with others and learnt to look towards therapy as a way of illuminating some of these difficulties. If we do not respect our own feelings and experience, it is difficult to respect others'.

But a Protestant culture has only taught us to reject feelings and emotions that are judged as unacceptable to our reason.[12] We are constantly critical of ourselves and critical of others as a way of defending ourselves. Little of what we do is good enough, and, as I have argued, we are plagued by feelings that if others knew what we were really like, then they would surely reject us. So we protect the images that we place before others and judge others critically for being taken in by what we show them. They do not know us as we truly are. But often we do not seek to know ourselves in this way, for we are fearful about what we might discover.

As feminism challenges the idea that people can be possessions of each other, so ecology challenges our possessive relationship to nature. Nature is not there to serve human needs and, equally, women exist as individuals in their own right who, in taking responsibility for themselves, learn to value what is meaningful for them. This challenges a tradition of Weberian rationalism that thinks that meanings and values can be assigned by reason alone. For often it is through our feelings rather than our reason alone that we can work out what matters to us, what brings fulfilment in our lives.

But a Protestant moral culture never focuses upon this issue for it assumes that we will be eternally dissatisfied. If we expect little for ourselves, then we never have to make ourselves vulnerable to others. Our attention is always moving into the future and we are constantly envious of what we think others have. As men, distance often serves as a form of self-protection. We learn not to make ourselves vulnerable, and often we do not have to be, for our male identities are firmly set within the public realm of work.

Both feminism and ecology provide a challenge to a Marxist theory that assumes that we are only creative in our labour and that we only produce ourselves through production. It is at this deeper ontological level that Marxism resonates with particular aspects of the dominant masculinity. Not only does it serve to reinforce the notion that what matters takes place in our creative activity as individuals, but too often this notion of creative activity has been identified with work, if not paid work. The underpinning metaphor seems to be that of the individual alone with *his* creation. This tends to reinforce gender divisions because it is men's work and men's time that matters in the organisation of relationships and families, since often it is the greater source of income.

Historically, it has reinforced a productivist ethic that has been blind to the value and fulfilment that can be drawn from other parts of people's lives. It reinforces the notion that creativity has to do with work and it denies or diminishes the creativity that can be expressed in other areas of life.

In defence of orthodox Marxism, it could be said that work and production have for so long been central in people's everyday existence and survival that it is a luxury to bring forward these other needs. But this is a destructive argument, as the experience of Eastern Europe has shown, for it has so often been used to minimise the importance of truth, integrity and dignity in people's lives. It has also encouraged men to take their private lives and sexual relationships for granted, assuming that women could be relied upon to do the emotional work required to keep them going. As men, we are often blind to the energy and involvement that is necessary to sustain relationships.

Often it comes as a shock to us when our partners say that they have had enough, for we grow up within a Protestant culture to assume that there is always something that we can do to make things better. But this is not true and it is often painful to recognise that once distrust and silent disapproval has taken over, it can be impossible to reform the situations. The injuries have been too many and the distances created too great for forgiveness to be possible. We have seen that, as men, we reason that someone has to be to blame for the breakdown, for we think that it has to be somebody's 'fault'. It is hard for us to learn that it takes two to tango and that, as men, we are equally responsible for what goes on in our relationships. Too often the energy is so focused upon our work that we take the other areas of our lives for granted. Often we take pride in letting our partners make decisions for us, without realising how this means that we are failing to take responsibility for ourselves. Often we are taking our partners for granted.

This is significant because Marxism supposedly recognises that it is relationships with others rather than material goods that bring fulfilment into our lives. Central to Marx's critique of capitalism is his insight that production for profits takes precedence over the fulfilment of human needs. Exchange values come to dominate within a capitalist society and the only values that can be recognised are the values that are assigned on the market. In part, Marx welcomes the ways that traditional values were undermined in this process, for they tended to legitimate arbitrary distinctions of blood and family ties.

In *Capital* (Marx 1976) Marx investigated the ways that exchange values are embodied within a capitalist economy organised around production for profits. Against this, he explores the contradictions that are created in the relationship between the production of goods and the meeting of human needs. But within this contradiction between use values and exchange values, it is easy to lose a sense of the importance of human relationships as a source of human fulfilment.[13] This was certainly lost within a tradition of orthodox Marxism that identified socialism with the socialisation of the means of production. This worked to legitimate a centralised state authority that talked about the people but which often defended its own privileges, seeing civil society as a threat to its powers.

The strength of a libertarian socialist tradition as it emerged in the late 1960s was its challenge to abiding centralised state structures. It insisted that people learn to control the terms in which services were provided so that it was suspicious of a social democratic tradition that saw equality as a matter of the allocation of resources. In this way, it was sceptical of educational and welfare institutions that arrogantly assumed that they 'knew best' and that people should be grateful for whatever they were provided with. Against this there was a sense that this dependency amounted to a denial of freedom and responsibility and that if people were to be free, they should have more control over crucial areas of their lives.

But, unfortunately, the dissatisfaction with bureaucratic state institutions, whether it be hospital or housing offices, was articulated on the libertarian Right that in both England and America was able to take crucial moral and political initiatives. It spoke with conviction and this shattered a period of consensus politics in which there was a prevailing feeling that politicians took the people for granted, just telling them what they wanted to hear. There was a crisis of credibility in which people were ready to say 'a plague on both your houses!' Thatcherism sometimes caught this mood, appearing to stand for a clearly defined set of beliefs whilst others did not really seem to believe in anything.[14]

Thatcherism articulated a vision of freedom as choice, which worked particularly well when it promised to give working-class people the chance to buy their council houses. It could seem as if this was extending a freedom that socialism had proved itself unable to deliver. It allowed people in work to feel better off. It was able to identify socialism with a belief in the state in a period in which people had become suspicious of bureaucratic authorities. The morality of the market was hegemonised so that the extension of the market appeared as an extension of freedom. Paradoxically, this often meant a concentration of state powers rather than a decentralisation, for it challenged the autonomy of local authorities and appropriated to itself, for instance, in the sphere of education, the right to dictate the form and content of education.

Thatcherism did not really trust people to make decisions for themselves, for it only trusted the movements of the market. It could not recognise a plurality of values, for it assumed that the market as the only guarantee of freedom was always right. But it was able to appropriate the idea of liberty for itself, and the Left libertarian tradition, which sought to give people more effective control of their everyday lives and bring freedom and equality into a different relationship, was temporarily lost from view. It has been this loss of political memory that has allowed the events of Eastern Europe to be understood as a defeat for socialism and a reassertion of capitalist values. But there are different traditions of socialism and such a dualistic vision is blind to their potential re-emergence.

MORALITY, JUSTICE AND EQUALITY

The development of Green politics has brought some of these issues of freedom, control and authority into a new focus in its challenge to the statist politics of social democratic traditions that see economic growth as an end in itself. Issues of justice and morality only emerge later when it becomes a matter of the distribution of resources, so that the organisation of a capitalist economy goes largely unquestioned.

It has been a strength of Green politics to say that economics is inseparable from morality. This is not simply a technical and practical issue. Further, it challenges an abiding distinction between morality and politics that holds that morality has to do with individual conscience and decision while politics has to do with the allocation of resources and the regulation of competing interests. This often fosters the feeling that the individual alone is powerless and ineffective, unable to effect anything in the world of politics.

Ecological politics has broken the spell of this passivity, empowering individuals to feel that their individual action can affect the wellbeing of the planet. If I continue to use spray cans with CFCs, then I am hurting the planet. Ecology has also invoked a revitalised sense of equality and community, for we share a common fate as regards the planet. So it is that a planetary consciousness tends to create new forms of community and association. It sets questions of value at the centre of our lives. It challenges a positivist tradition that sought to marginalise and diminish questions of value as if they are 'merely' a personal concern. We have learnt that individual actions can have consequences far beyond themselves. They can resonate in different worlds. People are offered a different sense of personal responsibility and a different sense of connection with others.

A socialist tradition has for too long been concerned to think of justice as a matter of the distribution of resources. It was at this level that social democratic politics tended to define its difference from conservative and liberal politics. It has taken feminist and ecological politics to awaken us to a prior sense of justice, as Simone Weil construes it in her essay 'Human personality', that has to do with the ways that we violate others in our treatment of them. Weil thinks of the situation of a young girl being dragged into a brothel against her will. She argues that to think of this in terms of a liberal language of the infringement of rights is to fail to illuminate the moral realities of the situation. To think in terms of rights is to fail to appreciate the injury of violation. In treating someone in this way, we do an injustice to them.[15]

This helps restore the priority of justice as a language that has to do with the ways that we treat each other. It links to the way we treat ourselves as well as the way that we treat animals and nature. It makes issues of abuse – whether it be the different ways that we abuse ourselves through not listening to our emotions and feelings or the ways we abuse others in our relationships with them – of central moral and political importance. Both feminism and ecology have served to redefine the nature of politics through the ways they have rejected traditional definitions of 'the political' that see it as primarily focused upon issues of distribution and exploitation within the public sphere.

So there is a developing challenge to a capitalist morality and politics that assumes that nature is there to be used and that the only dignity and value it can aspire to is that which is provided for it by its usefulness to human beings. This fails to appreciate the integrity and autonomy of animals and plants. They do not simply exist in relation to humans but in their own right.[16] This challenges a tradition of Enlightenment modernity which would seek in Kantian terms to ground our dignity as human beings in an independent faculty of reason that supposedly makes us superior to animals and nature. This is to define our humanity as a relationship of superiority which provides us with nature as something that has been reduced to dead and inert 'matter'. As matter, nature can make no claims upon us; it is there waiting to be grasped and ordered according to the laws of reason. We are no longer the guardians of nature, as Genesis might have it, but nature is there for us to use and exploit as we see fit.[17]

The theological resonances remain significant, for Kant and the Enlightenment tradition prepare us to accept a secularised form of Protestantism, as if it were the impartial and universal voice of reason. It is the connection between Protestantism and the spirit of capitalism that Max Weber does so much to illuminate. Often the issue of secularism is misconceived, for it is rarely appreciated that we are dealing with a Protestant form of secularism. This is part of the inheritance that a Western culture has sought to impose as part of its identification of progress and science with modernity.

But unless the 'religious' sources of particular forms of modernity are more clearly explored, our challenges are bound to be more superficial than they need be. This containment persists in the challenges that have been made to Enlightenment conceptions of reason. Often within discussions of post-modernity, we end up with forms of relativism that refuse to give priority to particular notions of reason and the claims that it makes to define a linear form of progress and development.[18] If this opens up the possibility of different ways of knowing, so that we are not tied to an identification of knowledge with a perceptual grasp of reality, it often misses how an Enlightenment modernity has been structured around a pervasive distinction between reason and nature.

For Kant, this meant that it is only as rational beings that we can be moral agents. It is only if we act out of a sense of duty that our lives can have any dignity or moral worth. Our emotions and feelings are sources of unfreedom, for they seek to determine our behaviour externally. It is only with reason that we can have an inner relationship, so it is only reason that is the source of freedom and dignity. This is a philosophical vision that has helped define modernity.[19] It is in challenging this vision that feminism, ecology and forms of traditional and humanistic therapy can be taken as providing issues that help define a different vision of 'post-modernity'. In their different ways, they recognise the dignity and integrity of our emotional lives and recognise the need for us to develop more of an ongoing relationship with them. This cannot be achieved through suppression, nor simply as a matter of will and determination.

Rather, it calls for a different exploration of our experience in which we are ready to share the tension between what we experience and what we think we rationally ought to feel or experience. This recognises that integrity has to do as much with being true to our feelings as being true to our thoughts. The dignity of our emotions and feelings does not depend upon their conforming with what we would want them to be. Part of recognising the dignity of our emotional lives is in acknowledging that our feelings cannot be reduced to thoughts or to mental states. They have a logic and reality of their own which connects in particular ways with what we think and how we act.

As we learn to listen and respond to our inner natures, we can recognise that what brings us fulfilment is different from the goals and ends that we have set by reason alone. We become more aware of feelings as a source of values, for it is often what we feel most deeply about that we value and want to cherish in our lives. It also awakens us to the fact that, especially as men, we find it difficult to draw support from each other, locked as we are within competitive relationships in which it is hard not to believe that in showing our vulnerability to others, they will take advantage of this or somehow use it against us. Within a rationalistic masculinity so tied to priding itself in its independence and self-sufficiency that it is hard to learn the value of relationships with others. So often we pay lip-service to relationships but this becomes rhetorical within a culture of liberal individualism.

Similarly, Marxism has a language of relationships which, at different periods, has resonated with the support and solidarities of working-class experience.[20] But as the realities of these communities are subverted and undermined, the language of community and association seems to become increasingly hollow. In its orthodox forms, Marxism has most easily concerned itself with attacks on private property as the source of injustice and exploitation. It has invoked its own form of duty and called upon individuals to subordinate their selfish interests to identify themselves with the higher interests supposedly represented by the state.

In ways that are rarely appreciated, Marxism has, in practice, often been sustained by its own vision of duty and self-denial.[21] People learn to look to the state rather than to the help of fellow citizens. Charity is just one form of association that died in the Soviet Union as people learnt to ridicule it as a form of paternalism. In any case, in a society in which the means of production had been socialised, there was no need for charity. With a Protestant ethic, Marxism often shares a sense of life being an endless struggle to redeem a flawed conception of nature. It shares a moral framework in which it is deemed wrong to give to ourselves, for this is a form of selfishness. Morality has to do with selflessness. Within a capitalist society, as Weber grasped, work and money become ends in themselves.

People learn to pride themselves on the renunciations they make. Within the Soviet Union, people were taught to put the interests of the state above their own personal interests. People learn to identify themselves with the production goals of the state. But gradually they become disenchanted as their lives fail to improve and the fear and corruption of the state leads to a cynical detachment from politics. In these situations, consumer goods can seem to provide the only meaningful compensation. Nothing which is not tangible can be trusted. If Soviet Marxism is not to be discredited completely, it has to find ways of meeting the consumption needs of its population.

It has been ecological politics that has raised the issue of fulfilment, of whether people have to be eternally dissatisfied as they are within a Protestant ethic, or whether they can ever be satisfied with what they have. This is a crucial issue for the West, particularly in its relationships with the South. The way that our visions of modernity have been cast within a Protestant mould has meant that our social and political theory has largely been built on the assumption that human beings need infinitely to appropriate. We constantly need more, for we can never fulfil the dark hole that we carry within us. This is the source of the possessive individualism that still remains at the heart of liberal moral and political theory.[22]

So a dynamic is set up in which we are constantly striving after goals we set ourselves and that we have little experience or conception of self-acceptance or self-nourishment. Within a Protestant moral culture, it is easy to carry a sense that we are undeserving, so that we have to earn the love of others. Within a culture of self-denial, as I have portrayed it, it can be difficult to accept the support and love of others if we have never had to learn how to accept and love ourselves. The extent of our recognition of our emotional lives as men is limited to the private sphere of relationships. Often this is sharply divided from the ways that we feel obliged to present ourselves in public where we systematically conceal our vulnerability so as not to give others an advantage over us. Within the public realm, emotions are a sign of weakness, an indication that we cannot really cope. More generally, as men, we learn to suppress our emotions and feelings, for to engage with them is often dismissed as a sign of self-indulgence. Therapy cannot be used as a support and clarification in our everyday lives, for we often learn that it is only for the sick or the mad. We fear its polluting effects if we have contact with it.

MASCULINITY, THERAPY AND EMOTION

I have argued that, as men, we are often blind to the injuries that we do to ourselves. As we learn to suppress our emotional lives, fixed in the notion that our emotions have to be rationally justified before we can allow ourselves to have them, we lock ourselves into a ceaseless mental struggle with ourselves. Often so much more is going on inside as mental anguish and tension than we ever allow ourselves to express out of a fear of what others might think about us. Our emotions, thoughts and feelings are locked inside us as we assume that we have to work things out for ourselves within our inner lives.

It can feel a weakness even to share ourselves with our sexual partners, thinking that this will only diminish us in their eyes. We can so easily withdraw and withhold out of a sense that it is a sign of weakness to need the understanding and support of others. So often within a Protestant moral culture we learn that to share ourselves emotionally with others is to burden them with a load that it is our lot to carry for ourselves. In this way, we rarely learn how to form bridges to others, how to deepen our relationship with them.

So it is that, as men, we are often very hard on ourselves. We are constantly critical of ourselves for failing to live up to the goals and standards that we set for ourselves. We can feel undeserving and punishing of ourselves. At the same time, we can protect ourselves from the attacks that we so often expect from others, either by being harder on ourselves or putting ourselves down before others have had a chance, or else by feeling superior and diminishing the experience of others. In whatever way we do it, we block our contact with others, especially with men, from whom we feel the threat of competition.

It is a strength of humanistic forms of therapy that they can help us identify some of these strategies that might have become so second-nature to us that it is very difficult to identify these patterns for ourselves. Therapy can remind us of a shared humanity in showing that we all withhold in different ways out of a culturally induced fear that we might be rejected or found inadequate in some way of other. It can remind us that often we do want the contact and understanding of others, even if we seem to be constantly rejecting it out of a fear that showing our emotional vulnerability will inevitably lead to rejection. In this sense, group therapy can be a profoundly egalitarian practice, for it provides a space in which we can experience the shared character of our emotions and feelings. As we learn of the different ways that we have hardened ourselves against our emotions, we recognise some of the processes through which we have injured and forsaken aspects of our humanity.

This is not to deny the significance of gender, class and ethnic differences but it can help to place them in a different context. Differences of material and social power are in no way dissolved, but as we experience people struggling with the difficulties of emotional expression, say about their grief at the loss of a parent, it can touch something in ourselves. As people express the pain of a grief that has been locked up for years, an unexpressed grief that has for so long cast a shadow over an individual life, it can awaken us to our own suppressed feelings of compassion and love. The very fact that this sharing takes place in a group situation can awaken a sense of human equality and can reveal to us aspects of a humanity we have long put aside.

As you experience the pain that someone is carrying because of the loss of their mother, you recognise that this has to be lived through, it cannot be taken away. As someone comes to terms with the grief, anger and sadness they felt, they are facing themselves in an important moment of truth.[23] It is crucial to recognise that this is a process and that as people learn to express, as well as to acknowledge, their grief, then things begin to change for them. This can be a slow and painful path and, as you move on this path, different facets of the relationship might well be brought into focus. It might be that it is only after some of the anger has been expressed at the death, that someone can begin to feel some of the loss.

In different ways, this provides a challenge to rationalistic modes of modernity. Someone might block the expression of their anger with the idea that it is 'irrational' to feel anger at someone who has died, especially someone who has done so much for them. They can then discount and suppress these feelings, thinking that they are a sign of ingratitude or that they reflect some basic flaw in the personality that should best be hidden away lest it reflects badly on the person. This can make it hard to *explore* and *investigate* the anger that we feel, recognising that it is through such a process that we might understand it more. This is to recognise the dignity and integrity of our emotional lives, allowing them to have a voice of their own, rather than judging them according to the dictates of reason. So that rather than dismissing this anger as 'irrational' and so as something shameful, I might be interested in exploring what it means.

This is to challenge a rationalistic tradition that sees an independent faculty of reason as the only source of meaning. Within a Kantian tradition, emotions and feelings are supposedly part of a given nature. Since they are 'given', they cannot be a creative part of ourselves, nor can they be a source of knowledge. But so it is that we learn to use reason to fix our experience, with the idea that emotions have to be a kind of judgement, as if the anger we feel at a mother who has died is necessarily the way that we will always feel. There is no sense of emotional life as part of a *process* of experience that includes our thoughts and our behaviour.

It becomes difficult to acknowledge the ways that our attitudes and beliefs might change, for we assume that they change because of the impersonal reasons that we are offered. Within a rationalistic culture, it can be difficult to acknowledge that someone can be suffering from grief, for we tend to be dismissive of this as 'merely' psychological, which is another way of throwing doubt on the 'reality' of the suffering or sickness. As men brought up to identify our masculinity with reason, it can be particularly difficult to recognise some of these issues.

Since, as I have argued, we are constantly denying our emotions and feelings since their acknowledgement is felt as a sign of weakness which compromises our sense of masculine identity, this renders invisible the emotional injuries that we are constantly doing to ourselves, for we learn to take pride in these suppressions as proof and validation of our masculinity. This makes us less sensitive to the damage that we do to ourselves since it is a way of hardening ourselves against our experience. Wilhelm Reich learnt to think of this as a process of armouring, for it is a somatic way of organising our muscular structure so that we do not have to feel the pain of our experience. We learn to experience it as a source of pride. We learn to be cool and unaffected, as if to be unaffected by life is something to be proud of.

Therapy also provided a challenge to modernity in its recognition that people can grow and develop. Individuals are not fixed as rational selves guiding their lives by reason alone, but people change as a result of their experience of life. Experience is not simply given. It can be transformative. This is something that the libertarian politics of the 1960s and 1970s appreciated, as Havel readily acknowledges when reflecting on 1968. He recognised how pervasive it was for an older generation 'to approach reality by way of certain abstract categories' while his generation, as I have already quoted, 'tend to use as a starting point reality as it exists at the moment', allowing general concepts to form on the basis of this reality (quoted by W.L. Webb, *The Guardian*, 30/1 Dec 1989).

Similarly, it is a strength of *Gestalt* as well as other forms of humanistic therapy to focus upon the quality of 'here and now' experience, allowing conceptions to emerge which illuminate it. This is no less theoretical a vision but it is theoretical in a different way. It breaks with a psychoanalytic tradition that has its theoretical categories worked out in advance, recognising that too often the theoretical categories freeze and we tend to organise observations, say of young children, to fit with a theoretical framework. To treat theory as auto-nomous in this way seems to be endemic within a rationalistic intellectual culture.

It makes it difficult to recognise the breaks with this tradition when they happen. So, for instance, it can be easy to diminish the insights embodied in alternative forms of therapy by claiming that they are not theoretical. This is to hold tight to a particular conception of theoretical work which treats the analyst as the source of truth. A different vision of therapy is signalled in the insistence within the humanistic tradition that therapy is something that people have to be continually doing for themselves, if they are with integrity to be working with others. It is not something simply to be experienced as a part of training.

MASCULINITY, MODERNITY AND EMOTIONAL LIFE

Modernity is characterised by a desire for control. Its vision was formed within a masculinist framework as the new sciences of the seventeenth century were understood as part of a new masculine philosophy.[24] Since it is presented to us as a universal category, we are often blind to the gender assumptions that have been built into our inherited visions of reason. As we seek to control external nature, so we learn to trust ourselves as men, with the control that we exercise over our emotional lives. Often we never learn the difference between control and suppression, and, within a Kantian tradition, we think we are being rational through subordinating our 'inclinations'.

I have argued that this weakens and undermines a sense of autonomy and independence, although Kant takes these to be the outcome of reason alone. A sense of moral self is traditionally taken to be a strength of Kantian theory when it is compared with utilitarianism. Kant is seen as able to sustain a sense of individual dignity and integrity, refusing to sacrifice individual dignity to larger social goals. His vision can seem to sustain freedom and dignity. I have argued that its failure to come to terms with our emotional lives as much as its failure to come to terms with history and culture, treating them equally as externally determining and conditioning our individual freedom, makes it incapable of illuminating the relationship of emotional life to morality and politics. Rather it leaves us with an attenuated conception of the individual and a limited conception of morality, which it treats as a matter of reason alone.[25]

Within a rationalist vision of modernity, we inherit a sense of life as a series of rational actions. Freedom is a matter of being left alone to pursue the goals and ends that we set for ourselves. Emotions are a sign of weakness and they continually threaten to interfere with a life that has been firmly set in its tracks. To a large extent Marxism has remained trapped within this vision of modernity. Even if it has a language of relationships, it has never really been able to develop this. It has taken feminism, therapy and ecology to raise fundamental issues about the *quality* of life and relationships. In their different ways they have challenged the place of consumerism in our lives, trying to show the costs of the idolisation of individual success and economic growth, both in terms of our relationships with our partners and children and also in the injuries that we do to nature and the planet.

An experience might help to illuminate some of this. As a child of refugee parents, it was important for me to be accepted by the other children at school. I put enormous efforts into getting things right and I became adept at sensing what was expected of me by my teachers and peers. This is not an unfamiliar experience for immigrants, for there is often a sharp demarcation between school and life within the family at home. It is easy to feel that home is to be hidden away, for it tends to mark a difference with others that is threatening. It is as if home is to be kept private because it is hard to feel that who we are in the context of, say, the Jewish home is acceptable in the larger Christian world. Unwittingly, it becomes tinged with shame because it has no reality within the public world that was defined by school.

This might well make some immigrant children more externally defined, more placating and eager to please. For me it meant that I was able to sense the rules that were operating in any situation so that I could prove myself in their terms. It meant a cautious marginality that was not unsatisfying because I could prove myself intellectually, but reflected itself in a difficulty that I can still have of setting the terms for a particular activity or discussion. This is to stick my neck out in a way that can still feel too threatening.

It could be argued that Kant shows a way out of this by stressing the dangers of being externally defined for being able to develop a clear sense of identity. For Kant this can only be achieved by developing a relationship with an interior vision of reason. But it might be that reason is no less 'inner' or 'interior' than are our emotions and feelings 'external' or 'exterior'. A rationalist culture has drawn this distinction and we have become used to living it, but in different ways it does not reflect reality. If you grow up within a family in which very few emotions and feelings are expressed, and when they are it is seen as a sign of weakness, then it might be only with severe bodily injury or pain that you can feel *entitled* to look for some kind of parental sympathy or understanding. With this background, it might take considerable time and effort to learn to identify and give form to feelings and emotions.

It is somewhat paradoxical that within our culture 'how are you feeling?' is supposed to have an immediate response, for we assume that our feelings are given and immediate. But often this is a difficult question that we sidestep by saying 'fine' because we learn to assume that people are not really interested in knowing. Often it is women with more ongoing relationship to their emotional lives who are able to say how they feel. As men, we can come to realise how attenuated is our relationship to our emotional lives. It is as if they have been suppressed for so long as we have learnt to get on with 'the business of life' that our personal life and relationships are often experienced as distractions.

As men, we often experience ourselves trying so hard but feeling, at least in our relationships, that things often go wrong. It is as if we would prefer a set of rules that we could follow so that we can rationalise our relationships in a similar way that we can rationalise our work. So it is that a man might switch from work to home feeling that he has to be 'on duty' as soon as he comes through the door. It is hard for him to recognise that if he has not learnt to nourish himself, to give time and space to himself, then it is hard to give to others. Children are very quick to pick this up and are rightfully angry that as a father you are just 'going through the motions with them' but are not really *there*. In a way not illuminated by Kant, it is only when we have connected with our emotions and feelings about the day that we can really be there for others.

It is not then simply a matter of facing the next task which duty has set before us. The rational self is not a presence in the way that Derrida's notion of deconstruction has it. Nor is it simply an issue of recognising that the self exists in unintegrated fragments, as a plurality of identities.[26] This does not touch the ways that Western conceptions of modernity enshrine a particular masculinist vision of the rational self. It is in the diminishment of emotional life that traditions of postmodernism have failed to address the crucial demarcations between reason and nature.

As a child, it might be threatening to contact my emotions and feelings if I feel they are going to betray me and throw into question the ways that I have presented myself to others, say at school. Within a Protestant moral culture, we learn to suppress our emotions and feelings, for they might well reveal an animal nature. Expressing them will prove that our natures are rotten after all and that we are worthless human beings. This makes it more difficult to develop a clearer sense of self. In contrast to Kant, I argue that it is in contacting our emotions and feelings that we draw more reality in our lives and contact with others.

For example, if a boy has been caned at school but was too shy to seek an explanation so that he grew up feeling that this arbitrary punishment could befall him at any moment, then it is hardly surprising if he feels constantly vigilant, distrustful and on his guard with adults. He does not know where the next attack is going to come from so that he has got to be constantly on the alert. This is to adrenalise your experience constantly and so it is to weaken your immune system. It is to be constantly prepared for an unseen danger. This experience is not unfamiliar to men, for, within a competitive culture, we learn that we have to be constantly on our guard. In this context it is hard to trust, especially other men who we fear will take any opportunity to put us down. We learn never to drop our guards. This injures our relationships for it is difficult to trust someone enough to allow ourselves to be vulnerable with them. We are so accustomed to the resulting loneliness and isolation that we do not identify the pain for what it is.

If, as boys, we go home from school only to be told by parents that we must have deserved the punishment that we received and that in any case this is what happens if you do not 'keep your nose to the grindstone', we learn not to share ourselves. Many children feel intensely alone in their experience at school, but since this is how it has always been, they do not expect any different. So it is, for instance, that boys can experience their fellows being humiliated in front of the whole class – the boy with a stutter being told that if he cannot talk then he should shut up. We do not learn to identify the physical abuse for what it is but rather the abuse and the humiliation become normalised and taken for granted.

As we join in the laughter, we collude in the pain. We might feel that something unspeakably wrong has taken place, a violation, but we learn to pass over these feelings in silence. This has been a central part of an education into masculinity. Many of us carry memories of being terrified at school, but, within a culture that has institutionalised and normalised abuse, it is difficult to name it for what it is. More than most examples we could give, it shows up the poverty of our moral and political traditions, whether liberal or Marxist, for they diminish these violations as 'private' and so in some way less 'real'. It is a strength of Simone Weil's writing that she refuses these strategies, insisting that injustice as the violation of a person be rediscovered as central to our language of morality and justice.

As adults looking back on these experiences we often learn to make light about them. We think that because we have 'survived' these experiences they could not have been that bad. As a way of not having to deal with the unspoken injuries and humiliations, many families send the next generation to a similar fate. For the cycle is not broken unless we are prepared to break it ourselves. Especially as men, it can be difficult to face the pain and humiliations of our personal histories, for we have learnt to pride ourselves in being able 'to take it'. We do not want others to think that we are 'wingeing' or 'complaining' because they could easily use this against us.

Alice Miller's crucial work in *For Your Own Good* (1983) has helped illuminate the ways that parents who love their children will abuse them without really understanding how.[27] If a child is hit 'for its own good', then he or she will not be allowed to *feel* the anger and resentment. The child will be silenced so that these feelings will have to be suppressed. In this sense, the integrity of the child will be undermined. This is something that Kant gives us no language for. Often the child is made to feel bad about herself or himself. This is reflected in the broader culture in which we silence children in their complaints about school, thinking that 'you cannot expect any child to like school'. We stop listening to our children. Soon they stop listening to themselves, and, as boys, will often take out their unspoken and unrecognised pain in being violent and taking it out on others, often smaller than themselves. More often, girls seem to turn this pain against themselves as they internalise the blame.

Sadly, it is often children who have been abused themselves who seem to go on and abuse their own children. It is as if taking it out on others is a way of controlling the unacknowledged pain that is carried inside. For as Freud grasped, the fact that we learn to suppress emotions and feelings does not mean that they do not return to haunt our experience. Our moral theory is still trapped within Kant's rationalist framework that assumed that if we do not attend to our 'inclinations', they will wither and die. Often to suppress our emotions and feelings can itself be a form of abuse and if we cannot recognise within our inherited moral culture the abuse that we do to ourselves, then it is hard to identify the ways that we abuse others.

It has taken feminism to illuminate the ways that women have been constantly abused and subordinated when, as men, we thought we were treating them equally. This has sharpened our sense of what it means to exist as a person in our own right. More, it has shown emotions and feelings are important sources, as against Kant, for individual dignity and integrity. As women learnt to discount their feelings of anger and fear at the ways they were being treated, so they were being untrue to themselves, but it was only in the context of a movement with other women that these relationships could be challenged as women learnt to appreciate themselves in their own terms, rather than constantly evaluating themselves in the eyes of men.

For men it has been hard to learn how to take more responsibility for our emotional lives and learn how to draw more support from each other as men. Gay men have learnt to do this, particularly in the light of AIDS, which has forced a reconsideration of many aspects of their relationships. Heterosexual men have been slow to learn from our gay brothers and from each other. Often it is only as relationships with women break down that we begin to consider our personal lives. We can be so estranged from our emotional lives that we fear being overwhelmed if we give our feelings of anger, resentment or loneliness some form of expression. We have learnt to take security in the sharp boundaries that separate the 'personal' from the 'public', so that it is threatening when these boundaries begin to lose rationale or stand in the way of our living fuller, more meaningful, lives.

In this way, feminism, therapy and ecology all challenge in their different ways the inherited relationship between the personal and the political, the emotional and the rational, the private and the public, the cultural and the natural. In their different ways they all make us sensitive to the ways that we treat ourselves, for the ways that we listen to ourselves will often be reflected in our relationships with others. They all call upon us to change ourselves as part of a process of changing the world and healing the planet.

MEN, FEMINISM AND MODERNITY

Enlightenment modernity tends to confuse control with domination. The only control that we can feel secure with is that which silences through its domination. Kant teaches us to silence our inclinations as sources of knowledge, for they can only interfere with a path set by reason. He assumed that women, as closer to nature, could only be 'rational' in their relationship with men. On their own they could not be complete and autonomous beings because they could not be rational. Feminism has challenged this legitimation for women's subordination. But, as men, we grow up in the shadow of this rationalism, assuming that we have appropriated reason as our own. We assume the right to talk for others and to know what is best for others, even if we are supposedly ready to listen.

As men we remain threatened by the independence and autonomy of women. This touches a deep fear that is tied in with the very definitions of male identity which we have inherited. It is as if it remains difficult at some level, whatever our rationalisations, not to feel that women are 'ours'. Possessiveness is so deeply rooted within our culture and so subtly tied in with the organisation of identities, that it is hard to work it through. Even to acknowledge the depths at which feminism threatens us as men would be a first step.

This abiding sense of possession, control and domination is deeply rooted within modernity. We inherit a vision of nature as being there to serve us. Even the planetary warnings of the greenhouse effect are treated as confronting us with 'problems' calling for a particular 'solution'. We rarely face the ethical issues which underpin our relationship to animals and nature. Our identities as 'rational selves' have been so firmly set within a Cartesian/Kantian tradition as in opposition to nature, that we easily get lost when thinking about a different relationship to nature.[28]

Possibly a start would be to reconsider our relationship to our 'rational' selves, so that we begin to reverance ourselves as part of nature, rather than assuming that to be human is to be 'rational' and this is to set us irrevocably in opposition to nature. As men, we seem particularly tied to the notion that our task, even in personal relationships, is to come up with some kind of practical solution to change the situation. Often our partners might be looking for support and validation, say of their frustration or upsetness at work, but often what we offer is an immediate solution to make the situation better. Often they want the experience of being listened to, rather than being told that it might be time to change their jobs.

It is partly because we relate to our own emotional lives in this way, thinking that if we change the situation some uncomfortable or unwelcome feeling might go away, that we offer this advice to others. But this can be a way of short-circuiting a process, for it does not give us time and space within which we might learn from these emerging feelings. As men, we have learnt to distrust our feelings as a source of knowledge so that we just want to rid ourselves and others of them as soon as we can.

Not only is this reflected in our personal relationships, as feminism or therapy might illuminate, but it is also a feature in our dealings with nature, as ecology has it. Often we are well on the way to finding solutions before really understanding the nature of the problems that we face. Sometimes it is in pushing into action that we can curb and control uncomfortable feelings that might be breaking the surface. It can certainly be easier to offer solutions than to listen to the hurt we have caused to those who are close to us. It can equally be hard to listen to the injuries and sufferings that we have helped create for others. Sometimes our friends just want us to listen to what they have to say *and take it in* before we rush into ceaseless activities. This would involve recognising that issues in relationships which confront us with human problems cannot be approached, let alone solved, as if they are technical problems of cause and effect.

As men brought up within an Enlightenment culture, it is easy to assume that every problem can be thought about 'rationally' or 'scientifically' so that we can weigh the considerations on different sides before we come to a 'solution'. It was important for Wittgenstein in his later writings to explore the idea that there is not a single pattern or language game to which different aspects of our experience can be subsumed. Reason operated in quite different ways in the different parts of our lives and what works for us at work might prove quite inappropriate, if not insensitive, if we try to operate in our relationships in this way. At work as an engineer, you might apply British standards to all your calculations, but it is dehumanising to try and operate in a similar manner in your relationships or with yourself. A different kind of exploration is called for.

The women's movement has argued that women's subordination cannot be thought about simply as an issue of extending rights to women that men already enjoy. This is not a 'problem' that can be solved without changes both in what men do and in how we grow up to be. As men, it is difficult to recognise that nothing we might be able to do can restore a relationship that has died. We assume that if things are not working in a relationship, then someone must be to blame and there must be a solution that we can work out through reason.

It is painful to recognise that relationships are not like machines that can be fixed or a part replaced. These mechanical metaphors have come to dominate our thinking and experience since the Scientific Revolutions of the seventeenth century. They inform not only the ways that we think about our relationships with nature, but also our sense of social relationships. It is in their image that we learn to treat our bodies as if they are machines. This remains the guiding metaphor of allopathic medicine.[29]

ECOLOGY, FEMINISM AND POLITICS

If it is difficult to recognise that our relationships could have died because of our neglect, since we never learnt as men that they needed to be tended and cared for. Too often we take them as part of the background against which we live out our individual lives as men. As we never learn to nourish ourselves, so we never learn to nourish our relationships. We learn to prove ourselves through effort and activities. We never learn in our schooling how to care for ourselves or others. We think that things will look after themselves, only needing some kind of attention if they break down or collapse.

Similarly, it is difficult to recognise that the injuries that we have done to the planet cannot be undone. As Bill McKibbon points out in *The End of Nature* (1990), 'we can only stabilise the situation at some sort of fairly horrific level; we cannot solve it'. He recognises that we might work out ways of trimming our way of life but 'our impulse will be to adapt not ourselves but the earth. We will try, I think, to figure out a new way to continue our domination and hence our accustomed lifestyles'.[30]

It seems as if the hardest thing is to change ourselves because so much of our modernist discourse, somewhat paradoxically given its literary expressions, seems to turn us away from the self. Even if we learn with Freud and psychoanalysis to interpret our experience and so to develop a more refined sensitivity to ourselves, this is different from a commitment to change ourselves and relationships, as alternative therapies have stressed. It is this meeting with our emotional selves, through an intellectual and cultural transformation, that has come to have a vital significance for the healing of the planet.

McKibbon (1990) is convinced that we will prefer to develop new forms of domination by different and more destructive means. In his words, 'we may well find a way to keep from choking on our cake, only to gag on the icing later.' For these new tools, say of planetary management of scarce resources, will be

> deployed – in the service of an ideology, a philosophy, that man is at the centre of creation and it is therefore right for him to do whatever pleases him. The notion is deeply ingrained – all of us act on it every day.
>
> (McKibbon 1990)

The gender designations speak for themselves. Unless, as men, we learn to relate differently to ourselves, we will extend our control over women just as we seek to do over nature, as environmentalists learn to control the earth's resources that remain.

These attempts at 'macro-management', as it is called, remain fairly crude. We might, for instance, be able to keep track of the movements of fish through satellite, but they are still wild creatures able to grow at their own pace. But it is a different kind of assault of nature that occurs in genetic engineering when animal blends are developed. In England, researchers have crossed a goat and a sheep. As McKibbon (1990) reports it, Christmas-tree growers are now cloning trees with branches at the proper 45° angle and, as the advert has it, 'thick needles that do not fall off to litter the living room floor'.

Often we fail to recognise the significance of such developments, either because we have a belief in the benign character of scientific progress, or at least its inevitability, or just because we prefer to pretend that it is not happening. As with issues in our relationships, we live in the hope that if we do not attend to them, they might just disappear or go away. Some people do not worry about genetic engineering because they think it is just an extension of traditional practices, such as selective breeding. But, as McKibbon points out,

> nature puts definite limits on such activity: one could cross two peas, but not a pea with a pine, much less with a pig, much less with a person. There were restraints, in other words limits. And our understanding of what those limits were helped to define nature in our minds.
>
> (McKibbon 1990)

We are in danger of losing any sense of the autonomy and independence of nature, any sense that it should be respected in its own right. Since the scientific revolutions, we have tended to see nature as matter. It is as if nature died before our eyes. This meant that it was there at the service of humans and that the only dignity that it could aspire to was in its usefulness to human lives. So it is that, as men, we have learnt to take nature for granted, as feminism alerted us to the ways we were taking women for granted. We sought to make nature in our own image just as we sought to make women as a reflection of our masculine fantasies. But as women have revolted, so has nature. We have been rudely reminded as men that domination has its limits.

It was a weakness of the libertarian politics of the 1960s and 1970s that they had no sense of limits. It was a period of relative affluence and of youth. In Bob Dylan's words, we were to be 'forever young'. We had little sense that we would grow into the future because our attention was so focused upon the present. We were prepared to let the future look after itself. In many ways, as I have shown, this was unrealistic and naïve. We were blind to our own cycle of life and to the limits that nature would put on our own lives. In this sense, our politics and morality were very much shaped in the image of the Enlightenment. The vision was also masculine in the sense that it tended to revolve around ourselves, even when it was concerned with the plight of the Vietnam war. We were concerned to be morally and politically right. We would not let authorities stand in the way of our freedom.

It took time to recognise how self-centred this was, for, in many ways, it assumed that we could make the world in our own image. It was part of a rationalist tradition in that it did not recognise limits. In this sense, it was part of a politics of domination, for it saw the world and people as essentially malleable, as waiting to be 'formed' according to 'our' conceptions. We knew best and it was up to others to listen. It was as if the world existed as some kind of projection of our consciousness, gradually being transformed into what we would want it to be. It was not there as a limit to our activity and certainly not as some kind of partner with which we could have genuine contact as we transformed the world together.

Feminism made it clear that women did not exist simply as pro- jections of the male consciousness. Women existed as individuals in their own right with experience, understanding, values and dreams of their own. They did not exist to agree or accommodate themselves to the world according to us as men. This itself challenges men to explore the narcissism of their vision. It is here that psychoanalysis can be illumin- ating. Though Freud remains in part trapped in the notion of the world as some kind of projection of the individual consciousness and of relationships as providing us with 'objects' for our libidinal desire, he also makes a crucial distinction between rationalisation and reality.

Psychotherapy at least supposedly seeks to question the fictions that we create for ourselves so that we can accept more reality in our lives. But more negatively, it is significant that the analyst sits behind the 'patient' as he or she lies on a couch. They do not engage person to person – and they do not even have to make eye contact with each other. The analyst is supposedly to serve as some kind of mirror or screen that will encourage the all-important transference of infantile wishes and desires to take place. This is supposedly an important learning experience and it has obviously been important in many people's lives, but it still seems an awkward context if two people are somehow unable to meet in their shared experience of life.[31] In this sense it can leave open questions of the forms of contact that can provide for fuller connection between people.

Women insisted that men learn to meet them face to face so that their independent reality, values and visions were appreciated. Women refused to live primarily in relation to their partners and children. Men had to learn to communicate their needs for themselves and could no longer rely on women to do the emotional work for them. So it was that men had to learn to relate to women as equals, rather than as their own projections. This was threatening because it brought into question many long-standing assumptions that men had learnt to make about themselves. Having to meet women in their autonomy and independence was a challenge to the domination that men had assumed.

Similarly, ecology has taught people increasingly to recognise the integrity and dignity of animals and nature. It has helped question the assumption that nature exists in relation to people so that the domination of nature can be taken as a sign of progress. People have had to learn that they exist as part of a broader conception of nature. Ecology has also helped challenge an economics of growth, raising questions about the fulfilment of human needs. It questions a conception of possessive individualism that has underpinned so much of our Western moral and political theory.

This is to put consumerism into some broader context rather than to deny the needs it serves. It calls us to take greater responsibility for the suffering and poverty experienced by so many as we rework relationships between rich and poor nations.[32] The experience of poverty in the midst of plenty, of private affluence and public squalor, remains an indictment of the capitalist market. If markets are to be reintroduced in Eastern Europe, some important lessons have to be learnt, if people's hopes are not to be dashed. Some will prosper but many more will suffer.

In Eastern Europe, civil society has been subordinated to a state that is supposedly its higher realisation.[33] This vision of state socialism has lost all credibility. People have recovered a sense of their own dignity and self-respect as they have challenged these regimes in popular movements. New forms of solidarity are being created that embody a new freedom and democracy. There is a vision that people can live in truth and dignity as a new form of politics takes root. But this is also a precarious time since old nationalist identities which have for so long been suppressed begin to surface again.

It is as if the centralised state control had sought to banish any identities that would conflict with itself, imposing its own form of universality. Distinctions of gender, ethnicity, religion were all declared superficial or accidental with no foundation in reality. It was declared that, as human beings, we are all the same and we should have the same opportunities and health and educational provision. At least in the public sphere there was some egalitarian sense, even though there was enormous fear, privilege and corruption and enormous inequalities of wealth and power. But as this vision of socialism is discredited, it means that in the West it can no longer be pointed to as the only alternative to capitalism.

The Enlightenment helped foster dreams of a society structured according to reason. In many ways, Marxism remained a child of the Enlightenment, for it thought that if society could be reconstructed according to reason, then people would be able to live in freedom and equality. Too often this fostered the notion that the rulers knew best because they have reason, science or theory on their side. This utopian vision has come to an end as we learn that we have to take more responsibility for our own lives and relationships. We cannot leave it up to others. We have to discern our own needs and desires. Reason cannot be relied upon to do the work for us.

Feminism has taught men that women cannot be taken for granted. They have to set their own terms for participation in the public realm. As the relationship between public and private is redefined and as women learn to value their own experience, forms of knowledge and visions, they learn to empower themselves. Similarly ecology teaches us that nature has its own dignity and integrity and that unless we learn to respect it in forming a transformed relationship with it, there can be no healing of the planet.

But only as we learn to heal ourselves as we learn to integrate and accept the conflicts, pain and joys of our emotional life will we be able to treat others more equally. This is a way in which we can help to check a movement towards violence and abuse within personal life, family and civil society. As we accept more of the reality of our own lives, it could help us to live more equally with others. As we learn to listen to ourselves, so it makes it easier to listen to others. This could help in the transformation of our inherited visions of morality and politics.

Notes

1 Introduction: identity, politics and experience

1 For useful discussions of the changing character of politics in the 1980s, see the articles gathered together by Stuart Hall and Martin Jacques in *The politics of Thatcherism* and also Andrew Gamble's *The free economy and the strong state* and *Britain in decline*. See also *New times: the changing face of politics in the 1990s*, ed Stuart Hall and Martin Jacques, which attempts to connect structural changes with issues of identity and post-modernism.

2 For an understanding of the impact of Althusser on the British Left in this period, see E.P. Thompson 'The poverty of theory' in *The poverty of theory and other essays*. What these developments in theory meant for our appreciation of sexual politics in the late 1970s is brought out in Victor J. Seidler, 'Trusting ourselves: Marxism, human needs and sexual politics' in *One-dimensional Marxism: Althusser and the politics of culture*, ed Simon Clarke *et al.*, pp. 103/156. See also Ted Benton's *The rise and fall of structural Marxism* for a more internal understanding of this movement of ideas. Its antagonism to issues of experience and nature still haunt discussions around post-structuralism and post-modernity.

3 For an understanding of Laing's work see *The divided self* and *The politics of experience* which had an enormous appeal in the early 1970s. See also R.D. Laing and A. Esterson, *Sanity, madness and the family* and David Cooper's *The grammar of living*. In 1967 in the Roundhouse in London there was a large gathering of intellectuals including R.D. Laing, David Cooper, Jules Henri and Herbert Marcuse, whose work had been largely marginalised up to then in English academic life. This was later published as *The dialectics of liberation*, ed D. Cooper. For later critical evaluation of Laing's work see Andrew Collier, *R.D. Laing: the philosophy and politics of psychotherapy*, and *Laing and anti-psychiatry* ed Robert Boyers and Robert Orrill. Some of the concerns around issues of identity, fragmentation and displacement that have become critical in discussions around post-modernity were initially brought into focus in these works loosely and misleadingly organised around the notion of 'anti-psychiatry'.

4 See Sheila Rowbotham's elaboration of these themes in 'Women's liberation and the new politics' reprinted in *The body politic* ed Michelene Wandor, pp. 3/30. See also her *Woman's consciousness, man's world* for a personal sense of the issues and conflicts that were given expression in the development of

feminism. Sheila Rowbotham's collection of essays, *Dreams and dilemmas*, helps to place some of the ideas that were growing in the 1970s in the context of discussions in the women's movement.

5 For a useful discussion of liberal conceptions of freedom and autonomy which touches on some of these themes in a different context, see the essay by Ronald Dworkin 'Liberalism' and T.M. Scanlon 'Rights, goals and fairness' in *Public and private morality*, ed Stuart Hampshire, and Michael Sandel's critical discussion in *Liberalism and the limits of justice*. For insightful feminist discussions of some of these issues, see Ellen Kennedy and Susan Mendus, *Women in western political philosophy*, Genevieve Lloyd's *The man of reason: 'male' and 'female' in western philosophy*, and *Feminist challenges: social and political theory*, ed Carole Pateman and Elizabeth Gross.

6 The historical sources of this conception of possessive individualism are well set out in C.B. Macpherson's *The political theory of possessive individualism*. Some of these ideas are discussed in an illuminating way by Charles Taylor in his paper 'Atomism' in *Philosophy and the human sciences: philosophical papers 2*, pp. 187/210.

7 See Bernard Williams on the nature of respect in his article 'The idea of equality' reprinted in his *Problems of the self* and the discussion of respect and inequality in Victor J. Seidler's *Kant, respect and injustice: the limits of liberal moral theory*. It is a central theme in this work to explore the difficulties of sustaining a liberal account of equal respect within a society characterised by unequal relationships of power and subordination.

8 For some influential statements of some of the sensibility and politics that was developing out of the Black movement which seems to be so often marginalised in accounts of this period, see Eldridge Cleaver's *Soul on ice* (1969), Franz Fanon's *Black skin, white mask*, George Jackson's *Soledad brother* and Malcolm X's *The Autobiography of Malcolm X*.

9 The way that men responded to the ideas and challenges of the women's movement is a theme in Victor J. Seidler, *Rediscovering masculinity: reason, language and sexuality*. See also *The making of masculinities*, Harry Brod ed, and Jeff Hearn, *The gender of oppression*.

10 The situationist literature of Guy Debord and Raoul Vaneigem was a real influence of the time, especially in the events of May 1968. See, for instance, Guy Debord *The society of the spectacle* and the collection of situationist writings, *Leaving the 20th century*, ed Chris Gray. More recently in the work of Jean Baudrillard, some of the notions have become important in contemporary understandings of media, culture and society. It has taken considerable time for these insights to be assimilated and they have received significance within a very different cultural and political climate. See, for instance, his *Simulations* and *In the shadow of the silent majorities*.

11 Attempts to bring Marx and Freud into relationship with each other were variously the source of a renewed interest in the writings of Wilhelm Reich and the Frankfurt School. See, for instance, the useful historical discussion in Reich's *The function of the orgasm* and the essays collected by Lee Baxendall as *Sex-pol essays – 1929-1934*. There was a broad interest in Marcuse's writings, especially perhaps his analysis in *One-dimensional man* and *Eros and civilisation*. See also Bruce Brown, *Marx, Freud and the critique of everyday life*, Eli Zaretsky's *Capitalism, the family and personal life* and Anne Foreman's *Femininity as alienation*. For more recent work, see *Social*

amnesia by Russell Jacoby and *Neurosis and civilisation* by Michael Schneider; coming from a structuralist tradition which tends to accept Lacan's reading of Freud, see *Psychoanalysis and feminism* by Juliet Mitchell, and *Sexuality* and *Sexuality and its discontents* by Jeffrey Weeks.

12 The different ways that issues of respect and equality are to be reconciled within a vision of individuality in the writings of Kant, Kierkegaard and Simone Weil are discussed in Victor J. Seidler, *The moral limits of modernity: love, inequality and oppression.*

2   Consciousness-raising

1 The notion of 'second nature' is briefly alluded to by Georg Lukàcs in *History and class consciousness.* It supposedly indicates the ways that certain culturally defined modes of behaviour become so firmly established and taken for granted that they shape our very conception of self.

2 Some of these issues about political activity and self-denial were explored by Sheila Rowbotham in her essay in *Beyond the fragments: feminism and the making of socialism,* (eds) Sheila Rowbotham, Lynne Segal and Hilary Wainwright, entitled 'The women's movement and organising for socialism'.

3 This self-definition of men as 'Men against Sexism' can be followed in the newsletters that were a regular feature in the 1970s and early 1980s. It brought together different tendencies but in the early years it often perpetuated a negative conception of masculinity as essentially oppressive to women. Often it did not leave enough space for the exploration and reworking of different masculinities. In this sense, *Achilles' Heel* represented a different current of thought and feeling.

4 For an appreciation of some of these tendencies within the gay liberation movement, see, for instance, the collection edited by Gay Left Collective, *Homosexuality: power and politics.* See also Jeffrey Weeks's later reflections in *Sexuality and its discontents* and in 'Questions of identity' in *The cultural construction of sexuality* ed Pat Caplan, pp. 31/44.

5 This rationalistic conception of rationality is alluded to by Bernard Williams in his *Ethics and the limits of philosophy.* If he had connected this to particular forms of dominant masculinity, he might have found ways of exploring how this notion is lived out in our everyday lives. But his treatment is full of suggestive ideas. The connection between masculinity and reason is a theme in Victor J. Seidler's *Rediscovering masculinity: reason, language and sexuality.*

6 This discussion of 'character forms' owes much to the writings of Wilhelm Reich. See in particular his insightful *Character analysis* where he goes beyond a Freudian theory that is concerned with individual symptoms. See also his *The sexual revolution* where, somewhat crudely, these notions are invoked within a social context. These ideas had a pervasive influence on Erich Fromm and on the Frankfurt School, though they were rarely acknowledged. An interesting discussion which bears on some of these issues is provided by Russell Jacoby in *The repression of psychoanalysis: Otto Fenichel and the political Freudians.*

7 An understanding of some of these changes in work processes is provided by Harry Braverman's *Labor and monopoly capital* and the extensive discussions that have followed that work. See, for instance, Bob Young

'Labour and monopoly capital' in *Radical science journal* no.4 (1976), pp. 81/93, and Russell Jacoby 'Essay review of Braverman', *Telos* (Fall, 1976) pp. 196/206. See also *The division of labour: the labour process and class struggle in modern capitalism*, Andre Gorz (ed), and the special issue of *Insurgent sociologist* devoted to Braverman's work, nos. 2 and 3 (Fall 1978).

8 The ways that men's dependency on their partners is often denied because it conflicts with the images that men want to present of themselves as 'independent' and 'self-sufficient' and the consequent devaluation of the 'emotional work' that women are expected to do has been a theme in feminist psychotherapy. See Susie Orbach and Luise Eichenbaum, *What do women want?* and *Understanding women*. See also Sheila Ernst and Marie Maguire, *Living with the sphinx: papers from the Women's Therapy Centre*.

3 Feminism

1 These conceptions coincide with particular interpretations of Marx's work, namely the extent to which a more orthodox conception of Marxism as a form of economic determinism is adhered to. It is only if we can show that a particular form of human misery and suffering has a 'material basis' that we are permitted to talk of 'oppression' at all. Many women have taken themselves to be breaking with Marx when they have felt it necessary to challenge this conceptualisation of their experience which they have correctly perceived as a minimisation and denial of so much of what they are struggling to get acknowledged and recognised. Again, some of these issues were usefully illuminated in the discussion provoked by *Beyond the fragments: feminism and the making of socialism*, Sheila Rowbotham, Lynne Segal and Hilary Wainwright (eds).

2 Some of these issues are usefully set out in Simon Clarke's essay 'Althusserian Marxism' in *One-dimensional Marxism* pp. 7/102. For a useful introduction to Althusser's writing see his *For Marx* and *Lenin and philosophy and other essays*. This writing had considerable influence in the move towards theory in the mid-1970s and away from an earlier politics of experience that had thrown up so many painful questions and contradictions.

3 Reich's discussions in *The sexual revolution* and 'What is class consciousness?' reprinted in *Sex-Pol* are still critical for an understanding of the weakness of an interpretation of Marxism as economic determinism. He shows how it disfigures our sense of the conditions for a transformation of personal and sexual relationships. At the same time, his visit to Russia helped him grasp the significance of compulsory marriage and its relationship to property and legal relations. For an important biography of Reich, see Myron Sharaf's *Fury on earth: a biography of Wilhelm Reich*. Some of these issues are also critically explored in Eli Zaretsky's *Capitalism, the family and personal life* and Russell Jacoby's *Social amnesia*.

4 There have been numerous discussions around the family, partly sparked off by Christopher Lasch's work, *Haven in a heartless world*. See, for instance, *What is to be done about the family?*, Lynne Segal (ed), and *The anti-social family*, Michele Barrett and Mary McIntosh. See also *Rethinking the family: feminist questions*, ed B. Thorne and M. Yalom.

5 For writings which show the experience of women in socialist societies, see

Hilda Scott's *Women and socialism: experiences from Eastern Europe* which shows that, where women are given access to the labour market, it is often not on equal terms.

6 For an interesting discussion of the relationship of sex and class, see Ann Phillips and Barbara Taylor, 'Sex and skill: notes towards a feminist economics', *Feminist review* No. 6, 1980. See also Anna Coote and Beatrix Campbell, *Sweet freedom: the struggle for women's liberation*, and *The economics of women and work*, A.H. Lamsden (ed).

7 An introduction to the Frankfurt School is provided by Martin Jay's *The dialectical imagination – a history of the Frankfurt School and Institute of Social Research* and David Held's *An introduction to critical theory: from Horkheimer to Habermas*. For a seminal statement of Horkheimer's conception of critical theory, see his useful essay 'Traditional and critical theory' reprinted in his collection *Critical theory*. There are also interesting discussions of these issues in *The positivist dispute in German sociology*, ed David Frisby.

8 This vision of 'common sense' is central to Gramsci's reworking of the relationship of Marxism to morality within the *Prison notebooks*. It is introduced in Part 3 of the notebooks under the general heading 'The philosophy of praxis' made up of (1) 'The study of philosophy', pp. 323/77, and (2) 'Problems of Marxism', pp. 378/472.

9 Marx's *Economic and philosophical manuscripts of 1844*, where it is said that as production is increased, the worker is degraded. This is an idea appreciated by Simone Weil in her 'Reflections concerning the causes of liberty and social oppression' in *Oppression and liberty*. These ideas are explored in the chapter 'Work' in Lawrence Blum and Victor J. Seidler's *A truer liberty: Simone Weil and Marxism*, pp. 143/93.

10 These arrangements have been multifarious, which is itself something to be understood within the contexts of development of late capitalism, and which leaves 'the family' in an ambivalent situation. Some of these issues are usefully brought together in *What is to be done about the family?*, ed Lynne Segal. See also David Morgan, *Social theory and the family*.

11 The situationists analysed capitalist society as increasingly a society of the spectacle. See, for instance, the collection of situationist writing *Leaving the 20th century*, ed Chris Gray. Issues of identity and fragmentation have also emerged as central concerns in the discussions around 'post-modernity'. See, for instance, Jean Baudrillard's *Simulations* and *In the shadow of silent majorities*. For a useful discussion of Baudrillard's work see Douglas Kellner, *Jean Baudrillard: from Marxism to postmodernism and beyond*.

12 Laing's work was important in identifying and establishing this idea of the 'unreality' of social life, particularly the ways that people could constantly fail to reaffirm and legitimate each other's experience but would constantly undermine it. See in particular the studies collected in *Sanity, madness and the family* by R.D. Laing and A. Esterson.

13 Adorno's work is insightfully introduced in Susan Bucks-Morss's *The origin of negative dialectics* and by Gillian Rose's *The melancholy science: an introduction to the thought of Adorno*. For a sense of Marcuse's writings in this period, see *Negations*, particularly the essays on 'Philosophy and critical theory' and 'On hedonism'. For a more general presentation of Marcuse's work, see Douglas Kellner *Herbert Marcuse and the crisis of Marxism*.

14 This is something discussed in Victor J. Seidler's 'Trusting ourselves: Marxism, human needs and sexual politics' in *One-dimensional Marxism*. It is also a theme in his *The moral limits of modernity: love, inequality and oppression*. The different traditions that western culture has invoked to describe the self are well illuminated in Charles Taylor's *Sources of the self*.

15 The ways that men are moved 'out of touch' with their inner emotional lives and often learn to use language as a way of concealing this inner impoverishment of experience is a theme in Victor J. Seidler, *Rediscovering masculinity: reason, language and sexuality*, ch 7 'Language', pp. 123/42.

4 Self-denial

1 Our dominant moral traditions within an Enlightenment culture have tended to focus on the morality of individual actions. They have centred around issues of individual right actions and so around questions of 'what ought I to do?' This is certainly true of Kant, and in crucial ways, it is true of our utilitarian moral tradition too. This makes it difficult to think seriously about the formulation and organisation of 'character' within a particular moral tradition. People who have been drawn to these issues such as Erich Fromm and the Frankfurt School at least help to open up the question of the relationship of morality to politics. Recently, hopes for a reconstructed Aristotelian tradition have been favoured as a way out of some of these issues. See, for instance, Bernard Williams's *Ethics and the limits of philosophy* and Alastair MacIntyre's *After virtue*.

2 The ways in which we might talk about 'injury' or 'damage' in a way that goes beyond a Kantian idea of treating people as means to our own ends or a utilitarian vision of limiting individual satisfaction and desire is explored in the concluding chapter, entitled 'Liberalism and the autonomy of morality' of Victor J. Seidler's *Kant, respect and injustice: the limits of liberal moral theory*, pp. 118/223. It is also an abiding strength of the moral and political writings of Simone Weil that she recognises the centrality of these concerns for the revitalisation of our social and ethical tradition. See Lawrence Blum and Victor J. Seidler, *A truer liberty: Simone Weil and Marxism*.

3 A useful example of the kind of social research that can be done if you keep some of these notions in mind is provided by Richard Sennett and Jonathan Cobb in *The hidden injuries of class*. See also Lillian Rubin, *Worlds of pain: life in the working-class family*.

4 Durkheim's conception of morality reflects an attempt to socialise and secularise Kant's ethical vision by placing society in the space that Kant reserves for reason. Durkheim's later conception of morality is clearly presented in the introduction to the *Elementary forms of the religious life* and in the essay 'The dualism of human nature' reprinted in Kurt Woolfe, *Emile Durkheim, 1858-1917*. See also the discussions in Durkheim's *Sociology and philosophy* and the assessments offered by Steven Lukes in *Emile Durkheim* and by Anthony Giddens in *Durkheim*.

5 See, for instance, the interesting discussion of the relationship of feminism to moral theory in Genevieve Lloyd's *The men of reason: 'male' and 'female' in western philosophy*, and Jean Grimshaw's *Feminist philosophers*. See also E. Kennedy and S. Mendus *Women in western political philosophy* and

Feminist challenges: social and political theory, ed Carole Pateman and Elizabeth Gross.

6 Some of these issues about the nature of dependency are discussed by Luise Eichenbaum and Susie Orbach in *What do women want?* They recognise how much men have invested in burying their needs for dependency. It is not their task to illuminate the sources of this situation.

7 See, for instance, the ways that relationships are discussed by Sheila Rowbotham in *Woman's consciousness, man's world*.

8 See the discussion in Elena Belotti, *Little girls*, and the theoretical exploration of women's gender identity in Nancy Chodorow's *The reproduction of mothering*. See also the illuminating discussions of fathers by their daughters in *Fathers: reflections by daughters*, ed Ursula Owen.

9 C.B. Macpherson's *The political theory of possessive individualism* can help us place some of the contradictions within liberal theory in historical context, although not with specific reference to sexual politics. See also his essays collected in *Democratic theory: essays in retrieval* and the introductory essay by Isaiah Berlin to his *Four essays on liberty*.

10 See the discussion of power in Steven Lukes' *Power: a radical view*. This is still, somewhat paradoxically, a relatively unexplored area within social theory. It has come into prominence with the influence of Foucault's writing. See, for instance, the collection of essays and interviews with Foucault collected in *Power/knowledge*, ed Colin Gordon. Some of the difficulties with Foucault's conception of power are discussed in Victor J. Siedler's 'Reason, desire and male sexuality' in *The cultural construction of sexuality*, ed Pat Caplan. See also *Foucault: a critical reader* ed David Hoy, particularly the essays by Charles Taylor, 'Foucault on freedom and truth' and Michael Walzer, 'The politics of Michel Foucault'.

11 The identification of masculinity with reason is explored briefly in Brian Easlea's *Science and sexual oppression*, particularly in chapter 3, and by Victor J. Seidler in *Rediscovering masculinity: reason, language and sexuality*.

12 Issues about emotions, dependency and relationship are also illuminated by Luise Eichenbaum and Susie Orbach in *Understanding women*, which talks about the development of feminist psychotherapy. See also the papers of the Women's Therapy Centre in London which raise further issues in these approaches in *Living with the sphinx: papers from the Women's Therapy Centre*, Sheila Ernst and Marie MacGuire (eds). See also the discussion in Lilian Rubin's *Intimate strangers*.

13 Issues about women's work in the context of the family are discussed in *What is to be done about the family?* ed Lynne Segal, and, within a structuralist framework, by Michele Barrett and Mary McIntosh in *The anti-social family*.

14 It is a strength of Nancy Chodorow's *The reproduction of mothering* to bring out the limits of understanding women's subordination and gender identity in terms of socialisation theory, largely built upon the conception of role expectations.

15 Freud's understandings of the nature of gender identity as a process that is usually precarious are clearly set out by Jeffrey Weeks in *Sexuality and its discontents*, ch 6, 'Sexuality and the unconscious'. For a useful collection of Freud's own writings on this theme see *Sexuality* in the Penguin Freud library.

16 The relationship of Protestantism to a developing conception of masculinity can be read as an implicit theme in Max Weber's *The Protestant ethic and the*

spirit of capitalism. This has been usefully explored in David Morgan's 'Men, masculinity and the process of sociological enquiry' in *Doing feminist research*, ed Helen Roberts.

17 The ways in which men can be trained into being observers of our own experience and relationships is a theme in Victor J. Seidler's *Rediscovering masculinity: reason, language and sexuality*, ch 9, 'Intimacy'.

5 Morality

1 Erich Fromm's *Fear of freedom* was influenced by a reading of Max Weber's *The Protestant ethic and the spirit of capitalism* as well as Tawney's *Religion and the rise of capitalism*. The danger of talking in terms of characters is that we slip into reifying these into fixed categories and so lose a sense both of the possibilities of change and of the ways that people are continually remaking their characters through the way they live their experience and relationships.

2 For a useful, if somewhat abstract, discussion of the nature of ideology, see the discussions by Jorge Larrain in *The concept of ideology* and in *Marxism and ideology*. But for me the discussion by Gramsci in Part 3 of the *Prison notebooks* entitled 'The philosophy of praxis' remains crucial. A careful reading of this shows that Gramsci himself undercuts the attempts which have been made to present his writings on ideology within a structuralist framework, as well as giving us indications of some of the weaknesses of structuralist Marxism itself, particularly its categorical separation between Marxism as a philosophy and as a science of history and politics. This was precisely the weakness that Gramsci challenged in the orthodox Marxism of the Second International as well as in what was to become Soviet Marxism.

3 I would question the ways that the relationship between capitalism and patriarchy is usually conceived within a structuralist tradition, as if they exist as independent and autonomous structures that can somehow be related to each other. This is a central weakness in Michele Barrett's *Women's oppression today*. See the article 'The trouble with patriarchy' by Sheila Rowbotham that has been reprinted in her *Dreams and dilemmas* pp. 207/14.

4 Some of the weaknesses in Althusserian Marxism were dismissed in an illuminating, if sometimes exaggerated form, by E.P. Thompson in 'The poverty of theory' in *The poverty of theory and other essays* and by S. Clarke *et al.* in *One-dimensional Marxism: Althusser and the politics of culture*.

5 The ways that a liberal moral culture has secularised and legitimated Christian conceptions of love and equality is investigated in Victor J. Seidler's *The moral limits of modernity: love, inequality and oppression*.

6 Kant's vision of respect and the abstract conception of humanity it often carries with it is discussed in Victor J. Seidler's *Kant, respect and injustice: the limits of liberal moral theory*.

7 To see how this acceptance of 'self-interest' as rational developed, see the instructive study *The passions and the interests* by A. Hirschman. For a sense of the centrality of the discussion between egoism and altruism which accepts egoism as defining a 'common-sense' rationality for a liberal moral culture, see Bernard Williams's *Morality*. For critical discussions of this see Lawrence Blum's *Friendship, altruism and morality* and Mary Midgley *Heart and mind: the varieties of moral experience*.

8 For some illuminating discussions of the difficulties of equality in the emerging conditions of capitalism, see Alexis de Toqueville's *Democracy in America*. See also questions raised by Simone Weil in her essay 'Human personality' in *Selected essays 1934–43* ed R. Rees, and the discussion of her work in Victor J. Seidler, *The moral limits of modernity: love, inequality and oppression*.

9 Some of the implications of the identification of masculinity with reason for the place of women and relationships within moral and political theory are drawn out in Susan Moller Okin's *Women in western political thought*. For Kant's own vision of sexual relationships between the sexes see Kant's *Anthropology*. This is briefly discussed by Hans Fink in *Social philosophy*, and by Victor J. Seidler in *Kant, respect and injustice: the limits of liberal moral theory*. See also 'Kant: an honest but narrow-minded bourgeois?' by Susan Mendus, in *Women in western political philosophy*, ed Ellen Kennedy and Susan Mendus, pp. 21/43.

10 For an exploration of tensions surrounding inequality and the relationships between rich and poor in Kant's thought, see Victor J. Seidler, *Kant, respect and injustice: the limits of liberal moral theory*. See also Galvano della Volpe *Rousseau and Marx*, chs 1 and 4.

11 The relationship between dignity and work is centrally important for Simone Weil. It is discussed in Lawrence Blum and Victor J. Seidler, *A truer liberty: Simone Weil and Marxism*, ch 6, 'Work', pp. 143/93.

12 An interesting sense of both the power and limitations of a Lacanian or structuralist reading of Freud can be gained from Juliet Mitchell's *Women: The longest revolution: essays in feminism, literature and psychoanalysis*. See also Juliet Mitchell and Jacqueline Rose, *Feminine sexuality: Jacques Lacan and the Ecole Freudienne* and Jane Gallop, *Feminism and psychoanalysis: the daughter's seduction*.

13 This vision of the 'inner self' that nobody really sees, understands or appreciates is a powerful aspect of the Protestant inheritance. It disconnects us from our work and social relations which seem to have no bearing upon this inner self. It is a way that we can make ourselves invulnerable to the indignities and humiliations of social life. This theme is briefly set in historical context by Herbert Marcuse in the introductory chapter to *Reason and revolution*. It is also discussed in Raymond Williams's *Modern tragedy*.

14 The way that education can be organised to undermine our intrinsic joy in learning itself is well illuminated in *Letter to a teacher* by the schoolchildren of Barbiana. See also John Holt, *How children fail*, and George Dennison, *The lives of children*. Some of these experiments in free school were usefully evaluated by Allen Graubard in *Free the children*. Sadly, they were too readily dismissed as forms of 'progressivism' by the Left in the late 1970s, which was increasingly drawn to Marxist accounts of the reproduction of skills. When the libertarian Right sought to open the discussion of standards in education in the 1980s, many teachers had already lost confidence, through the abstract critiques of 'progressivism', in their educational practice.

15 John Stuart Mill's *Autobiography* went through different editions. These are variously discussed, as is his relationship with Harriet Taylor whose ideas are said to have had a real impact on Mill, in Alice Rossi ed (1970).

16 For an interesting feminist discussion of the universality of reason as a masculine convention, see Genevieve Lloyd, *The man of reason: 'male' and 'female' in western philosophy*. It is also a theme in the developmental work of Carol Gilligan, *In a different voice: psychological theory and women's*

development. See also the discussion of Gilligan's work in Seyla Benhabib, 'The generalised and the concrete other: the Kohlberg-Gilligan controversy and feminist theory' in *Feminism as critique: essays on the politics of gender in late capitalism*, ed Seyla Benhabib and Drucilla Cornell.

17 Mill's crucial discussion of individuality is to be found in chapter 3 in *On liberty.* For a useful discussion see Isaiah Berlin's essay 'John Stuart Mill and the ends of life' in *Four essays on liberty*, pp. 173/206. See also the essay by Charles Taylor, 'What's wrong with negative liberty' in *Philosophy and the human sciences*, pp. 211/24, and Alan Ryan, *J.S. Mill* ch 5, where some of the difficulties in placing *On liberty* in Mill's intellectual history are explored.

6 Emotional life

1 Michel Foucault's *A history of sexuality* has focused discussion on the difficulties of invoking a concept of repression. He would have us dispense with it altogether. I am doubtful, thinking that we will thereby lose significant insights. See Victor J. Seidler 'Reason, desire and male sexuality' in *The cultural construction of sexuality* ed Pat Caplan pp. 82/112.

2 Georg Lukàcs' insightful, if somewhat generalised, account of reification is to be found in 'Reification and the consciousness of the proletariat' in his *History and class consciousness*, pp. 83/122. A useful introduction is provided by A. Arato and P. Breines in *The young Lukàcs and western Marxism*.

3 For some understanding of the way that psychoanalysis illuminates the connection between the suppression of emotions and the place of fantasies in our lives, see Freud's *Introductory lectures*. See also Philip Rieff's *Freud: The mind of a moralist*, O. Mannoni's *Freud* and, possibly the most illuminating study yet, Peter Gay's *Freud* (1990).

4 The relationship between individuality, experience and language within a structuralist tradition is explored in Victor J. Seidler's *Rediscovering masculinity: reason, language and sexuality.*

5 The relationship between factories and the gradual acceptance of factory discipline is discussed in Z. Bauman's *Memories of class.* For important treatments of this period, see Edward Thompson's *The making of the English working class* and Eric Hobsbawm's *The age of revolution.*

6 The weak and attenuated conception of individuality that we inherit within a liberal moral culture that so often prides itself in its individualism is a continuing theme in Victor J. Seidler's *Kant, respect and injustice: the limits of liberal moral theory.* Too often socialism has seen individualism and individuality as essentially market conceptions that need to be challenged by forms of community and collectivism. It has rarely seen its task as bringing into balance a richer individuality within an accessible community. This involves a challenge to the statist conception of the Left.

7 The issue of fantasy and its relationship to any sense of 'truth' or 'reality' is an ongoing issue within psychoanalytic theory. It was raised in brute form by the publication of J.M. Masson, *Freud: the assault on truth: Freud's suppression of the seduction thesis.* This is a more difficult issue than often presented, confused by the idea that if we talk of 'truth' or 'reality', we must be suggesting a single history that is gradually uncovered, as if our fantasies are simply a smokescreen that conceals an underlying emotional reality. This does not have to be

the issue at all and we can recognise the importance of fantasy in our lives without thinking that we have thereby to give equal weight or significance to each narrative or historical reconstruction of our early childhood. Against a Lacanian or post-structuralist reading of Freud I think it is vital to maintain the vision of truth as we are brought into a deeper contact with ourselves.

8 For a useful introduction to Melanie Klein's focus on early childhood, see Hanna Segal's *Introduction to the work of Melanie Klein*. See also Klein's writings, *Love, guilt and reparations and other works 1921–1945* and *Envy and gratitude and other writings 1946-1963*.

9 See Freud's *Civilisation and its discontents* which some argue was partly a response to Reich's attempts to politicise psychoanalysis. For Reich's account of the history, see the early chapters of *The function of the orgasm* (1942) and, for his relationship to Freud, see *Reich speaks of Freud* (1972c). For accounts of Reich's life and work see David Boadella's *Wilhelm Reich: the evolution of his work* and Myron Sharaf's *Fury on earth: a biography of Wilhelm Reich*. See also Russell Jacoby, *The repression of psychoanalysis: Otto Fenichel and the political Freudians*.

10 It is this picture of emotional life as essentially 'inner' that Wittgenstein set out to challenge in parts of his *Philosophical investigations*. He brings us into a different relationship to the pervasive distinction between 'inner' and 'outer' that is drawn within an Enlightenment culture. It was his recognition of the continuing hold of an Enlightenment rationalism that made him feel more generally out of sympathy with his time. It was also behind an abiding sense that his work could neither be understood nor appreciated. See Wittgenstein's remarks brought together as *Culture and Value* edited by Peter Winch.

7 Work

1 Marx's discussion of the wage contract that is presented as a contract between equals in a way that hides the underlying relations of class power, is to be found in *Wages, prices and profits*. A fuller exploration of the idea of contract as providing the basis for liberal conceptions of equality is to be found in the *Grundrisse* and in Marx's *Critique of the Gotha Programme*.

2 Harry Braverman's *Labor and monopoly capital* was important in getting issues of the labour process taken seriously. See also the useful collection of articles brought together by André Gorz, *The division of labour: the labour process and class struggle in modern capitalism*. The CSE journal *Capital and class* as well as the journal *Work* provide ways of following developments in this reconceptualisation of work. See also Victor Seidler's 'The labour process and politics' in the *CSE conference papers, 1979*.

3 These connections between the labour process and the indignities of work is a central insight of Simone Weil's writing on work. Too much recent discussion of work is bereft of moral insight and language, as if it were simply an issue of economic organisation and quantifiable forms of exploitation. See Lawrence Blum and Victor J. Seidler, *A truer liberty: Simone Weil and Marxism*, ch 6, 'Work'.

4 Goffman's work in many ways shows a mirror to contemporary identities. It is subtle and in many ways persuasive while at the same time lacking any

moral insight, for morality itself is yet another image that we would project of ourselves. An early challenge to the direction of this work was provided by Alvin Gouldner in *The coming crisis of western sociology*.

5 An understanding of the ways that men in particular are divided against their natures, identified as we are with reason and culture, is a theme in Susan Griffin's *Pornography and silence*. She offers a powerful and suggestive analysis of some of the tensions that are inherited within dominant forms of masculinity and the fears that men carry at the revelations of our natures. So much structuralist social theory finds it impossible to learn from such insights because it draws a categorical distinction between 'nature' and 'culture' and seeks to banish 'nature' as if it were given and not itself being continually historically reconstituted. I have argued in *Rediscovering masculinity: reason, language and sexuality* that recognising the gendered nature of masculinity can help us challenge the pervasiveness of these implicit – if often not well thought out – structuralist distinctions.

6 It is rare for the study of work to take on issues about how men feel and learn to cope with their feelings at work, especially within relationships of subordination. Within our positivist traditions, emotions and feelings are too often regarded as individual and subjective responses to the workplace, which have relatively little consequence in themselves. It is a significant contribution of Wilhelm Reich's essay on 'Class consciousness' that he challenges – as Gramsci does in different terms – the rationalism and intellectualism of so much Marxist discussion of the development of class consciousness. A Leninist tradition formulated around Lenin's early *What is to be done?* is conceived too narrowly in terms of bringing 'political' consciousness to a proletariat that is otherwise limited to an 'economistic' form of trade union consciousness, and has blocked the possibility of formulating different questions. More recent phenomenologically inspired work in industrial sociology looking at the 'meanings' that workers ascribe to their experience too often normalises the situation and renders invisible the frustrations and humiliations which are integral to relationships of subordination. Again, Simone Weil asks some challenging questions about the nature of authority and discipline in the labour process. See the discussion in Lawrence Blum and Victor J. Seidler, *A truer liberty: Simone Weil and Marxism*, ch 6, 'Work'.

7 Sometimes it is difficult to face these questions of ideology head-on, for our social theory has been too used to considering them abstractly, somehow divorced from particular forms of oppression and subordination. It is an enduring strength of Gramsci's work, especially in the *Prison notebooks*, to keep these crucial connections firmly in view.

8 For a discussion of men's particular relationships to language see Victor J. Seidler's *Rediscovering masculinity: reason, language and sexuality*, ch 7, 'Language', pp. 123/42. For a useful discussion of recent developments in language theory as they bear upon social theory, see Frederik Jameson's *The prison house of language*, and Deborah Cameron's *Feminism and linguistic theory*.

8 Violence

1 Anne-Marie Fearon, 'Come in, Tarzan, your time is up' in *Shrew*, issue on 'Feminism and non-violence', spring 1978.

2 These universalised images of men and male violence are explored in Susan Brownmiller's *Against our will: men, women and rape*. Susan Griffin has also argued that rape and male violence play a central role in establishing and perpetuating male power, and they are a recurring theme in Andrea Dworkin's *Pornography: men possessing women*. Lynne Segal in *Slow motion: changing masculinities, changing men*, argues against Brownmiller's universalism, using some of Roy Porter's work – 'Rape – does it have a historical meaning?' in *Rape*, S. Tomaselli and R. Porter (eds) – to show that rape has not always been used as the principal agent to subordinate women. At the same time she recognises the significance of the ideas that not all men are potential rapists and that some women face greater risk of male violence than others – 'both these statements, however, are not just controversial but explosive in feminist discourse. They need the most careful study.' (p. 240).

3 Adorno questions our accepted understandings of bourgeois society which tend to marginalise issues of bodily threat and violence, in *Minima moralia*. It is a recurring insight in his writings. A useful introduction to his writings is provided by Susan Bucks-Morss in *The origin of negative dialectics: Theodor W. Adorno, Walter Benjamin and the Frankfurt Institute*. See also *The melancholy science: an introduction to the thought of Theodor W. Adorno* by Gillian Rose.

4 Scorsese seems well aware of some of the issues of masculinity and violence, which are in many ways the central themes of *Raging Bull*. These issues of displacement, violence and control are never far from the surface of the film. But hopefully the argument that I am making does not depend on a familiarity with the film, though obviously this helps.

5 This refers to the collective discussion within the *Achilles' heel* collective as we were preparing the issue on violence. A number of the articles in the issue reflect the discussions we were having. See also the article by Tony Eardley on 'Violence and sexuality' in *The sexuality of men*, ed. M. Humphries and A. Metcalf.

6 See the article on 'Masculinity and violence' by David Morgan in *Women, violence and social control*, ed J. Hanmer and M. Maynard. It is also illuminating to connect these issues with the different views expressed in Susan Griffin's *Pornography and silence* and Lynne Segal's *Is the future female? – troubled thoughts on contemporary feminism*.

7 Issues about men and masculinity as they emerge within the trade union movement are usefully discussed in a roundtable discussion, 'Mending the broken heart of socialism' in *Male order: unwrapping masculinity*, edited by Rowena Chapman and Jonathan Rutherford. See also the discussion in Lynne Segal's *Slow motion: changing masculinities, changing men*, ch 10, where in her attempt to make a relatively uncontentious point that we need to think in terms of 'masculinities' rather than any single masculinity, she tends to misconstrue the *Achilles' heel* project. We affirmed men's engagement in trade union struggles and in political struggles against patriarchy but said that in our experience, men's support for feminism will tend to remain 'abstract' if it does not allow for the importance of consciousness-raising. Nor did we see masculinity simply as 'a personality issue' rather than as constructed around assumptions of social power. She offers another version of the false idea that sexual politics in the 1970s, at least as it influenced men, was only concerned with the personal and the psychological and not with the

political. This allows her to argue that 'like some feminists' we were supposedly travelling on a road 'which would finally reduce politics in its entirety to the individual struggles in personal life' (p. 283).

8 An interesting set of discussions around issues of abuse are presented in Lina Gordon's *Heroes of their own lives: the politics and history of family violence*, in Jan Pahl's *Private violence and public policy*, and in Patricia Mrazek and C. Henry Kempe, *Sexually abused children and their families*. See also the work that was done by such groups as 'Emerge' in the United States, who were working with men who abused in Boston, in 'Emerge: a men's counselling service on domestic violence: organising and implementing services for men who batter', copyright 1981, Emerge Inc.; and the work Ray Wyre has being doing amongst others in England reported in *Men, women and rape*.

9 Developments in working with men are presented and explored in the newsletter 'Working with men' ed Trefor Lloyd. This shows how the 1980s saw an enormous spread and diversity of men's involvement with anti-sexist activities.

9 Fascism

1 For an interesting discussion of the growth and development of fascism in Britain in the 1930s, see the personal account of J.E. Jacobs, *Out of the ghetto: my youth in the East End: communism and fascism 1913-1939*.

2 Wilhelm Reich's discussion of fascism in his *The mass psychology of fascism*, for all its shortcomings in its mechanical rendering of Marxism, remains a source of powerful insights. See the interesting discussion of Reich's work in Klaus Theweleit's *Male fantasies vol. 1: women, floods, bodies, history*.

3 Reich's 'What is class consciousness?' raises crucial issues of power and consciousness that echo some of Gramsci's insights in his *Prison notebooks*. It is usefully presented with other writings of the period in Lee Baxendall (ed) *Sex-pol essays: 1929-1934*. See also the discussions in Bertell Ollman, *Social and sexual revolution: essays on Marx and Reich*, which appreciate issues of sexuality and emotional life that are so often absent within Marxist discussions. Reich himself has too often been dismissed for his 'biologism' that became one of the deadly sins which Althusser's structuralist Marxism invoked to diminish his work. Sadly, it has meant that we have often failed to learn from him as he was written out, as were Lukàcs, Gramsci and the Frankfurt School for a while. For a sustained, if somewhat rhetorical, challenge to Reich see *Freud or Reich? – psychoanalysis and illusion* by Janine Chasseguet-Smirgel and Dela Grunberger.

4 The attraction of the New Right for women is a theme that is usefully explored by Beatrix Campbell in *Iron ladies*. This book was breaking new ground in refusing to dismiss what women had to say but in being ready to listen without feeling obliged to agree. See also discussions of the Right in the United States in Andrea Dworkin, *Right-wing women: the politics of domesticated females*.

5 For a useful discussion of Fordism, see the essay by Gramsci 'Americanism and Fordism' in the *Prison notebooks*, where Gramsci draws connections with issues of masculinity. See also André Gorz (ed) *The division of labour: the labour process and class struggle in modern capitalism*; Michael Aglietta, *A*

theory of capitalist regulation: the US experience; and Alain Lipietz, *The enchanted world* and *Miracles and mirages: the crisis of global Fordism in the 1980s*. There is a growing conviction that we have shifted to a different phase of post-Fordism which relies less on mass production in large factories but is more concerned with smaller-scale production for particular markets. See, for instance, the discussion of this restructuring of the labour process in S. Lash and J. Urry, *The end of organised capitalism*, and M.J. Piore and C.F. Sabel, *The second industrial divide*. See also the critical discussion of the 'post-Fordist' notion of a new mode of regulation of modern capitalism in Michael Rustin, 'The politics of post-Fordism: or, the Trouble with "New Times"', *New Left Review* 175, May/June 1989 pp. 54/77.

6 For an early and remarkable discussion on the effects of rationalisation on work, see Simone Weil's 'Factory journal' in *Simone Weil: formative writings 1924–1941* pp. 151/226 ed Dorothy Tuck McFarland and Wilhelmina Van Ness. See also the discussion in Lawrence Blum and Victor J. Seidler, *A truer liberty: Simone Weil and Marxism* ch 6, 'Work', pp. 143/93. See also the collection of papers, *The labour process and class struggle* ed C.S.E. and subsequent issues of *Capital and class* that have fostered a sensitivity to the crucial importance of these issues.

7 David Edgar has written insightfully about some of these connections between age, work and racism. See, for instance, Trevor Blackwell and Jeremy Seabrook, *A world still to win: the reconstruction of the post-war working class*. See also *The politics of Thatcherism*, ed Stuart Hall and Martin Jacques, and Stuart Hall's *The hard road to renewal*.

8 It may be that as men feel less power in relation to their work they are more assertive of their power in the family. This might be one way of explaining why physical violence is more common in some working-class communities than in comfortably middle-class ones. Since working-class men have fewer opportunities to exercise power they may resort to force more often. But this does not mean that men who enjoy control over their work are in any general way less tyrannical or emotionally available in their families than men who do not. Beatrix Campbell in *Wigan Pier revisited* points out that miners, traditionally a group of workers with a very strong sense of community and control over work, with a very positive self and social valuation in terms of work, often imposed miserable conditions on their wives and resisted pit head baths, the introduction of which transformed the lives and homes of their families overnight. I am grateful to Ed Mason for pointing this out as well as for his other insightful remarks on this chapter. I hope I have been able to take most of them into account.

9 The Frankfurt School discussed some of these issues of familial authority in the context of Max Horkheimer's essay 'Authority and the family' which is reprinted in *Critical theory: selected essays* by Max Horkheimer. See the interesting discussion of some of its themes in Jessica Benjamin, 'Authority and the family revisited: or, a world without fathers?' and in Victor J. Seidler, 'Fathering, authority and masculinity' in *Male order: unwrapping masculinity* ed R. Chapman and J. Rutherford. For useful introductions to critical theory see Martin Jay, *The dialectical imagination: a history of the Frankfurt School*, and David Held, *An introduction to critical theory: from Horkheimer to Habermas*. See also *The essential Frankfurt School reader*, Andrew Arato and Eike Gebhardt (eds).

10 Issues of nationalism and identity are thought about in an interesting way in Benedict Anderson's *Imagined communities*. See also the provocative discussions of the issue of roots and rootedness in Simone Weil's *The need for roots*.

11 Issues of the family in relation to politics are discussed in *What is to be done about the family?*, ed Lynne Segal. See also Lillian Rubin, *Intimate strangers*, and Sheila Rowbotham, *The past is before us: feminism in action since the 1960s*.

10 Therapy

1 This remains a critical assumption. Though the issues it raises are alive in the feminist idea that there can be no revolution without women's liberation, they get sidetracked in structuralist Marxist ideas about socialism as a more 'advanced mode of production'. The idea of society as a structured totality seems to pre-empt a serious discussion of prefigurative politics. See Victor J. Seidler's discussion in 'Trusting ourselves: Marxism, human needs and sexual politics' in Simon Clarke *et al.*, *One-dimensional Marxism*, pp. 103/136.

2 This rings true of Reich's essay 'Dialectical materialism and psychoanalysis', which is to be found along with other useful writings in *Sex-pol: essays 1924-1934*, ed Lee Baxendall.

3 See, for instance, the somewhat dismissive treatment of Reich in Juliet Mitchell's influential *Psychoanalysis and feminism*. Within her structuralist paradigm there is no space to appreciate the significance of his work. The beginnings of a fuller appreciation are to be found in Myron Sharaf's *Fury on earth: a biography of Wilhelm Reich*.

4 Georg Lukàcs sets the terms of 'the antimonies of bourgeois thought' in his crucial essay entitled 'Reification and the consciousness of the proletariat' in *History and class consciousness*, pp. 83/222. He sets the crucial terms for discussion without providing an adequate formulation for their resolution, which he would want to identify with the historical mission of the proletariat.

5 Possibly Gramsci's *Prison notebooks* comes closest to a formulation of how individuality is socially and hisorically formed without thereby reducing individuals to effects of social structures. But it can be difficult to rework some of the themes since the writings of Korsch, Lukàcs and Gramsci tend to be dismissed within an Althusserian structuralist tradition that would see them collectively as a form of humanist Marxism that relies upon an essentialist conception of human nature. If Gramsci is redeemed, as, for instance, in *Gramsci and Marxist theory*, ed Chantale Mouffe, it is as a theorist of hegemony, itself redefined within structuralist terms as invoking a science of history and politics.

6 See, for instance, Max Horkheimer's interesting *The eclipse of reason* which focuses upon the historical development of individualism.

7 See Marcuse's early collection of writings, largely drawn from the 1930s when he was still in Frankfurt, *Negations: essays in critical theory* especially the essays 'Philosophy and critical theory', 'On hedonism' and 'The concept of essence'.

8 Marcuse's late interest in feminist ideas is shown in the interview he gave on the Frankfurt School, later published in Brian Magee's *Men of ideas* as 'Marcuse and the Frankfurt School: dialogue with Herbert Marcuse', pp. 62/73.

9 Adorno's *Minima moralia* is full of acute and telling insight that has been largely unexplored within recent social theory but is beginning to get renewed attention as connections between post-structuralism and critical theory become apparent. See, for instance, Peter Dews, *Logics of disintegration: post-structuralism and the claims of critical theory*.

10 This could echo an earlier discussion between Marcuse and Erich Fromm in the 1950s about the possibility of 'happiness' in capitalist society. Marcuse tended to voice the view that to talk of happiness was only to debase the notion since it is to create expectations that cannot possibly be fulfilled. Even though this seems like a radical impulse I think it is in reality part of the conservative strain in the Frankfurt School that made it impossible for Adorno, for instance, to recognise any radical impulse in the movements of the 1960s. I imagine that Marcuse towards the end of his life shifted his view about this.

11 As Reich was used to legitimate the personal and sexual experimentation, so he was often blamed when things did not turn out as people had planned. The deeper challenge that Reich makes to the instrumentality of personal relationships where people are out of touch with their own bodily experience was missed. This was an insight that could have been gleaned from David Boadella's *Wilhelm Reich: the evolution of his work* and the collection of essays he edited, *In the wake of Reich*. But unfortunately this work has been marginalised till quite recently, possibly because the issues it brings to the surface are too unsettling for rationalistic forms of psychoanalytic theory. It threatens the form of control that psychoanalytic theory can seem to promise.

12 The work of the Birmingham-based Centre for Contemporary Cultural Studies was important in bringing these issues into a clearer focus. See, for instance, *Resistance through rituals*, ed Stuart Hall and Tony Jefferson. See also Dick Hebdige's *Subculture* and Paul Willis's *Learning to labour*, which have both helped to open up these areas of discussion. See also the useful essays collected in *Gender and generation*, ed A. McRobbie and M. Nava.

13 Laing's *The divided self* contains a powerful challenge to medical objectification. It raises issues about the organisation of medical knowledge that were to be raised within a different theoretical tradition by Michel Foucault in *Madness and civilisation* and *Birth of the clinic*. Strangely, these different kinds of work could complement each other though they are rarely brought into the same discussion. Laing's work has been discussed in such work at Peter Sedgwick's *Psychpol* and edited work, *Laing and antipsychiatry*, ed Robert Boyers and Robert Orrill, but sadly it is yet to find its proper place within social theory.

14 The challenges of the women's movement to prevailing conceptions of masculinity is discussed by Bob Connell in *Gender and power*, in Jeff Hearn's *The gender of oppression* and in Victor J. Seidler's *Rediscovering masculinity: reason, language and sexuality*.

15 The discussion of the relationship of Marxism to morality is still relatively neglected. See the useful questions raised by Steven Lukes in *Marxism and morality*. There has been considerable discussion raised by the formulations of Allen Wood which would deny the significance of morality in his reformulation of Marxism as a form of economic determinism. See Allen Wood, *Karl Marx* and Richard W. Miller, *Analyzing Marx: morality, power and history*, as well as the collection edited by Kay Nielsen and Steven Patten

on *Marx and morality* as a special issue of the *Canadian journal of philosophy*, Supplementary Vol. 7 1981.

16 The relationship between structuralist theory, feminism and the analysis of men and masculinity is a continuing theme in Victor J. Seidler's *Rediscovering masculinity: reason, language and sexuality*. I argue that a structuralist tradition, while bringing into focus some important questions and concerns, is part of the problem rather than the solution.

17 For a useful introduction to Lacan, see Sherry Turkle, *Psychoanalytic politics: Freud's French Revolution*; David Macey, *Lacan in context*; B. Benvenuto and Roger Kennedy, *The Works of Jacques Lacan: an introduction*; Jacques Lacan, *Ecrits: a selection*, and Juliet Mitchell and Jacqueline Rose (eds) *Feminine sexuality: Jacques Lacan and the Ecole Freudienne*.

18 See G. Deleuze and F. Guattari's major work in the field, *Anti-Oedipus: capitalism and schizophrenia*. For a sense of the development of Gualtari's work, see the collection of essays brought together as *Molecular revolution*.

19 For a sense of the development of feminist psychotherapy, see Susie Orbach and Luise Eichenbaum *Outside in, inside out* and *What do women want?* Also, see the collection from the Women's Therapy Centre, London, *Living with the sphinx*, ed Sheila Ernst and Marie Maguire.

20 Alexander Lowen's *Bioenergetics* is a useful introduction setting out some of the historical relationship to Reich. See also his *The betrayal of the body*. See also David Boadella, *In the wake of Reich* for a broader grasp of developments in body-related therapies, Stanley Kellerman, *Your body speaks its mind* and Ken Dychwald, *Bodymind*.

21 The development of these new forms of therapy within the context of the Growth Movement has taken many different directions. A useful introduction is provided in *In our own hands*, ed Sheila Ernst and Lucy Goodison. For gestalt, see Fritz Perls, *Gestalt therapy verbatim*; Joel Fagan and Irma Lee Shepherd (eds), *Gestalt therapy now*; Claude Steiner (ed) *Readings in radical psychiatry*. For encounter, see William Shultz, *Joy*, though it tends to be overly optimistic and somewhat uncritical; Hogie Wyckoff, *Solving women's problems* gives a different approach to group interaction with an awareness of women's needs. Michael Rossman's *New age blues* provides political critique of the Growth Movement from an insider's viewpoint.

22 An important questioning of this tradition of political militancy is provided in *Beyond the fragments: feminism and the making of socialism*, Sheila Rowbotham, Lynne Segal and Hilary Wainwright. It is important to recognise different libertarian traditions of socialist thought so that the revolutions in Eastern Europe are not themselves taken as discrediting socialism, but the traditions of authoritarian statist conceptions that the Eastern European regimes represented. For many it also brings into question basic assumptions of Leninist theory and practice.

23 Issues of men's relationship to language are explored further in *Rediscovering masculinity: reason, language and sexuality*, ch 7 'Language'.

24 Eileen Fairweather's article 'The Feelings Behind the Slogans' was reprinted in a collection of early writings on the women's movement by The Women's Press. It first appeared in *Spare Rib*.

25 Some discussion of the difficulties of talking about socialism since its

language, especially in Eastern Europe, has been so debased and discredited, is found in Václav Havel, *Living in truth* (1987). For some stimulating reflections on these recent events see Timothy Garton Ash, 'We the people: the revolution of 89' and 'Tearing down the curtain' published in 1990 by the *Observer*.

26 The relationship between masculinity and self-sufficiency is also a theme in Victor J. Seidler's *Kant, respect and injustice: the limits of liberal moral theory*, where it is connected to inherited notions of freedom and independence.

27 For some interesting discussions of developments in feminist psychotherapy see, for instance, Jean Baker Miller (ed), *Psychoanalysis and women*; Jean Strouse (ed), *Women and analysis*; Susie Orbach and Luise Eichenbaum, *What do women want?* and *Outside in/inside out* (expanded version, *Understanding women: a feminist psychoanalytic approach*).

28 Some sense of feminist discussion about the possibilities of men changing is given in Lynne Segal's *Slow motion: changing masculinities, changing men*. See also Alice Jardine and Paul Smith (eds), *Men in feminism*, and Gillian Hanscome and Martin Humphries (eds), *Heterosexuality*.

29 Questions of dignity and respect have been further explored in Victor J. Seidler, *The moral limits of modernity: love, inequality and oppression*.

30 Issues relating psychotherapy to the public sphere have been a central focus for the journal *Free associations*; see the various attempts to integrate psychoanalysis and Marxism. See also Jessica Benjamin, *Bonds of love: psychoanalysis, feminism and the problem of domination*; Joel Kovel, *The age of desire: case histories of a radical psychoanalyst*; Richard Lichtman, *The production of desire*; and Michael Schneider, *Neurosis and civilisation*. See also the useful collection, *Capitalism and infancy*, ed Barry Richards, which partly centres on these questions.

11 Politics

1 A useful discussion of democratic theory which helped to place it within a historical context is provided by C.B. Macpherson, *Democratic theory: essays in retrieval* and *The life and times of liberal democracy*. See also the stimulating discussion in Benjamin Barber, *Strong democracy*, which argued that the little democracy we have had in the West has been repeatedly compromised by the liberal institutions and philosophy that underpin it.

2 For an appreciation of these new social movements see, for instance, Sheila Rowbotham, *Dreams and dilemmas*; Anna Coote and Beatrix Campbell, *Sweet freedom*; Wini Breines, *Community and organisation in the New Left: 1962-1968*; and *They should have served that cup of coffee*, ed Dick Cluster.

3 A useful introduction to situationist writings that seem to have re-emerged influentially in the writings of Jean Baudrillard in the late 1980s is provided by Guy Debord, *The Society of the spectacle*. For an exploration of Baudrillard's development, see Douglas Kellner, *Jean Baudrillard: from Marxism to postmodernism and beyond*.

4 For a sense of the Left's responses to Thatcherism in England, see the useful collection, *The politics of Thatcherism*, ed Stuart Hall and Martin Jacques, and the more recent collection, *New times: the changing structural face of politics in the 1990s*.

5 To understand the relationship of Althusser to politics, see Victor J. Seidler, 'Trusting ourselves: Marxism, human needs and sexual politics' in *One-dimensional Marxism*, ed Simon Clarke *et al.*, pp. 103/56. See also E.P. Thompson's essay, 'The poverty of theory' in *The poverty of theory and other essays* and Ted Benton, *The rise and fall of Marxism*.

6 An important discussion of the Leninist models of political militancy was initiated by the publication of *Beyond the fragments: feminism and the making of socialism*, Sheila Rowbotham, Lynne Segal and Hilary Wainwright. See also the discussions of Leninism in *Lenin and the cultural revolution* by Carmen Claudin-Urondo, *The intellectual origins of Leninism* by Alain Besancon, and *The radical tradition* by Richard Gombin.

7 Alice Miller has written in an insightful way about the emotional life of children and adults. See, for instance, her *The drama of the gifted child* and *For your own good: hidden cruelty in child-rearing and the roots of violence*. If the connections to masculinity are often left implicit, they are no less vital for a fuller appreciation of her work.

8 Useful insights into the workings of relationships that are practical as well as potentially profound are provided by Virginia Satir in *Peoplemaking*. See also her *Conjoint family therapy*.

9 For useful background essays to understand some of the recent movements in Eastern Europe, see Timothy Garton Ash, *The uses of adversity*. See also his *The Polish revolution: Solidarity*, and Paul Lewis, ed, *Eastern Europe: legitimation and political crisis*.

10 The strengths of a structuralist account of women's oppression, if also its weakness, can be gained from Michele Barrett's *Women's oppression today*. See also the work on the family by Michele Barrett and Mary McIntosh, *The anti-social family*.

11 The weakness of a technical conception of the relations of production was pinpointed by Lukàcs as part of his critique of orthodox Marxism. See, for instance, 'Technology and social relations' in *Marxism and human liberation*, ed E. San Juan, Jr. It is also a point made by Simon Clarke in his 'Althusserian Marxism' in *One-dimensional Marxism*, ed Simon Clarke *et al.*.

12 A useful historical account of the development of the gay movement is provided by Jeffrey Weeks's *Coming out: homosexual politics in Britain*. See also his *Sex, politics and society: the regulation of sexuality since 1800*. For accounts that focus more explicitly upon a lesbian experience, see Lillian Faderman, *Surpassing the love of men*; E.M. Ettorre, *Lesbians, women and society*; D.G. Wolfe, *The lesbian community*.

13 For some different reflections on the implications of the absent father for the growth and development of children, see Alexander Mitscherlich, *Society without the father*, Max Horkheimer's essay, 'Authority and the family' in his *Critical theory: selected essays*, and Victor J. Seidler's 'Fathering, authority and masculinity' in *Male order: unwrapping masculinity*, ed K. Chapman and J. Rutherford. For more Jungian inspired reflections, see *The father* ed Andrew Samuel.

14 Gramsci's discussion of the importance of a moral critique of 'common sense' is in the *Prison notebooks*, 'The study of philosophy', pp. 321/42. A useful introductory discussion to Gramsci is provided by Carl Boggs's *Gramsci's Marxism*. See also Victor J. Seidler's 'Trusting ourselves: Marxism, human needs and sexual politics' in *One-dimensional Marxism*, ed Simon Clarke *et al.*, pp. 103/56.

15 For some useful, if very different, reflections upon the relationship of psychology to politics, see, for instance, Russell Jacoby's *Social amnesia*; Claude Steiner (ed), *Readings in radical psychiatry*; Bruce Brown, *Marx, Freud and the critique of everyday life*; Eli Zaretsky, *Capitalism, the family and personal life*; Joel Kovel, *The age of desire: Case histories of a radical psychoanalyst*; and Jeffrey Weeks, *Sexuality and its discontents*.

16 This has been a theme in the earlier chapters on 'Self-Denial' and 'Morality', as well as in Victor J. Seidler's *Kant, respect and injustice: the limits of liberal moral theory*.

17 For interesting discussions of male sexuality, see *The sexuality of men*, ed M. Humphries and A. Metcalf. See also Victor J. Seidler's *Rediscovering masculinity: reason, language and sexuality*.

18 Some sense of how women conceive relationships with men as well as relationships with each other is explored in *Sex and love: new thoughts on old contradictions*, ed Sue Cartledge and Joanna Ryan.

19 Notions of respect, dignity and integrity and the difficulties which an Enlightenment rationalism has with them are explored in Victor Seidler's *The moral limits of modernity: love, inequality and oppression*.

20 For an understanding of some of these tendencies in Eastern Europe, see the essay by Timothy Garton Ash, 'Does central Europe exist?' in *The uses of adversity*, pp. 161/91. See also *Antipolitics: an essay* by György Konrad, and *Letters from prison and other essays* by Adam Michnik.

21 This vision of the liberal state is discussed by R. Dworkin in his essay 'Liberalism' in *Public and private morality*, ed Stuart Hampshire. This vision of neutrality in relation to visions of the good life is a feature of recent liberal theory that was not known to its earlier expressions. For some critical remarks on this tradition of work, see Michael Sandel, *Liberalism and the limits of justice* and the concluding chapter to Victor J. Seidler's *Kant, respect and injustice: the limits of liberal moral theory* entitled 'Liberalism and the autonomy of morality'.

22 For a discussion of women's relationship to language and silence, see Sheila Rowbotham, 'Women's liberation and the new politics', reprinted in *Dreams and dilemmas* pp. 5/32. A more generalised discussion was provoked by Dale Spender's *Man-made language*. See the different critical responses in Deborah Cameron's *Feminism and linguistic theory* and Lynne Segal's *Is the future female?*

23 Some psychological reflections that draw on conceptions of child development to show that boys learn a different relationship to principles, wanting to decide issues through reason alone, are found in Carol Gilligan's *In a different voice: psychological theory and women's development*.

24 Stanley Cavell's 'The availability of the later Wittgenstein' in *Must we mean what we say?*, pp. 44/72, brings out difficulties in the interpretation of Wittgenstein's later writings. See also his *The claim of reason* and Norman Malcolm's work on the development of Wittgenstein which brings out how his understanding of the relationship of language to experience changes in his *Nothing is hidden*.

25 A sense of these discussions in the women's movement is provided by Sheila Rowbotham's *Dreams and dilemmas* and her *The past is before us: feminism in action since the 1960s*.

26 Tensions between orthodox Marxism as science and as moral challenge to

unequal and oppressive relationships are explored by Simone Weil in *Oppression and liberty*. It is a crucial work since forms of Marxism as technological determinism have reasserted themselves within an Anglo-American tradition of analytical Marxism. For a critical introduction to Weil's social and political theory, see Lawrence Blum and Victor J. Seidler's *A truer liberty: Simone Weil and Marxism*.

12 Conclusion: recreating politics – socialism, feminism and ecology

1 Simone Weil's discussion of the inadequacies of our prevailing moral and political traditions to illuminate the realities we face in contemporary industrialised societies is a theme in Lawrence Blum and Victor J. Seidler's *A truer liberty: Simone Weil and Marxism*, ch 4, 'Liberty', pp. 80/106.

2 Discussions which provide useful background to the revolutionary changes in Eastern Europe are provided by Timothy Garton Ash in *The uses of adversity*. See also the special edition of Granta 30 (1990).

3 Walter Schwartz (*The Guardian*, 3 Jan 1990). See also more extended discussion in Walter and Dorothy Schwartz, *Breaking through*, (1987).

4 The relationship of psychoanalytic theory to the 'reality' of a person's experience has provoked enormous discussion most recently with the publication of J. Masson's *Freud: The assault on truth – Freud's suppression of the seduction theory*. See also Janet Malcolm *In the Freud archives* and J. Masson's further response in *Against therapy*. The sides are clearly drawn but the important issues involved still seem far from clear to me. The issues have been usefully discussed within the journal *Free associations* and by Edgar Levenson in *The ambiguity of change*.

5 'Does Central europe exists?' by Timoth Garton Ash has been reprinted in his *The uses of adversity*, pp. 161/98.

6 An attempt to reinstate a conception of justice that is grounded in people's treatment of each other as prior to distributive conceptions of justice since they sustain autonomy and independence which the latter take for granted, is a central concern in Victor J. Seidler's *The moral limits of modernity: love, inequality and oppression*.

7 A useful discussion of Freud on the issue of validating personal pain and suffering is promoted by Philip Rieff's *Freud: the mind of the moralist*. See also Sherry Turkle, *Psychoanalytic politics: Freud's French Revolution* for useful background on how Freud's work was received in France.

8 For some discussion of feminism's problematic relationship with psychoanalysis we need to consider the importance of Juliet Mitchell's *Psychoanalysis and feminism*, which in large part set the terms for a reconsideration of Freud's work after the early challenges of, for instance, Kate Millett in *Sexual politics*. See, for instance, Jane Gallop, *Feminism and psychoanalysis: the daughter's seduction*, and Juliet Mitchell and Jacqueline Rose (eds) *Feminine sexuality: Jacques Lacan and the Ecole Freudienne*. Different terms were set from those offered by Lacan, by Jean Baker Miller in *Toward a new psychology of women*, by Dorothy Dinnerstein's *The rocking of the cradle and the ruling of the world*, by Janet Sayers's *Sexual contradictions: psychology, psychoanalysis and feminism* and by Jessica

Benjamin's *Bonds of love: psychoanalysis, feminism and the problem of domination.*

9 A useful discussion of the different forms of masculinities is provided by Bob Connell in *Gender and power* and, largely following the theoretical position he establishes, Lynne Segal in *Slow motion: changing masculinities, changing men.* See also Tim Carrigan, Bob Connell and John Lee, 'Towards a sociology of masculinity' in Harry Brod (ed), *The making of masculinities: the new men's studies.*

10 The historical sources for possessive forms of individualism are explored by C.B. Macpherson in *The political theory of possessive individualism.* Different aspects of Macpherson's work have been explored in *Powers, possessions and freedom*, ed Alkis Kontos. See, in particular, an essay by Charles Taylor entitled 'Atomism', reprinted along with his 'The nature and scope of distributive justice' and 'Kant's theory of freedom' in his *Philosophy and the human sciences: philosophical papers 2.*

11 Locke's conception of freedom is at the core of Robert Nozick's influential libertarian view, worked out in *Anarchy, state and utopia.*

12 This rejection of our emotional selves within an Enlightenment rationalism is a continuing theme in Susan Griffin's writings. See, for instance, *Women and nature* and *Pornography and silence.* It helps her to draw out vital connections between sexism, racism and anti-Semitism which are too often treated as having discrete histories rather than as located within a culture of modernity where they belong.

13 For an insightful discussion of the distinction between use values and exchange values in Marx's writings, see Roman Rosdolsky's *The making of Mark's 'Capital'.* See also I.I. Rubin, *Essays on Marx's theory of value.* The danger seems to be that too much is squeezed into the conception of use value to allow for the economic analysis to be sustained.

14 Useful discussions of Thatcherism are provided by *The politics of Thatcherism*, ed Martin Jacques and Stuart Hall. See also Andrew Gamble, *The Conservative nation* and *New times: the changing face of politics in the 1980s*, ed Stuart Hall and Martin Jacques.

15 Simone Weil's discussion of different conceptions of justice is in 'Human personality' in *Selected Essays, 1934-1943*, ed Richard Rees. It is a theme that remains a touchstone with all her writings. It is discussed in Victor J. Seidler's *The moral limits of modernity: love, inequality and oppression*, chs 7 and 9.

16 The relationship of humans to other animals and to nature generally as it has been presented within a Western philosophical tradition is an important theme explored by Mary Midgley. See, for instance, the pioneering study *Beast and man* and the brief but insightful *Animals and why they matter.* See also interesting discussion in Tom Regan, *The case for animal rights.*

17 It is misleading, if not worse, to think of the Genesis notion of the dominion of nature as supporting the idea of the domination of nature. Crucial distinctions need to be made. See, for instance, Mary Daly, *Beyond God the Father*; Virginia Mollenkott, *Women, men and the Bible*; Elaine Pagels, *The gnostic gospels* and *Feminist interpretation of the Bible*, ed Letty M. Russell.

18 Discussions of the relationship of modernity to post-modernity have come to assume a central, if uneasy, position within social theory. Useful introductions are provided by Hal Foster (ed), *Post-modern culture*, and the special number of *Theory, culture and society* entitled 'Postmodernism', Vol. 5 Nos. 2/3 June

1988. See in particular Zygmunt Bauman, 'Is there a post-modern sociology?' pp. 217/38 and Douglas Kellner, 'Postmodernism as social theory' pp. 239/70.

19 The ways in which morality has been identified with reason within Enlightenment visions of modernity and the limits that this has placed upon our moral consciousness is a theme in Victor J. Seidler, *The moral limits of modernity: love, inequality and oppression.*

20 The relationship of Marxism to working-class experience was a theme increasingly appreciated by Raymond Williams. See his *The country and the city* and *Politics and letters.*

21 The relationship of Marxism to morality is explored by Herbert Marcuse in *Soviet Marxism: a critical analysis*; Steven Lukes in *Marxism and morality*; Richard W. Miller, *Analysing Marx: morality, power and history*; a special issue of the *Canadian journal of philosophy*, supplementary vol. V11 on 'Marx and morality' ed K. Nielson and Steven C. Patten; Anthony Skillen, *Ruling illusions*; and Douglas Kellner, *Critical theory; Marxism and modernity.*

22 For some reflections on the way that possessive conceptions of individualism still inform liberal moral and political theory, see C.B. Macpherson, *Democratic theory: essays in retrieval* and *The real world of democracy.*

23 Social theory has been slow to recognise the implications of important work done by Elizabeth Kübler-Ross on the processes of death and bereavement. See, for instance, her *On death and dying*. See also Stanislav Grof and Joan Halifax, *The human encounter with death.*

24 A useful discussion of the relationship of the Scientific Revolutions to particular conceptions of masculinity is found in Brian Easlea, *Science and sexual oppression*, ch 3, 'Male Sexism and the 17th Century Scientific Revolution', Benjamin Farrington's *The philosophy of Francis Bacon*, and Susan Griffin's *Woman and nature*. It is useful to read these works next to such works as E.A. Burtt, *The metaphysical foundations of modern physical science* and Joseph Needham, *The great titration.*

25 The idea that Kant leaves us with a weak and attenuated conception of the person can be difficult to hear since it is taken to be a strength of his moral rationalism when compared with utilitarianism, which is often taken to be the only viable alternative. This is a central argument in Victor J. Seidler's *Kant, respect and injustice: the limits of liberal moral theory.*

26 The discussion around post-modernity is often flawed because of the dualities of structuralism that still inform its terms. It is as if the visions of post-modernity are set in contrast with a sense of modernity that went before, and it is because we have barely appreciated how our conceptions of modernity were organised around a distinction between reason and nature, that we fail to recognise how feminism, ecology and forms of psychotherapy, in challenging this separation, are challenging the vision of the rational self which has guided modernity. This sets the distinction between the supposedly unified Cartesian self and the fragmented identities of post-modernity within a different perspective. Some useful reflections are provided in *Feminism/Post-modernism*, ed Linda Nicolson.

27 A useful introduction to Alice Miller's pioneering work is her *The drama of the gifted child and the search for the true self*. See also *For your own good: hidden cruelty in child-rearing and the roots of violence.*

28 An awareness of the centrality of mechanical notions and relationships within our inherited conceptions of modernity is provided by F. Capra in *The turning point*. See also Carolyn Merchant, *The death of nature*. For an alternative, more holistic vision which seems to be growing in clarity and focus, see, for instance, James Lovelock, *Gaia: a new look at life on earth*; F. Capra, *The tao of physics*; Gary Zukav, *The dancing Wu Li masters*. For the political implications, see André Gorz, *Ecology as politics*; Walter and Dorothy Schwarz, *Breaking through*; Trevor Blackwell and Jeremy Seabrook, *The politics of hope*.

29 For introductions to different visions of holistic conceptions in medicine, see, for instance, E.K. Ledermann, *Mental health, human conscience*; John Berger, *A fortunate man*; and George Vithoulkas *Homeopathy*.

30 As well as Bill McKibbon, *The end of nature*, it is useful to read Jonathan Schell, *The fate of the earth*; Susan Griffin, *Woman and nature*; Rudolph Bahro *Socialism and survival* and *From red to green*; Peter Russell, *The awakening earth*; James Lovelock, *Gaia: a new look at life on earth*; Jonathon Porritt, *Seeing green*; André Gorz, *Ecology as politics*.

31 Issues of reality and relationship within a psychoanalytic process are discussed in an interesting way by Edgar Levensen in *The ambiguity of change*.

32 Relationships between rich and poor nations, between North and South, have been explored in relevant ways by Susan George, *How the other half dies*; Francis Lappé and Joseph Collins, *Food first*; Peter Worsley, *The three worlds*; and Michael Redclift, *Development and the environmental crisis*.

33 The relationship between state and civil society has become a central theme in the movements for democracy in Eastern Europe. See, for instance, John Keane, *Democracy and civil society*, and the collection edited by him, *Civil society and the state*.

Bibliography

Adorno, T.W. (1968) 'Sociology and psychology' in *New Left Review* No.46, Nov 1967, and No.47, Jan 1968.
—— (1974) *Minima moralia*, trans C.E.N. Jephcott, London: New Left Books.
Aglietta, M. (1979) *A theory of capitalist regulation: the US experience*, London: Verso.
Althusser, L. (1969) *For Marx*, London: New Left Books.
—— (1971) *Lenin and philosophy and other essays*, London: New Left Books.
—— (1972) *Essays in self-criticism*, London: New Left Books.
Altman, D. (1982) *The homosexualization of America, the Americanization of the homosexual*, New York: St. Martin's Press.
Anderson, B. (1983) *Imagined communities*, London: Verso.
Arato, A. and Breines, P. (1979) *The young Lukàcs and western Marxism*, London: Pluto.
Arato, A. and Gebhardt, E. (eds) (1978) *The essential Frankfurt School reader*, Oxford: Blackwell.
Ash, T.G. (1983) *The Polish revolution: Solidarity*, London: Jonathan Cape.
—— (1989) *The uses of adversity*, Cambridge: Granta Books with Penguin Books.
—— (1990) *We the people: the revolution of 89*, Harmondsworth: Granta, Penguin.
Bahro, R. (1982) *Socialism and survival*, London: Heretic Books.
—— (1984) *From red to green*, London: Verso.
Barber, B. (1984) *Strong democracy*, Berkeley: University of California Press.
Barnes, H. (1981) *Sartre and Flaubert*, Chicago: Chicago University Press.
Barrett, M. (1980) *Women's oppression today*, London: Verso.
Barrett, M. and McIntosh, M. (1987) *The anti-social family*, London: Verso.
Bateson, G. (1979) *Mind and nature: a necessary unity*, New York: E.P. Dutton.
Baudrillard, J. (1981) *For a critique of the political economy of the sign*, St. Louis: Telos Press.
—— (1983a) *Simulations*, New York: Semiotext(e).
—— (1983b) *In the shadow of the silent majorities*, New York: Semiotext(e).
Bauman, Z. (1980) *Memories of class*, London: Routledge & Kegan Paul.
Belotti, E.G. (1971) *Little girls*, London: Readers & Writers.
Benhabib, S. and Cornell, D. (1987) *Feminism as critique: essays in the politics of gender*, Cambridge: Polity.
Benjamin, J. (1977) 'Authority and the family revisited', *New German Critique* 13 pp. 35/57.

—— (1990) *The bonds of love: psychoanalysis, feminism and the problem of domination*, London: Virago.

Benton, T. (1984) *The rise and fall of structural Marxism*, London: Macmillan.

Benvenuto B. and Kennedy, R. (1987) *The works of Jacques Lacan: An introduction*, London: Free Association Books.

Berger, J. (1962) *A fortunate man*, Harmondsworth: Penguin.

Berger, P. and Pulberg, S. 'Reification and the sociological critique of consciousness' in *New Left Review*, No. 35, Jan 1966.

Berlin, I. (1969) *Four essays on liberty*, Oxford: Oxford University Press.

—— (1981) *Against the current*, Oxford: Oxford University Press.

Besancon, A. (1974) *The intellectual origins of Leninism*, Oxford: Blackwell.

Blackwell, T. and Seabrook, J. (1985) *A world still to win*, London: Faber.

—— (1988) *The politics of hope*, London: Faber.

Blum, L. (1980) *Friendship, altruism and morality*, London: Routledge.

Blum, L. and Seidler, V.J. (1989) *A truer liberty: Simone Weil and Marxism*, New York and London: Routledge.

Boadella, D. (ed) (1976) *In the wake of Reich*, London: Coventire.

—— (1988) *Wilhelm Reich: The evolution of his work*, London: Routledge.

Boggs, C. (1976) *Gramsci's Marxism*, London: Pluto Press.

Boyers, R. and Orrill, R. (eds) (1972) *Laing and anti-psychiatry*, Harmondsworth: Penguin.

Braverman, H. (1974) *Labor and monopoly capital*, New York: Monthly Review Press.

Breines, W. (1982) *Community and organisation in the New Left 1962-68*, New York: Praeger.

Brinton, M. *Authoritarian conditioning, sexual repression and the irrational in politics*, Solidarity Pamphlet No. 33, June 1930.

Brod, H. (1987) *The making of masculinities: the new men's studies*, Boston: Allen & Unwin.

Brown, B. (1974) *Marx, Freud and the critique of everyday life*, Monthly Review Press.

Brownmiller, S. (1975) *Against our will: men, women and rape*, Harmondsworth: Penguin.

Buber, M. (1957) 'Distance and relation' in *Psychiatry* 20.

Bucks-Morss, S. (1977) *The origin of negative dialectics*, Brighton: Harvester Press.

Burtt, E.A. (1932) *The metaphysical foundations of modern physical science*, London: Routledge & Kegan Paul.

Cameron, D. (1985) *Feminism and linguistic theory*, London: Macmillan.

Campbell, B. (1984) *Wigan Pier revisited*, London: Virago.

—— (1987) *Iron ladies: why women vote Tory*, London: Virago.

Caplan, P. (ed) (1987) *The cultural construction of sexuality*, London: Tavistock.

Capra, F. (1975) *The turning point*, London: Wildwood House.

—— (1986) *The tao of physics*, London: Wildwood House.

Cartledge, S. and Ryan, J. (eds) (1983) *Sex and love: new thoughts on old contradictions*, London: The Women's Press.

Cavell, S. (1969) *Must we mean what we say?*, New York: Scribners.

—— (1980) *The claim of reason*, Oxford: Oxford University Press.

Chapman, R. and Rutherford, J. (eds) (1988) *Male order: unwrapping masculinity*, London: Lawrence & Wishart.

Chasseguet-Smirgel, J. and Grunberger, B. (1986) *Freud or Reich?*, London: Free Association Books.

Chodorow, N. (1978) *The reproduction of mothering*, Berkeley: University of California Press.

Clarke, S., Lovell, T., Robins, K. and Seidler, V.J. (1980) *One-dimensional Marxism*, London: Allison & Busby.

Claudin-Urondo, C. (1977) *Lenin and the cultural revolution*, Brighton: Harvester.

Cleaver, E. (1969) *Soul on ice*, London: Cape.

Cluster, D. (1979) *They should have served that cup of coffee*, Boston: South End Press.

Cockburn, C. (1980) *Brothers*, London: Pluto Press.

Collier, A. (1977) *R.D. Laing: The philosophy and politics of psychotherapy*, Brighton: Harvester Press.

Connell, R.W. (1987) *Gender and power*, Cambridge: Polity Press.

Cooper, D. (ed) (1968) *The dialectics of liberation*, Harmondsworth: Penguin Books.

—— (1970) *Psychiatry and anti-psychiatry*, London: Paladin.

—— (1974) *The grammar of living*, London: Allen Lane.

Coote, A. and Campbell, B. (1982) *Sweet freedom: the struggle for women's liberation*, London: Picador.

Coward, R. (1984) *Female desire*, London: Paladin.

Daly, M. (1973) *Beyond God the Father*, Boston: Beacon Press.

—— (1978) *Gyn/ecology: the metaethics of radical feminism*, London: The Women's Press.

De Cecco, J. and Shiveley, H. (1984) *Bisexual and homosexual identities*, New York: Haworth Press.

Debord, G. (1970) *The society of the spectacle*, Detroit: Black & Red.

Debray, R. (1970) *Prison writings*, Harmondsworth: Penguin.

Deleuze, G. and Guattari, F. (1977), *Anti-Oedipus: capitalism and schizophrenia*, New York: The Viking Press.

Dennison, G. (1971) *The lives of children*, Harmondsworth: Penguin Education.

Dews, P. (1987) *Logics of disintegration: post-structuralism and the claims of critical theory*, London: Verso.

Derrida, J. (1976) *Of grammatology*, Baltimore: The Johns Hopkins University Press.

Dinnerstein, D. (1976) *The rocking of the cradle and the ruling of the world*, London: Souvenir Press.

Dunayevskaya, R. (1971) *Marxism and freedom*, London: Pluto Press.

Durkheim, E. (1915) *The elementary forms of the religious life*, London: Allen & Unwin.

—— (1957) *Professional ethics and civil morals*, London: Routledge & Kegan Paul.

—— (1960) *Moral education*, New York: Free Press.

—— (1974) *Sociology and philosophy*, New York: Free Press.

Dworkin, A. (1981) *Pornography: men possessing women*, London: The Women's Press.

—— (1987) *Right-wing women: the politics of domesticated females*, London: The Women's Press.

Dychwald, K. (1978) *Bodymind*, London: Wildwood House.

Easlea, B. (1981) *Science and sexual oppression*, London: Weidenfeld & Nicholson.
Easthope, A. (1985) *What a man's gotta do*, London: Paladin.
Ehrenreich, B. (1983) *The hearts of men*, London: Pluto Press.
——— (1986) *Re-making love: the feminization of sex*, New York: Anchor Press.
Ehrenreich, B. and English, D. (1979) *For her own good*, London: Pluto Press.
Eisenstein, H. and Jardine, A. (1980) *The future of difference*, Boston: G.K. Hall.
Eisenstein, Z. (1986) *The radical future of liberal feminism*, New York: Longman.
Elshtain, J.B. (1981) *Public man, private woman: women in social and political thought*, Princeton: Princeton University Press.
Erikson, E. (1964) *Insight and responsibility*, New York: W.W. Norton.
Ernst, S. and Goodison, L. (1981) *In our own hands*, London: The Women's Press.
Ernst, S. and Maguire, M. (1987) *Living with the sphinx: papers from the Women's Therapy Centre*, London: The Women's Press.
Esterson, A. (1972) *The leaves of spring*, Harmondsworth: Penguin Books.
Ettorre, E.M. (1980) *Lesbians, women and society*, London: Routledge.
Faderman, L. (1976) *Surpassing the love of men*, London: Junction Books.
Fagan, J. and Shepherd, I.L. (eds) (1972) *Gestalt therapy now*, Harmondsworth: Penguin.
Fanon, F. (1970) *Black skin, white masks*, London: Paladin.
Farrington, B. (1964) *The philosophy of Francis Bacon*, Liverpool: Liverpool University Press.
Fearon, A.-M. (1978) 'Come in Tarzan, your time up' in *Shrew*, feminism and non-violence issue.
Fernbach, D. (1970) 'Sexual oppression and political practice' in *New Left Review*, No.64
——— (1981) *The spiral path*, London: Gay Men's Press.
Firestone, S. (1970) *The dialectics of sex*, New York: Bantam Books.
Foreman, A. (1977) *Femininity as alienation*, London: Pluto Press.
Foster, H. (ed) (1985) *Postmodern culture*, London: Pluto.
Foucault, M. (1971) *Madness and civilization*, London: Tavistock.
——— (1973) *The birth of the clinic*, London: Tavistock.
——— (1979a) *Discipline and punish: the birth of the prison*, London: Allen Lane.
——— (1979b) *A history of sexuality*, London: Allen Lane.
——— (1980) *Power/knowledge*, Brighton: Harvester Press.
Francke, L.B. (1979) *The ambivalences of abortion*, London: Allen Lane.
Fraser, N. (1988) *Unruly practices: power, discourse and gender*, Oxford: Polity.
Freud, S. (1900) *The interpretation of dreams*, Standard Edition, Vol.4–5, London: Hogarth.
——— (1930) *Civilisation and its discontents*, London: Hogarth Press.
——— (1973) *Introductory lectures on psychoanalysis*, Harmondsworth: Pelican Freud Library.
——— (1975) *Three essays on the theory of sexuality*, Harmondsworth: Pelican Freud Library.
Friedenberg, E. (1973) *R.D. Laing*, London: Fontana Books.
Frisby, D. (ed) (1976) *The positivist dispute in German sociology*, London: Heinemann.
Fromm, E. (1946) *Fear of freedom*, London: Routledge & Kegan Paul.
——— (1973) *The crisis of psychoanalysis*, Harmondsworth: Penguin Books.

Frosch, S. (1987) *The politics of psychoanalysis*, London: Macmillan.
Gallop, J. (1982) *Feminism and psychoanalysis: the daughter's seduction*, London: Macmillan.
Gamble, A. (1984) *The conservative nation*, London: Macmillan.
—— (1988) *The free economy and the strong state*, London: Macmillan.
—— (1990) *Britain in decline*, London: Macmillan.
Gay, P. (1990) *Freud*, Harmondsworth: Penguin.
Gay Left Collective (ed) (1980) *Homosexuality: power and politics*, London: Allison & Busby.
George, S. (1976) *How the other half dies*, Harmondsworth: Penguin.
Giddens, A. (1978) *Durkheim*, London: Fontana.
Gilligan, C. (1982) *In a different voice: psychological theory and women's development*, Cambridge: Harvard.
Goffman, E. (1959) *The presentation of self in everyday life*, New York: Doubleday Anchor Books.
Gombin, R. (1978) *The radical tradition*, London: Methuen.
Gordon, L. (1988) *Heroes of their lives: the politics and history of family violence*, New York: Viking.
Gorz, A. (1967) *Strategy for labour*, Boston: Beacon Books.
—— (ed) (1976) *The division of labour: the labour process and class struggle in modern capialism*, Brighton: Harvester.
—— (1983) *Ecology as politics*, London: Pluto Press.
Gould, C. and Wartofsky, M. (1976) *Women's philosophy: towards a theory of liberation*, New York: Capricorn Press.
Gouldner, A. (1970) *The coming crisis of western sociology*, London: Heinemann.
Gramsci, A. (1971) *Prison notebooks*, London: Lawrence & Wishart.
Granta 30 (1990) *New Europe*, Harmondsworth: Granta, Penguin.
Graubard, A. (1972) *Free the children*, New York: Vintage.
Gray, C. (ed) (1974) *Leaving the 20th century*, London: Free Fall Publications.
Gray, J.N. and Peltzynski (1984) *Conceptions of liberty in political theory*, London: Althorne Press.
Griffin, S. (1980) *Pornography and silence*, London: The Women's Press.
—— (1982) *Woman and nature*, London: The Women's Press.
Grimshaw, J. (1986) *Feminist philosophers*, Brighton: Harvester.
Grof, S. and Halifax, J. (1977) *The human encounter with death*, New York: E.P. Dutton.
Guattari, F. (1984) *Molecular revolution*, Harmondsworth: Penguin Books.
Habermas, J. (1971) *Toward a rational society*, London: Heinemann.
—— (1981) 'Modernity versus post-modernity' in *New German Critique*: 22 pp 3-14.
—— (1986) *Habermas, autonomy and solidarity: interviews with Jürgen Habermas*, ed Peter Dews, London: Verso.
Hall, S. (1988) *The hard road to renewal*, London: Verso.
Hall, S. and Jacques, M. (eds) (1983) *The politics of Thatcherism*, London: Lawrence & Wishart.
—— (1990) *New times: the changing face of politics in the 1990s*, London: Lawrence & Wishart.
Hall, S. and Jefferson, T. (eds) (1977) *Resistance through rituals*, London: Hutchinson University Library.
Hampshire, S. (ed) (1978) *Public and private morality*, Cambridge: Cambridge University Press.

Hanmer, J. and Maynard, M. (eds) (1987) *Women, violence and social control*, London: Macmillan.

Hanscombe, G. and Humphries, M. (eds) (1987) *Heterosexuality*, London: Gay Men's Press.

Harding, S. (1986) *The science question in feminism*, Ithaca: Cornell University Press.

Harding, S. and Hintikka, H. (eds) (1983) *Discovering reality: feminist perspectives on epistemology, metaphysics, methodology and philosophy of science*, Dordrecht: D. Reidel.

Havel, V. (1987) *Living in truth*, ed J. Vladislav London: Faber & Faber.

Hearn, J. (1987) *The gender of oppression*, Brighton: Harvester Press.

Hebdige, D. (1979) *Subculture: the meaning of style*, London: Methuen.

Held, D. (1980) *An introduction to critical theory: from Horkheimer to Habermas*, London: Hutchinson.

Henriques, J. *et al.* (1984) *Changing the subject: psychology, social regulation and subjectivity*, London: Methuen.

Hirschmann, A. (1977) *The passions and the interests*, Princeton: Princeton University Press.

Hite, S. (1981) *The Hite report on male sexuality*, London: Macdonald.

Hobsbawm, E. (1977) *The age of revolution*, London: Abacus.

Hoch, P. (1979) *White hero, black beast*, London: Pluto Press.

Hollis, M. and Lukes, S. (1982) *Rationality and relativism*, Oxford: Blackwell.

Holt, J. (1969) *How children fail*, Harmondsworth: Penguin.

Horkheimer, M. (1972a) *The eclipse of reason*, New York: OUP 1947, Seabury Press.

—— (1972b) *Critical theory: selected essays*, New York: Seabury Press.

Hoy, D.C. (1986) *Foucault: a critical reader*, Oxford: Blackwell.

Humphries, M. and Metcalf, A. (1985) *The sexuality of men*, London: Pluto Press.

Irigaray, L. (1985) *Speculum of the other woman*, Ithaca: Cornell University Press.

Jackson, G. (1971) *Soledad brother: the prison letters of George Jackson*, Harmondsworth: Penguin.

Jacobs, J. (1978) *Out of the ghetto: fascism and communism 1913-1939*, London: Janet Simon.

Jacoby, R. (1975) *Social amnesia*, Boston: Beacon Books.

—— (1983) *The repression of psychoanalysis: Otto Fenichel and the political Freudians*, New York: Basic Books.

Jameson, F. (1972) *The prison house of language*, Princeton: Princeton University Press.

Jardine, A. and Smith, P. (1987) *Men in feminism*, London: Methuen.

Jay, M. (1973) *The dialectical imagination – a history of the Frankfurt School and Institute of Social Research*, London: Heinemann.

Kant, I. (1974) *Anthropology from a pragmatic point of view*, trans Mary Gregor, The Hague: Martinus Nijhoff.

Kaufman, M. (ed) (1987) *Beyond patriarchy*, Toronto: OUP.

Keane, J. (1985) *The power of the powerless: citizens against the state in central-Eastern Europe*, London: Hutchinson.

—— (1988a) *Democracy and civil society*, London: Verso.

—— (ed) (1988b) *Civil society and the state*, London: Verso.

Kellerman, S. (1975) *Your body speaks its mind*, New York: Simon & Schuster.
Kellner, D. (1984) *Herbert Marcuse and the crisis of Marxism*, London: Macmillan.
—— (1988a) *Critical theory, Marxism and modernity*, Cambridge: Polity Press.
—— (1988b) *Jean Baudrillard: from Marxism to postmodernism and beyond*, Cambridge: Polity Press.
Kennedy, E. and Mendus, S. (1987) *Women in western political philosophy*, Brighton: Harvester.
Kimmel, M. (1987) *Changing men*, London: Sage Publications.
Klein, M. (1975a) *Envy and gratitude and other writings 1946–1963*, London: Virago.
—— (1975b) *Love, guilt and reparation and other works 1921–1945*, London: Virago.
Konrad, G. (1986) *Antipolitics: an essay*, London: Paladin.
Kontos, A. (ed) (1979) *Powers, possessions and freedom*, Toronto: Toronto University Press.
Korsch, K. (1970) *Marxism and philosophy*, trans F. Halliday, New York: Monthly Review Press.
Kovel, J. (1981) *The age of desire: case histories of a radical psychoanalyst*, New York: Pantheon Books.
Kübler-Ross, E. (1970) *On death and dying*, London: Tavistock.
Lacan, J. (1977) *Ecrits: a selection*, London: Tavistock.
Laing, R.D. (1970a) *The divided self*, Harmondsworth: Penguin Books.
—— (1970b) *The politics of experience*, Harmondsworth: Penguin Books.
—— (1971) *The politics of the family*, Harmondsworth: Penguin Books.
Laing, R.D. and Esterson, A. (1970) *Sanity, madness and the family*, Harmondsworth: Penguin Books.
Lamsden, A.H. (ed) (1980) *The economics of women and work*, Harmondsworth: Penguin.
Lappé, F. and Wilkins, J. (1982) *Food first*, London: Sphere.
Larrain, J. (1979) *The concept of ideology*, London: Hutchinson.
—— (1983) *Marxism and ideology*, London: Macmillan.
Lasch, C. (1971) *Everyday life in the modern world*, New York: Harpers Row.
—— (1977) *Haven in a heartless world*, New York: Basic Books.
Lash, S. and Urry, J. (1987) *The end of organised capitalism*, Cambridge: Cambridge University Press.
Lederman, E.K. (1984) *Mental health and human conscience*, Amersham: Avebury.
Lefèbvre, H. (1968) *Dialectical materialism*, London: Cape.
Lenin, V.I. (1905) 'What is to be done?' in V.I. Lenin (ed) *Selected writings*, Moscow: Lawrence & Wishart.
Lenin, V.I. (1972) *Collected writings: philosophical notebook*, Vol. 38, Moscow: Progress Publishers.
Levene, M. (1979) *Gay men: the sociology of male homosexuality*, New York: Harpers & Row.
Levenson, E. (1983) *The ambiguity of change*, New York: Basic Books.
Lewis, C. and O'Brien, M. (eds) (1987) *Reassessing fatherhood*, London: Sage Publications.
Lichtman, R. (1982) *The production of desire*, New York: Free Press.
Lipietz, A. (1985) *The enchanted world*, London: Verso.

—— (1987) *Miracles and mirages: the crisis of global Fordism in the 1980s*, London: Verso.

Lloyd, G. (1984) *The men of reason: 'male' and 'female' in western philosophy*, London: Methuen.

Lovelock, J. (1979) *Gaia: a new look at life on earth*, Oxford: OUP.

Lowen, A. (1963) *The betrayal of the body*, London: Collier Macmillan.

—— (1976) *Bioenergetics*, Harmondsworth: Penguin.

Lukàcs, G. (1970) *History and class consciousness*, London: Merlin Press.

Lukes, S. (1973) *Individualism*, Oxford: Blackwell.

—— (1975) *Power: a radical view*, London: Macmillan.

—— (1985) *Marxism and morality*, Oxford: Oxford University Press.

—— (1975) *Emile Durkheim*, Harmondsworth: Peregrin Books.

Lyotard, J-F. (1985) *The Post-modern condition*, Manchester: Manchester University Press.

Macey, D. (1988) *Lacan in context*, London: Verso.

MacIntyre, A. (1981) *After virtue*, London: Duckworths.

McKibbon, B. (1990) *The End of Nature*, Harmondsworth: Penguin.

McLellan, D. (1989) *The young Hegelians and Karl Marx*, London: Macmillan.

McMillan, C. (1982) *Women, reason and nature*, Oxford: Blackwell.

Macpherson, C.B. (1962) *The political theory of possessive individualism*, Oxford: Oxford University Press.

—— (1972) *The real world of democracy*, Oxford: Oxford University Press.

—— (1973) *Democratic theory*, Oxford: Oxford University Press.

—— (1977) *The life and times of liberal democracy*, Oxford: Oxford University Press.

McRobbie, A. and Nava, M. (eds) (1985) *Gender and generation*, London: Macmillan.

Magee, B. (1978) *Men of ideas*, London: BBC.

Malcolm, N. (1986) *Nothing is hidden*, Oxford: Blackwell.

Malcolm X (1968) *Autobiography of Malcolm X*, Harmondsworth: Penguin.

Mannoni, O. (1972) *Freud: the theory of the unconscious*, London: New Left Books.

Marcuse, H. (1961) *Soviet Marxism: a critical analysis*, New York: Vintage.

—— (1964) *One-dimensional man*, Boston: Beacon Books.

—— (1967) *Reason and revolution*, London: Routledge.

—— (1968) *Negations*, London: Allen Lane.

—— (1972) *Studies in critical philosophy*, London: New Left Books.

—— (1974) *Eros and civilisation*, Boston: Beacon Press.

Marx, K. (1973a) *Grundrisse*, Harmondsworth: Pelican Marx Library.

—— (1973b) *Wages, prices and profits*, Peking: Foreign Languages Press.

—— (1975) *Economic and Philosophical Manuscripts of 1844*, Harmondsworth: Pelican Marx Library.

—— (1976) *Capital Vol. 1* trans. B. Fowkes, Harmondsworth: Penguin.

Marx, K. and Engels, F. (1968) *Collected works*, London: Lawrence & Wishart.

Masson, J. (1984) *Freud: the assault on truth*, London: Faber & Faber.

—— (1990) *Against therapy*, London: Fontana.

Merchant, C. (1980) *The death of nature; women and the scientific revolution*, San Francisco: Harper & Row.

Michnik, A. (1985) *Letters from prison and other essays*, trans M. Latynski, Berkeley: University of California Press.

Midgley, M.(1978) *Beast and man*, Sussex: Harvester Press.
—— (1981) *Heart and mind: the varieties of moral experience*, London: Methuen.
—— (1983) *Animals and why they matter*, Harmondsworth: Penguin Books.
Midgley, M. and Hughes, J. (1983) *Women's choices: philosophical problems facing feminism*, London: Weidenfeld & Nicolson.
Mill, J.S. (1964) *On Liberty*, London: Everyman Library, Dent.
—— (1971) *Autobiography*, ed J. Sturinger, Oxford: Clarendon Press.
Miller, A. (1981) *The drama of the gifted child*, New York: Basic Books.
—— (1983a) *For your own good: hidden cruelty in child-rearing and the roots of violence*, London: Faber & Faber.
—— (1983b) *Prisoners of childhood*, New York: Basic Books.
Miller, J.B. (ed) (1973) *Psychoanalysis and women*, Harmondsworth: Penguin.
—— (1976) *Toward a new psychology of women*, Harmondsworth: Penguin.
Miller, R.W. (1984) *Analyzing Marx: morality, power and history*, Princeton: Princeton University Books.
Millett, K. (1971) *Sexual politics*, London: Virago.
Mitchell, J.(1971) *Women's estate*, Harmondsworth: Penguin.
—— (1975) *Psychoanalysis and feminism*, Harmondsworth: Penguin.
—— (1984) *Women: the longest revolution*, London: Virago.
Mitchell, J. and Rose, J. (eds) (1982) *Feminine sexuality: Jacques Lacan and the Ecole Freudienne*, London: Macmillan.
Mitscherlich, A. (1970) *Society without the father*, New York: Schocken Books.
Mollenkott, V. (1977) *Women, men and the Bible*, Abingdon Press.
Morgan, D. (1975) *Social theory and the family*, London: Routledge.
Mort, F. (1987) *Dangerous sexualities*, London: Routledge.
Mouffe, C. (1979) *Gramsci and Marxist theory*, London: Routledge.
Mrazek, P. and Kempe, C. (1981) *Sexually abused children and their families*, Oxford: Pergamon Press.
Needham, J. (1969) *The great titration*, London: Allen & Unwin.
Nicolson, L. (1990) *Feminism/postmodernism*, New York: Routledge.
Nielsen, K. and Patten, S. (eds) (1981) *Marx and Morality*, special issue of *Canadian Journal of Philosophy* Supplementary vol 7.
Nozick, R. (1974) *Anarchy, state and utopia*, New York: Basic Books.
O'Brien, M. (1981) *The politics of reproduction*, London: Routledge.
Observer (1990) *Tearing down the curtain*, London: Hodder & Stoughton.
Okin, S.M. (1980) *Women in western political thought*, London: Virago Press.
Ollman, B. (1979) *Social and sexual revolutions*, London: Pluto Press.
Orbach, S. and Eichenbaum, L. (1982) *Outside in/inside out*, Harmondsworth: Penguin.
—— (1983) *Understanding women*, Harmondsworth: Penguin.
—— (1984) *What do women want?*, London: Fontana.
Owen, U. (1983) *Fathers: reflections by daughters*, London: Virago.
Pagels, E. (1982) *The Gnostic gospels*, Harmondsworth: Penguin Books.
Pahl, J. (1985) *Private violence and public policy*, London: Routledge.
Pateman, C. 'The disorder of women: women, love and the sense of justice' in *Ethics* 91, pp 20-34.
Pateman, C. and Gross, E. (eds) (1986) *Feminist challenges: social and political theory*, London: Allen & Unwin.
Perls, F. (1969) *Gestalt therapy verbatim*, Uttar: Real People Press.
Piore, M.J. and Sabel, C.F. (1984) *The second industrial divide*, New York.

Plummer, K. (ed) (1981) *The making of the modern homosexual*, London: Hutchinson.

Porritt, J. (1984) *Seeing green*, Oxford: Blackwell.

Rawls, J. (1972) *A theory of justice*, Oxford: Clarendon Press.

Redclift, M. (1984) *Development and the environmental crisis*, London: Methuen.

Regan, T. (1988) *The case for animal rights*, London: Routledge.

Reich, W. (1942) *The function of the orgasm*, New York: Farrar, Strauss & Giroux.

—— (1970) *The mass psychology of fascism*, New York: Farrar, Strauss & Giroux.

—— (1972a) *Character analysis*, New York: Simon & Schuster.

—— (1972b) *Sex-pol essays: 1929–1934*, ed Lee Baxendall, New York: Vintage.

—— (1974) *The sexual revolution*, New York: Farrar, Strauss & Giroux.

Reiche, R. (1970) *Sexuality and class struggle*, London: New Left Books.

Richards, B. (ed) (1984) *Capitalism and infancy*, London: Free Association Books.

Ricoeur, P. (1970) *Freud and philosophy*, New Haven: Yale University Press.

Rieff, P. (1965) *Freud: the mind of the moralist*, London: Methuen.

Roberts, H. (ed) (1981) *Doing feminist research*, London: Routledge.

Rorty, R. (1979) *Philosophy and the mirror of nature*, Princeton: Princeton University Press.

Rosdolsky, R. (1977) *The making of Marx's 'Capital'*, London: Pluto Press.

Rose, G. (1978) *The melancholy science: an introduction to the thought of Theodor W. Adorno*, London: Macmillan.

—— (1981) *Hegel contra sociology*, London: Athlone Press.

—— (1988) *Dialectic of nihilism: post-structuralism and law*, Oxford: Blackwell.

Rossi, A. (ed) *John Stuart Mill and Harriet Taylor Mill: essays on sex and equality*, Chicago and London: University of Chicago Press.

Rossman, M. (1979) *New age blues or the politics of consciousness*, New York: E.P. Dutton.

Rowbotham, S. (1973) *Woman's consciousness, man's world*, Harmondsworth: Penguin.

—— (1983) *Dreams and dilemmas*, London: Virago.

—— (1989) *The past is before us: feminism in action since the 1960s*, London: Pandora.

Rowbotham, S., Segal, L. and Wainwright, H. (eds) (1980) *Beyond the fragments: feminism and the making of socialism*, London: Merlin Press.

Rubin, I.I. (1972) *Essays on Marx's theory of value*, Detroit: Black & Read.

Rubin, L.B. (1960) *Worlds of pain: life in the working-class family*, New York: Basic Books.

—— (1983) *Intimate strangers*, London: Fontana.

Russell, L. (ed) (1985) *Feminist interpretation of the Bible*, Oxford: Blackwell.

Russell, P. (1982) *The awakening earth*, London: Routledge.

Ryan, A. (1974) *J.S. Mill*, London: Routledge & Kegan Paul.

Sabel, C.F. (1982) *Work and politics: the division of labour in industry*, Cambridge.

Samuels, A. (ed) (1985) *The father: contemporary Jungian perspectives*, London: Free Association Books.

San Juan, E. (ed) (1973) *Marxism and human liberation*, New York: Dell Publishing.

Sandel, M. (1983) *Liberalism and the limits of justice*, Cambridge: Cambridge University Press.

Satir, V. (1978a) *Conjoint family therapy*, London: Souvenir Press.

—— (1978b) *Peoplemaking*, London: Souvenir Press.

Sayers, J. (1986) *Sexual contradictions*, London: Tavistock.

Schatzman, M. (1973) *Soul murder: persecution in the family*, New York: Random House.

Schmidt, A. (1971) *The concept of nature in Marx*, London: New Left Books.

Schneider, M. (1975) *Neurosis and civilisation*, New York: The Seabury Press.

School of Barbiana (1969) *Letter to a teacher*, Harmondsworth: Penguin.

Schroyer, T. 'The dialectical foundations of critical theory' in *Telos*, No. 12, Summer 1972, pp 93-114.

Schumpeter, J. (1966) *Capitalism, socialism and democracy*, London: Unwin.

Schur, M. (1972) *Freud: living and dying*, New York: International Universities Press.

Schutz, W. (1968) *Joy*, Harmondsworth: Penguin.

Schwarz, W. and Schwarz, D. (1987) *Breaking through*, London: Green Books.

Scott, H. (1973) *Women and socialism*, London: Allison & Busby.

Sedgwick, P. (1982) *Psycho-politics*, London: Pluto Books.

Segal, H. (1964) *Introduction to the Work of Melanie Klein*, London: Heineman.

Segal, L. (ed) (1983) *What is to be done about the family?*, Harmondsworth: Penguin.

—— (1987) *Is the future female?*, London: Virago.

—— (1990) *Slow motion: changing masculinities, changing men*, London: Virago.

Seidler, V.J. (1986) *Kant, respect and injustice: the limits of liberal moral theory*, London: Routledge.

—— (1989) *Rediscovering masculinity: reason, language and sexuality*, London: Routledge.

—— (1990) *The moral limits of modernity: love, inequality and oppression*, London: Macmillan.

Sennett, R. and Cobb. J. (1970) *The hidden injuries of class*, New York: Vintage Books.

Sharaf, M. (1985) *Fury on earth: a biography of Wilhelm Reich*, London: Macmillan.

Skillen, A. (1977) *Ruling illusions*, Brighton: Harvester Press.

Snitow, A., Stansell, C. and Thompson (eds) *Powers of desire*, New York: Monthly Review Press.

Spender, D. (1980) *Man-made language*, London: Routledge & Kegan Paul.

Stanko, E. (1985) *Intimate intrusions: women's experience of male violence*, London: Routledge.

Steiner, C. (ed) (1975) *Readings in radical psychiatry*, New York: Grove Press.

Strouse, J. (ed) (1974) *Women and analysis*, New York: Dell Books.

Sullivan, H.S. (1953) *The interpersonal theory of psychiatry*, New York: W.W. Norton.

Tawney, R. (1926) *Religion and the rise of capialism*, London: John Murray.

Taylor, C. (1973) *Sources of the self*, Cambridge: Harvard University Press.

—— (1979) *Hegel and modern society*, Cambridge: Cambridge University Press.

—— (1985) *Philosophy and the human sciences: philosophical papers 2*, Cambridge: Cambridge University Press.

Therbon, G. (1980) *The ideology of power and the power of ideology*, London: New Left Books.

Theweleit, K. (1987 and 1989) *Male fantasies*, vols. 1 and 2, Cambridge: Polity Press.

Thompson, E.P. (1970) *The making of the English working class*, Harmondsworth: Penguin Books.

—— (1979) *The poverty of theory and other essays*, London: Merlin Press.

Thorne, B. and Yalom, M. (eds) *Rethinking the family: feminist questions*, New York: Longman.

Tillich, P. (1954) *The courage to be*, London: Fontana.

Tocqueville, A. de (1952) *Democracy in America*, New York: Vintage.

Tomaselli, S. and Porter, R. (eds) (1986) *Rape*, Oxford: Blackwell.

Trilling, L. (1951) *The liberal imagination*, New York: Viking Books.

—— (1972) *Sincerity and authenticity*, Oxford: Oxford University Press.

Turkle, S. (1979) *Psychoanalytic politics: Freud's French Revolution*, London: André Deutsch.

Vance, S. (ed) (1984) *Pleasure and danger: explaining female sexuality*, London: Routledge.

Vithoulkas, G. (1985) *Homeopathy*, Wellingborough, Thorsons.

Volpe, G. della (1978) *Rousseau and Marx*, trans J. Fraser, London: Lawrence & Wishart.

Waltzer, M. (1983) *Spheres of justice*, New York: Basic Books.

Wandor, M. (1972) *The body politic: women's liberation in Britain 1969-1972*, London: Stage 1.

Weber, M. (1930) *The Protestant ethic and the spirit of capitalism*, London: Allen & Unwin.

Weeks, J. (1977) *Coming out: homosexual politics in Britain*, London: Quartet Books.

—— (1981) *Sex, politics and society*, London: Longman.

—— (1984) *Sexuality*, London: Horwood/Tavistock.

—— (1985) *Sexuality and its discontents*, London: Routledge.

Weil, S. (1952) *The need for roots*, London: Routledge & Kegan Paul.

—— (1958) *Oppression and liberty*, London: Routledge & Kegan Paul.

—— (1962) *Selected essays 1934-43*, trans R. Rees, Oxford: Oxford University Press.

—— (1988) *Formative writings 1924-1941*, ed D.T. Macfarland and Van Ness, London: Routledge.

Williams, B. (1937) *Problems of the self*, Cambridge: Cambridge University Press.

—— (1972) *Morality: an introduction to ethics*, Cambridge: Cambridge University Press.

—— (1985) *Ethics and the limits of philosophy*, London: Fontana.

Williams, R. (1958) *Culture and society*, Harmondsworth: Penguin Books.

—— (1973) *The country and the city*, London: Chatto & Windus.

—— (1979a) *Modern tragedy*, London: Verso.

—— (1979b) *Politics and letters*, London: New Left Books.

Willis, P. (1977) *Learning to labour*, London: Saxon House, Gower.

Winnicott, D.W. (1974) *Playing and reality*, Harmondsworth: Penguin Books.

Wittgenstein, L. (1963) *Philosophical investigations*, Oxford: Blackwell.

—— (1980) *Culture and value*, ed Peter Winch, Oxford: Blackwell.

Wolfe, D.G. (1979) *The lesbian community*, San Francisco: University of California Press.
Wood, A. (1960) *Karl Marx*, London: Routledge & Kegan Paul.
Woolfe, K. (1960) *Emile Durkheim 1858-1917*, Columbus: Ohio State University Press.
Worsley, P. (1984) *The three worlds*, London: Weidenfeld & Nicolson.
Wyckoff, H. (1977) *Solving women's problems*, New York: Grove Press.
Wyre, R. (1986) *Men, women and rape*, Oxford: Perry Publications.
Zaretsky, E. (1976) *Capitalism, the family and personal life*, London: Pluto Press.
Zukav, G. (1979) *The dancing Wu Li masters*, London: Rider Hutchinson.

Index